THREE CUPS OF TEA

ONE MAN'S MISSION TO PROMOTE PEACE . . .
ONE SCHOOL AT A TIME

GREG MORTENSON

and

DAVID OLIVER RELIN

VIKING
an imprint of
PENGUIN BOOKS

VIKING

Published by the Penguin Group
Penguin Group (Australia)
250 Camberwell Road, Camberwell, Victoria 3124, Australia
(a division of Pearson Australia Group Pty Ltd)
Penguin Group (USA) Inc.
375 Hudson Street, New York, New York 10014, USA
Penguin Group (Canada)
90 Eglinton Avenue East, Suite 700, Toronto ON M4P 2Y3, Canada
(a division of Pearson Penguin Canada Inc.)
Penguin Books Ltd
80 Strand, London WC2R 0RL, England
Penguin Ireland
25 St Stephen's Green, Dublin 2, Ireland
(a division of Penguin Books Ltd)
Penguin Books India Pvt Ltd
11 Community Centre, Panchsheel Park, New Delhi – 110 017, India
Penguin Books (NZ) Ltd,
67 Apollo Drive, Rosedale, North Shore 0632, New Zealand
(a division of Pearson New Zealand Ltd)
Penguin Books (South Africa) (Pty) Ltd
24 Sturdee Avenue, Rosebank, Johannesburg 2196, South Africa

Penguin Books Ltd, Registered Offices: 80 Strand, London, WC2R 0RL, England

First published in the United States of America by Viking Penguin,
a member of Penguin Group (USA) Inc. 2006
Published in Penguin Books 2007
This edition published by Penguin Group (Australia)
a division of Pearson Australia Group Pty Ltd, 2007

5 7 9 10 8 6

Designed by Elke Sigal · Set in Stempel Garamond
Printed and bound in Australia by McPherson's Printing Group, Maryborough, Victoria

ISBN: 978 0670 91742 6

penguin.com.au

"An inspiring account of how one man can make a difference."
—*The Oregonian*

"A riveting account of how a failed K2 attempt serendipitously sparked a remarkably successful program building schools for girls in Pakistan and Afghanistan's most desolate regions."
—*Daily Camera* (Boulder)

"Greg Mortenson represents the best of America. He's my hero. And after you read *Three Cups of Tea*, he'll be your hero, too."
—Mary Bono, U.S. Representative (California)

"As a former climber, Greg Mortenson knows something about hardship. But when you read *Three Cups of Tea*, you realize that the summit he is striving for as a humanitarian is much more difficult than any mountain."
—Conrad Anker

THREE CUPS OF TEA

GREG MORTENSON is the director of the Central Asia Institute. A former mountaineer and military veteran, he spends several months each year building schools in Pakistan and Afghanistan. He lives in Montana with his wife and two children.

DAVID OLIVER RELIN is a globe-trotting journalist who has won more than forty national awards for his writing and editing. A former teaching/writing fellow at the Iowa Writers' Workshop, he is a frequent contributor to *Parade* and *Skiing Magazine*. He lives in Portland, Oregon.

to
Irvin "Dempsey" Mortenson
Barry "Barrel" Bishop
and
Lloyd Henry Relin
for showing us the way, while you were here

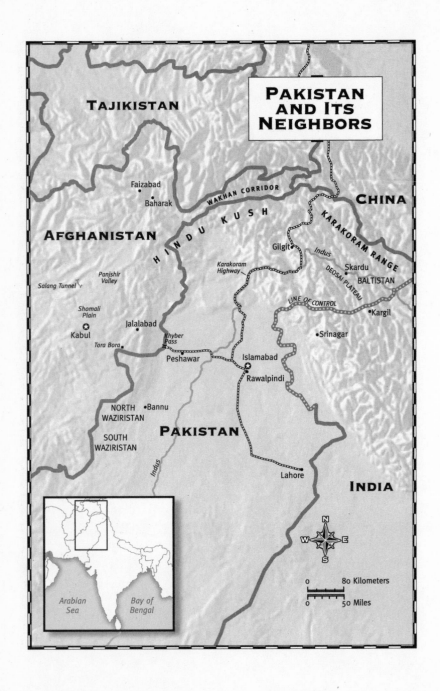

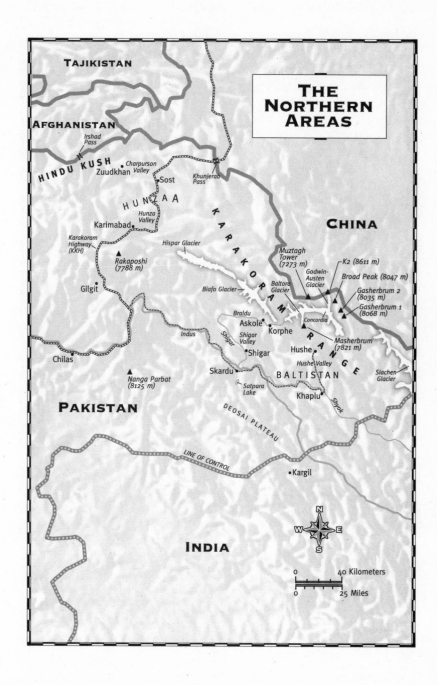

TAJIKISTAN

AFGHANISTAN

Irshad Pass

HINDU KUSH

Charpurson Valley
Zuudkhan

Sost

Khunjerab Pass

HUNZA

Hunza Valley

Karimabad

Karakoram Highway (KKH)

▲ *Rakaposhi (7788 m)*

Hispar Glacier

KARAKORAM

Gilgit

Blafo Glacier

Braldu
Askole •
Indus

Shigar

Shigar Valley
• Shigar

Chilas

▲ *Nanga Parbat (8125 m)*

Skardu •

Satpara Lake

RANGE

THE
NORTHERN
AREAS

CHINA

Muztagh Tower (7273 m)

Godwin-Austen Glacier
Baltoro Glacier

• Korphe

Concordia

▲ K2 (8611 m)
▲ Broad Peak (8047 m)
▲ *Gasherbrum 2 (8035 m)*
▲ *Gasherbrum 1 (8068 m)*

Hushe •
▲ *Masherbrum (7821 m)*

Hushe Valley

Siachen Glacier

BALTISTAN

Khaplu •
Shyok

PAKISTAN

DEOSAI PLATEAU

LINE OF CONTROL

• Kargil

INDIA

N
W   E
S

0   40 Kilometers
0   25 Miles

CONTENTS

THREE CUPS OF TEA

IN MR. MORTENSON'S ORBIT

THE LITTLE RED light had been flashing for five minutes before Bhangoo paid it any attention. "The fuel gages on these old aircraft are notoriously unreliable," Brigadier General Bhangoo, one of Pakistan's most experienced high-altitude helicopter pilots, said, tapping it. I wasn't sure if that was meant to make me feel better.

I rode next to Bhangoo, looking down past my feet through the Vietnam-era Alouette's bubble windshield. Two thousand feet below us a river twisted, hemmed in by rocky crags jutting out from both sides of the Hunza Valley. At eye level, we soared past hanging green glaciers, splintering under a tropical sun. Bhangoo flew on unperturbed, flicking the ash of his cigarette out a vent, next to a sticker that said "No smoking."

From the rear of the aircraft Greg Mortenson reached his long arm out to tap Bhangoo on the shoulder of his flight suit. "General, sir," Mortenson shouted, "I think we're heading the wrong way."

Brigadier Bhangoo had been President Musharraf's personal pilot before retiring from the military to join a civil aviation company. He was in his late sixties, with salt-and-pepper hair and a mustache as clipped and cultivated as the vowels he'd inherited from the private British colonial school he'd attended as boy with Musharraf and many of Pakistan's other future leaders.

The general tossed his cigarette through the vent and blew out his breath. Then he bent to compare the store-bought GPS unit he balanced on his knee with a military-grade map Mortenson folded to highlight what he thought was our position.

"I've been flying in northern Pakistan for forty years," he said, waggling his head, the subcontinent's most distinctive gesture. "How

is it you know the terrain better than me?" Bhangoo banked the Alouette steeply to port, flying back the way we'd come.

The red light that had worried me before began to flash faster. The
bobbing needle on the gauge showed that we had less than one hundred liters of fuel. This part of northern Pakistan was so remote and
inhospitable that we'd had to have friends preposition barrels of aviation fuel at strategic sites by jeep. If we couldn't make it to our drop
zone we were in a tight spot, literally, since the craggy canyon we flew
through had no level areas suitable for setting the Alouette down.

Bhangoo climbed high, so he'd have the option of auto-rotating
toward a more distant landing zone if we ran out of fuel, and jammed
his stick forward, speeding up to ninety knots. Just as the needle hit E
and the red warning light began to beep, Bhangoo settled the skids at
the center of a large H, for helipad, written out in white rocks, next to
our barrels of jet fuel.

"That was a lovely sortie," Bhangoo said, lighting another cigarette. "But it might not have been without Mr. Mortenson."

Later, after refueling by inserting a handpump into a rusting barrel
of aviation fuel, we flew up the Braldu Valley to the village of Korphe,
the last human habitation before the Baltoro Glacier begins its march
up to K2 and the world's greatest concentration of twenty-thousand-
foot-plus peaks. After a failed 1993 attempt to climb K2, Mortenson
arrived in Korphe, emaciated and exhausted. In this impoverished
community of mud and stone huts, both Mortenson's life and the lives
of northern Pakistan's children changed course. One evening, he went
to bed by a yak dung fire a mountaineer who'd lost his way, and one
morning, by the time he'd shared a pot of butter tea with his hosts and
laced up his boots, he'd become a humanitarian who'd found a meaningful path to follow for the rest of his life.

Arriving in Korphe with Dr. Greg, Bhangoo and I were welcomed
with open arms, the head of a freshly killed ibex, and endless cups of
tea. And as we listened to the Shia children of Korphe, one of the
world's most impoverished communities, talk about how their hopes
and dreams for the future had grown exponentially since a big American arrived a decade ago to build them the first school their village had
ever known, the general and I were done for.

"You know," Bhangoo said, as we were enveloped in a scrum of
120 students tugging us by the hands on a tour of their school, "flying

2

with President Musharraf, I've become acquainted with many world leaders, many outstanding gentlemen and ladies. But I think Greg Mortenson is the most remarkable person I've ever met."

Everyone who has had the privilege of watching Greg Mortenson operate in Pakistan is amazed by how encyclopedically well he has come to know one of the world's most remote regions. And many of them find themselves, almost against their will, pulled into his orbit. During the last decade, since a series of failures and accidents transformed him from a mountaineer to a humanitarian, Mortenson has attracted what has to be one of the most underqualified and overachieving staffs of any charitable organization on earth.

Illiterate high-altitude porters in Pakistan's Karakoram have put down their packs to make paltry wages with him so their children can have the education they were forced to do without. A taxi driver who chanced to pick Mortenson up at the Islamabad airport sold his cab and became his fiercely dedicated "fixer." Former Taliban fighters renounced violence and the oppression of women after meeting Mortenson and went to work with him peacefully building schools for girls. He has drawn volunteers and admirers from every stratum of Pakistan's society and from all the warring sects of Islam.

Supposedly objective journalists are at risk of being drawn into his orbit, too. On three occasions I accompanied Mortenson to northern Pakistan, flying to the most remote valleys of the Karakoram Himalaya and the Hindu Kush on helicopters that should have been hanging from the rafters of museums. The more time I spent watching Mortenson work, the more convinced I became that I was in the presence of someone extraordinary.

The accounts I'd heard about Mortenson's adventures building schools for girls in the remote mountain regions of Pakistan sounded too dramatic to believe before I left home. The story I found, with ibex hunters in the high valleys of the Karakoram, in nomad settlements at the wild edge of Afghanistan, around conference tables with Pakistan's military elite, and over endless cups of *paiyu cha* in tearooms so smoky I had to squint to see my notebook, was even more remarkable than I'd imagined.

As a journalist who has practiced this odd profession of probing into people's lives for two decades, I've met more than my share of public figures who didn't measure up to their own press. But at Korphe and every other Pakistani village where I was welcomed like long-lost family, because another American had taken the time to forge ties there, I saw the story of the last ten years of Greg Mortenson's existence branch and fork with a richness and complexity far beyond what most of us achieve over the course of a full-length life.

This is a fancy way of saying that this is a story I couldn't simply observe. Anyone who travels to the CAI's fifty-three schools with Mortenson is put to work, and in the process, becomes an advocate. And after staying up at all-night *jirgas* with village elders and weighing in on proposals for new projects, or showing a classroom full of excited eight-year-old girls how to use the first pencil-sharpener anyone has ever cared to give them, or teaching an impromptu class on English slang to a roomful of gravely respectful students, it is impossible to remain simply a reporter.

As Graham Greene's melancholy correspondent Thomas Fowler learned by the end of *The Quiet American*, sometimes, to be human, you have to take sides.

I choose to side with Greg Mortenson. Not because he doesn't have his flaws. His fluid sense of time made pinning down the exact sequence of many events in this book almost impossible, as did interviewing the Balti people with whom he works, who have no tenses in their language and as little attachment to linear time as the man they call Dr. Greg.

During the two years we worked together on this book, Mortenson was often so maddeningly late for appointments that I considered abandoning the project. Many people, particularly in America, have turned on Mortenson after similar experiences, calling him "unreliable," or worse. But I have come to realize, as his wife Tara Bishop often says, "Greg is not one of us." He operates on Mortenson Time, a product, perhaps, of growing up in Africa and working much of each year in Pakistan. And his method of operation, hiring people with limited experience based on gut feelings, forging working alliances with necessarily unsavory characters, and, above all, winging it, while unsettling and unconventional, has moved mountains.

For a man who has achieved so much, Mortenson has a remarkable lack of ego. After I agreed to write this book, he handed me a page of notepaper with dozens of names and numbers printed densely down the margin in tiny script. It was a list of his enemies. "Talk to them all," he said. "Let them have their say. We've got the results. That's all I care about."

I listened to hundreds of Mortenson's allies and enemies. And in the interest of security and/or privacy I've changed a very few names and locations.

Working on this book was a true collaboration. I wrote the story. But Greg Mortenson lived it. And together, as we sorted through thousands of slides, reviewed a decade's worth of documents and videos, recorded hundreds of hours of interviews, and traveled to visit with the people who are central to this unlikeliest of narratives, we brought this book to life.

And as I found in Pakistan, Mortenson's Central Asia Institute does, irrefutably, have the results. In a part of the world where Americans are, at best, misunderstood, and more often feared and loathed, this soft-spoken, six-foot-four former mountaineer from Montana has put together a string of improbable successes. Though he would never say so himself, he has single-handedly changed the lives of tens of thousands of children, and independently won more hearts and minds than all the official American propaganda flooding the region.

So this is a confession: Rather than simply reporting on his progress, I want to see Greg Mortenson succeed. I wish him success because he is fighting the war on terror the way I think it should be conducted. Slamming over the so-called Karakoram "Highway" in his old Land Cruiser, taking great personal risks to seed the region that gave birth to the Taliban with schools, Mortenson goes to war with the root causes of terror every time he offers a student a chance to receive a balanced education, rather than attend an extremist *madrassa*.

If we Americans are to learn from our mistakes, from the flailing, ineffective way we, as a nation, conducted the war on terror after the attacks of 9/11, and from the way we have failed to make our case to the great moderate mass of peace-loving people at the heart of the Muslim world, we need to listen to Greg Mortenson. I did, and it has been one of the most rewarding experiences of my life.

—David Oliver Relin
Portland, Oregon

CHAPTER 1

FAILURE

When it is dark enough, you can see the stars.

—Persian proverb

IN PAKISTAN'S KARAKORAM, bristling across an area barely one hundred miles wide, more than sixty of the world's tallest mountains lord their severe alpine beauty over a witnessless high-altitude wilderness. Other than snow leopard and ibex, so few living creatures have passed through this barren icescape that the presence of the world's second-highest mountain, K2, was little more than a rumor to the outside world until the turn of the twentieth century.

Flowing down from K2 toward the populated upper reaches of the Indus Valley, between the four fluted granite spires of the Gasherbrums and the lethal-looking daggers of the Great Trango Towers, the sixty-two-kilometer-long Baltoro Glacier barely disturbs this still cathedral of rock and ice. And even the motion of this frozen river, which drifts at a rate of four inches a day, is almost undetectable.

On the afternoon of September 2, 1993, Greg Mortenson felt as if he were scarcely traveling any faster. Dressed in a much-patched set of mud-colored *shalwar kamiz*, like his Pakistani porters, he had the sensation that his heavy black leather mountaineering boots were independently steering him down the Baltoro at their own glacial speed, through an armada of icebergs arrayed like the sails of a thousand ice-bound ships.

At any moment, Mortenson expected to find Scott Darsney, a fellow member of his expedition, with whom he was hiking back toward civilization, sitting on a boulder, teasing him for walking so slowly. But the upper Baltoro is more maze than trail. Mortenson hadn't yet realized that he was lost and alone. He'd strayed from the main body of the glacier to a side spur that led not westward, toward Askole, the village fifty miles farther on, where he hoped to find a jeep driver willing to transport him out of these mountains, but south, into an impenetrable maze of shattered icefall, and beyond that, the high-altitude killing zone where Pakistani and Indian soldiers lobbed artillery shells at one another through the thin air.

Ordinarily Mortenson would have paid more attention. He would have focused on life-and-death information like the fact that Mouzafer, the porter who had appeared like a blessing and volunteered to haul his heavy bag of climbing gear, was also carrying his tent and nearly all of his food and kept him in sight. And he would have paid more mind to the overawing physicality of his surroundings.

In 1909, the duke of Abruzzi, one of the greatest climbers of his day, and perhaps his era's most discerning connoisseur of precipitous landscapes, led an Italian expedition up the Baltoro for an unsuccessful attempt at K2. He was stunned by the stark beauty of the encircling peaks. "Nothing could compare to this in terms of alpine beauty," he recorded in his journal. "It was a world of glaciers and crags, an incredible view which could satisfy an artist just as well as a mountaineer."

But as the sun sank behind the great granite serrations of Muztagh Tower to the west, and shadows raked up the valley's eastern walls, toward the bladed monoliths of Gasherbrum, Mortenson hardly noticed. He was looking inward that afternoon, stunned and absorbed by something unfamiliar in his life to that point—failure.

Reaching into the pocket of his *shalwar,* he fingered the necklace of amber beads that his little sister Christa had often worn. As a three-year-old in Tanzania, where Mortenson's Minnesota-born parents had been Lutheran missionaries and teachers, Christa had contracted acute meningitis and never fully recovered. Greg, twelve years her senior, had appointed himself her protector. Though Christa struggled to perform simple tasks—putting on her clothes each morning took upward of an hour—and suffered severe epileptic seizures, Greg pressured his mother, Jerene, to allow her some measure of independence. He helped Christa find work at manual labor, taught her the routes of the Twin Cities' public buses, so she could move about freely, and, to their mother's mortification, discussed the particulars of birth control when he learned she was dating.

Each year, whether he was serving as a U.S. Army medic and platoon leader in Germany, working on a nursing degree in South Dakota, studying the neurophysiology of epilepsy at graduate school in Indiana in hopes of discovering a cure for Christa, or living a climbing bum's life out of his car in Berkeley, California, Mortenson insisted that his little sister visit him for a month. Together, they sought out the spectacles that brought Christa so much pleasure. They took in the Indy 500, the Kentucky Derby, road-tripped down to Disneyland, and he guided her through the architecture of his personal cathedral at that time, the storied granite walls of Yosemite.

For her twenty-third birthday, Christa and their mother planned to make a pilgrimage from Minnesota to the cornfield in Deyersville, Iowa, where the movie that Christa was drawn to watch again and again, *Field of Dreams*, had been filmed. But on her birthday, in the small hours before they were to set out, Christa died of a massive seizure.

After Christa's death, Mortenson retrieved the necklace from among his sister's few things. It still smelled of a campfire they had made during her last visit to stay with him in California. He brought it to Pakistan with him, bound in a Tibetan prayer flag, along with a plan to honor the memory of his little sister. Mortenson was a climber and he had decided on the most meaningful tribute he had within him. He would scale K2, the summit most climbers consider the toughest to reach on Earth, and leave Christa's necklace there at 28,267 feet.

He had been raised in a family that had relished difficult tasks, like building a school and a hospital in Tanzania, on the slopes of Mount Kilimanjaro. But despite the smooth surfaces of his parents' unquestioned faith, Mortenson hadn't yet made up his mind about the nature of divinity. He would leave an offering to whatever deity inhabited the upper atmosphere.

Three months earlier, Mortenson had positively skipped up this glacier in a pair of Teva sandals with no socks, his ninety-pound pack beside the point of the adventure that beckoned him up the Baltoro. He had set off on the seventy-mile trek from Askole with a team of ten English, Irish, French, and American mountaineers, part of a poorly financed but pathologically bold attempt to climb the world's second-highest peak.

Compared to Everest, a thousand miles southeast along the spine of the Himalaya, K2, they all knew, was a killer. To climbers, who call it "The Savage Peak," it remains the ultimate test, a pyramid of razored granite so steep that snow can't cling to its knife-edged ridges. And Mortenson, then a bullishly fit thirty-five-year-old, who had summited Kilimanjaro at age eleven, who'd been schooled on the sheer granite walls of Yosemite, then graduated to half a dozen successful Himalayan ascents, had no doubt when he arrived in May that he would soon stand on what he considered "the biggest and baddest summit on Earth."

He'd come shatteringly close, within six hundred meters of the summit. But K2 had receded into the mists behind him and the necklace was still in his pocket. How could this have happened? He wiped his eyes with his sleeve, disoriented by unfamiliar tears, and attributed them to the altitude. He certainly wasn't himself. After seventy-eight days of primal struggle at altitude on K2, he felt like a faint, shriveled caricature of himself. He simply didn't know if he had the reserves left to walk fifty more miles over dangerous terrain to Askole.

The sharp, shotgun crack of a rockfall brought him back to his surroundings. He watched a boulder the size of a three-story house accelerate, bouncing and spinning down a slope of scree, then pulverize an iceberg on the trail ahead of him.

Mortenson tried to shake himself into a state of alertness. He looked out of himself, saw how high the shadows had climbed up the eastern peaks, and tried to remember how long it had been since he'd seen a sign of other humans. It had been hours since Scott Darsney had disappeared down the trail ahead of him. An hour earlier, or maybe more, he'd heard the bells of an army mule caravan carrying ammunition toward the Siachen Glacier, the twenty-thousand-foot-high battlefield a dozen miles southeast where the Pakistani military was frozen into its perpetual deadly standoff with the Indian army.

He scoured the trail for signs. Anywhere on the trail back to Askole, there would be debris left behind by the military. But there were no mule droppings. No cigarette butts. No food tins. No blades of the hay the mule drivers carried to feed their animals. He realized it didn't look much like a trail at all, simply a cleft in an unstable maze of boulders and ice, and he wondered how he had wandered to this spot. He tried to summon the clarity to concentrate. But the effects of prolonged exposure to high altitude had sapped Mortenson of the ability to act and think decisively.

He spent an hour scrambling up a slope of scree, hoping for a vantage point above the boulders and icebergs, a place where he might snare the landmark he was looking for, the great rocky promontory of Urdukas, which thrust out onto the Baltoro like a massive fist, and haul himself back toward the trail. But at the top he was rewarded with little more than a greater degree of exhaustion. He'd strayed eight miles up a deserted valley from the trail, and in the failing light, even the contours of peaks that he knew well looked unfamiliar from this new perspective.

Feeling a finger of panic probing beneath his altitude-induced stupor, Mortenson sat to take stock. In his small sun-faded purple daypack he had a lightweight wool Pakistani army blanket, an empty water bottle, and a single protein bar. His high-altitude down sleeping bag, all his warm clothes, his tent, his stove, food, even his flashlight and all his matches were in the pack the porter carried.

He'd have to spend the night and search for the trail in daylight. Though it had already dropped well below zero, he wouldn't die of exposure, he thought. Besides, he was coherent enough to realize that stumbling, at night, over a shifting glacier, where crevasses yawned hundreds of feet down through wastes of blue ice into subterranean pools, was far more dangerous. Picking his way down the mound of scree, Mortenson looked for a spot far enough from the mountain walls that he wouldn't be crushed by rockfall as he slept and solid enough that it wouldn't split and plunge him into the glacier's depths.

He found a flat slab of rock that seemed stable enough, scooped icy snow into his water bottle with ungloved hands, and wrapped himself in his blanket, willing himself not to focus on how alone and exposed he was. His forearm was lashed with rope burns from the rescue, and he knew he should tear off the clotted gauze bandages and drain pus from the wounds that refused to heal at this altitude, but he couldn't quite locate the motivation. As he lay shivering on uneven rock, Mortenson watched as the last light of the sun smoldered blood red on the daggered summits to the east, then flared out, leaving their afterimages burning in blue-black.

Nearly a century earlier, Filippo De Filippi, doctor for and chronicler of the duke of Abruzzi's expedition to the Karakoram, recorded the desolation he felt among these mountains. Despite the fact that he was in the company of two dozen Europeans and 260 local porters, that they carried folding chairs and silver tea services and had European newspapers delivered to them regularly by a fleet of runners, he felt crushed into insignificance by the character of this landscape. "Profound silence would brood over the valley," he wrote, "even weighing down our spirits with indefinable heaviness. There can be no other place in the world where man feels himself so alone, so isolated, so completely ignored by Nature, so incapable of entering into communion with her."

Perhaps it was his experience with solitude, being the lone American child among hundreds of Africans, or the nights he spent bivouacked three thousand feet up Yosemite's Half Dome in the middle of a multiday climb, but Mortenson felt at ease. If you ask him why, he'll credit altitude-induced dementia. But anyone who has spent time in Mortenson's presence, who's watched him wear down a congressman or a reluctant philanthropist or an Afghan warlord with his doggedness, until he pried loose overdue relief funds, or a donation, or the permission he was seeking to pass into tribal territories, would recognize this night as one more example of Mortenson's steely-mindedness.

The wind picked up and the night became bitterly crystalline. He tried to discern the peaks he felt hovering malevolently around him, but he couldn't make them out among the general blackness. After an hour under his blanket he was able to thaw his frozen protein bar against his body and melt enough silty icewater to wash it down, which set him shivering violently. Sleep, in this cold, seemed out of the question. So Mortenson lay beneath the stars salting the sky and decided to examine the nature of his failure.

The leaders of his expedition, Dan Mazur and Jonathan Pratt, along with French climber Etienne Fine, were thoroughbreds. They were speedy and graceful, bequeathed the genetic wherewithal to sprint up technical pitches at high altitude. Mortenson was slow and bearishly strong. At six-foot-four and 210 pounds, Mortenson had attended Minnesota's Concordia College on a football scholarship.

Though no one directed that it should be so, the slow, cumbersome work of mountain climbing fell naturally to him and to Darsney. Eight separate times Mortenson served as pack mule, hauling food, fuel, and oxygen bottles to several stashes on the way to the Japanese Couloir, a tenuous aerie the expedition carved out within six hundred meters of K2's summit, stocking the expedition's high camps so the lead climbers might have the supplies in place when they decided to dash to the top.

All of the other expeditions on the mountain that season had chosen to challenge the peak in the traditional way, working up the path pioneered nearly a century earlier, K2's Southeastern Abruzzi Ridge. Only they had chosen the West Ridge, a circuitous, brutally difficult route, littered with land mine after land mine of steep, technical pitches, which had been successfully scaled only once, twelve years earlier, by Japanese climber Eiho Otani and his Pakistani partner Nazir Sabir.

Mortenson relished the challenge and took pride in the rigorous route they'd chosen. And each time he reached one of the perches they'd clawed out high on the West Ridge, and unloaded fuel canisters and coils of rope, he noticed he was feeling stronger. He might be slow, but reaching the summit himself began to seem inevitable.

Then one evening after more than seventy days on the mountain, Mortenson and Darsney were back at base camp, about to drop into well-earned sleep after ninety-six hours of climbing during another resupply mission. But while taking a last look at the peak through a telescope just after dark, Mortenson and Darsney noticed a flickering light high up on K2's West Ridge. They realized it must be members of their expedition, signaling with their headlamps, and they guessed that their French teammate was in trouble. "Etienne was an *Alpiniste*," Mortenson explains, underlining with an exaggerated French pronunciation the respect and arrogance the term can convey among climbers. "He'd travel fast and light with the absolute minimum amount of gear. And we had to bail him out before when he went up too fast without acclimatizing."

Mortenson and Darsney, doubting whether they were strong enough to climb to Fine so soon after an exhausting descent, called for volunteers from the five other expeditions at base camp. None came forward. For two hours they lay in their tents resting and rehydrating, then they packed their gear and went back out.

Descending from their seventy-six-hundred-meter Camp IV, Pratt and Mazur found themselves in the fight of their lives. "Etienne had climbed up to join us for a summit bid," Mazur says. "But when he got to us, he collapsed. As he tried to catch his breath, he told us he heard a rattling in his lungs."

Fine was suffering from pulmonary edema, an altitude-induced flooding of the lungs that can kill those it strikes if they aren't immediately evacuated to lower ground. "It was terrifying," Mazur says. "Pink froth was pouring out of Etienne's mouth. We tried to call for help, but we'd dropped our radio in the snow and it wouldn't work. So we started down."

Pratt and Mazur took turns clipping themselves to Fine, and rapelling with him down the West Ridge's steepest pitches. "It was like hanging from a rope strapped to a big sack of potatoes," Mazur says. "And we had to take our time so we wouldn't kill ourselves."

With his typical understatement, Mortenson doesn't say much about the twenty-four hours it took to haul himself up to reach Fine other than to comment that it was "fairly arduous."

"Dan and Jon were the real heroes," he says. "They gave up their summit bid to get Etienne down."

By the time Mortenson and Darsney met their teammates, on a rock face near Camp I, Fine was lapsing in and out of conciousness, suffering also from cerebral edema, the altitude-induced swelling of the brain. "He was unable to swallow and attempting to unlace his boots," Mortenson says.

Mortenson, who'd worked as an emergency room trauma nurse for the freedom the irregular hours gave him to pursue his climbing career, gave Fine injections of Decadron to ease the edema and the four already exhausted climbers began a forty-eight-hour odyssey of dragging and lowering him down craggy rock faces.

Sometimes Fine, ordinarily fluent in English, would wake enough to babble in French, Mortenson says. At the most technical pitches, with a lifelong climber's instinct for self-preservation, Fine would rouse himself to clip his protective devices onto the rope, before melting back into deadweight, Mortenson remembers.

Seventy-two hours after Mortenson and Darsney set out, the group had succeeded in lowering Fine to flat ground at their advance base camp. Darsney radioed the Canadian expedition below, who relayed his request to the Pakistani military for a high-altitude Lama helicopter rescue. At the time, it would have been one of the highest helicopter rescues ever attempted. But the military HQ replied that the weather was too bad and the wind too strong and ordered Fine evacuated to lower ground.

It was one thing to issue an order. It was quite another for four men in the deepest animal stages of exhaustion to attempt to execute it. For six hours, after strapping Fine into a sleeping bag, they communicated only in grunts and whimpers, dragging their friend down a dangerous technical route through the icefall of the Savoia Glacier.

"We were so exhausted and so beyond our limits that, at times, we could only crawl ourselves as we tried to get down," Darsney remembers.

Finally, the group approached K2 base camp, towing Fine in the bag behind them. "All the other expeditions strolled about a quarter mile up the glacier to greet us and give us a hero's welcome," Darsney says. "After the Pakistani army helicopter came and evacuated Etienne, the Canadian expedition members cooked up a huge meal and everyone had a party. But Greg and I didn't stop to eat, drink, or even piss, we just fell into our sleeping bags like we'd been shot."

For two days, Mortenson and Darsney drifted in and out of the facsimile of sleep that high altitude inflicts on even those most exhausted. As the wind probed at their tents, it was accompanied by the sound of metal cook kit plates, engraved with the names of the forty-eight mountaineers who'd lost their lives to the Savage Mountain, clanging eerily on the Art Gilkey Memorial, named for a climber who died during a 1953 American expedition.

When they woke, they found a note from Pratt and Mazur, who'd headed back up to their high camp. They invited their teammates to join them for a summit attempt when they recovered. But recovery was beyond them. The rescue, coming so quickly on the heels of their resupply climb, had ripped away what reserves they had.

When they finally emerged from their tent, both found it a struggle simply to walk. Fine had been saved at a great price. The ordeal would eventually cost him all his toes. And the rescue cost Mortenson and Darsney whatever attempt they could muster at the summit they had worked so hard to reach. Mazur and Pratt would announce to the world that they'd stood on the summit a week later and return home to glory in their achievement. But the number of metal plates chiming in the wind would multiply, as four of the sixteen climbers who summited that season died during their descent.

Mortenson was anxious that his name not be added to the memorial. So was Darsney. They decided to make the trek together back toward civilization, if they could. Lost, reliving the rescue, alone in his thin wool blanket in the hours before dawn, Greg Mortenson struggled to find a comfortable position. At his height, he couldn't lie flat without his head poking out into the unforgiving air. He had lost thirty pounds during his days on K2, and no matter which way he turned, uncushioned bone seemed to press into the cold rock beneath him. Drifting in and out of consciousness to a groaning soundtrack of the glacier's mysterious inner machinery, he made his peace with his failure to honor Christa. It was his body that had failed, he decided, not his spirit, and every body had its limits. He, for the first time in his life, had found the absolute limit of his.

CHAPTER 2

THE WRONG SIDE OF THE RIVER

Why ponder thus the future to foresee,
and jade thy brain to vain perplexity?
Cast off thy care, leave Allah's plans to him—
He formed them all without consulting thee.

—Omar Khayyam, *The Rubaiyat*

MORTENSON OPENED HIS eyes.

The dawn was so calm that he couldn't make sense of the frantic desire he felt to breathe. He untangled his hands from the blanket's tight cocoon with nightmarish inefficiency, then flung them toward his head, where it lay, exposed to the elements on a bare slab of rock. His mouth and nose were sculpted shut beneath a smooth mask of ice. Mortenson tore the ice free and took his first deep, satisfying breath. Then he sat up, laughing at himself.

He had slept just enough to be thoroughly disoriented. As he stretched and tried to rub some feeling back into the numb spots the rocks had imprinted on him, he took in his surroundings. The peaks were painted in garish, sugary colors—all pinks and violets and baby blues—and the sky, just before sunrise, was windless and clear.

The details of his predicament trickled back in along with the circulation in his limbs—still lost, still alone—but Mortenson wasn't worried. Morning made all the difference.

High above the Baltoro, a *gorak* circled hopefully, its large black wings brushing the vista of candied peaks. With hands clawed from the cold, Mortenson jammed his blanket into his small purple pack and tried unsuccessfully to unscrew his half-full water bottle. He stowed it carefully and told himself he'd drink it as soon as his hands thawed. The *gorak,* seeing Mortenson stir, flapped away down the glacier, seeking another source of breakfast.

Maybe it was however much sleep he'd managed, but Mortenson sensed he was thinking more clearly. Looking back up the valley the way he'd come, he realized if he retraced his steps for a few hours, he couldn't help running into the trail.

He set off north, stumbling a bit over boulders, straining just to jump the narrowest of crevasses with his still-numb legs, but he made what he considered acceptable progress. The song floated up out of his childhood as it so often did, keeping pace with his steps. *"Yesu ni refiki Yangu, Ah kayee Mbinguni"* ("What a friend we have in Jesus, He lives in Heaven"), he sang in Swahili, the language they had used in the plain church building, with its distant view of Kilimanjaro, at services every Sunday. The tune was too ingrained for Mortenson to consider the novelty of this moment—an American, lost in Pakistan, singing a German hymn in Swahili. Instead, among this moonscape of boulders and blue ice, where pebbles he kicked would disappear down crevasses for seconds, before splashing into subterranean rivers, it burned with a nostalgic warmth, a beacon from the country he had once called home.

An hour passed this way. And then another. Mortenson hauled himself up a steep trail out of the gulch he had been traveling in, dropped to his hands and knees to scramble over a cornice, and stood at the top of a crest just as the rising sun climbed free of the valley walls.

It was as if he'd been shot through the eyes.

The panorama of colossi blinded him. Gasherbrum, Broad Peak, Mitre Peak, Muztagh Tower—these ice-sheathed giants, naked in the embrace of unfiltered sunlight, burned like bonfires.

Mortenson sat on a boulder and drank from his water bottle until it was empty. But he couldn't drink in enough of this setting. Wilderness photographer Galen Rowell spent years, before his 2002 death in a plane crash, trying to capture the transcendent beauty of these mountains that escort the Baltoro down to lower ground. His images startle, but Rowell always felt they failed compared to the experience of simply standing there, dwarfed by the spectacle of what he considered the most beautiful place on earth, a place he dubbed "the throne room of the mountain gods."

Though Mortenson had already been there for months, he drank in the drama of these peaks like he'd never seen them before. "In a way, I never had," he explains. "All summer, I'd looked at these mountains as goals, totally focused on the biggest one, K2. I'd thought about their elevation and the technical challenges they presented to me as a climber. But that morning," he says, "for the first time, I simply saw them. It was overwhelming."

He walked on. Maybe it was the architectural perfection of the mountains—the broad set-backs and buttresses of maroon and ochre granite that built, with symphonic intensity, toward the lone soaring finale of their peaks—but despite his weakened state, his lack of food and warm clothing, his poor odds of surviving if he didn't find some of both sometime soon, Mortenson felt strangely content. He filled his water bottle from a fast-running trickle of glacial meltwater and winced from the cold as he drank. Food won't be a problem for days, he told himself, but you must remember to drink.

Toward late morning, he heard the faintest tinkling of bells and tacked toward them to the west. A donkey caravan. He searched for the stone cairns that marked the main route down the Baltoro, but found only rock strewn in its most random arrangements. Over a sharp lip of lateral moraine, the debris band that forms at the edge of a glacier, he was suddenly face to face with a five-thousand-foot wall blocking any hope of further progress. He realized he must have passed over the trail without noticing it, so returned the way he came, forcing himself to look down for signs, not up at the mesmerization of the peaks. After thirty minutes, he spotted a cigarette butt, then a cairn. He walked down the still indistinct trail toward bells that he could hear more clearly now.

He couldn't spot the caravan. But, finally, a mile or more distant, he made out a man's form, standing on a boulder that overhung the glacier, silhouetted against the sky. Mortenson shouted, but his voice wouldn't carry that far. The man vanished for a few moments, then reappeared on a boulder a hundred yards closer. Mortenson bellowed with as much force as he had in him, and this time, the man turned sharply toward him, then climbed quickly down from his perch and dropped out of sight. Down in the center of the glacier, among a catacomb of boulders, in dusty, stone-colored clothes, Mortenson wasn't visible, but he could make his voice echo off the rock.

He couldn't manage to run, so trotted, panting, toward the last spot he'd seen the man and shouted every few minutes with a roar that surprised him every time he heard himself produce it. Then, there the man was, standing on the far side of a wide crevasse, with an even wider smile. Dwarfed by Mortenson's overloaded North Face backpack, Mouzafer, the porter he had hired to haul him and his gear back down to inhabited regions, searched for the narrowest section of the crevasse, then leaped over it effortlessly, with more than ninety pounds on his back.

"Mr. Gireg, Mr. Gireg," he shouted, dropping the pack and wrapping Mortenson in a bear hug. "*Allah Akbhar!* Blessings to Allah you're alive!"

Mortenson crouched, awkwardly, crushed almost breathless by the strength and vigor of the man, a foot shorter and two decades older than himself.

Then Mouzafer released him and began slapping Mortenson happily on the back. Whether from the cloud of dust coming off his soiled *shalwar* or from Mouzafer's blows, Mortenson began coughing, then doubled over, unable to stop.

"*Cha*, Mr. Gireg," Mouzafer prescribed, worriedly assessing Mortenson's weakened condition. "*Cha* will give you strength!" Mouzafer led Mortenson to a small cave out of the wind. He tore two handfuls of sagebrush from the bunch he'd strapped to his pack, rummaged through the pockets of the sun-faded, oversized purple Gore-Tex jacket he wore, a castoff from one of the countless expeditions he'd guided through the Baltoro, found a flint and a metal pot, and sat down to prepare tea.

Mortenson had first met Mouzafer Ali four hours after leaving K2 with Darsney. The three-mile walk to the base camp of Broad Peak, which had taken only forty-five minutes when they had strolled over earlier in the summer to visit a female member of a Mexican expedition whom Darsney had been trying, all summer, to seduce, had become a four-hour ordeal of stumbling on altitude-spindled legs under weight they couldn't imagine carrying for more than sixty miles.

Mouzafer and his friend Yakub had completed their assignment for the Mexican team and were headed home down the Baltoro unladen. They offered to carry Mortenson and Darsney's heavy packs all the way to Askole for four dollars a day. The Americans had happily agreed and though they were down to their last handful of rupees, planned to present the men with more when they'd made it out of the mountains.

Mouzafer was a Balti, the mountain people who populated the least hospitable high-altitude valleys in northern Pakistan. The Balti had originally migrated southwest from Tibet, via Ladakh, more than six hundred years ago, and their Buddhism had been scoured away as they traveled over the rocky passes and replaced by a religion more attuned to the severity of their new landscape—Shiite Islam. But they retained their language, an antique form of Tibetan. With their diminutive size, toughness, and supreme ability to thrive at altitudes where few humans choose even to visit, they have physically reminded many mountaineers climbing in Baltistan of their distant cousins to the east, the Sherpa of Nepal. But other qualities of the Balti, a taciturn suspicion of outsiders, along with their unyielding faith, have prevented Westerners from celebrating them in the same fashion as they fetishize the Buddhist Sherpa.

Fosco Maraini, a member of the 1958 Italian expedition that managed the first ascent of Gasherbrum IV, a rugged neighbor of K2, was so appalled and fascinated by the Balti, that his erudite book about the expedition, *Karakoram: The Ascent of Gasherbrum IV*, reads more like a scholarly treatise on the Balti way of life than a memoir of mountaineering triumph. "They connive, and complain and frustrate one to the utmost. And beyond their often-foul odor, they have an unmistakable air of the brigand," Maraini wrote. "But if you are able to overlook their roughness, you'll learn they serve you faithfully, and they are high-spirited. Physically they are strong; above all in the show of resistance they can put up to hardship and fatigue. You can see thin little men with legs like storks', shouldering forty kilos day after day, along tracks that would make the stranger think twice before he ventured on them carrying nothing at all."

Mouzafer crouched in the cave, blowing violently on the sagebrush he'd lit with a flint until it bloomed into flame. He was ruggedly handsome, though his missing teeth and sun-weathered skin made him look much older than a man in his mid-fifties. He prepared *paiyu cha*, the butter tea that forms the basis of the Balti diet. After brewing green tea in a blackened tin pot, he added salt, baking soda, and goat's milk, before tenderly shaving a sliver of *mar*, the aged rancid yak butter the Balti prize above all other delicacies, and stirred it into the brew with a not especially clean forefinger.

Mortenson looked on nervously. He'd smelled *paiyu cha* ever since arriving in Baltistan, and its aroma, which he describes as "stinkier than the most frightening cheese the French ever invented," had driven him to invent any number of excuses to avoid drinking it.

Mouzafer handed him a smoking mug.

Mortenson gagged at first, but his body wanted the salt and warmth and he swallowed it all. Mouzafer refilled the mug. Then dipped it full again.

"*Zindabad!* Good! Mr. Gireg," Mouzafer said after the third cup, pounding Mortenson delightedly on the shoulder, clouding the tiny cave with more of Mortenson's surplus of dust.

Darsney had gone on ahead toward Askole with Yakub, and for the next three days, until they were off the Baltoro, Mouzafer never let Mortenson out of his sight. On the trail that Mortenson still struggled to follow, but Mouzafer saw as clearly as the New Jersey Turnpike, the porter held Mortenson's hand as they walked, or insisted that his charge walk directly on the heels of the cheap plastic Chinese high-tops that he wore without socks. Even during his five daily prayer sessions, Mouzafer, a fastidious man of faith, would steal a glance away from Mecca to make sure Mortenson was still nearby.

Mortenson made the best of their proximity and quizzed Mouzafer on the Balti words for all they saw. Glacier was *gangs-zhing*, avalanche *rdo-rut*. And the Balti had as many names for rock as the Inuit have for snow. *Brak-lep* was flat rock, to be used for sleeping or cooking upon. *Khrok* was wedge-shaped, ideal for sealing holes in stone homes. And small round rocks were *khodos*, which one heated in a fire, then wrapped in dough to make skull-shaped *kurba*, unleavened bread, which they baked every morning before setting out. With his ear for languages, Mortenson soon had a basic Balti vocabulary.

Picking his way down a narrow gorge, Mortenson stepped off ice and onto solid ground for the first time in more than three months. The snout of the Baltoro Glacier lay at the bottom of a canyon, black with debris and sculpted to a point like the nose of a 747. From this aperture, the subterranean rivers traveling under sixty-two kilometers of ice shot into the open with an airblast like a jet engine's exhaust. This foaming, turbulent waterspout was the birthplace of the Braldu

River. Five years later, a Swedish kayaker arrived with a documentary film crew and put in at this same spot, attempting to run the Braldu to the Indus River, all eighteen hundred miles to the Arabian Sea. He was dead, smashed against boulders by the primordial strength of the Braldu, minutes after he hit the water.

Mortenson saw his first flower in months, a five-petaled pink rose-hip, and he knelt to examine it, marking as it did his return from eternal winter. Reeds and sagebrush dotted the riverbanks as they walked down, and life, meager though it was in this rocky river gorge, seemed lush to Mortenson. The autumn air down at eleven thousand feet had a weight and luxury he'd forgotten.

Now that they had left the dangers of the Baltoro behind, Mouzafer hiked ahead, setting up camp and preparing dinner each evening before Mortenson arrived. Though Mortenson occasionally strayed where the trail forked toward a shepherd's summer pasture, he soon found the path again and it seemed a simple enough business to follow the river until he found the smoke of Mouzafer's campfire each evening. Walking on his weak and aching legs wasn't as simple, but, since he had no choice, he soldiered on, stopping more and more often to rest.

On his seventh day after leaving K2, high on a ledge on the south bank of the Braldu River Gorge, Mortenson saw his first trees. They were five poplars, bowed by strong wind, and waving like the fingers of a welcoming hand. They had been planted in a row, indicating human influence, rather than the raw force of the Karakoram, a force that sent shelves of ice and slabs of rock racing down mountainsides where they indiscriminately blotted out creatures as insignificant as a lone human. The trees told Mortenson he'd made it down alive.

Lost in contemplation of the greenery, he failed to see the main trail fork down to the river, where it led to a *zamba*, a "bridge" of yak hair rope lashed together and strung across the torrent between two boulders. For the second time, Mortenson had lost his way. The bridge led to his destination, Askole, eight miles farther on the north side of the river. Instead, he stayed high on the ledge that led along the river's south bank, walking toward the trees.

The poplars petered out into apricot orchards. Here, at ten thousand feet, the harvest had already ended by mid-September. Piles of ripe fruit were stacked on hundreds of flat woven baskets. They bathed the underleaves of the apricot trees with their fiery reflection.

There were women kneeling by the baskets, splitting the fruit and setting aside their pits to be pried open for the nutty meat of their kernels. But they pulled their shawls over their faces when they saw him and ran to put trees between themselves and the *Angrezi*, the strange white man.

Children had no such reservations. Mortenson gathered a comet's tail as he passed into tawny fields where other women peered at him over growths of buckwheat and barley, which they were at work harvesting with scythes. The children fingered his *shalwar*, searched his wrists for the watch he didn't wear, and took turns holding his hands.

For the first time in many months, Mortenson became aware of his appearance. His hair was long and unkempt. He felt huge, and filthy. "By that time it had been more than three months since I'd had a shower," he says. He stooped, trying not to tower over the children. But they didn't seem to find him threatening. Their *shalwar kamiz* were as stained and torn as his own, and most were barefoot despite the cold.

Mortenson smelled the village of Korphe a mile before he approached it. The scent of juniper woodsmoke and unwashed humanity was overwhelming after the sterility of altitude. Thinking he was still on the correct trail, he assumed he was approaching Askole, which he'd passed through three months earlier on his way to K2, but nothing looked familiar. By the time he reached the village's ceremonial entrance, a simple archway constructed of poplar beams standing alone at the edge of a potato field, he was leading a procession of fifty children.

He looked ahead, hoping to see Mouzafer waiting at the outskirts of town. Instead, standing on the other side of the gate, wearing a *topi*, a lambswool pillbox cap the same distinguished shade of gray as his beard, a wizened old man, with features so strong they might have been carved out of the canyon walls, waited. His name was Haji Ali and he was the *nurmadhar*, the chief, of Korphe.

"*As-salaam Alaaikum*," Haji Ali said, shaking Mortenson's hand. He escorted him through the gate with the hospitality that is unforgivable for the Balti not to extend, led him first to a ceremonial brook, where he instructed Mortenson to wash his hands and face, and then on to his home.

Korphe was perched on a shelf eight hundred feet above the Braldu River, which clung in unlikely fashion to the side of the canyon wall like a rock climber's sleeping platform bolted into the side of a sheer cliff. The tightly packed warren of square three-story stone homes, built without adornment, would have been almost indistinguishable from the canyon walls but for the riot of apricots, onions, and wheat piled colorfully on their flat roofs.

Haji Ali led Mortenson into a hut that looked no nobler than the others. He beat a pile of bedding until its dust was distributed throughout the *balti*, the large, central room, placed cushions at the spot of honor close to an open hearth, and installed Mortenson there.

There was no talk as tea was prepared, only the shuffle of feet and placement of pillows as twenty male members of Haji Ali's extended family filed in and took their places around the hearth. Most of the acrid smoke from a yak dung fire under the teapot escaped, mercifully, through a large open square in the ceiling. When Mortenson looked up, he saw the eyes of the fifty children who had followed him, ringing the opening in the ceiling as they lay on the roof. No foreigner had ever been to Korphe before.

Haji Ali worked his hand vigorously in the pocket of his embroidered vest, rubbing rancid pieces of ibex jerky against leaves of a strong green chewing tobacco known as *naswar*. He offered a piece to Mortenson, after it had been thoroughly seasoned, and Mortenson choked down the single most challenging mouthful of his life, as the gallery of spectators chuckled appreciatively.

When Haji Ali handed him a cup of butter tea, Mortenson drank it with something similar to pleasure.

The headman leaned forward, now that the required threshold of hospitality had been crossed, and thrust his bearded face in front of Mortenson's.

"Cheezaley?" he barked, an indispensable Balti word that means, roughly, "What the hell?"

With snatches of Balti, and a lot of gesticulating, Mortenson told the crowd now watching him with rapt attention that he was American, that he'd come to climb K2 (which produced appreciative murmurs from the men), that he had become weak and sick and had walked here to Askole to find a jeep willing to take him on the eight-hour journey down to Skardu, Baltistan's capital.

Mortenson sank back on his cushions, having drained his final reserve, between the endless days of walking and the effort it took to convey so much information. Here, warm by the hearth, on soft pillows, snug in the crush of so much humanity, he felt the exhaustion he'd been holding at arm's length surge up over him.

"Met Askole" ("not Askole"), Haji Ali said, laughing. He pointed at the ground by his feet. *"Korphe,"* he said.

Adrenaline snapped Mortenson back upright. He'd never heard of Korphe. He was positive it hadn't appeared on any map he'd ever studied of the Karakoram, and he'd studied dozens. Rousing himself, he explained that he had to get to Askole and meet a man named Mouzafer who was carrying all his belongings.

Haji Ali gripped his guest by the shoulders with his powerful hands and pushed him back on the pillows. He summoned his son Twaha, who had traveled down to Skardu often enough to acquire a smattering of Western vocabulary, and instructed him to translate. "Today walking Askole no go. Big problem. Half one days trekking," said the man, who was an unmistakable incarnation of his father, minus the beard. *"Inshallah,* tomorrow Haji send find man Mouzafer. Now you slip."

Haji Ali stood and waved the children away from the darkening square of sky. The men melted from the hearth back to their homes. Despite the anxiety swirling through his thoughts, his anger at himself for having strayed from the trail again, his complete and utter sense of displacement, Greg Mortenson slipped, and fell unshakably asleep.

CHAPTER 3

"PROGRESS AND PERFECTION"

"Tell us, if there were one thing we could do for your village,
what would it be?"
"With all respect, Sahib, you have little to teach us in strength
and toughness. And we don't envy you your restless spirits.
Perhaps we are happier than you? But we would like our children to
go to school. Of all the things you have, learning is the one
we most desire for our children."

—Conversation between Sir Edmund Hillary and Urkien Sherpa,
from *Schoolhouse in the Clouds*

SOMEONE HAD TUCKED a heavy quilt over him. He was snug beneath it and Mortenson luxuriated in the warmth. It was the first night he'd spent indoors since late spring. By the faint light of coals in the hearth, he could see the outline of several sleeping figures. Snoring came from all corners of the room, in all different calibers. He rolled back over and added his own.

The next time he woke, he was alone and blue sky showed clearly through the square in the ceiling. Haji Ali's wife, Sakina, saw him stir and brought a *lassi,* a fresh-baked *chapatti,* and sweet tea. She was the first Balti woman who had ever approached him. Mortenson thought that Sakina had perhaps the kindest face he'd ever seen. It was wrinkled in a way that suggested smile lines had set up camp at the corners of her mouth and eyes, then marched toward each other until they completed their conquest. She wore her long hair elaborately braided in the Tibetan fashion, under an *urdwa,* a wool cap adorned with beads and shells and antique coins. She stood, waiting, for Mortenson to sample his breakfast.

He took a bite of warm *chapatti* dunked in *lassi,* wolfed all that he'd been served, and washed it down with sugary tea. Sakina laughed appreciatively and brought him more. If Mortenson had known how scarce and precious sugar was to the Balti, how rarely they used it themselves, he would have refused the second cup of tea.

Sakina left him and he studied the room. It was spartan to the point of poverty. A faded travel poster of a Swiss chalet, in a lush meadow alive with wildflowers, was nailed to one wall. Every other object, from blackened cooking tools to oft-repaired oil lanterns, seemed strictly functional. The heavy quilt he had slept under was made of plush maroon silk and decorated with tiny mirrors. The blankets the others had used were thin worn wool, patched with whatever scraps had been at hand. They had clearly wrapped him in the finest possession in Haji Ali's home.

Late in the afternoon, Mortenson heard raised voices and walked, with most of the rest of the village, to the cliff overlooking the Braldu. He saw a man pulling himself along in a box suspended from a steel cable strung two hundred feet above the river. Crossing the river this way saved the half day it would take a trekker to walk upriver and cross at the bridge above Korphe, but a fall would mean certain death. When the man was halfway across the gorge, Mortenson recognized Mouzafer, and saw that he was wedged into the tiny cable car, just a box cobbled together from scrap lumber, riding on top of a familiar-looking ninety-pound pack.

This time the backslapping from Mouzafer's greeting didn't catch him unprepared, and Mortenson managed not to cough. Mouzafer stepped back and looked him up and down, his eyes wet, then raised his hands to the sky, shouting *Allah Akbhar!* and shook them as if manna had already begun piling up around his feet.

At Haji Ali's, over a meal of *biango*, roasted hen that was as wiry and tough as the Balti people who had raised the birds, Mortenson learned that Mouzafer was well known throughout the Karakoram. For three decades he had served as one of the most skilled high-altitude porters in the Himalaya. His accomplishments were vast and varied and included accompanying famed climber Nick Clinch on the first American ascent of Masherbrum in 1960. But what Mortenson found most impressive about Mouzafer was that he'd never mentioned his accomplishments in all the time they'd spent walking and talking.

Mortenson discreetly handed Mouzafer three thousand rupees, far more than the wages they'd agreed on, and promised to visit him in his own village, when he'd fully healed. Mortenson had no way of knowing then that Mouzafer would remain a presence in his life over the next decade, helping to guide him past the roadblocks of life in northern Pakistan with the same sure hand he had shown avoiding avalanches and skirting crevasses.

With Mouzafer, Mortenson met up with Darsney and made the long journey by jeep down to Skardu. But after sampling the pedestrian pleasures of a well-prepared meal and a comfortable bed at a renowned mountaineers' lodge called the K2 Motel, Mortenson felt something tugging him back up into the Karakoram. He felt he had found something rare in Korphe and returned as soon as he could arrange a ride.

From his base in Haji Ali's home, Mortenson settled into a routine. Each morning and afternoon he would walk briefly about Korphe, accompanied, always, by children tugging at his hands. He saw how this tiny oasis of greenery in a desert of dusty rock owed its existence to staggering labor, and admired the hundreds of irrigation channels the village maintained by hand that diverted glacial meltwater toward their fields and orchards.

Off the Baltoro, out of danger, he realized just how precarious his own survival had been, and how weakened he'd become. He could barely make it down the switchback path that led to the river and there, in the freezing water, when he took off his shirt to wash, he was shocked by his appearance. "My arms looked like spindly little toothpicks, like they belonged to somebody else," Mortenson says.

Wheezing his way back up to the village, he felt as infirm as the elderly men who sat for hours at a time under Korphe's apricot trees, smoking from hookahs and eating apricot kernels. After an hour or two of poking about each day he'd succumb to exhaustion and return to stare at the sky from his nest of pillows by Haji Ali's hearth.

The *nurmadhar* watched Mortenson's state carefully, and ordered one of the village's precious *chogo rabak*, or big rams, slaughtered. Forty people tore every scrap of roasted meat from the skinny animal's bones, then cracked open the bones themselves with rocks, stripping the marrow with their teeth. Watching the ardor with which the meat was devoured, Mortenson realized how rare such a meal was for the people of Korphe, and how close they lived to hunger.

As his strength returned, his power of perception sharpened. At first, in Korphe, he thought he'd stumbled into a sort of Shangri-La. Many Westerners passing through the Karakoram had the feeling that the Balti lived a simpler, better life than they did back home in their developed countries. Early visitors, casting about for suitably romantic names, dubbed it "Tibet of the Apricots."

The Balti "really seem to have a flair for enjoying life," Maraini wrote in 1958, after visiting Askole and admiring the "old bodies of men sitting in the sun smoking their picturesque pipes, those not so old working at primitive looms in the shade of mulberry trees with that sureness of touch that comes with a lifetime's experience, and two boys, sitting by themselves, removing their lice with tender and meticulous care.

"We breathed an air of utter satisfaction, of eternal peace," he continued. "All this gives rise to a question. Isn't it better to live in ignorance of everything—asphalt and macadam, vehicles, telephones, television—to live in bliss without knowing it?"

Thirty-five years later, the Balti still lived with the same lack of modern conveniences, but after even a few days in the village, Mortenson began to see that Korphe was far from the prelapsarian paradise of Western fantasy. In every home, at least one family member suffered from goiters or cataracts. The children, whose ginger hair he had admired, owed their coloring to a form of malnutrition called kwashiorkor. And he learned from his talks with Twaha, after the *nurmadhar*'s son returned from evening prayer at the village mosque, that the nearest doctor was a week's walk away in Skardu, and one out of every three Korphe children died before reaching their first birthday.

Twaha told Mortenson that his own wife, Rhokia, had died during the birth, seven years earlier, of his only child, his daughter, Jahan. The maroon, mirrored quilt that Mortenson felt honored to sleep under had been the centerpiece of Rhokia's dowry.

Mortenson couldn't imagine ever discharging the debt he felt to his hosts in Korphe. But he was determined to try. He began distributing all he had. Small useful items like Nalgene bottles and flashlights were precious to the Balti, who trekked long distances to graze their animals in summer, and he handed them out to the members of Haji Ali's extended family. To Sakina, he gave his camping stove, capable of burning the kerosene found in every Balti village. He draped his wine-colored L.L. Bean fleece jacket over Twaha's shoulders, pressing him to take it even though it was several sizes too large. Haji Ali he presented with the insulated Helly Hansen jacket that had kept him warm on K2.

But it was the supplies he carried in the expedition's medical kit, along with his training as a trauma nurse, that proved the most valuable. Each day, as he grew stronger, he spent longer hours climbing the steep paths between Korphe's homes, doing what little he could to beat back the avalanche of need. With tubes of antibiotic ointment, he treated open sores and lanced and drained infected wounds. Everywhere he turned, eyes would implore him from the depths of homes, where elderly Balti had suffered in silence for years. He set broken bones and did what little he could with painkillers and antibiotics. Word of his work spread and the sick on the outskirts of Korphe began sending relatives to fetch "Dr. Greg," as he would thereafter be known in northern Pakistan, no matter how many times he tried to tell people he was just a nurse.

Often during his time in Korphe, Mortenson felt the presence of his little sister Christa, especially when he was with Korphe's children. "Everything about their life was a struggle," Mortenson says. "They reminded me of the way Christa had to fight for the simplest things. And also the way she had of just persevering, no matter what life threw at her." He decided he wanted to do something for them. Perhaps, when he got to Islamabad, he'd use the last of his money to buy textbooks to send to their school, or supplies.

Lying by the hearth before bed, Mortenson told Haji Ali he wanted to visit Korphe's school. Mortenson saw a cloud pass across the old man's craggy face, but persisted. Finally, the headman agreed to take Mortenson first thing the following morning.

After their familiar breakfast of *chapattis* and *cha*, Haji Ali led Mortenson up a steep path to a vast open ledge eight hundred feet above the Braldu. The view was exquisite, with the ice giants of the upper Baltoro razored into the blue far above Korphe's gray rock walls. But Mortenson wasn't admiring the scenery. He was appalled to see eighty-two children, seventy-eight boys, and the four girls who had the pluck to join them, kneeling on the frosty ground, in the open. Haji Ali, avoiding Mortenson's eyes, said that the village had no school, and the Pakistani government didn't provide a teacher. A teacher cost the equivalent of one dollar a day, he explained, which was more than the village

31

could afford. So they shared a teacher with the neighboring village of Munjung, and he taught in Korphe three days a week. The rest of the time the children were left alone to practice the lessons he left behind.

Mortenson watched, his heart in his throat, as the students stood at rigid attention and began their "school day" with Pakistan's national anthem. "Blessed be the sacred land. Happy be the bounteous realm, symbol of high resolve, land of Pakistan," they sang with sweet raggedness, their breath steaming in air already touched with winter. Mortenson picked out Twaha's seven-year-old daughter, Jahan, standing tall and straight beneath her headscarf as she sang. "May the nation, the country, and the state shine in glory everlasting. This flag of crescent and star leads the way to progress and perfection."

During his recuperation in Korphe, Mortenson had frequently heard villagers complain about the Punjabi-dominated Pakistani government, which they considered a foreign, lowland power. The common refrain was how a combination of corruption and neglect siphoned off what little money was meant for the people of Baltistan as it made the long journey from Islamabad, the capital, to these distant mountain valleys. They found it ironic that the Islamabad government would fight so hard to pry away this piece of what had once been Kashmir from India, while doing so little for its people.

And it was obvious that most of the money that reached this altitude was earmarked for the army, to finance its costly standoff with Indian forces along the Siachen Glacier. But a dollar a day for a teacher, Mortenson fumed, how could a government, even one as impoverished as Pakistan's, not provide that? Why couldn't the flag of crescent and star lead these children such a small distance toward "progress and perfection"?

After the last note of the anthem had faded, the children sat in a neat circle and began copying their multiplication tables. Most scratched in the dirt with sticks they'd brought for that purpose. The more fortunate, like Jahan, had slate boards they wrote on with sticks dipped in a mixture of mud and water. "Can you imagine a fourth-grade class in America, alone, without a teacher, sitting there quietly and working on their lessons?" Mortenson asks. "I felt like my heart was being torn out. There was a fierceness in their desire to learn, despite how mightily everything was stacked against them, that reminded me of Christa. I knew I had to do something."

But what? He had just enough money, if he ate simply and stayed in the cheapest guest houses, to travel by jeep and bus back to Islamabad and catch his flight home.

In California he could look forward to only sporadic nursing work, and most of his possessions fit in the trunk of "La Bamba," the burgundy gas-guzzling Buick that was as close as he had to a home. Still, there had to be something.

Standing next to Haji Ali, on the ledge overlooking the valley, with such a crystalline view of the mountains he'd come halfway around the world to measure himself against, climbing K2 to place a necklace on its summit suddenly felt beside the point. There was a much more meaningful gesture he could make in honor of his sister's memory. He put his hands on Haji Ali's shoulders, as the old man had done to him dozens of times since they'd shared their first cup of tea. "I'm going to build you a school," he said, not yet realizing that with those words, the path of his life had just detoured down another trail, a route far more serpentine and arduous than the wrong turns he'd taken since retreating from K2. "I *will* build a school," Mortenson said. "I promise."

CHAPTER 4

SELF-STORAGE

Greatness is always built on this foundation: the ability
to appear, speak and act, as the most common man.

—Shams-ud-din Muhammed Hafiz

THE STORAGE SPACE smelled like Africa. Standing on the verge of this
unlocked six-by-eight-foot room, a closet really, with rush-hour traffic boiling past on busy San Pablo Avenue, Mortenson felt the dislocation that only forty-eight hours of air travel can inflict. On the flight
out of Islamabad he had felt so full of purpose, scheming a dozen different ways to raise money for the school. But back in Berkeley, California, Greg Mortenson couldn't orient himself. He felt blotted out
under the relentlessly sunny skies, among prosperous college students
strolling happily toward their next espresso, and his promise to Haji
Ali felt more like a half-remembered movie he'd dozed through on
one of his three interminable flights.

Jet lag. Culture shock. Whatever name you gave the demons of
dislocation, he'd been assailed by them often enough in the past.
Which was why he'd come here, as he always did after returning from
a climb—to Berkeley Self-Storage stall 114. This musty space was
Mortenson's anchor to himself.

He reached into the fragrant dark, fumbling for the string that illuminated the overhead bulb, and when he found and tugged it, he saw
dusty mountaineering books stacked against the walls, a caravan of
fine elephants carved out of African ebony that had been his father's,
and sitting on top of a dog-eared photo album, GiGi, a coffee-colored
stuffed monkey that had been his closest companion back where
memory fringes into mere sensory recall.

He picked up the child's toy, and saw that the animal's African

34

kapok stuffing was leaking out a seam in its chest. He pressed it to his nose, inhaling, and was back by the sprawling cinder-block house, in the courtyard, under the all-enveloping limbs of their pepper tree. In Tanzania.

Like his father, Mortenson had been born in Minnesota. But in 1958, when he was only three months old, his parents had packed him along on the great adventure of their lives, a posting to work as missionaries teaching in Tanzania, in the shadow of the continent's highest peak, Mount Kilimanjaro.

Irvin Mortenson, Greg's father, was born of the well-intentioned Lutheran stock that Garrison Keillor has mined for so much material. As with the taciturn men of Lake Wobegon, language was a currency he was loath to spend carelessly. Well over six feet, and a raw-boned athlete like his son, Irvin Mortenson was nicknamed "Dempsey" as an unusually stout baby, and the boxer's name blotted out his given name for the rest of his life. The seventh and final child in a family economically exhausted by the Great Depression, Dempsey's athletic prowess—he was an all-state quarterback on his high-school football team and an all-state guard on the basketball team—got him out of Pequot Lakes, a tiny fish-crazy town in northern Minnesota, and sent him on a path to the wider world. He attended the University of Minnesota on a football scholarship, earning a degree in physical education while nursing the bruises inflicted by defensive linemen.

His wife, Jerene, swooned for him shortly after her family moved to Minnesota from Iowa. She, too, was an athlete and had been the captain of her high-school basketball team. They married impulsively, while Dempsey, then serving in the army, was on leave from Fort Riley, Kansas, on a three-day pass. "Dempsey had the travel bug," Jerene says. "He had been stationed in Japan and had loved seeing more of the world than Minnesota. He came home one day while I was pregnant with Greg and said, 'They need teachers in Tanganyika. Let's go to Africa.' I couldn't say no. When you're young you don't know what you don't know. We just did it."

They were posted to a country neither knew much about beyond the space it occupied on the map of East Africa between Kenya and Rwanda. After four years working in the remote Usambara Mountains, they moved to Moshi, which means "smoke" in Swahili, where the family was billeted by their Lutheran missionary society in a

Greek gun dealer's sprawling cinder-block home, which had been seized by the authorities. And with the sort of serendipity that so often rewards impetuousness, the entire family fell fiercely in love with the country that would be renamed Tanzania after independence in 1961. "The older I get, the more I appreciate my childhood. It was paradise," Mortenson says.

More so than the house, which wrapped comfortably around a lush courtyard, Mortenson saw the enormous pepper tree as home. "That tree was the image of stability," Mortenson says. "At dusk, the hundreds of bats that lived in it would swarm out to hunt. And after it rained, the whole yard smelled like pepper. That smell was exquisite."

With both Dempsey and Jerene wearing their faith lightly, the Mortenson home became more of a community than a religious center. Dempsey taught Sunday school. But he also laid out a softball diamond with the trunk of the pepper tree as a backstop and launched Tanzania's first high-school basketball league. But it was two all-consuming projects that came to dominate Dempsey and Jerene's lives.

Dempsey threw every molecule of himself into the great achievement of his life—raising money for and founding Tanzania's first teaching hospital, the Kilimanjaro Christian Medical Center. Jerene labored with the same single-mindedness to establish the Moshi International School, which catered to a cosmopolitan melting pot of expatriates' children. Greg attended the school, swimming happily in a sea of cultures and languages. The divisions between different nationalities meant so little to him that he was upset when they fought with each other. During a time of intense conflict between India and Pakistan, Greg was disturbed by the graphic way Indian and Pakistani students played war at recess, pretending to machine gun and decapitate each other.

"Otherwise, it was a wonderful place to go to school," he says. "It was like a little United Nations. There were twenty-eight different nationalities and we celebrated all the holidays: Hanukkah, Christmas, Diwali, the Feast of Id."

"Greg hated going to church with us," Jerene remembers, "because all the old African ladies always wanted to play with his blond hair." Otherwise, Mortenson grew up happily oblivious to race. He soon mastered Swahili with such accentless perfection that people presumed he was Tanzanian on the phone. He sang archaic European hymns in his church choir, and joined an otherwise all-African dance troupe that competed in a nationally televised tribal dance contest for Saba Saba, Tanzania's independence day.

At age eleven, Greg Mortenson scaled his first serious mountain. "Ever since I was six, I'd been staring at the summit and begging my father to take me there." Finally, when Dempsey deemed his son old enough to make the climb, rather than enjoying his trip to the top of Africa, Greg says, "I gagged and puked my way up Kilimanjaro. I hated the climb. But standing on the summit at dawn, seeing the sweep of African savannah below me, hooked me forever on climbing."

Jerene gave birth to three girls: Kari, Sonja Joy, and finally, when Greg was twelve, Christa. Dempsey was often away for months at a time, recruiting funds and qualified hospital staff in Europe and America. And Greg, already over six feet by the time he turned thirteen, shuffled easily into the role of man of the house when his father was absent. When Christa was born, her parents took her to be baptized and Greg volunteered to serve as her godfather.

Unlike the three oldest Mortensons, who quickly grew to their parents' scale, Christa remained small and delicate-boned. And by the time she started school, it was apparent she differed profoundly from the rest of her family. As a toddler, Christa had a terrible reaction to a smallpox vaccination. "Her arm turned completely black," Jerene says. And she believes that toxic injection of live bovine virus marked the beginning of Christa's brain dysfunction. At age three, she contracted severe meningitis, and in her frantic mother's eyes, never emerged whole after the illness. By eight, she began suffering frequent seizures and was diagnosed as an epileptic. But between these episodes, Christa also ailed. "She learned to read right away," Jerene says. "But they were just sounds to her. She didn't have a clue what the sentences meant."

A still-growing Greg became a looming presence over anyone who would consider teasing his littlest sister. "Christa was the nicest of us," he says. "She faced her limitations with grace. It would take her forever to dress herself in the morning, so she'd lay her clothes out the night before, trying not to take up too much of our time before school. She was remarkably sensitive to other people."

"In some ways, she was like my dad," Mortenson says. "They were both listeners." Dempsey listened, especially, to the young, ambitious Africans in Moshi. They were eager for opportunity, but postcolonial Tanzania—then, as now, one of the poorest nations on

Earth—had little to offer them beyond menial agricultural work. When his teaching hospital was up and partially running, he insisted, against the wishes of many foreign members of the board, that they focus on offering medical scholarships to promising local students, rather than simply catering to expat children and the offspring of East Africa's wealthy elite.

Just after Greg's fourteenth birthday, the 640-bed hospital was finally completed, and the president of Tanzania, Julius Nyerere, spoke at the ribbon-cutting. Greg's father purchased gallons of *pombe*, the local banana beer, and cut down all the bushes in their yard to better accommodate the five hundred locals and expats he'd invited to a barbecue celebrating the hospital's success. Standing on a stage he'd built for musicians under the pepper tree, Dempsey, wearing a traditional black Tanzanian outfit, stood and addressed the community he'd come to love.

After fourteen years in Africa, he'd put on weight, but he held himself straight as he spoke, and looked, his son thought, if not like the athlete he'd once been, then still formidable. He began by thanking his Tanzanian partner at the hospital, John Moshi, who Dempsey said was just as responsible for the medical center's success as he was. "I have a prediction to make," he said in Swahili, looking so at peace with himself that Greg remembers, for once, his father didn't seem awkward speaking in front of a crowd. "In ten years, the head of every department at the Kilimanjaro Christian Medical Center will be a Tanzanian. It's your country. It's your hospital," he said.

"I could feel the swell of pride from the Africans," Mortenson remembers. "The expats wanted him to say, 'Look what we've done for you.' But he was saying, 'Look what you've done for yourselves and how much more you can do.'

"My dad got blasted by the expats for that," Mortenson says. "But you know what? It happened. The place he built is still there today, the top teaching hospital in Tanzania, and a decade after he finished it, all the department heads were African. Watching him up there, I felt so proud that this big, barrel-chested man was my father. He taught me, he taught all of us, that if you believe in yourself, you can accomplish anything."

With both the school and hospital well-established, the Mortensons' work was done in Tanzania. Dempsey was offered a tempting job—establishing a hospital for Palestinian refugees on Jerusalem's Mount of Olives—but the Mortensons decided it was time for their children to experience America.

Greg and his sisters were both excited and anxious about moving back to what they still considered their country, despite the fact that they'd only been there on brief visits half a dozen times. Greg had read the entry on each of the fifty states in the family's set of encyclopedias, trying to both picture and prepare for America. For fourteen years, their relatives in Minnesota had written of family functions the African Mortensons had to miss and sent newspaper clippings about the Minnesota Twins, which Greg preserved in his room and reread at night, artifacts from an exotic culture he hoped to understand.

The Mortensons crated up their books and weavings and woodcarvings and moved into Jerene's parents' old four-story home in St. Paul, before buying an inexpensive pale green home in a middle-class suburb called Roseville. On his first day of American high school, Greg was relieved to see so many black students roaming the halls of St. Paul Central. He didn't feel so far from Moshi. Word quickly spread that the big, awkward fifteen-year-old had come from Africa.

Between classes, a tall, sinewy basketball player wearing a Cadillac hood ornament around his neck on a gold chain shoved Mortenson up against a drinking fountain, while his friends closed in menacingly. "You ain't no African," he sneered, then the pack of boys began raining blows on Mortenson while he tried to cover his head, wondering what he'd done. When they finally stopped, Mortenson lowered his arms, his lips trembling. The leader of the group wound up and smashed his fist into Mortenson's eye. Another boy picked up a trash can and upended it onto his head. Mortenson stood by the drinking fountain, the reeking can covering his head, listening as laughter faded down the hallway.

In most respects, Mortenson proved adaptable to American culture. He excelled academically, especially in math, music, and the sciences, and, of course, he had the genetic predisposition to succeed at sports.

After the Mortensons moved to the suburbs, Greg's looming presence on the Ramsey High School football team as a defensive lineman broke open a path of, if not friendship, then camaraderie with other students. But in one respect, he remained out of sorts with American life. "Greg has never been on time in his life," his mother says. "Ever since he was a boy, Greg has always operated on African time."

The family's work in Africa had been rewarding in every way except monetarily. Paying tuition at an expensive private school was out of the question, so Mortenson asked his father what he should do. "I went to college on the GI Bill," Dempsey said. "You could do worse." In April of his senior year, Greg visited an army recruiting office in St. Paul and signed on for a two-year tour of duty. "It was a very weird thing to do, right after Vietnam," Greg says. "And kids at my school were amazed I'd even consider the military. But we were broke."

Four days after his high-school graduation, Mortenson landed in basic training at Fort Leonard Wood, Missouri. While most of his classmates were sleeping in during the summer before college, he was jarred awake the first morning at five by a drill sergeant kicking and shaking his bunk and shouting, "Drop your cocks and grab your socks!"

"I decided I wasn't going to let this guy terrify me," Mortenson says. So he greeted Senior Drill Sergeant Parks the next morning at five, sitting fully dressed in the dark on his tightly made cot. "He cussed me out for failing to get eight hours' sleep while I was on government time, made me do forty push-ups, then marched me over to HQ, gave me a stripe, and marched me back to my bunk. 'This is Mortenson, he's your new platoon leader,' the sergeant said. 'He outranks all you mofos so do what the man say.'"

Mortenson was too quiet to effectively order his fellow soldiers around. But he excelled in the army. He was still supremely fit from football and the high-school track team, so the rigors of basic training weren't as memorable to Mortenson as the poor morale he found endemic in the post-Vietnam military. He was taught advanced artillery skills and tactics, then embarked on his lifelong interest in medicine when he received training as a medic, before being posted to Germany with the Thirty-third Armored Division. "I was really naïve when I enlisted, but the army has a way of shocking that out of you," Mortenson says. "A lot of guys after Vietnam were hooked on heroin. They'd OD in their bunks and we'd have to go and collect their bodies." He also remembers one winter morning when he had to collect the corpse of a sergeant who'd been beaten and left in a snowy ditch to die, because his fellow soldiers found out he was gay.

Posted to Bamberg, Germany, near the East German border, Mortenson perfected the ability he would have for the rest of his life, thanks to the military's irregular hours, to fall asleep anywhere, at a moment's notice. He was an exemplary soldier. "I never fired a gun at anyone," Mortenson says, "but this was before the Berlin Wall fell and we spent a lot of time looking through our M-16 scopes at the East German guards." On watch, Mortenson was authorized to fire at the Communist snipers if they shot at East German civilians trying to escape. "That happened occasionally, but never while I was on watch," Mortenson says, "thank God."

Most of the white soldiers he knew in Germany would spend weekends "catching the clap, getting drunk, or shooting up," Mortenson says, so he'd catch free military flights with black soldiers instead—to Rome or London or Amsterdam. It was the first time Mortenson had ever traveled independently and he found it, and the company, exhilarating. "In the army my best friends were black," Mortenson says. "In Minnesota, that always seemed awkward, but in the military race was the least of your worries. In Germany I felt really accepted, and for the first time since Tanzania, I wasn't lonely."

Mortenson was awarded the Army Commendation Medal, for evacuating injured soldiers during a live-fire exercise. He was honorably discharged after two years, glad he'd served and now saddled with his second-most-unbreakable habit, after arriving late—the inability to drive a car forward into a parking space. Long after his discharge, he'd still back every vehicle—a jeep in Baltistan, his family Toyota on a trip to the mall—into a space as the army teaches, so it's facing forward and prepared for a quick escape under fire.

He headed to tiny Concordia College in Moorhead, Minnesota, on a football scholarship, where his team won the 1978 NAIA II National Championship. But he quickly grew weary of the homogeneous population at the small, unworldly campus, and transferred to the more diverse University of South Dakota, in Vermillion, on a GI scholarship.

Jerene was a student, working toward her Ph.D. in education, and Dempsey had found a poorly paying, uninspiring job working long hours in the basement of the state capital, on creditor/debtor legislation, so money was tighter than ever for the Mortensons. Greg worked his way through college, washing dishes in the school cafeteria, and as an orderly on the overnight shift at Dakota Hospital. Each month, he secretly sent a portion of his earnings home to his father.

In April 1981, Greg's second year in Vermillion, Dempsey was diagnosed with cancer. He was forty-eight years old. Greg was then a chemistry and nursing student, and when he learned that his father's cancer had metastasized and spread to his lymph nodes and liver, he realized how quickly he could lose him. While cramming for tests and holding down his student jobs, Mortenson endured the six-hour drive home to Minnesota every other weekend to spend time with his father. And at every two-week interval, he was shocked by how quickly Dempsey was deteriorating.

Mortenson, already well-versed in medicine, persuaded Dempsey's doctors to discontinue radiation, knowing his father's condition was terminal and determined that he should have a chance to enjoy what little time he had. Greg offered to drop out of school and care for his father full-time, but Dempsey told his son, "Don't you dare." So the biweekly visits went on. When the weather was fine, he would carry his father outside, shocked by how much weight he had lost, to a lawn chair where he'd sit in the sun. Dempsey, still fixated, perhaps, on the lush grounds of their compound in Moshi, took great care with his herb garden, and ordered his son to leave no weeds standing.

Late at night, while Greg wrestled with sleep, he'd hear the sound of Dempsey typing, painstakingly constructing the ceremony for his own funeral. Jerene would doze on the couch, waiting for the typewriter to fall silent so she could accompany her husband to bed.

In September, Greg visited his father for the last time. Dempsey by then was confined to the Midway Hospital in St. Paul. "I had a test the next morning and didn't want to arrive home in the middle of the night, but I couldn't leave him," Greg remembers. "He wasn't very comfortable with affection, but he kept his hand on my shoulder the whole time I was there. Finally, I got up to leave and he said, 'It's all done. It's all okay. Everything's taken care of.' He was remarkably unafraid of death."

As in Moshi, where Dempsey had thrown a mammoth party to mark the successful end of their time in Africa, Dempsey, having detailed the ceremony to mark the end of his time on Earth, down to the last hymn, died at peace the following morning.

At the overflowing Prince of Peace Lutheran Church in Roseville, mourners received a program that Dempsey had designed called "The Joy of Going Home." Greg gave his father a sendoff in Swahili, calling him *Baba, kaka, ndugu,* "Father, brother, friend." Proud of his military service, Dempsey was laid to rest at the Twin Cities' Ft. Snelling National Cemetery.

With Dempsey dead, and an honors degree in both nursing and chemistry in hand, Mortenson felt remarkably untethered. He considered, and was accepted to Case Western University medical school, but couldn't imagine waiting five more years before earning any money. After his father's death, he began to obsess about losing Christa, whose seizures had become more frequent. So he returned home for a year to spend time with his youngest sister. He helped her find a job assembling IV solution bags at a factory and rode the St. Paul city bus with her a dozen times until she was able to learn the route herself. Christa took great interest in her brother's girlfriends and asked him detailed questions about sex that she was too shy to discuss with her mother. And when Greg learned Christa was dating, he had a nurse talk to her about sex education.

In 1986, Mortenson began a graduate program in neurophysiology at Indiana University, thinking idealistically that with some inspired hard work he might be able to find a cure for his sister. But the wheels of medical research grind too slowly for an impatient twenty-eight-year-old, and the more Mortenson learned about epilepsy, the further away any possible cure seemed to recede. Wading through his dense textbooks, and sitting in labs, he found his mind drifting back to intricate veins of quartz inlaid into granite on The Needles, spiky rock formations in South Dakota's Black Hills, where he'd learned the fundamentals of rock climbing the previous year with two college friends.

He felt the tug with increasing urgency. He had his grandmother's old burgundy Buick, which he'd nicknamed La Bamba. He had a few thousand dollars he'd saved, and he had visions of a different sort of life, one more oriented toward the outdoors, like the life he'd loved in Tanzania. California seemed the obvious place, so he packed La Bamba and bombed out West.

As with most pursuits he has ever cared deeply about, Greg Mortenson's learning curve with climbing was as steep as the rock faces he was soon scaling. To hear him describe those first years in California, there was hardly an interval between the week-long course he took on Southern California's Suicide Rocks and leading climbs of twenty-thousand-foot-plus peaks in Nepal. After a regimented childhood in

his mother's highly structured home, then the army, college, and graduate school, the freedom of climbing, and working just enough to climb
some more, was intoxicatingly new. Mortenson began a career as a
trauma nurse, working overnight and holidays at Bay Area emergency
rooms, taking the shifts no one else wanted in exchange for the freedom
to disappear when the mountains called.

The Bay Area climbing scene can be all-consuming, and Mortenson let himself be swallowed by it. He joined a climbing gym, City
Rock, in an old Emeryville warehouse, where he spent hour after hour
refining his moves. He began running marathons and worked out constantly between expeditions to climb the north face of Mount Baker,
Annapurna IV, Baruntse, and several other Himalayan peaks. "From
1989 to 1992 my life was totally about climbing," Mortenson says.
And the lore of mountaineering had almost as strong a pull on him as
the process of measuring himself against unyielding rock. He amassed
an encyclopedic knowledge of the history of climbing and combed the
Bay Area's used-book stores for nineteenth-century accounts of
mountaineering derring-do. "My pillow those years was a mountaineer's bible called *Freedom of the Hills*," Mortenson says.

Christa came to visit him each year, and he'd try to explain his
love for the mountains to his sister, driving her to Yosemite and tracing his finger along the half-dozen routes he'd taken up the monolithic
granite slab of Half-Dome.

On July 23, 1992, Mortenson was on Mount Sill, in the eastern
Sierra, with his girlfriend at the time, Anna Lopez, a ranger who spent
months alone in the backcountry. At four-thirty in the morning, they
were descending a glacier where they had bivouacked for the night
after summiting, when Mortenson tripped, did a complete forward
flip, then started sliding down the steep slope. His momentum sent
him toppling down the glacier, flipping him five feet in the air with
each bounce and slamming him against the compacted snow and ice.
His heavy pack twisted and ripped his left shoulder out of joint,
breaking his humerus bone. He fell eight hundred vertical feet, until
he managed to jam the tip of his ice axe into the snow and stop himself
with his one working arm.

After Mortenson spent a hallucinatory twenty-four hours stumbling in pain down the mountain and out to the trailhead, Anna drove
him to the nearest emergency room, in Bishop, California. Mortenson

called his mother from the hospital to tell her he'd survived. What he heard hurt him more than his fall. At the same hour that Greg was crashing down Mount Sill, his mother opened Christa's bedroom door to wake her for the trip they'd planned for her twenty-third birthday, to the Field of Dreams in Dyersville, Iowa, where the movie had been filmed. "When I went to wake her Christa was on her hands and knees, like she was trying to get back into bed after going to the bathroom," Jerene says. "And she was blue. I guess the only good thing you could say is that she had died so quickly of a massive seizure that she was just frozen in place."

Mortenson attended the funeral in Minnesota with his arm in a sling. Jerene's brother, Pastor Lane Doerring, gave a eulogy, in which he added an appropriate twist to Christa's favorite movie's most famous line. "Our Christa's going to wake up and say, 'Is this Iowa?' And they'll say 'No, this is heaven'," he told a sobbing crowd of mourners at the same church where they'd bid Dempsey good-bye.

In California, Mortenson felt more meaninglessly adrift than he could ever remember. The phone call from Dan Mazur, an accomplished climber Mortenson knew by his reputation for single-mindedness, felt like a lifeline. He was planning an expedition to K2, mountaineering's ultimate test, and he needed an expedition medic. Would Mortenson consider coming? Here was a path, a means by which Mortenson could get himself back on course and, at the same time, properly honor his sister. He'd climb to the summit those of his avocation respected most, and he'd dedicate his climb to Christa's memory. He'd find a way to wring some meaning out of this meaningless loss.

Gingerly, Mortenson lowered GiGi from his face, and laid the monkey back on top of the photo album. An eighteen wheeler rumbled by out on San Pablo, shaking the little room as it passed. He walked out of the storage space and retrieved his climbing gear from the trunk of La Bamba.

Hanging his harness, his ropes, his crampons, carabiners, hex-bolts, and Jumar ascenders neatly on the hooks where they'd rested only briefly between trips for the last five years, these tools that had carried him across continents and up peaks once thought unassailable by humans seemed powerless. What tools did it take to raise money?

How could he convince Americans to care about a circle of children sitting in the cold, on the other side of the world, scratching at their lessons in the dirt with sticks? He pulled the light cord, extinguishing the particularity of the objects in the storage space. A shard of California sun gleamed in the stuffed monkey's scuffed plastic eyes before Mortenson padlocked the door.

CHAPTER 5

580 LETTERS, ONE CHECK

Let sorrowful longing dwell in your heart.
Never give up, never lose hope.
Allah says, "The broken ones are my beloved."
Crush your heart. Be broken.

—Shaikh Abu Saeed Abil Kheir, aka Nobody, Son of Nobody

THE TYPEWRITER WAS too small for Mortenson's hands. He kept hitting two keys at once, tearing out the letter, and starting over, which added to the cost. A dollar an hour to rent the old IBM Selectric seemed reasonable, but after five hours at downtown Berkeley's Krishna Copy Center, he'd only finished four letters.

The problem, apart from the inconvenient way IBM had arranged the keys so close together, was that Mortenson wasn't sure, exactly, what to say. "Dear Ms. Winfrey," he typed, with the tips of his forefingers, starting a fifth letter, "I am an admirer of your program. You strike me as someone who really cares what is best for people. I am writing to tell you about a small village in Pakistan called Korphe, and about a school that I am trying to build there. Did you know that for many children in this beautiful region of the Himalaya there are no schools at all?"

This is where he kept getting stuck. He didn't know whether to come right out and mention money, or just ask for help. And if he asked for money, should he request a specific amount? "I plan to build a five-room school to educate 100 students up to the fifth grade," Mortenson typed. "While I was in Pakistan climbing K2, the world's second-highest peak (I didn't quite make it to the top) I consulted with local experts. Using local materials and the labor of local craftsmen, I feel sure I can complete the school for $12,000."

47

And here came the hardest part. Should he ask for it all? "Anything you could contribute toward that amount would be a blessing," Mortenson decided to say. But his fingertips failed him and the last word read "bledding." He tore the sheet out and started over.

By the time he had to head to San Francisco, for his night shift at the UCSF Medical Center emergency room, Mortenson had completed, sealed, and stamped six letters. One for Oprah Winfrey. One for each network news anchor, including CNN's Bernard Shaw, since he figured CNN was becoming as big as the other guys. And a letter he'd written spontaneously to the actress Susan Sarandon, since she seemed so nice, and so dedicated to causes.

He wheeled La Bamba through rush-hour traffic, steering the Buick with a single index finger. Here was a machine perfectly suited to the size of Mortenson's hands. He parked, leaned out the passenger window, and slid the letters into the maw of a curbside collection box at the Berkeley Post Office.

It wasn't much to show for a full day's work, but at least he'd started somewhere. He'd get faster, he told himself. He would have to, since he'd set himself a firm goal of five hundred letters. Easing La Bamba into westbound Bay Bridge traffic, he felt giddy, like he'd lit a fuse and an explosion of good news would soon be on the way.

In the ER, a shift could disappear in a blur of knife wounds and bleeding abcesses. Or, in the small hours, with no life-threatening admissions, it could crawl imperceptibly toward morning. During those times, Mortenson catnapped on cots, or talked with doctors like Tom Vaughan. Tall, lean, spectacled, and serious, Vaughan was a pulmonologist and a climber. He had climbed Aconcagua, in the Andes, the highest mountain outside Asia. But it was his experience as expedition doctor during a 1982 American attempt on Pakistan's Gasherbrum II that forged a bond between the doctor and the nurse.

"You could see K2 from Gasherbrum II," Vaughan says. "It was incredibly beautiful, and scary. And I had a lot of questions for Greg about what it was like to climb it." Vaughan had been part of an attempt on what's usually considered the easiest of the eight-thousand-meter peaks. But during his season on the mountain, no member of his team summited, and one member of the expedition,

Glen Brendeiro, was swept over a cliff by an avalanche and never found.

Vaughan had a sense of what kind of accomplishment it took to nearly summit a killer peak like K2. Between crises, they spoke of the grandeur and desolation of the Baltoro, which they both believed to be the most spectacular place on earth. And Mortenson quizzed Vaughan intently about the research he was doing on pulmonary edema, the altitude-induced swelling of the lungs that caused so many deaths and injuries among climbers.

"Greg was incredibly fast, calm, and competent in an emergency," Vaughan remembers. "But when you'd talk to him about medicine, his heart didn't seem to be in it. My impression of him at that time was that he was just treading water until he could get back to Pakistan."

Mortenson's mind may have been focused on a mountain village twelve thousand miles away. But he couldn't take his eyes off a certain resident in anesthesiology who swept him off-balance every time he encountered her—Dr. Marina Villard. "Marina was a natural beauty," Mortenson says. "She was a climber. She didn't wear makeup. And she had this dark hair and these full lips that I could hardly look at. I was in agony whenever I had to work with her. I didn't know if I should ask her out, or avoid her so I could think straight."

To save money while he was trying to raise funds for the school, Mortenson decided not to rent an apartment. He had the storage space. And La Bamba's backseat was the size of a couch. Compared to a drafty tent on the Baltoro, it seemed like a reasonably comfortable place to sleep. He kept up his membership at City Rock, as much for access to a shower as for the climbing wall he scaled most days to stay in shape. Each night, Mortenson prowled the Berkeley Flats, a warehouse district by the bay, searching for a dark and quiet enough block so that he could sleep undisturbed. Wrapped in his sleeping bag, his legs stretched almost flat in the back of La Bamba, he'd find Marina flitting through his thoughts last thing before falling asleep.

During days he wasn't working, Mortenson hunted and pecked his way through hundreds of letters. He wrote to every U.S. senator. He haunted the public library, scanning the kind of pop culture magazines he would never otherwise read for the names of movie stars and pop singers, which he added to a list he kept folded inside a Ziploc bag. He copied down addresses from a book ranking the one hundred richest Americans. "I had no idea what I was doing," Mortenson remembers. "I just kept a list of everyone who seemed powerful or popular or important and typed them a letter. I was thirty-six years old and I didn't even know how to use a computer. That's how clueless I was."

One day Mortenson tried the door of Krishna Copy and found it unexpectedly locked. He walked to the nearest copy shop, Lazer Image on Shattuck Avenue, and asked to rent a typewriter.

"I told him, we don't have typewriters," remembers Lazer Image's owner, Kishwar Syed. "This is 1993, why don't you rent a computer? And he told me he didn't know how to use one."

Mortenson soon learned that Syed was Pakistani, from Bahawal Puy, a small village in the central Punjab. And when Syed found out why Mortenson wanted to type letters, he sat Mortenson in front of an Apple Macintosh and gave him a series of free tutorials until his new friend was computer literate.

"My village in Pakistan had no school so the importance of what Greg was trying to do was very dear to me," Syed says. "His cause was so great it was my duty to devote myself to help him."

Mortenson was amazed by the computer's cut and paste and copy functions. He realized he could have produced the three hundred letters it had taken him months to type in one day. In a single caffeine-fueled weekend session under Syed's tutelage, he cut and pasted his appeal for funds feverishly until he reached his goal of five hundred letters. Then he blazed on, as he and Syed brainstormed a list of dozens more celebrities, until Mortenson had 580 appeals in the mail. "It was pretty interesting," Mortenson says. "Someone from Pakistan helping me become computer literate so I could help Pakistani kids get literate."

After sending off the letters, Mortenson returned to Syed's shop on his days off and put his new computer skills to work, writing sixteen grant applications seeking funds for the Korphe School.

When they weren't hunched over a keyboard together, Mortenson and Syed discussed women. "It was a very sad and beautiful time in our lives," Syed says. "We talked often of loneliness and love." Syed was engaged to a woman his mother had chosen for him in Karachi. And he was at work saving money for their wedding before he brought her to America.

Mortenson confided about his crush on Marina and Syed strategized endlessly, inventing ways his friend could ask her out. "Listen to Kish," he counseled. "You're getting old and you need to start a family. What are you waiting for?"

Mortenson found himself tongue-tied whenever he tried to ask Marina out. But during down time at the UCSF Medical Center, he started telling Marina stories about the Karakoram, and his plans for the school. Trying not to lose himself in this woman's eyes, Mortenson retreated into his memories as he talked. But when he'd look up, after chronicling Etienne's rescue, or his lost days on the Baltoro, or his time in Korphe under the care of Haji Ali, Marina's eyes would be shining. And after two months of these conversations, she ended Mortenson's agony by asking him out on a date.

Mortenson had lived with monkish frugality since his return from Pakistan. Most days he breakfasted on the ninety-nine-cent special—coffee and a cruller—at a Cambodian doughnut shop on MacArthur Avenue. Often, he didn't eat again until dinner, when he'd fill up on a three-dollar burrito at one of downtown Berkeley's taquerias.

For their first date, Mortenson drove Marina to a seafood restaurant on the water in Sausalito and ordered a bottle of white wine, gritting his teeth at the cost. He threw himself into Marina's life vertiginously, jumping in with both feet. Marina had two girls from a previous marriage, Blaise, five, and Dana, three. And Mortenson soon felt almost as attached to them as he did to their mother.

On some weekends when the girls stayed with their father, he and Marina would drive to Yosemite, sleep in La Bamba, and climb peaks like Cathedral Spire all weekend. When the girls were home, Mortenson took them to Indian Rock, a scenic outcropping in the breathtaking Berkeley Hills, where he taught them the fundamentals of rock climbing. "It felt like I suddenly had my own family," Mortenson says, "which I realized I really wanted. And if the fundraising for the school had been going better I might have been completely happy."

Jerene Mortenson had been anxiously following her son's odyssey from her new home in River Falls, Wisconsin. After finishing her Ph.D., she had been hired as principal of the Westside Elementary School. Jerene convinced her son to visit, and to give a slide show and speech to six hundred students in her school. "I'd been having a really hard time explaining to adults why I wanted to help students in Pakistan,"

Mortenson says. "But the kids got it right away. When they saw the pictures, they couldn't believe that there was a place where children sat outside in cold weather and tried to hold classes without teachers. They decided to do something about it."

A month after returning to Berkeley, Mortenson got a letter from his mother. She explained that her students had spontaneously launched a "Pennies for Pakistan" drive. Filling two forty-gallon trash cans, they collected 62,345 pennies. When he deposited the check his mother sent along for $623.45 Mortenson felt like his luck was finally changing. "Children had taken the first step toward building the school," Mortenson says. "And they did it with something that's basically worthless in our society—pennies. But overseas, pennies can move mountains."

Other steps came all too slowly. Six months had passed since Mortenson had sent the first of the 580 letters and finally he got his one and only response. Tom Brokaw, like Mortenson, was an alumnus of the University of South Dakota. As football players they had both been coached by Lars Overskei, a fact Mortenson's note made clear. Brokaw sent a check for one hundred dollars and a note wishing him luck. And one by one, letters arrived from foundations like hammer blows to his hopes, notifying Mortenson that all sixteen grant applications had been rejected.

Mortenson showed Brokaw's note to Tom Vaughan and admitted how poorly his efforts at fundraising were progressing. Vaughan supported the American Himalayan Foundation and decided to see if the organization could help. He wrote a short item about Mortenson's K2 climb, and his efforts to build a school for Korphe, that was published in the AHF's national newsletter. And he reminded the AHF's members, many of whom were America's elite mountaineers, of Sir Edmund Hillary's legacy in Nepal.

After conquering Mount Everest with Tenzing Norgay in 1954, Hillary returned often to the Khumbu Valley. And he set himself a task that he described as more difficult than summiting the world's tallest peak—building schools for the impoverished Sherpa communities whose porters had made his climb possible.

In his 1964 book about his humanitarian efforts, *Schoolhouse in the Clouds*, Hillary spoke with remarkable foresight about the need for aid projects in the world's poorest and most remote places. Places like Khumbu, and Korphe. "Slowly and painfully, we are seeing worldwide acceptance of the fact that the wealthier and more technologically advanced countries have a responsibility to help the undeveloped ones," he wrote. "Not only through a sense of charity, but also because only in this way can we ever hope to see any permanent peace and security for ourselves."

But in one sense, Hillary's path was far easier than Mortenson's quixotic quest. Having conquered the planet's tallest peak, Hillary had become one of the world's most famous men. When he approached corporate donors for help funding his effort to build schools, they fell over themselves competing to support his "Himalayan Schoolhouse Expedition." *World Book Encyclopedia* signed on as the chief sponsor, bankrolling Hillary with fifty-two thousand 1963 dollars. And Sears Roebuck, which had recently started selling Sir Edmund Hillary brand tents and sleeping bags, outfitted the expedition and sent a film crew to document Hillary's work. Further funds piled up as Hillary's representatives sold European film and press rights and obtained an advance for a book about the expedition before Hillary left for Nepal.

Mortenson not only had failed to summit K2, he had returned home broke. And because he was anxious about spoiling things by leaning too heavily on Marina, he still spent the majority of his nights in La Bamba. He had become known to the police. And they roused him in the middle of the night with flashlights and made him trace sleepy orbits of the Berkeley Flats, half awake at the wheel, searching for parking spots where they wouldn't find him before morning.

Lately, Mortenson had felt a rift developing with Marina about money. Sleeping in La Bamba on their weekend climbing trips had clearly lost its charm for her. He handled it poorly when, one cold afternoon in early spring, on their way to Yosemite, she suggested they splurge and stay at the historic Ahwahnee Hotel, a grand WPA-era jewel of rustic western architecture. A single weekend in the Ahwahnee would cost the rough equivalent of all the money he'd raised for the school so far. And after Mortenson bluntly refused, their weekend in the damp car simmered with unspoken tension.

One typically cold, foggy day of San Francisco summer, Mortenson arrived for a shift of work and Tom Vaughan handed him a page torn from his prescription pad. "This guy read the piece about you in the newsletter and called me," Vaughan said. "He's a climber and some kind of scientist. He also sounded, frankly, like a piece of work. He asked me if you were a drug fiend who would waste his money. But I think he's rich. You should give him a call." Mortenson looked at the paper. It said "Dr. Jean Hoerni" next to a Seattle number. He thanked Vaughan and tucked it into his pocket on his way into the ER.

The next day, in the Berkeley Public Library, Mortenson looked up Dr. Jean Hoerni. He was surprised to find hundreds of references, mostly in newspaper clippings about the semiconductor industry.

Hoerni was a Swiss-born physicist with a degree from Cambridge. With a group of California scientists who dubbed themselves the "Traitorous Eight," after defecting from the laboratory of infamously tempestuous Nobel laureate William Shockley, he had invented a type of integrated circuit that paved the way for the silicon chip. One day while showering, Hoerni solved the problem of how to pack information onto a circuit. Watching the water run in rivulets over his hands, he theorized that silicon could be layered in a similar fashion onto a circuit, dramatically increasing its surface area and capacity. He called this the "planar process" and patented it.

Hoerni, whose brilliance was equaled only by his orneryness, jumped jobs every few years, repeatedly butting heads with his business partners. But along his remarkable career path, he founded half a dozen companies that would eventually, after his departure, grow into industry behemoths like Fairchild Semiconductors, Teledyne, and Intel. By the time Hoerni called Tom Vaughan trying to track down Mortenson, he was seventy, and his personal fortune had grown into the hundreds of millions.

Hoerni was also a climber. As a younger man, he had attempted Everest and scaled peaks on five continents. As physically tough as he was tough-minded, he once survived a cold night at high altitude by stuffing his sleeping bag with newspaper. He then wrote a letter to the editor of the *Wall Street Journal*, praising it as "by far the warmest paper published."

Hoerni had a special fondness for the Karakoram, where he'd gone trekking, and told friends he had come away struck by the discrepancy between the exquisite mountain scenery and the brutal lives of the Balti porters.

Mortenson changed ten dollars into quarters and called Hoerni at his home in Seattle from the library's pay phone. "Hi," he said, after several expensive minutes passed and Hoerni finally came to the phone. "This is Greg Mortenson. Tom Vaughan gave me your number and I'm calling because—"

"I know what you're after," a sharp voice with a French accent interrupted. "Tell me, if I give you fund for your school, you're not going to piss off to some beach somewhere in Mexico, smoke dope, and screw your girlfriend, are you?"

"I . . ." Mortenson said.

"What do you say?"

"No sir, of course not. I just want to educate children." He pronounced "educate" with the guileless midwestern cadence with which he always flavored his favorite word. "Eh-jew-kate." "In the Karakoram. They really need our help. They have it pretty rough there."

"I know," Hoerni said. "I am there in '74. On my way to the Baltoro."

"Were you there for a trek, or with a—"

"So. What, exactly, will your school cost?" Hoerni barked. Mortenson fed more quarters into the phone.

"I met with an architect and a contractor in Skardu, and priced out all the materials," Mortenson said. "I want it to have five rooms, four for classes, and one common room for—"

"A number!" Hoerni snapped.

"Twelve thousand dollars," Mortenson said nervously, "but whatever you'd like to contribute toward—"

"Is that all?" Hoerni asked, incredulous. "You're not bullshitting? You can really build your school for twelve grand?"

"Yes sir," Mortenson said. He could hear his own heartbeat in his ears. "I'm sure of it."

"What is your address?" Hoerni demanded.

"Uh, that's an interesting question."

Mortenson walked giddily through the crowd of students on Shattuck Avenue toward his car. He figured this was one night he had a rock-solid excuse for not sleeping in La Bamba.

A week later, Mortenson opened his PO box. Inside was an envelope containing a receipt for a twelve-thousand-dollar check Hoerni had sent, in Mortenson's name, to the AHF and a brief note scrawled on a piece of folded graph paper: "Don't screw up. Regards, J.H."

* * *

The first editions went first. Mortenson had spent years prowling Berkeley's Black Oak Books, especially the back room, where he'd found hundreds of historical books about mountaineering. He carried six crates of them in from the car. Combined with several of his father's rare books from Tanzania, they brought just under six hundred dollars from the buyer.

While he waited for Hoerni's check to clear, Mortenson converted everything else he owned into enough cash to buy his plane ticket and pay his expenses for however long he'd have to be in Pakistan. He told Marina that he was going to follow this path he'd been on since he met her all the way to the end—until he fulfilled the promise he made to the children of Korphe. When he came back, he promised her, things would be different. He'd work full-time, find a real place to live, and lead a less haphazard life.

He took his climbing gear to the Wilderness Exchange on San Pablo Avenue, a place where much of his disposable income had vanished in the years since he'd become a devoted climber. It was only a four-minute drive to the shop from his storage space, but Mortenson remembers the passage as indelibly as a cross-country road trip. "I felt like I was driving away from a life I'd led ever since I'd come to California," he says. He left with almost fifteen hundred dollars more in his pocket.

The morning before his flight, Mortenson drove Marina to work, then made his most difficult divestment. At a used-car lot in Oakland, he backed La Bamba into a space and sold it for five hundred dollars. The gas guzzler had carried him faithfully from the Midwest to his new existence as a climber in California. It had housed him for a year while he struggled to find his way through the fundraising wilderness. Now, the proceeds from the car would help send him to the other side of the Earth. He patted the big burgundy hood, pocketed the money, and carried his duffel bag toward the taxi waiting to take him to the next chapter of his life.

CHAPTER 6

RAWALPINDI'S ROOFTOPS AT DUSK

Prayer is better than sleep.

—from the *hazzan,* or call to worship

HE WOKE, CURLED around the money, drenched in sweat. Twelve thousand eight hundred dollars in well-thumbed hundreds were stacked in a worn green nylon stuff sack. Twelve thousand for the school. Eight hundred to see him through the next several months. The room was so spartan there was no place to hide the pouch except under his clothes. He patted the money reflexively as he'd taken to doing ever since he'd left San Francisco and swung his legs off the wobbly *charpoy* and onto the sweating cement floor.

Mortenson pushed a curtain aside and was rewarded with a wedge of sky, bisected by the green-tiled minaret from the nearby Government Transport Service Mosque. The sky had a violet cast that could mean dawn or dusk. He tried to rub the sleep out of his face, considering. Dusk, definitely. He had arrived in Islamabad at dawn and must have slept all day.

He had stitched together half of the globe, on a fifty-six-hour itinerary dictated by his cut-rate ticket, from SFO to Atlanta, to Frankfurt to Abu Dhabi to Dubai and, finally, out of this tunnel of time zones and airless departure lounges to the swelter and frenzy of Islamabad airport. And here he was in leafy Islamabad's teeming twin city, low-rent Rawalpindi, in what the manager of the Khyaban Hotel assured him was his "cheapliest" room.

Every rupee counted now. Every wasted dollar stole bricks or books from the school. For eighty rupees a night, or about two dollars, Mortenson inhabited this afterthought, an eight-by-eight-foot glassed-in cubicle on the hotel's roof that seemed more like a garden shed than a guest room. He pulled on his pants, unglued his *shalwar* shirt from his chest, and opened the door. The early evening air was no cooler, but at least it had the mercy to move.

Squatting on his heels, in a soiled baby-blue *shalwar kamiz*, the hotel's *chokidar* Abdul Shah regarded Mortenson through his one unclouded eye. "*Salaam Alaaikum*, Sahib, Greg Sahib," the watchman said, as if he'd been waiting all afternoon just in case Mortenson stirred, then rose to run for tea.

In a rusted folding chair on the roof, next to a pile of cement blocks hinting at the hotel's future ambitions, Mortenson accepted a chipped porcelain pot of sticky sweet milk tea and tried to clear his head enough to come up with a plan.

When he'd stayed at the Khyaban a year earlier, he'd been a member of a meticulously planned expedition. Every moment of every day had been filled with tasks, from packing and sorting sacks of flour and freeze-dried food, to procuring permits and arranging plane tickets, to hiring porters and mules.

"Mister Greg, Sahib," Abdul said, as if anticipating his train of thought, "may I ask why you are coming back?"

"I've come to build a school, *Inshallah*," Mortenson said.

"Here in 'Pindi, Greg Sahib?"

As he worked his way through the pot of tea, Mortenson told Abdul the story of his failure on K2, his wanderings on the glacier, and the way the people of Korphe had cared for the stranger who wandered into their village.

Sitting on his heels, Abdul sucked his teeth and scratched his generous belly, considering. "You are the rich man?" he asked, looking doubtfully at Mortenson's frayed running shoes and worn mud-colored *shalwar*.

"No," Mortenson said. He couldn't think of any way to put the past year of fumbling effort into words. "Many people in America gave a little money for the school, even children," Mortenson said, finally. He took out the green nylon pouch from under his shirt and showed the money to Abdul. "This is exactly enough for one school, if I'm very careful."

Abdul rose with a sense of resolve. "By the merciful light of Allah Almighty, tomorrow we make much bargain. We must bargain very well," he said, sweeping the tea things into his arms and taking his leave.

From his folding chair, Mortenson heard the electronic crackle of wires being twisted together in the minaret of the GTS Mosque, before the amplified wail of the *hazzan* implored the faithful to evening prayer. Mortenson watched a flock of swallows rise all at once, still in the shape of the tamarind tree where they'd been perched in the hotel garden, before wheeling away across the rooftops.

Across Rawalpindi, *muezzins'* cries from half a dozen other mosques flavored the darkening air with exhortations. Mortenson had been on this roof a year earlier, and had heard the texture of dusk in Rawalpindi as part of the exotic soundtrack to his expedition. But now, alone on the roof, the *muezzins* seemed to be speaking directly to him. Their ancient voices, tinged with a centuries-old advocacy of faith and duty, sounded like calls to action. He swept aside the doubts about his ability to build the school that had nagged at him for the last year, as Abdul had briskly cleared the tea tray. Tomorrow it was time to begin.

Abdul's knock was timed to the morning call of the *muezzin*. At four-thirty, as the electronic crackle of a microphone switched on, and in the amplified throat-clearing before slumbering Rawalpindi was called to prayer, Mortenson opened the door to his shed to find Abdul gripping the edges of the tea tray with great purpose.

"There is a taxi waiting, but first tea, Greg Sahib."

"Taxi?" Mortenson said, rubbing his eyes.

"For cement," Abdul said, as if explaining an elementary arithmetic lesson to an unusually slow student. "How can you build even one school without the cement?"

"You can't, of course," Mortenson said, laughing, and gulped at the tea, willing the caffeine to get to work.

At sunrise they shot west, on what had once been the Grand Trunk Road, ribboning the twenty-six hundred kilometers from Kabul to Calcutta, but which had now been demoted to the status of National Highway One, since the borders with Afghanistan and India were so often closed. Their tiny yellow Suzuki subcompact seemed to have no suspension at all. And as they juddered over potholes at hundred kilometers an hour, Mortenson, wedged into the miniature backseat, struggled to keep his chin from smacking against his huddled knees.

When they reached Taxila at six it was already hot. In 326 B.C., Alexander the Great had billeted his army here on the last, easternmost push of his troops to the edge of his empire. Taxila's position, at the confluence of the East-West trade routes that would become the Grand Trunk Road, at the spot where it bisected the Silk Road from China, shimmering down switchbacks from the Himalaya, had been one of the strategic hubs of antiquity. Today's Taxila contained the architectural flotsam of the ancient world. It had once been the site of Buddhism's third-largest monastery and a base for spreading the Buddha's teachings north into the mountains. But today, Taxila's historic mosques were repaired and repainted, while the Buddhist shrines were moldering back into the rock slabs from which they'd been built. The dusty sprawl, hard by the brown foothills of the Himalaya, was a factory town now. Here the Pakistani army produced replicas of aging Soviet tanks. And four smoke plumes marked the four massive cement factories that provided the foundation for much of Pakistan's infrastructure.

Mortenson was inclined to enter the first one and begin bargaining, but again, Abdul scolded him like a naïve student. "But Greg, Sahib, first we must take tea and discuss cement."

Balanced unsteadily on a toy stool, Mortenson blew on his fifth thimbleful of green tea and tried to decipher Abdul's conversation with a trio of aged tea-shop customers, their white beards stained yellow with nicotine. They seemed to be conversing with great passion and Mortenson was sure the details about cement were pouring out.

"Well," Mortenson asked after he'd left a few dirty rupee notes on the table. "Which factory? Fetco? Fauji? Askari?"

"Do you know they couldn't say," Abdul explained. "They recommended another tea shop where the owner's cousin used to be in the cement business."

Two more tea shops and countless cups of green tea later, it was late morning before they had an answer. Fauji cement was reputed to be reasonable and not too adulterated with additives to crumble in Himalayan weather. Purchasing the hundred bags of cement Mortenson estimated the school would require was anticlimactic. Girding himself for hard bargaining, Mortenson was surprised when Abdul walked into the office of Fauji cement, meekly placed an order, and asked Mortenson for a hundred-dollar deposit.

"What about the bargaining?" Mortenson asked, folding the receipt that promised one hundred bags would be delivered to the Khyaban Hotel within the week.

Patiently regaling his pupil once again, Abdul lit a reeking Tander brand cigarette in the overheated taxi and waved away the smoke along with Mortenson's worries. "Bargain? With cement can not. Cement business is a . . ." he searched for a word to make things clear to his slow-witted American ". . . Mafia. Tomorrow in Rajah Bazaar much *bes,* much bargain."

Mortenson wedged his knees under his chin and the taxi turned back toward 'Pindi.

At the Khyaban Hotel, pulling the shirt of his dust-colored *shalwar* over his head in the men's shower room, Mortenson felt the material rip. He lifted the back of the shirt to examine it and saw that the fabric had torn straight down the middle from shoulder to waist. He removed as much road dust as he could with the trickling shower, then put his only set of Pakistani clothes back on. The ready-bought *shalwar* had served him well all the way to K2 and back but now he'd need another.

Abdul intercepted Mortenson on the way to his room, tsk-tsking at the tear, and suggested they visit a tailor.

They left the oasis of the Khyaban's greenery and stepped out into 'Pindi proper. Across the street, a dozen horse-drawn taxi-carts stood at the ready, horses foaming and stamping in the dusty heat while an elderly man with a hennaed beard haggled energetically over the price.

Mortenson looked up and noticed for the first time the billboard painted in glowing primary colors at the swarming intersection of Kashmir and Adamjee roads. "Please patronize Dr. Azad," it read, in English. Next to a crudely but energetically drawn skeleton with miniature skulls glowing in its lifeless eyes, Dr. Azad's sign promised "No side effects!"

The tailor didn't advertise. He was tucked into a concrete hive of shops off Haider Road that either had been decaying for a decade, or was waiting forlornly for construction to be completed. Manzoor Khan may have been squatting in a six-foot-wide storefront, before a fan, a few bolts of cloth and a clothesmaker's dummy, but he exuded an imperial dignity. The severe black frames of his eyeglasses and his precisely trimmed white beard gave him a scholarly air as he drew a measuring tape around Mortenson's chest, looked startled at the re- sults, measured again, then jotted numbers on a pad.

"Manzoor, Sahib, wishes to apologize," Abdul explained, "but your *shalwar* will need six meters of cloth, while our countrymen take only four. So he must charge you fifty rupees more. I think he says true," Abdul offered.

Mortenson agreed and asked for two sets of *shalwar kamiz*. Abdul climbed up onto the tailor's platform and energetically pulled out bolts of the brightest robin's egg blue and pistachio green. Mortenson, picturing the dust of Baltistan, insisted on two identical sets of mud brown. "So the dirt won't show," he told a disappointed Abdul.

"Sahib, Greg Sahib," Abdul pleaded, "much better for you to be the clean gentleman. For many men will respect you."

Mortenson pictured the village of Korphe, where the population survived through the interminable winter months in the basements of their stone and mud homes, huddled with their animals around smol- dering yak dung fires, in their one and only set of clothing.

"Brown will be fine," Mortenson said.

As Manzoor accepted Mortenson's deposit, a *muezzin*'s wail pierced the hive of small shops. The tailor quickly put the money aside and unfurled a faded pink prayer mat. He aligned it precisely.

"Will you show me how to pray?" Mortenson asked, impulsively.

"Are you a Muslim?"

"I respect Islam," Mortenson said, as Abdul looked on, approvingly.

"Come up here," Manzoor said, delighted, beckoning Mortenson onto the cluttered platform, next to a headless dummy, pierced with pins. "Every Muslim must wash before prayer," he said. "I've already made *wudu* so this I will show you the next time." He smoothed out the bolt of brown cloth Mortenson had chosen next to his mat and instructed the American to kneel beside him. "First, we must face Mecca, where our holy prophet, peace be upon him, rests," Monzoor said. "Then we must kneel before the All-Merciful Allah, blessed be his name."

Mortenson struggled to kneel in the tailor's tiny cubbyhole and accidentally kicked the dummy, which waggled over him like a disap- proving deity.

"No!" said Manzoor, pincering Mortenson's wrists in his strong hands and folding Mortenson's arms together. "We do not appear before Allah like a man waiting for a bus. We submit respectfully to Allah's will."

Mortenson held his arms stiffly crossed and listened as Manzoor began softly chanting the essence of all Islamic prayer, the *Shahada*, or bearing witness.

"He is saying Allah is very friendly and great," Abdul said, trying to be helpful.

"I understood that."

"*Kha-mosh!* Quiet!" Manzoor Khan said firmly. He bent stiffly forward from the waist and prostrated his forehead against his prayer mat.

Mortenson tried to emulate him, but bent only partway forward, stopping when he felt the flaps of his torn shirt gaping inelegantly and the breath of the fan on his bare back. He looked over at his tutor. "Good?" he asked.

The tailor studied Mortenson, his eyes taking his pupil in piercingly through the thick black frames of his glasses. "Try again when you pick up your *shalwar kamiz*," he said, rolling his mat back up into a tight cylinder. "Perhaps you will improve."

His glass box on the roof of the Khyaban gathered the sun's full force all day and sweltered all night. During daylight, the sound of mutton being disjointed with a cleaver echoed unceasingly from the butcher shop below. When Mortenson strained to sleep, water gurgled mysteriously in pipes below his bed, and high on the ceiling, a fluorescent tube stayed unmercifully on. Mortenson had searched every surface inside and outside the room for a switch and found none. Thrashing against damp, well-illuminated sheets some hours before dawn, he had a sudden insight. He stood on the rope bed, swaying and balancing, then reached carefully toward the fixture and succeeded in unscrewing the tube. In complete darkness, he slept blissfully until Abdul's first firm knock.

At sunrise, the Rajah Bazaar was a scene of organized chaos that Mortenson found thrilling. Though operating with only his left eye,

Abdul took Mortenson's arm and threaded him neatly through a shifting maze of porters carrying swaying bales of wire on their heads and donkey carts rushing to deliver blocks of burlap-covered ice before the already formidable heat shrank their value.

Around the periphery of a great square were shops selling every implement he could imagine related to the erection and destruction of buildings. Eight shops in a row offered nearly identical displays of sledgehammers. Another dozen seemed to trade only in nails, with different grades gleaming from coffin-sized troughs. It was thrilling, after so much time spent in the abstraction of raising money and gathering support, to see the actual components of his school sitting arrayed all around him. That nail there might be the final one pounded into a completed Korphe school.

But before he let himself get too giddy, he reminded himself to bargain hard. Under his arm, wrapped in newspaper, was the shoebox-sized bundle of rupees he'd received at the money-changer for ten of his hundred-dollar bills.

They began at a lumber yard, indistinguishable from the almost-identical businesses flanking it on both sides, but Abdul was firm in his choice. "This man is the good Muslim," he explained.

Mortenson let himself be led down a long, narrow hallway, through a thicket of wooden roof struts leaning unsteadily against the walls. He was deposited on a thick pile of faded carpets next to Ali, the proprietor, whose spotless lavender *shalwar* seemed a miracle amidst the dust and clamor of his business. Mortenson felt more self-conscious than ever about his own torn and grease-spotted *shalwar*, which Abdul had at least stitched together until his new clothes were ready. Ali apologized that tea was not yet brewed and sent a boy running for three bottles of warm Thums Up brand orange soda while they waited.

For two crisp hundred-dollar bills, Abdul Rauf, an architect whose office consisted of a cubicle in the lobby of the Khyaban hotel, had drawn plans of the L-shaped five-room school Mortenson envisioned. In the margins, he had detailed the materials constructing the two-thousand-square-foot structure would require. Lumber was certain to be the school's single greatest expense. Mortenson unrolled the plans and read the architect's tiny printing: "Ninety-two eight-foot two-by-fours. Fifty-four sheets of four-by-eight-foot plywood sheeting." For this the architect had allotted twenty-five hundred dollars. Mortenson handed the plans to Abdul.

As he sipped at the tepid orange soda through a leaky straw, Mortenson watched Abdul reading the items aloud and winced as Ali's practiced fingers tapped the calculator balanced on his knee.

Finally, Ali adjusted the crisp white prayer cap on his head and stroked his long beard before naming a figure. Abdul shot up out of his cross-legged crouch and clasped his forehead as if he'd been shot. He began shouting in a wailing, chanting voice ripe with insult. Mortenson, with his remarkable language skills, already understood much everyday Urdu. But the curses and lamentations Abdul performed contained elaborate insults Mortenson had never heard. Finally, as Abdul wound down and bent over Ali with his hands cocked like weapons, Mortenson distinctly heard Abdul ask Ali if he was a Muslim or an infidel. This gentleman honoring him by offering to buy his lumber was a *hamdard*, a saint come to perform an act of *zakat*, or charity. A true Muslim would leap at the chance to help poor children instead of trying to steal their money.

Throughout Abdul's performance Ali's face remained serenely disengaged. He sipped at his Thums Up cozily, settling in for however long Abdul's diatribe lasted.

Tea arrived before he could be troubled to respond to Abdul's charges. All three added sugar to the fragrant green tea served in unusually fine bone china cups, and for a moment the only sound in the room was the faint clinking of spoons as they stirred.

Ali took a critical sip, nodded with approval, and then called down the hall with instructions. Abdul, still scowling, placed his teacup by his crossed legs untasted. Ali's faintly mustachioed teenage son appeared bearing two cross-sections of two-by-four. He placed them on the carpet on both sides of Mortenson's teacup like bookends.

Swirling his tea in his mouth like an aged Bordeaux, Ali swallowed, then began a professorial lecture. He indicated the block of wood on Mortenson's right. Its surface was violated by dark knots and curlicues of grease. Porcupiney splinters stood out on either end. He lifted the wood, turned it lengthways like a telescope, and peered at Mortenson through wormholes. "Local process," he said in English.

Ali indicated the other length of wood. "English process," he said. It was free of knots, and trimmed on a diagonal with a neat rip cut. Ali held it under Mortenson's nose with one hand and fanned his other hand underneath, conjuring the Kaghan Valley, the pristine pine forest from which it had recently departed.

Ali's son returned with two sheets of plywood, which he placed atop stacked cinder blocks. He took his sandals off and climbed on top of them. He couldn't have weighed more than one hundred pounds, but the first sheet buckled beneath him, bowing with an ominous screetch. The second sheet flexed only a few inches. At Ali's request the boy began jumping up and down to drive home the point. The wood still stood firm.

"Three-ply," Ali said to Mortenson, with a disgusted curl of his lips, refusing even to glance toward the first sheet. "Four-ply," he said beaming with pride at the platform where his son still bounced safely.

He switched back to Urdu. Following his exact language wasn't necessary. Obviously, he was explaining, one could acquire lumber at a pittance. But what sort of lumber? There was the unsavory product other unscrupulous merchants might sell. Go ahead and build a school with it. It might last one year. Then a tender boy of seven would be reciting from the Koran one day with his classmates when the floorboards would give way with a fearful crack and his arteries would be severed by this offensive and unreliable substance. Would you sentence a seven-year-old to bleed slowly to death because you were too frugal to purchase quality lumber?

Mortenson drained a second cup of tea and fidgeted on the dusty pile of carpets while the theatrics continued. Three times Abdul stalked toward the door as if to leave and three times Ali's asking price dropped a notch. Mortenson upended the empty pot. Well into the second hour, Mortenson found the limit of his patience. He stood and motioned for Abdul to walk out with him. There were three dozen similar negotiations they'd have to navigate if he hoped to load a truck and leave for Baltistan the day after tomorrow and he felt he couldn't spare another minute.

"*Baith, baith!* Sit, sit!" Ali said, grasping Mortenson's sleeve. "You are the champion. He has already crushed my price!"

Mortenson looked at Abdul. "Yes, he says true. Greg Sahib. You will pay only eighty-seven thousand rupees." Mortenson crunched the numbers in his head—twenty-three hundred dollars. "I told you," Abdul said. "He is the good Muslim. Now we will make a contract."

Mortenson struggled to smother his impatience as Ali called for another pot of tea.

In the late afternoon of the second full day of haggling, Mortenson, swollen with tea, sloshed toward the Khyaban with Abdul on the back of a cart pulled by a small horse that looked even more exhausted than they felt. His *shalwar* pocket was crammed with receipts for hammers, saws, nails, sheets of corrugated tin roofing, and lumber worthy of supporting schoolchildren. All the materials would be delivered beginning at dawn the next day to the truck they'd hired for the three-day trip up the Karakoram Highway.

Abdul had proposed they take a taxi back to the hotel. But Mortenson, stung by the quick depletion of his stack of rupees every time he paid another deposit, insisted on economizing. The two-mile trip took more than an hour, through streets fugged with exhaust from black, unmuffled Morris taxis.

At the hotel, Mortenson rinsed off the dust of the day's bargaining by dumping bucket after bucket of lukewarm water over his head, not bothering to remove his *shalwar,* then hurried to the tailor's hoping to retrieve his new clothes before the shop closed for Friday evening prayers.

Manzoor Khan was smoothing Mortenson's completed *shalwar* with a coal-fired iron, and humming along to a woman's voice wailing an Urdu pop song. The tinny tune echoed through the complex from a cobbler's radio down the hall, accompanied by the melancholy sound of steel shutters being pulled down at day's end.

Mortenson slid into the clean, oatmeal-colored *shalwar* shirt, which was crisp and still warm from the iron. Then, modestly shielded by the knee-length shirttails, he pulled on his baggy new pants. He tied the *azarband,* the waiststring, with a tight bow and turned toward Manzoor for inspection.

"*Bohot Kharab!*" very horrible, Manzoor pronounced. He lunged toward Mortenson, grabbed the *azarband,* which hung outside the infidel's trousers, and tucked it inside the waistband. "It is forbidden to wear as such," Manzoor said. Mortenson felt the tripwires that surrounded him in Pakistani culture—the rigid codes of conduct he was bound to stumble into—and resolved to try to avoid further explosions of offense.

Manzoor polished his glasses with his own shirttail, revealing his modestly tied trousers, and inspected Mortenson's outfit carefully. "Now you look 50 percent Pakistani," he said. "Shall you try again to pray?"

Manzoor shuttered his shop for the evening and led Mortenson outside. The tropical dusk was quickly tamping down the daylight, and with it, some of the heat. Mortenson walked arm in arm with the tailor, toward the tiled minaret of the GTS Mosque. On both sides of Kashmir Road men walked similarly in twos and threes past closed and closing shops. Since driving is frowned upon during evening prayer, traffic was unusually light.

Two blocks before the intimidating minaret of the GTS Mosque, which Mortenson assumed to be their destination, Manzoor led him into the wide, dusty lot of a CalTex gas station, where more than a hundred men were bent to *wudu*, the ritual washing required before prayer. Manzoor filled a *lota*, or water jug, from a tap and instructed Mortenson in the strict order in which ablutions were to be performed. Imitating the tailor, Mortenson squatted and rolled up his pant legs and his sleeves, and began with the most unclean parts, splashing water over his left foot, then his right. He moved on to his left hand and was rinsing his right when Manzoor, bending over to refill the *lota* before washing his face, farted distinctly. Sighing, the tailor knelt and began his ablutions again with his left foot. When Mortenson did the same, he corrected him. "No. Only for me. I am unclean," he explained.

When his hands were again properly pure, the tailor pressed a finger to his left nostril then his right, blowing, and Mortenson again mirrored his actions. Around them, a cacophony of hawking and spitting accompanied half a dozen distant calls to prayer. Imitating Manzoor, Mortenson rinsed his ears, then carefully swished water throughout what Muslims consider humans' holiest feature, the mouth, from which prayers ascend directly to Allah's ears.

For years, Mortenson had known, intellectually, that the word "Muslim" means, literally, "to submit." And like many Americans, who worshipped at the temple of rugged individualism, he had found the idea dehumanizing. But for the first time, kneeling among one hundred strangers, watching them wash away not only impurities, but also, obviously, the aches and cares of their daily lives, he glimpsed the pleasure to be found in submission to a ritualized fellowship of prayer.

Someone switched off the station's generator, and attendants cloaked the gaudy gas pumps beneath modest sheets. Manzoor took a small white prayer cap from his pocket and crushed it flat so it would stay on Mortenson's large head. Joining a row of men, Mortenson and Manzoor knelt on mats the tailor provided. Mortenson knew that beyond the wall they faced, where an enormous purple and orange sign advertised the virtues of CalTex gasoline, lay Mecca. He couldn't help feeling that he was being asked to bow to the salesmanship and refining skills of Texas and Saudi oilmen, but he put his cynicism aside.

With Manzoor he knelt and crossed his arms to address Allah respectfully. The men around him weren't looking at the advertisement on the wall, he knew, they were looking inward. Nor were they regarding him. As he pressed his forehead against the still-warm ground, Greg Mortenson realized that, for the first moment during all his days in Pakistan, no one was looking at him as an outsider. No one was looking at him at all. *Allah Akbhar,* he chanted quietly, God is great, adding his voice to the chorus in the darkened lot. The belief rippling around him was strong. It was powerful enough to convert a gas station into a holy place. Who knew what other wonders of transformation lay ahead?

CHAPTER 7

HARD WAY HOME

This harsh and splendid land
With snow-covered rock mountains, cold-crystal streams,
Deep forests of cypress, juniper and ash
Is as much my body as what you see before you here.
I cannot be separated from this or from you.
Our many hearts have only a single beat.

—from *The Warrior Song of King Gezar*

ABDUL'S KNOCK CAME well before dawn. Mortenson had been lying awake, on his string bed, for hours. Sleep had been no match for the fear of all that, this day, could go wrong. He rose and opened the door, trying to make sense of the sight of a one-eyed man holding out a pair of highly polished shoes for his inspection.

They were his tennis shoes. Abdul had clearly spent hours while Mortenson slept mending, scrubbing, and buffing his torn and faded Nikes, trying to transform them into something more respectable. Something a man setting out on a long and difficult journey might lace up with pride. Abdul had transformed himself for the occasion, too. His usually silvery beard was dyed deep orange from a fresh application of henna.

Mortenson took his tea, then washed with a bucket of cold water and the last bit of the Tibet Snow brand soap he'd been rationing all week. His handful of belongings only half-filled his old duffel bag. He let Abdul sling it over his shoulder, knowing the firestorm of offense he'd encounter if he tried to carry it himself, and bid his rooftop sweatbox a fond good-bye.

Conscious of his gleaming shoes, and seeing how much keeping up appearances pleased Abdul, Mortenson consented to hire a taxi for the trip to Rajah Bazaar. The black colonial-era Morris, flotsam abandoned in 'Pindi by the ebbing tide of British empire, purled quietly along still-sleeping streets.

Even in the faint light of the shuttered market square, they found their truck easily enough. Like most Bedfords in the country, little remained of the original 1940s vehicle that had once served as an army transport when Pakistan had been but a piece of British India. Most moving parts had been replaced half a dozen times by locally machined spares. The original olive paint, far too drab for this king of the Karakoram Highway, had been buried beneath a blizzard of decorative mirrors and metal lozenges. And every square inch of ungarnished surface area had been drowned out beneath an operatic application of "disco paint," at one of Rawalpindi's many Bedford workshops. Most of the brilliantly colored designs, in lime, gold, and lurid scarlet, were curlicues and arabesques consistent with Islam's prohibition against representative art. But a life-sized portrait of cricket hero Imran Khan on the tailgate, holding a bat aloft like a scepter, was a form of idol worship that provoked such acute national pride that few Pakistanis, even the most devout, could take offense.

Mortenson paid the taxi driver, then walked around the sleeping mammoth, searching for the truck's crew, anxious to begin the day's work. A sonorous rumbling led him to kneel underneath the truckbed, where three figures lay suspended in hammocks, two snoring in languid concert.

The *hazzan* woke them before Mortenson could, wailing out of a minaret on the far side of the square at a volume that made no allowance for the hour. While the crew groaned, hauled themselves out of the hammocks, spat extravagantly, and lit the first of many cigarettes, Mortenson knelt with Abdul and prepared to pray. It seemed to Mortenson that Abdul, like most Muslims, had an internal compass permanently calibrated toward Mecca. Though they faced the uninspiring prospect of their lumber yard's still-padlocked gates, Mortenson tried to look beyond his surroundings. With no water on hand, Abdul rolled up his pantlegs and sleeves and performed ritualized ablutions anyway, symbolically rubbing away impurities that couldn't be washed. Mortenson followed, then folded his arms and bent to morning prayer. Abdul glanced at him critically, then nodded with approval. "So," Mortenson said, "do I look like a Pakistani?"

Abdul brushed the dirt from the American's forehead, where it had been pressed to the cool ground. "Not Pakistan man," he said. "But if you say Bosnia, I believe."

Ali, in another set of immaculate *shalwar,* arrived to unlock the gate of his business. Mortenson *salaamed* to him, then opened a small black student's notebook he'd bought in the bazaar and began jotting some calculations. When the Bedford was fully loaded with his purchases, more than two-thirds of his twelve thousand dollars would already be spent. That left him only three thousand to pay laborers, to hire jeeps to carry the school supplies up narrow tracks to Korphe, and for Mortenson to live on until the school was completed.

Half a dozen members of Ali's extended family loaded the lumber first as the driver and his crew supervised. Mortenson counted the sheets of wood as they were wedged against the front of the truckbed, and confirmed they were in fact the reliable four-ply. He watched, contented, as a neat forest of two-by-fours grew on top of them.

By the time the sun illuminated the market, the temperature was already well over a hundred degrees. With a symphonic clanging, shopkeepers rolled up or folded back their businesses' metal gates. Pieces of the school threaded their way through the crowds toward the truck on porters' heads, carried by human-powered rickshaws, motor-cycle jeepneys, donkey carts, and another Bedford delivering one hundred bags of cement.

It was hot work in the truckbed, but Abdul hovered over the crew, calling out the name of every item as it was stowed to Mortenson, who checked them off his list. Mortenson watched, with increasing satisfaction, as each of the forty-two different purchases he and Abdul had haggled for were neatly stowed, axes nestling against mason's trowels, tucked together by a phalanx of shovels.

By afternoon, a dense crowd had gathered around the Bedford as word spread that an enormous infidel in brown pajamas was loading a truck full of supplies for Muslim schoolchildren. Porters had to push through a ring five people thick to make their deliveries. Mortenson's size-fourteen feet drew a steady stream of bouncing eyebrows and bawdy jokes from onlookers. Spectators shouted guesses at Mortenson's nationality as he worked. Bosnia and Chechnya were deemed the most likely source of this large mangy-looking man. When Mortenson, with his rapidly improving Urdu, interrupted the speculation to tell them he was American, the crowd looked at his sweat-soaked and dirt-grimed *shalwar*, at his smudged and oily skin, and several men told him they didn't think so.

Two of the most precious items—a carpenter's level and a weighted plumb line—were missing. Mortenson was sure he'd seen them delivered but he couldn't find them in the rapidly filling truck. Abdul led the search with fervor, heaving bags of concrete aside until he found the spot where they'd slipped to the bottom. He rolled them inside a cloth and gravely instructed the driver to shelter the tools safely in the cab all the way to Skardu.

By evening, Mortenson had checked off all forty-two items on his list. The mountain of supplies had reached a height of twenty feet and the crew labored to make the load secure before dark, stretching burlap sacking over the top and tying it down tightly with a webwork of thick ropes.

As Mortenson climbed down to bid Abdul good-bye, the crowd pressed in on him, offering him cigarettes and handfuls of battered rupee notes for his school. The driver was impatient to leave and revved his engine, sending spouts of black diesel smoke out the truck's twin stacks. Despite the noise and frenzy, Abdul stood perfectly still at the center of the crowd, performing a *dua*, a prayer for a safe journey. He closed his eye and drew his hands toward his face, fanning himself in Allah's spirit. He stroked his hennaed beard and chanted a fervent plea for Mortenson's wellbeing that was drowned by the blast of the Bedford's horn.

Abdul opened his eye and took Mortenson's large dirty hand in both of his. He looked his friend over, noting the shoes he'd polished the evening before were already blackened with grime, as was the freshly tailored *shalwar*. "I think not a Bosnian, Greg Sahib," he said, pounding Mortenson on the back. "Nowadays, you are the same as a Pakistan man."

Mortenson climbed on top of the truck and nodded to Abdul standing alone and exhausted at the edge of the crowd. The driver put the truck in gear. *Allah Akbhar!* the crowd shouted as one, *Allah Akbhar!* Mortenson held his arms aloft in victory and waved farewell until the small flame of his friend's hennaed beard was extinguished by the surging crowd.

Roaring west out of Rawalpindi, Mortenson rode on top of the Bedford. The driver, Mohammed, had urged him to sit in the smoky cab, but Mortenson was determined to savor this moment in style. The artists at the Bedford shop in 'Pindi had welded a jaunty extension to the truckbed, which hung over the cab like a hat worn at a rakish angle. On top of this hat brim hovering over the rattling cab, straddling supplies, Mortenson made a comfortable nest on burlap and bales of hay that swayed high over the highway their speed swallowed. For company he had crates of snowy white chickens Mohammed had brought to sell in the mountains, and untamed Punjabi pop music that shrilled out of the Bedford's open windows.

Leaving the dense markets of Rawalpindi, the dry, brown countryside opened, took on a flush of green, and the foothills of the Himalaya beckoned from beyond the late-day heat haze. Smaller vehicles made way for the massive truck, swerving onto the verge with every blast from the Bedford's air horns, then cheering when they saw the portrait of Imran Khan and his cricket bat passing them boldly by.

Mortenson's own mood felt as serene as the peaceful tobacco fields they sailed past, shimmering greenly like a wind-tossed tropical sea. After a hot week of haggling and fretting over every rupee, he felt he could finally relax. "It was cool and windy on top of the truck," Mortenson remembers. "And I hadn't been cool since I arrived in Rawalpindi. I felt like a king, riding high on my throne. And I felt I'd already succeeded. I was sitting on top of my school. I'd bought everything we needed and stuck to my budget. Not even Jean Hoerni could find fault with anything I'd done. And in a few weeks, I thought, the school would be built, and I could head home and figure out what to do with the rest of my life. I don't know if I've ever felt so satisfied."

Mohammed hit the brakes heavily then, pulling off the road, and Mortenson had to clutch at the chicken crates to avoid being thrown down onto the hood. He leaned over the side and asked, in Urdu, why they were stopping. Mohammed pointed to a modest white minaret at the edge of a tobacco field, and the men streaming toward it. In the silence after the Punjabi pop had been hastily muffled, Mortenson heard the call of the *hazzan* carried clearly on the wind. He hadn't known that the driver, who'd seemed so anxious to be on his way, was devout enough to stop for evening prayer. But there was much in this part of the world, he realized, that he barely understood. At least there would be plenty of opportunity, he told himself, searching for a foothold on the passenger door, to practice his praying.

After dark, fortified with strong green tea and three plates of *dhal chana*, a curry of yellow lentils, from a roadside stand, Mortenson lay back in his nest on top of the truck and watched individual stars pin-prick the fabric of twilight.

Thirty kilometers west of Rawalpindi, at Taxila, they turned north off Pakistan's principal thoroughfare toward the mountains. Taxila may have been a hub where Buddhism and Islam collided hundreds of years ago, before battling for supremacy. But for Mortenson's swaying school on wheels, the collision of tectonic plates that had occurred in this zone millions of years earlier was more to the point.

Here the plains met the mountains, this strand of the old Silk Road turned steep, and the going got unpredictable. Isabella Bird, an intrepid species of female explorer who could only have been produced by Victorian England, documented the difficulty of traveling from the plains of the Indian subcontinent into Baltistan, or "Little Tibet" as she referred to it, during her 1876 journey. "The traveler who aspires to reach the highlands cannot be borne along in a carriage or a hill cart," she wrote. "For much of the way he is limited to a foot pace and if he has regard to his horse he walks down all rugged and steep descents, which are many. 'Roads,' " she wrote, adding sarcastic quotation marks, "are constructed with great toil and expense, as nature compels the road-maker to follow her lead, and carry his track along the narrow valleys, ravines, gorges, and chasms which she has marked out for him. For miles at a time this 'road' . . . is merely a ledge above a raging torrent. When two caravans meet, the animals of one must give way and scramble up the mountain-side, where foothold is often perilous. In passing a caravan . . . my servant's horse was pushed over the precipice by a loaded mule and drowned."

The Karakoram Highway (KKH), the road their Bedford rumbled up with a bullish snorting from its twin exhausts, was a costly improvement over the type of tracks Bird's party traveled. Begun in 1958 by a newly independent Pakistan anxious to forge a transportation link with China, its ally against India, and in a perpetual state of construction ever since, the KKH is one of the most daunting engineering projects humans have ever attempted. Hewing principally to the rugged Indus River Gorge, the KKH has cost the life of one road worker for each of its four hundred kilometers. The "highway" was so impassable that Pakistani engineers were forced to take apart bulldozers, pack their components in on mules, and reassemble them before heavy work could begin. The Pakistani military tried flying in bulldozers on a Russian MI-17 heavy-lifting helicopter, but the inaugural flight, trying to maneuver through the high winds and narrow gorge, clipped a cliff and crashed into the Indus, killing all nine aboard.

In 1968, the Chinese, anxious to create an easy route to a new market for their manufactured goods, to limit Soviet influence in Central Asia, and to cement a strategic alliance against India, offered to supervise and fund the completion of the thirteen-hundred-kilometer route from Kashgar, in southwestern China, to Islamabad. And after more than a decade of deploying an army of road workers, the newly christened "Friendship Highway" was declared complete in 1978, sticking its thumb squarely in India's eye.

As they climbed, the air carried the first bite of winter and Mortenson wrapped a wool blanket around his shoulders and head. For the first time, he wondered whether he'd be able to complete the school before cold weather set in, but he banished the thought, propped his head against a bale of hay, and lulled by the slowly rocking truck, slept.

A rooster in a cage five feet from his head woke Mortenson without mercy at first light. He was stiff and cold and badly in need of a bathroom break. He leaned over the side of the truck to request a stop and saw the top of the bearish assistant's close-cropped head stretching out the window, and beyond it, straight down fifteen hundred feet to the bottom of a rocky gorge, where a coffee-colored river foamed over boulders. He looked up and saw they were hemmed in hard by granite walls that rose ten thousand feet on both sides of the river. The Bedford was climbing a steep hill, and slipped backward near its crest, as Mohammed fumbled with the shift, manhandling it until it clanked into first gear. Mortenson, leaning out over the passenger side of the cab, could see the truck's rear tires rolling a foot from the edge of the gorge, spitting stones out into the abyss as Mohammed gunned the engine. Whenever the tires strayed too near to the edge, the assistant whistled sharply and the truck swung left.

Mortenson rolled back on top of the cab, not wanting to interfere with Mohammed's concentration. When he'd come to climb K2, he'd been too preoccupied by his goal to pay much attention to his bus trip up the Indus. And on his way home, he'd been consumed with his plans to raise money for the school. But seeing this wild country again, and watching the Bedford struggling over this "highway" at fifteen miles an hour, he had a renewed appreciation for just how thoroughly these mountains and gorges cut Baltistan off from the world.

Where the gorge widened enough to permit a small village to cling to its edge, they stopped for a breakfast of *chapattis* and *dudh patti,* black tea sweetened with milk and sugar. Afterward Mohammed insisted, more emphatically than the night before, that Mortenson join them inside the cab, and he reluctantly agreed.

He took his place between Mohammed and the two assistants. Mohammed, as slight as the Bedford was enormous, could barely reach the pedals. The bearish assistant smoked bowl after bowl of hashish, which he blew in the face of the other assistant, a slight boy still struggling to grow his mustache.

Like the exterior, the inside of the Bedford was wildly decorated, with twinkling red lights, Kashmiri woodcarving, 3D photos of beloved Bollywood stars, dozens of shiny silver bells, and a bouquet of plastic flowers that poked Mortenson in the face whenever Mohammed braked too enthusiastically. "I felt like I was riding in a rolling brothel," Mortenson says. "Not that we were rolling all that much. It was more like watching an inchworm make progress."

On the steepest sections of the highway, the assistants would jump out and throw large stones behind the rear wheels. After the Bedford lurched forward a few feet, they'd collect the rocks and throw them under the tires again, repeating the Sisyphian process endlessly until the road flattened out. Occasionally a private jeep would pass them on the uphills, or an oncoming bus would rumble by, its female passengers mummified against road dust and prying male eyes. But mostly, they rolled on alone.

The sun disappeared early behind the steep valley walls and by late afternoon it was night-dark at the base of the ravine. Rounding a blind curve, Mohammed stood on the brakes and narrowly missed ramming the rear of a passenger bus. On the road ahead of the bus, hundreds of vehicles—jeeps, buses, Bedfords—were backed up before the entrance to a concrete bridge. With Mohammed, Mortenson climbed out to have a look.

As they approached the bridge, it was clear they weren't being delayed by the KKH's legendary propensity for rockfall or avalanche. Two dozen untamed-looking bearded men in black turbans stood guarding the bridge. Their rocket launchers and Kalashnikovs were trained lazily in the direction of a smart company of Pakistani soldiers whose own weapons were judiciously holstered. "No good," Mohammed said quietly, exhausting most of his English vocabulary.

One of the turbaned men lowered his rocket launcher and waved Mortenson toward him. Filthy from two days on the road, with a wool blanket wrapped over his head, Mortenson felt sure he didn't look like a foreigner.

"You come from?" the man asked in English, "America?" He held a propane lantern up and studied Mortenson's face. In the lamplight, Mortenson saw the man's eyes were fiercely blue, and rimmed with *surma,* the black pigment worn by the most devout, some would say fanatical, graduates of the fundamentalist *madrassas.* The men who were pouring over the western border this year, 1994, as foot soldiers of the force about to take control of Afghanistan, the Taliban.

"Yes, America," Mortenson said, warily.

"America number one," his interrogator said, laying down the rocket launcher and lighting a local Tander brand cigarette, which he offered to Mortenson. Mortenson didn't exactly smoke, but decided the time was right to puff appreciatively. With apologies, never meeting the man's eyes, Mohammed led Mortenson gently away by the elbow, and back to the Bedford.

As he brewed tea over a small fire by the tailgate of the truck, under Imran Khan's watchful eyes, and prepared to settle in for the night, Mohammed tapped into the rumor mill circulating among the hundreds of other stranded travelers. These men had blocked the bridge all day, and a squad of soldiers had been trucked up thirty-five kilometers from a military base at Pattan to see that it was reopened.

Between Mortenson's spotty Urdu and a number of conflicting accounts, he wasn't able to be sure he had the details properly sorted. But he understood that this was the village of Dasu, in the Kohistan region, the wildest part of Pakistan's North West Frontier Province. Kohistan was infamous for banditry and had never been more than nominally under control of Islamabad. In the years following 9/11 and America's war to topple the Taliban, these remote and craggy valleys would attract bands of Taliban and their Al Qaeda benefactors, who knew how easy it could be to lose oneself in these wild heights.

The gunmen guarding the bridge lived up a valley nearby and claimed that a contractor from the government in distant lowland Islamabad arrived with millions of rupees earmarked to widen their game trails into logging roads, so these men could sell their timber. But they said the contractor stole the money and left without improving their roads. They were blocking the Karakoram Highway until he was returned to them so they could hang him to death from this bridge.

After tea and a packet of crackers that Mortenson shared out, they decided to sleep. Despite Mohammed's warning that it was safer to spend the night in the cab, Mortenson climbed to his nest on top of the truck. From his perch by the sleeping chickens, he could see the fierce, shaggy Pashto-speaking Kohistanis on the bridge, illuminated by lanterns. The lowland Pakistanis who had come to negotiate with them spoke Urdu, and looked like a different species, girlishly trim, with neat blue berets and ammunition belts cinched tightly about their tiny waists. Not for the first time, Mortenson wondered if Pakistan wasn't more of an idea than a country.

He lay his head on a hay bale for a moment, sure he wouldn't be able to grasp any sleep this night, and awoke, in full daylight, to gunfire. Mortenson sat up and saw first the pink, inscrutable eyes of the white chickens regarding him blankly, then the Kohistanis standing on the bridge, firing their Kalashnikovs in the air.

Mortenson felt the Bedford roar to life, and saw black smoke belch out of the twin stacks. He leaned down into the driver's window. "Good!" Mohammed said, smiling up at him, revving the engine. "Shooting for happy, *Inshallah!*" He jammed the stick into gear.

Pouring out of doorways and alleys in the village, Mortenson saw, were groups of veiled women scurrying back to their vehicles, from the spots where they'd chosen to sequester themselves through the long night of waiting.

Passing over the Dasu bridge, in a long, dusty line of crawling vehicles, Mortenson saw the Kohistani who had offered him a cigarette and his colleagues pumping their fists in the air and firing their automatic weapons wildly. Never, not even on an army firing range, had

Mortenson experienced such intense gunfire. He didn't see any low-land contractor swinging from the bridge's girders and assumed the gunmen had extracted a promise of reparations from the soldiers.

As they climbed, the walls of the gorge rose until they blotted out all but a narrow strip of sky, white with heat haze. They were skirting the western flank of Nanga Parbat, at 26,658 feet the earth's ninth-loftiest peak, which anchors the western edge of the Himalaya. But the "Naked Mountain" was cloaked to Mortenson by the depths of the Indus Gorge. With a mountain climber's fixation, he felt it looming irresistibly to the east. For proof, he studied the surface of the Indus. Streams carrying meltwater from Nanga Parbat's glaciers boiled down ravines and over lichen-covered boulders into the Indus. They stippled the silty, mud-white surface of the river with pools of alpine blue.

Just before Gilgit, the most populous city in Pakistan's Northern Areas, they left the Karakoram Highway before it began its long switchback toward China over the world's highest paved road, the Khunjerab Pass, which crests at 15,520 feet, and instead followed the Indus east toward Skardu. Despite the growing chill in the air, Mortenson felt warmed by familiar fires. This riverine corridor carved between twenty-thousand-foot peaks so numerous as to be nameless was the entrance to his Baltistan. Though this lunar rockscape in the western Karakoram has to be one of the most forbidding on Earth, Mortenson felt he had come home. The dusty murk along the depths of the gorge and the high-altitude sun brushing the tips of these granite towers felt more like his natural habitat than the pastel stucco bungalows of Berkeley. His whole interlude in America, the increasing awkwardness with Marina, his struggle to raise money for the school, his insomniacal shifts at the hospital, felt as insubstantial as a fading dream. These juts and crags held him.

Two decades earlier, an Irish nurse named Dervla Murphy felt the same tug to these mountains. Traveling in the intrepid spirit of Isabella Bird, and ignoring the sage advice of seasoned adventurers who told her Baltistan was impassable in snow, Murphy crisscrossed the Karakoram in deep winter, on horseback, with her five-year-old daughter.

In her book about the journey, *Where the Indus Is Young*, the normally eloquent Murphy is so overcome attempting to describe her journey through this gorge that she struggles to spit out a description.

"None of the adjectives usually applied to mountain scenery is adequate here—indeed, the very word 'scenery' is comically inappropriate. 'Splendour' or 'grandeur' are useless to give a feeling of this tremendous ravine that twists narrow and dark and bleak and deep for mile after mile after mile, with never a single blade of grass, or weed, or tiny bush to remind one that the vegetable kingdom exists. Only the jade-green Indus—sometimes tumbling into a dazzle of white foam—relieves the gray-brown of crags and sheer precipices and steep slopes."

When Murphy plodded along the south bank of the Indus on horseback, she meditated on the horror of traversing this glorified goat path in a motor vehicle. A driver here must embrace fatalism, she writes, otherwise he "could never summon up enough courage to drive an overloaded, badly balanced, and mechanically imperfect jeep along track where for hours on end one minor misjudgement could send the vehicle hurtling hundreds of feet into the Indus. As the river has found the only possible way through this ferociously formidable knot of mountains, there is no alternative but to follow it. Without traveling through the Indus Gorge, one cannot conceive of its drama. The only sane way to cover such ground is on foot."

On top of the overloaded, badly balanced, but mechanically sound Bedford, Mortenson swayed with the twenty-foot pile of school supplies, yawning irremediably close to the ravine's edge every time the truck shimmied over a mound of loose rockfall. Hundreds of feet below, a shell of a shattered bus rusted in peace. With the regularity of mile markers, white *shahid,* or "martyr" monuments honored the death of Frontier Works Organization roadbuilders who had perished in their battles with these rock walls. Thanks to thousands of Pakistani soldiers the road to Skardu had been "improved" sufficiently since Murphy's day to allow trucks to pass on their way to support the war effort against India. But rockfall and avalanche, the weathered tarmac crumbling unpredictably into the abyss, and insufficient space for oncoming traffic meant that dozens of vehicles plummeted off the road each year.

A decade later, in the post-9/11 era, Mortenson would often be asked by Americans about the danger he faced in the region from terrorists. "If I die in Pakistan, it'll be because of a traffic accident, not a bomb or bullet," he'd always tell them. "The real danger over there is on the road."

He felt the opening in the quality of the light before he noticed where he was. Grinding down a long descent in late afternoon, the air brightened. The claustrophobic ravine walls widened then folded out into the distance, rising into a ring of snow-capped giants that surrounded the Skardu Valley. By the time Mohammed accelerated onto flatland at the bottom of the pass, the Indus had unclenched its muscles and relaxed to a muddy, meandering lakelike width. Along the valley floor, tawny sand dunes baked in the late sun. And if you didn't look up at the painfully white snow peaks that burned above the sand, Mortenson thought, this could almost be the Arabian Peninsula.

The outskirts of Skardu, awash in *pharing* and *starga,* apricot and walnut orchards, announced that the odyssey along the Indus was over. Mortenson, riding his school into Skardu, waved at men wearing the distinctive white woolen Balti *topis* on their heads, at work harvesting the fruit, and they waved back, grinning. Children ran alongside the Bedford, shouting their approval at Imran Khan and the foreigner riding atop his image. Here was the triumphal return he'd been imagining ever since he sat down to write the first of the 580 letters. Right now, right around the next curve, Mortenson felt certain, his happy ending was about to begin.

CHAPTER 8

BEATEN BY THE BRALDU

Trust in Allah, but tie up your camel.

—hand-lettered sign at the entrance to the Fifth Squadron airbase, Skardu

THE FIRST POPLAR branch smacked Mortenson in the face, before he had time to duck. The second tore the blanket off his head and left it hanging in the Bedford's wake. He flattened himself on the truck's roof and watched Skardu appear down a tunnel of cloth-wrapped tree trunks, girded against hungry goats.

A military green Lama helicopter flew slow and low over the Bedford, on its way from the Baltoro Glacier to Skardu's Fifth Aviation Squadron airbase. Mortenson saw a human figure shrouded in burlap and lashed to a gurney on the landing skid. Etienne had taken this same ride after his rescue, Mortenson thought, but he, at least, had lived.

By the base of the brooding eight-hundred-foot-high Karpocho, or Rock of Skardu, with its ruined fort standing sentinel over the town, the Bedford slowed to let a flock of sheep cross Skardu's bazaar. The busy street, lined with narrow stalls selling soccer balls, cheap Chinese sweaters, and neatly arranged pyramids of foreign treasure like Ovaltine and Tang, seemed overwhelmingly cosmopolitan after the deafening emptiness of the Indus Gorge.

This vast valley was fertile where the sand didn't drift. It offered relief from the rigors of the gorges and had been a caravan stop on the trade route from Kargil, now in Indian Kashmir, to Central Asia. But since Partition, and the closing of the border, Skardu had been stranded unprofitably at the wild edge of Pakistan. That is, until its reinvention as outfitter to expeditions trekking toward the ice giants of the Karakoram.

83

Mohammed pulled to the side of the road, but not far enough to let half a dozen jeeps pass. He leaned out the window and shouted to ask Mortenson directions over the indignant shrilling of horns. Mortenson climbed down off his rolling throne and wedged himself into the cab.

Where to go? Korphe was an eight-hour jeep ride into the Karakoram, and there was no way to telephone and tell them he'd arrived to fulfill his promise. Changazi, a trekking agent and tour operator who'd organized their attempt at K2, seemed like the person who could arrange to have the school supplies carried up the Braldu Valley. They stopped in front of Changazi's neatly whitewashed compound, and Mortenson knocked on a substantial set of green wooden doors.

Mohammed Ali Changazi himself swung open the doors. He was dressed in an immaculate starched white *shalwar* that announced he didn't degrade himself with the dusty business of this world. He was tall for a Balti. And with his precisely trimmed beard, noble nose, and startling brown eyes rimmed with blue, he cut a mesmerizing figure. In Balti, "Changazi" means "of the family of Genghis Khan," and can be used as a slang word conveying a terrifying type of ruthlessness. "Changazi is an operator, in every sense," Mortenson says. "Of course, I didn't know that then."

"Dr. Greg," Changazi said, enrobing as much of Mortenson as he was able in a lingering embrace. "What are you doing here? Trekking season is over."

"I brought the school!" Mortenson said slyly, expecting to be congratulated. After K2, he had discussed his plans with Changazi, who had helped him estimate a budget for the building materials. But Changazi seemed to have no idea what he was talking about. "I bought everything to build the school and drove it here from 'Pindi."

Changazi still seemed baffled. "It's too late to build anything now. And why didn't you buy supplies in Skardu?" Mortenson hadn't realized he could. As he was searching for something to say, they were interrupted by a blast from the Bedford's airhorns. Mohammed wanted to unload and start back toward 'Pindi right away. The truck crew unlashed the load and Changazi glanced admiringly at the valuable stacks of supplies towering above them.

"You can store all of this in my office," Changazi said. "Then we'll take tea and discuss what to do with your school." He looked Mortenson up and down, grimacing at the grease-caked *shalwar* and Mortenson's grime-blackened face and matted hair. "But why don't you have a wash first, and such like that," he said.

The bearish assistant handed Mortenson his plumb line and level, still wrapped neatly in Abdul's cloth. As load after load of cement and sheets of sturdy four-ply passed by an increasingly enthusiastic Changazi, Mortenson unwrapped the fresh bar of Tibet Snow soap his host provided. He set to work scouring away four days of road grit with a pot of water Changazi's servant Yakub heated over an Epigas cylinder that had probably been pilfered, he realized, from an expedition.

Mortenson, suddenly anxious, wanted to take an inventory of all the supplies, but Changazi insisted there would be time later. Accompanied by the call of the *muezzin*, Changazi led Mortenson to his office, where servants had unrolled a plush, scarcely used Marmot sleeping bag on a *charpoy* they'd placed between a desk and a dated wall map of the world. "Rest now," Changazi said, in a way that invited no argument. "I'll see you after evening prayer."

Mortenson woke to the sound of raised voices in an adjoining room. He stood and saw by the unrelenting mountain light scalpeling through the window that he'd blacked out once again and slept straight through until morning. In the next room, sitting cross-legged on the floor, next to a cold cup of untasted tea, was a small, scowling, solidly muscled Balti Mortenson recognized as Akhmalu, the cook who had accompanied his K2 expedition. Akhmalu stood and made a spitting motion toward Changazi's feet, the ultimate Balti insult, then, in the same instant, saw Mortenson standing in the doorway.

"Doctor Girek!" he said, and his face changed as quickly as a mountain crag fired by a shaft of sun. He ran to Mortenson, beaming, and wrapped him in a Balti bearhug. Over tea, and six slices of toasted white bread that Changazi served proudly with a fresh jar of Austrian lingonberry jam that he had mysteriously procured, Mortenson came to understand that a bout of tug-of-war had begun. News about the arrival of his building supplies had spread throughout Skardu. As the man who had cooked Mortenson's *dal* and *chapatti* for months, Akhmalu had come to stake his claim.

"Dr. Girek, you promise one time to me you come *salaam* my village," Akhmalu said. And it was true. He had. "I have one jeep waiting go to Khane village," he said. "We go now."

"Maybe tomorrow, or the next day," Mortenson said. He scanned Changazi's compound. An entire Bedford-load of building supplies worth more than seven thousand dollars had arrived the evening before, and now he didn't see so much as a hammer, not in this room, or the next, or the courtyard he could see clearly through the window.

"But my whole village will expect you, sir," Akhmalu said. "We have prepare special dinner already." The guilt of wasting a feast that a Balti village could barely afford was too much for Mortenson. Changazi walked with him to Akhmalu's hired jeep and climbed into the backseat before the question of his invitation could be considered.

The pavement ran out just east of Skardu. "How far is Khane?" Mortenson asked, as the rust-red Toyota Land Cruiser began bouncing over rocks scarcely smaller than its tires, up a narrow switchback to a ledge above the Indus River.

"Very far," Changazi said, scowling.

"Very near," Akhmalu countered. "Only three or seven hours."

Mortenson settled back into the seat of honor, next to the driver, laughing. He should have known better than to ask the time a journey took in Baltistan. Behind him, on the cargo seats, he felt the tension between the two men as palpably as the Toyota's unforgiving suspension. But ahead of him, through the windshield, with its spidery web-work of fissures, he saw the sixteen-thousand-foot-high panorama of the Karakoram's foothills tearing at a blameless blue sky with its fearsome assortment of brown, broken teeth, and felt unaccountably happy.

They bounced along a branch of the Indus for hours until it turned south toward India, then climbed up the Hushe Valley, alongside the Shyok River, with its chill blue glacial melt thundering over boulders recently departed, in geological time, from eroding cliffs on both sides of the slender valley. As the road worsened, the laminated 3D card depicting the great black-shrouded cube, the Kaaba of Mecca, that hung from the Toyota's rearview mirror, repeatedly smacked the windshield with the fervency of prayer.

The Al-Hajarul Aswad, a great black rock entombed within the walls of the Kaaba, is thought to be an asteroid. Many Muslims believe that it fell to earth in the time of Adam, as a gift from Allah, and its jet-black color indicates its ability to absorb the sins of the faithful who are fortunate enough to touch its once-white surface. Looking up at the boulder-strewn escarpments overhanging the road, Mortenson hoped that those celestial rocks would choose another moment to come crashing to earth.

Great brown crenulated walls hemmed in the terraced patchwork of potato and wheat fields as they climbed, like the battlements of castles constructed beyond the scale of human comprehension. By late afternoon, it was misty where the Hushe Valley narrowed to a pass. But Mortenson, who'd studied relief maps of the Karakoram for months as he waited out storms at K2 base camp, knew that one of the world's most formidable peaks, 25,660-foot Masherbrum, lay dead ahead.

Unlike most of the high peaks of the central Karakoram, Masherbrum was readily visible to the south, from what had once been the crown jewel of British India, Kashmir. That's why, in 1856, T. G. Montgomerie, a British Royal Engineers lieutenant, named the great gray wall rising above the snows "K1," or Karakoram 1, for the first peak in the remote region he was able to accurately survey. Its taller and more elusive neighbor twenty kilometers to the northeast became K2 by default, based on the later date of its "discovery." Mortenson stared at the whiteness, where Americans George Bell, Willi Unsoeld, and Nick Clinch had made the first ascent with their Pakistani partner Captain Jawed Aktar in 1960, willing Masherbrum's summit pyramid to pierce the clouds, but the mountain drew its cloak tight: The snowlight from its great hanging glaciers illuminated the mist from within.

The jeep stopped next to a *zamba*, swaying over the Shyok, and Mortenson got out. He'd never been comfortable crossing these yak-hair bridges, since they were engineered to support Balti half his weight. And when Akhmalu and Changazi piled on behind him, shaking the structure violently, he struggled to keep his feet beneath him. Mortenson grasped the twin handrails and shuffled his size-fourteen feet tightrope-walker-style along the single braided strand between him and the rapids fifty feet below. The *zamba* was slick with spray, and he concentrated so successfully on his feet that he didn't notice the crowd waiting to greet him on the far bank until he was nearly upon them.

A tiny, bearded Balti, wearing black Gore-Tex mountaineering pants and an orange T-shirt proclaiming "climbers get higher," helped

Mortenson onto the firm ground of Khane village. This was Jan-jungpa, who had been head high altitude porter for a lavish Dutch-led expedition to K2 during Mortenson's time on the mountain, and who possessed an uncanny ability to stroll over to base camp for a visit at the precise moment his friend Akhmalu was serving lunch. But Morten-son had enjoyed Janjungpa's company and his bravado, and mined him for stories about the dozens of expeditions he had led up the Baltoro. Westernized enough to extend his hand to a foreigner for a shake with-out invoking Allah, Janjungpa steered Mortenson through the narrow alleys between Khane's mud and stone homes, taking his elbow as they crossed irrigation ditches running ripe with waste.

Janjungpa led his large foreigner at the head of a procession of two dozen men, and two brown goats that followed with imploring yellow eyes. The men turned into a neat whitewashed home and climbed a ladder of carved logs toward the smell of cooking chicken.

Mortenson let himself be seated on cushions after his host beat the dust halfheartedly from them. The men of Khane crowded into the small room and arranged themselves in a circle on a faded floral carpet. From his seat, Mortenson had a fine view, over the rooftops of neigh-boring houses, toward the steep stone canyon that brought Khane its drinking water and irrigated its fields.

Janjungpa's sons rolled a pink, plasticized tablecloth onto the floor at the center of the circle, and arranged platters of fried chicken, raw turnip salad, and a stew of sheep liver and brains at Mortenson's feet. The host waited until Mortenson bit into a piece of chicken to begin. "I wish to thank Mr. Girek Mortenson for honoring us and coming to build a school for Khane village," Janjungpa said.

"A school for Khane?" Mortenson croaked, almost choking on the chicken.

"Yes, one school, as you promised," Janjungpa said, gazing in-tently around the circle of men as he spoke, as if delivering a summa-tion to a jury. "A climbing school."

Mortenson's mind raced and he looked from face to face, scanning them for signs that this was an elaborate joke. But the craggy faces of the men of Khane looked as stolid as the cliffs outside the window, looming impassively in the setting sunlight. He ran through months of his K2 memories. He and Janjungpa *had* discussed the need to pro-vide specialized mountaineering skills to Balti porters, who were often ignorant of the most basic mountain rescue techniques, and Janjungpa had dwelt at length on the Balti porters' high rate of injuries and low salaries. Mortenson could clearly remember him describing Khane and inviting him to visit. But he was quite sure they'd never discussed a school. Or a promise.

"Girek Sahib, don't listen to Janjungpa. He is the crazy man," Akhmalu said, and Mortenson felt flooded by relief. "He say the climbing school," Akhmalu continued, shaking his head violently. "Khane need the ordinary school, for Khane children, not for making the rich house for Janjungpa. This you should do." The relief evaporated as swiftly as it had come.

To his left, Mortenson saw Changazi reclining on a plump cushion, delicately stripping a chicken leg of its meat with his fingernails and smiling faintly. Mortenson tried to catch his eye, hoping Changazi would speak up and put an end to the madness, but a heated argument broke out in Balti, as two factions quickly formed behind Akhmalu and Janjungpa. Women climbed onto the adjoining rooftops, clutching their shawls against a bitter wind blowing down from Masherbrum, and trying to eavesdrop on the argument as it grew in volume.

"I never made any promise," Mortenson tried, first in English, and then when no one seemed to be listening, he repeated it in Balti. But it was as if the largest person in the room had become invisible. So he followed the argument, as well as he could. Repeatedly, he heard Akhmalu calling Janjungpa greedy. But Janjungpa parried every charge leveled against him by repeating the promise he claimed Mortenson had made to him.

After more than an hour, Akhmalu rose suddenly and pulled Mortenson up by the arm. As if he could steer the outcome his way by conducting Mortenson to his own home, Akhmalu led a still-shouting procession of men down the log ladder, across a muddy irrigation ditch and upstairs into his own home. Once the group was arranged on cushions in a smaller sitting room, Akhmalu's teenage son, who had been a kitchen boy on Mortenson's expedition, lay another procession of dishes at Mortenson's feet. A ring of wildflowers decorated the dish of turnip salad, and glistening kidneys floated prominently on the surface of the sheep organ stew, but otherwise the meal was almost identical to the banquet Janjungpa had served.

Akhmalu's son scooped a kidney, the choicest morsel, over a bowl of rice and handed it to Mortenson, smiling shyly, before serving the others. Mortenson pushed the kidney to one side of the bowl and ate only rice swimming in the greasy gravy, but no one seemed to notice. He was invisible again. The men of Khane ate as heartily as they argued, as if the previous argument and meal had never happened and each point of each faction's argument had to be shredded as thoroughly as the chicken and mutton bones they tore apart with their teeth.

Well into the argument's fourth hour, his eyes stinging from the cigarette smoke choking the room, Mortenson climbed up onto Akhmalu's roof and leaned back against a sheaf of newly harvested buckwheat that blocked the wind. The moon, on the rise, smoldered behind the eastern ridgeline. The wind had blown the peak of Masherbrum clear, and Mortenson stared a long time at its knife-edged summit ridges, sharpened eerily by moonlight. Just beyond it, Mortenson knew, could in fact feel, loomed the great pyramid of K2. How simple it had been to come to Baltistan as a climber, Mortenson thought. The path was clear. Focus on a peak, as he was doing now, and organize the men and supplies until you reached it. Or failed trying.

Through the large square hole in the roof, cigarette smoke and burning yak dung furnaced up out of the room below, fouling Mortenson's perch. And the argumentative voices of Khane's men rose with it, fouling Mortenson's mood. He took a thin jacket from his daypack, lay back on the buckwheat, and spread it over his chest like a blanket. The moon, nearly full, climbed clear of the jagged ridgeline. It balanced on top of the escarpment like a great white boulder about to fall and crush the village of Khane.

"Go ahead. Fall," Mortenson thought, and fell asleep.

In the morning, Masherbrum's south face was cloaked, once again, in clouds and Mortenson climbed down from the roof on stiff legs to find Changazi sipping milk tea. He insisted that Changazi get them back to Skardu before another round of meals and arguments could begin. Janjungpa and Akhmalu joined them in the jeep, not willing to abandon their chance of winning the argument by letting Mortenson escape.

All the way back to Skardu, Changazi wore the same thin-lipped smile. Mortenson cursed himself for wasting so much time. As if to emphasize the looming end of weather warm enough to build a school, Skardu was gripped in a wintry chill when they returned. Low clouds blotted out the encircling peaks and a fine rain seemed to hover constantly in the air, rather than having the mercy to fall and be finished.

Despite the plastic flaps folded down over the jeep windows, Mortenson's *shalwar kamiz* was soaked through by the time the jeep parked in front of Changazi's compound. "Please," Changazi said, staring at Mortenson's mud-caked, mud-colored *shalwar.* "I'll have Yakub heat some water."

"Before we do anything else, let's get a few things straightened out," Mortenson said, unable to keep the heat out of his voice. "First thing. Where are all my school supplies? I don't see them anywhere."

Changazi stood as beatifically still as a portrait of a revered prophet. "I had them shifted to my other office."

"Shifted?"

"Yes . . . shifted. To the safer place," he said, with the aggrieved air of a man forced to explain the obvious.

"What's wrong with right here?" Mortenson said.

"There are many dacoits about," Changazi said.

"I want to go see everything right now," Mortenson said, drawing himself up to his full height and stepping close to Changazi. Mohammed Ali Changazi closed his eyes and laced his fingers together, lashing his thumbs over each other. He opened his eyes, as if he hoped Mortenson might have disappeared. "It is late and my assistant has gone home with the key," Changazi said. "Also I must wash and prepare for evening prayer. But I promise you, tomorrow, you will have 100 percent satisfaction. And together, we will put aside these shouting village men and set to work on your school."

Mortenson woke at first light. Wearing Changazi's sleeping bag like a shawl, he stepped out into the damp street. The crown of eighteen-thousand-foot peaks that garlanded the town was still hidden behind low clouds. And without the mountains, Skardu, with its trash-strewn shuttered bazaar, its squat mud-brick and cinder-block buildings, seemed unaccountably ugly. During his time in California he'd made Skardu the gilded capital of a mythical mountain kingdom. And he'd remembered the Balti who peopled it as pure and fine. But he wondered, standing in the drizzle, if he'd invented the Baltistan he'd believed in. Had he been so happy to simply be alive after K2 that his exuberance had colored this place, and these people, beyond reason?

He shook his head, as if trying to erase his doubts, but they remained. Korphe was only 112 kilometers to the north, but it felt a world away. He'd find his supplies. Then he'd get himself somehow to Korphe. He'd come so far he had to believe in something, and so he chose that blighted place clinging to the Braldu Gorge. He'd get there before he'd give up hope.

Over breakfast, Changazi seemed unusually solicitous. He kept Mortenson's teacup topped up himself, and assured him they'd set out as soon as the driver arrived with his jeep. By the time the green Land Cruiser arrived, Janjungpa and Akhmalu had walked to Changazi's from the cheap truck driver's rest house where they'd spent the night. The group set out together in silence.

They drove west through sand dunes. Where the sand relented, burlap bags of recently harvested potatoes awaited collection at the edge of fields. They stood as tall as men and Mortenson, at first, mistook them for people waiting mutely in the mist. The wind gained force and blew scraps of cloud cover aside. Glimpses of snowfields flitted high overhead like hope, and Mortenson felt his mood lifting.

An hour and a half from Skardu, they left the main road and fishtailed up a rutted track to a cluster of large, comfortable-looking mud-and-stone homes sheltered by weedy willow trees. This was Kuardu, Changazi's home village. He led the awkward party through a pen, nudging sheep aside with his sandaled foot, and up to the second floor of the village's largest home.

In the sitting room, they reclined, not on the usual dusty flowered cushions, but on purple and green Thermarest self-inflating camping pads. The walls were decorated with dozens of framed photos of Changazi, distinctive in spotless white, posing with scruffy members of French, Japanese, Italian, and American expeditions. Mortenson saw himself, his arm hooked jauntily over Changazi's shoulder, on the way to K2, and he could hardly believe the photo was only a year old. His own face looking back at him from the photograph seemed to belong to someone a decade younger. Through the door, he could see women in the kitchen frying something over a pair of expedition-grade field stoves.

Changazi disappeared into another room and returned wearing a gray Italian cashmere crewneck over his *shalwar*. Five older men with unkempt beards and damp brown woolen *topis* cocked on their heads entered and gripped Mortenson's hand enthusiastically before taking their places on the camping pads. Fifty more Kuardu men filed in and wedged against each other around a plastic tablecloth.

Changazi directed a parade of servants who placed so many dishes in the space between the men that Mortenson had to fold his feet sideways to make room, and still more arrived. Half a dozen roast chickens, radishes and turnips carved into floral rosettes, a mound of biryani, studded with nuts and raisins, cauliflower *pakhora* fried in herbed batter, and what looked like the better part of a yak, swimming in a stew of chilis and potatoes. Mortenson had never seen so much food in Baltistan, and the dread that he'd been struggling to push down during the jeep ride rose up until he could taste its acidic tang in his throat.

"What are we doing here, Changazi," he said. "Where are my supplies?"

Changazi piled yak meat on a lavish mound of biryani and set it before Mortenson before he answered. "These are the elders of my village," he said, motioning to the five wizened men. "Here in Kuardu, I can promise you no arguments. They have already agreed to see that your school is built in our village before winter."

Mortenson stood up without answering and stepped over the food. He knew how rude it was to refuse this hospitality. And he knew that it was unforgivable to turn his back to the elders in this manner and step over their food with unclean feet, but he had to get outside.

He ran until he'd left Kuardu behind and lunged fiercely up a steep shepherd's path. He felt the altitude tearing at his chest but he pushed himself harder, running until he felt so light-headed the landscape began to swim. In a clearing overlooking Kuardu, he collapsed, struggling for breath. He hadn't cried since Christa's death. But there, alone in a windblown goat pasture, he buried his face in his hands and swabbed furiously at the tears that wouldn't stop.

When finally he looked up, he saw a dozen young children staring at him from the far side of a mulberry tree. They had brought a herd of goats here to graze. But the sight of a strange *Angrezi* sitting in the mud sobbing led them to neglect their animals, which wandered away up the hillside. Mortenson stood, brushing off his clothes, and walked toward the children.

He knelt by the oldest, a boy of about eleven. "What . . . are . . . you?" the boy said shyly, extending his hand for Mortenson to shake. The boy's hand disappeared in Mortenson's grasp. "I am Greg. I am good," he said.

"I am Greg. I am good," all of the children repeated as one.

"No, I am Greg. What is your name?" he tried again.

"No, I am Greg. What is your name," the children repeated, giggling.

Mortenson switched to Balti. *"Min takpo Greg. Nga America in."* ("My name is Greg. I come from America.") *"Kiri min takpo in?"* ("What is your name?")

The children clapped their hands, gleeful at understanding the *Angrezi.*

Mortenson shook each of their hands in turn, as the children introduced themselves. The girls wrapped their hands cautiously in their headscarves before touching the infidel. Then he stood, and with his back at the trunk of the mulberry tree, began to teach. *Angrezi,* he said, pointing to himself. "Foreigner."

"Foreigner," the children shouted in unison. Mortenson pointed to his nose, his hair, his ears and eyes and mouth. At the sound of each unfamiliar term the children exploded in unison, repeating it, before dissolving in laughter.

Half an hour later, when Changazi found him, Mortenson was kneeling with the children, drawing multiplication tables in the dirt with a mulberry branch.

"Doctor Greg. Come down. Come inside. Have some tea. We have much to discuss," Changazi pleaded.

"We have nothing to discuss until you take me to Korphe," Mortenson said, never letting his eyes leave the children.

"Korphe is very far. And very dirty. You like these children. Why don't you build your school right here?

"No," Mortenson, said, rubbing out the work of an earnest nine-year-old girl with his palm and drawing the correct number. "Six times six is thirty-six."

"Greg, Sahib, please."

"Korphe," Mortenson said. "I have nothing to say to you until then."

The river was on their right. It boiled over boulders big as houses. Their Land Cruiser bucked and surged as if it were trying to negotiate the coffee-colored rapids, rather than this "road" skirting the north bank of the Braldu.

Akhmalu and Janjungpa had given up at last. They said hasty, defeated farewells and caught a ride on a jeep heading back to Skardu rather than continue chasing Mortenson up the Braldu River Valley. During the eight hours it took the Land Cruiser to reach Korphe, Mortenson had ample time to think. Changazi sprawled against a sack of basmati rice in the back seat with his white wool *topi* pulled over his eyes and slept through the constant jolting of their progress, or seemed to.

Mortenson felt a note of regret toward Akhmalu. He only wanted the children of his village to have the school that the government of Pakistan had failed to provide. But Mortenson's anger at Janjungpa and Changazi, at their scheming and dishonesty, spilled over the gratitude he felt for Akhmalu's months of uncomplaining service at K2 base camp until it became the same disheartening dun color as the surface of this ugliest of rivers.

Perhaps he had been too harsh with these people: The economic disparity between them was simply too great. Could it be that even a partially employed American who lived out of a storage locker could seem like little more than a flashing neon dollar sign to people in the poorest region of one of the world's poorest countries? He resolved that, should the people of Korphe engage in a tug of war for his wealth, such as it was, he would be more patient. He would hear them all out, eat as many meals as necessary, before insisting that the school should benefit all, rather than enrich the headman Haji Ali, or anyone else.

It had been dark for hours by the time they arrived opposite Korphe. Mortenson jumped out of the jeep and scanned the far riverbank, but he couldn't tell if anyone was there. At Changazi's instruction, the driver honked his horn and flashed his headlights. Mortenson stepped into their beam and waved at the blackness until he heard a shout from the south side of the river. The driver turned the jeep so its lights were trained across the water. They spotlit the progress of a small man sitting in a rickety box suspended on a cable over the gorge, pulling himself toward them.

Mortenson recognized Haji Ali's son Twaha just before he jumped out of the cable car and crashed into him. Twaha wrapped his arms around Mortenson's waist and squeezed, pressing his head against the American's chest. He smelled densely of smoke and sweat. When he finally loosened his grip, Twaha looked up at Mortenson, laughing. "Father mine, Haji Ali, say Allah send you back someday. Haji Ali know everything, sir."

Twaha helped Mortenson fold himself into the cable car. "It was just a box really," Mortenson says. "Like a big fruit crate held together with a few nails. You pulled yourself along this greasy cable and tried not to think about the creaking sounds it made. Tried not to think about the obvious—if it broke, you'd fall. And if you fell, you were dead."

Mortenson wheeled himself slowly along the 350-foot cable, which swayed back and forth in the biting wind. He could feel spray in the air. And a hundred feet below, he could hear, but not see, the brute force of the Braldu scouring boulders smooth. Then on a bluff high above the far riverbank, silhouetted by the jeep's headlights, he saw hundreds of people lined up to greet him. It looked like the entire population of Korphe. And on the far right, at the highest point on the bluff, he saw an unmistakable outline. Standing like he was carved out of granite, his legs planted wide, his broad bearded head balanced like a boulder on his solid shoulders, Haji Ali studied Mortenson's clumsy progress across the river.

Haji Ali's granddaughter Jahan remembers that evening well. "Many climbers make promise to Braldu people and forget them when they find their way home. My grandfather told us many times that Doctor Greg was different. He would come back. But we were surprised to see him again so soon. And I was so surprised to see, once again, his long body. None of the Braldu people look like that. He was very . . . suprising."

While Jahan and the rest of Korphe looked on, Haji Ali offered loud praise to Allah for bringing his visitor back safely, then hugged his long body. Mortenson was amazed to see that the head of the man who had loomed so large in his imagination for the last year reached only as high as his chest.

By a roaring fire in Haji Ali's *balti*, there in the same spot where Mortenson had once washed up, lost and exhausted, he felt completely at home. He sat happily surrounded by the people he'd been thinking about all the months he'd wasted writing grant proposals and letters and flailing about for a way to come back here with the news that he could keep his promise. He was bursting to tell Haji Ali, but there were formalities of hospitality to which they had to attend.

From some hidden recess in her home, Sakina produced an ancient packet of sugar cookies and presented them to Mortenson on a chipped tray with his butter tea. He broke them into tiny pieces, took one, and passed the tray so they could be shared out to the crowd of Korphe men.

Haji Ali waited until Mortenson had sipped the *paiyu cha*, then slapped him on the knee, grinning. *Cheezaley!* He said, exactly as he had the first time Mortenson had come to his home a year earlier, "What the hell?" But Mortenson hadn't wandered into Korphe lost and emaciated this time. He'd labored for a year to get back to this spot, with this news, and he ached to deliver it.

"I bought everything we need to build a school," he said in Balti, as he'd been rehearsing. "All the wood, and cement and tools. It's all in Skardu right now." He looked at Changazi, who dipped a cookie in his tea, and flush with the moment, he felt affection even for him. He had, after all, after a few detours, brought him here. "I came back to keep my promise," Mortenson said, looking Haji Ali in the eye. "And I hope we can begin building it soon, *Inshallah.*"

Haji Ali thrust his hand into his vest pocket, absently worrying his store of ibex jerky. "Doctor Greg," he said in Balti. "By the most merciful blessings of Allah you have come back to Korphe. I believed you would and said so as often as the wind blows though the Braldu Valley. That's why we have all discussed the school while you were in America. We want very much a school for Korphe," Haji Ali said, fastening his eyes on Mortenson's. "But we have decided. Before the ibex can climb K2, he must learn to cross the river. Before it is possible to build a school, we must build a bridge. This is what Korphe needs now."

"Zamba?" Mortenson repeated, hoping there was some terrible misunderstanding. The fault must be with his Balti. "A bridge?" he said in English, so there could be no mistake.

"Yes, the big bridge, the stone one," Twaha said. "So we can carry the school to the Korphe village."

Mortenson took a long sip of tea, thinking, *thinking.* He took another.

CHAPTER 9

THE PEOPLE HAVE SPOKEN

All my fellows, why license is not deposed on
the beautiful eyes of a beautiful lady? They fire at men like a bullet.
They cut as surely as the sword.

—graffiti spray-painted on the world's oldest known Buddhist stone-carving,
in Satpara Valley, Baltistan

SAN FRANCISCO INTERNATIONAL Airport was awash with wild-eyed mothers clutching children. It was almost Christmas and thousands of overwrought travelers jostled each other, hurrying toward flights they hoped would deliver them to their families in time. But the level of panic in the stale air was palpable, as inaudible voices echoed through the terminal, announcing delay after delay.

Mortenson walked to baggage claim and waited for his shabby half-filled army duffel bag to appear on the conveyor of overstuffed suitcases. Slinging it over his shoulder, he scanned the crowd hopefully for Marina, as he had upstairs when he'd walked off his flight from Bangkok. But as he held that half smile peculiar to arriving travelers, he couldn't find her dark hair among the hundreds of heads in the crowd.

They'd spoken four days earlier, on a line whistling with feedback, from a public call office in 'Pindi, and he was certain she said she planned to meet him at the airport. But the six-minute call he'd booked had been cut before he'd been able to repeat his flight information. He was too worried about money to pay for another call. Mortenson dialed Marina's number from a kiosk of pay phones and got her answering machine. "Hey, sweetie," he said, and he could hear the strained cheer in his own voice. "It's Greg. Merry Christmas. How are you? I miss you. I got into SFO okay so I guess I'll take BART over to your—"

"Greg," she said, picking up. "Hey."

"Hi. Are you okay?" he said. "You sound kind of . . ."

"Listen," she said. "We have to talk. Things have changed since you left. Can we talk?"

"Sure," he said. He could feel the sweat prickling under his arms. It had been three days since his last shower. "I'm coming home," he said and hung up.

He feared coming home after failing to make any progress on the school. But the thought of Marina and Blaise and Dana had eased his dread on the long transpacific flight. At least, he thought, he was flying toward people he loved, not just away from failure.

He took a bus to the nearest BART station, rode the train, then transferred in San Francisco for a streetcar to the Outer Sunset. He turned Marina's words on the phone over, worrying them, trying to shake loose any meaning other than the obvious—she was leaving him. Until the conversation from 'Pindi, he hadn't called her for months, he realized. But she had to understand that was because he couldn't afford international calls if he was trying to keep the school on budget, didn't she? He'd make it up to her. Take Marina and the girls away somewhere with what little remained in his Berkeley bank account.

By the time he arrived in Marina's neighborhood, two hours had passed and the sun had sunk into the graying Pacific. He walked past blocks of neat stucco houses bedecked with Christmas bulbs, into a stiff sea breeze, then climbed the stairs to her apartment.

Marina swept her door open, gave Mortenson a one-armed hug, then stood in her entryway, pointedly not inviting him in.

"I'm just going to say this," she said. He waited, his bag still hanging from his shoulder. "I've started seeing Mario again."

"Mario?"

"You know Mario. From UCSF, an anesthesiologist?" Mortenson stood and stared blankly. "My old boyfriend, remember I told you we were . . ."

Marina kept talking. Presumably she was filling him in on the half dozen times he'd met Mario, the evenings they'd spent together in the ER, but the name meant nothing. He watched her mouth as she spoke. It was her full lips, he decided. They were the most beautiful thing about her. He couldn't focus on anything they were saying until he heard "so I reserved you a motel room."

Mortenson turned away while Marina was still talking and walked back out into the teeth of the sea breeze. It had gone fully dark and the duffel bag he'd hardly noticed until then suddenly felt so heavy he wondered if he could carry it another block. Fortunately the red neon sign of the Beach Motel throbbed from the next corner like an open wound requiring immediate attention.

In the cigarette-smelling faux-wood-paneled room, where he was admitted after parting with the last of the cash in his pocket, Mortenson showered, then searched through his duffel bag for a clean T-shirt to sleep in. He settled for the least stained one he could find and fell asleep with the lights and television on.

An hour later, in the midst of blank exhaustion so profound that dreams didn't come, Mortenson was yanked out of sleep by a pounding on the door. He sat up and looked around the motel room, imagining he was still in Pakistan. But the television was broadcasting words, in English, by someone named Newt Gingrich. And a star-spangled graphic across the screen said something that might have been a foreign language for all the sense Mortenson could make of it: "Minority Whip Touts Republican Takeover."

Lurching as if the room were bobbing above heavy seas, Mortenson reached the door and pulled it open. Marina was there, wrapped in his favorite yellow Gore-Tex parka. "I'm sorry. This isn't how I imagined it. Are you okay?" she asked, crushing his coat tight against her chest.

"It's . . . I guess . . . no," Mortenson said.

"Were you asleep?" Marina asked.

"Yes."

"Look, I didn't want it to happen like this. But I had no way to reach you in Pakistan." It was cold with the door open and Mortenson stood shivering in his underwear.

"I sent you postcards," he said.

"Telling me all about the price of roofing materials and, oh, how much it cost to rent a truck to Skardu. They were very romantic. You never said anything about us, except to keep pushing back the date you'd be home."

"When did you start dating Mario?" He forced himself to look away from Marina's lips and let his gaze settle on her eyes, but thought better of that and jerked his own down. Those, too, were too dangerous.

"That's not the point," she said. "I could tell from your postcards that I didn't exist for you once you left."

"That's not true," Mortenson said, wondering if it was.

"I don't want you to hate me. You don't hate me, do you?"

"Not yet," he said.

Marina uncrossed her arms and sighed. She had a bottle of Baileys liqueur in her right hand. She held it out and Mortenson took it. It looked about half full.

"You're a great guy, Greg," Marina said. "Good-bye."

"Bye," Mortenson said, shutting the door before he said something he'd regret.

He stood in the empty room, holding the half-full bottle. Or was it half empty? It wasn't the sort of thing he'd drink anyway, and he'd thought Marina knew him well enough to understand that. Mortenson didn't drink very often, certainly not alone, and there was little he loathed as much as sweet liqueur.

On the television, a strident, cocksure voice told an interviewer, "We are embarked on the second American Revolution and you have my solemn vow that with a new Republican majority in Congress, American life is about to be profoundly different. The people have spoken."

Mortenson strode across the room to the wastebasket. It was large, made of dull metal, and battered by the impurities of the thousands of people unfortunate enough to have passed through this room. He held the bottle out above it, straight-armed, and then let go. The Baileys clanged against the metal can with a sound, to Mortenson's ear, like a steel door slamming shut. He collapsed onto the bed.

Money competed with pain for supremacy in Mortenson's mind. After the holiday, when he tried to withdraw two hundred dollars from his checking account, the bank teller told him his balance was only eighty-three dollars.

Mortenson phoned his supervisor at the UCSF Medical Center, hoping to schedule a shift immediately, before his money crisis became critical. "You said you'd be back to cover Thanksgiving," he said. "And now you miss Christmas, too. You're one of the best we have, Greg, but if you don't show up you're useless to me. You're fired." A phrase from the televised speech the evening before lodged in Mortenson's mind, and he repeated it bitterly under his breath for days: "The people have spoken."

Mortenson called half a dozen acquaintances in his mountaineering circle until he found a climber's crash pad where he could stay until he could figure out what to do next. In a dilapidated green Victorian house on Berkeley's Lorina Street, Mortenson slept on the floor in an upstairs hallway for a month. Graduate students at Cal Berkeley and climbers returning from, or on their way to, Yosemite held boozy parties on the ground floor late into the night. In his sleeping bag, sprawled across the upstairs hallway, Mortenson tried not to listen to the sounds of sex that were uncomfortably audible through the thin walls. While he slept, people stepped over him on the way to the bathroom.

A qualified nurse is rarely unemployed for long. It's only a matter of motivation. And after a few bleary days riding public transportation to interviews, rainy days when he was acutely aware of the absence of La Bamba, he was hired to work the least desirable overnight shifts at the San Francisco General Trauma Center, and Berkeley's Alta Bates Burn Unit.

He managed to save enough to rent a room in a third-floor walkup on Berkeley's gritty Wheeler Street that was sublet to a Polish handyman named Witold Dudzinski. Mortenson spent a few companionable evenings with Dudzinski, who chain-smoked and drank ceaselessly from unmarked blue bottles of Polish vodka that he bought in bulk. But much as he enjoyed the first fond soliloquies about Pope John Paul, Mortenson learned that, after enough vodka, Dudzinski simply spoke to no one in particular. So most evenings, Mortenson retired to his room and tried not to think about Marina.

"I'd been left by girlfriends before," Mortenson says, "but this was different. This one really hurt. And there was nothing to do but deal with it. It took time."

Some merciful nights, Mortenson was able to lose himself and his worries in the whirl of activity. Confronted with the immediate needs of a five-year-old child with third-degree burns across half her torso, it was impossible to wallow in self-pity. And there was a deep satisfaction he could find in working swiftly, and alleviating pain, in a well-equipped Western hospital, where every medication, machine, and dressing necessary was on hand, rather than eight hours away down a frequently impassable jeep track, as had been the case during the seven weeks he'd lingered in Korphe.

Sitting by the *balti* in Haji Ali's home, after the old man had delivered the devastating news about the bridge, Mortenson had felt his mind race furiously, like a furry animal trying to escape a trap, then slow and settle itself, until he felt suprisingly still. He was aware that he'd reached the end of the line—his destination, Korphe, the last village before the land of eternal ice. Stamping out like he'd done in Kuardu, when complications appeared, would solve nothing. There was nowhere else to go. He had watched Changazi's thin-lipped smile grow wide, and understood that the man thought he'd won the tug-of-war for Mortenson's school.

Despite his disappointment, he couldn't feel angry at the people of Korphe. Of course they needed a bridge. How was he planning to build his school? Carry every board, every sheet of corrugated tin, one by one, in a rickety basket swaying dangerously over the Braldu? Instead he felt angry at himself for not planning better. He decided to stay in Korphe until he understood everything else he had to do to bring the school to life. A series of detours had brought him to this village. What was one more?

"Tell me about this bridge," he had asked Haji Ali, breaking the expectant silence in the home crowded with all of Korphe's adult men. "What do we need? How do we get started?"

Mortenson had hoped, at first, that building a bridge was something that could be accomplished quickly, and with little expense.

"We have to blast many dynamite and cut many many stone," Haji Ali's son Twaha said to Mortenson. Then an argument began in Balti, about whether to cut the stone locally, or have it jeeped in from farther down the valley. There was much heated discussion about what specific hillsides contained the best quality granite. On other points the men were in absolute agreement. Steel cables and wood planks would have to be purchased and transported from Skardu or Gilgit, costing thousands of dollars. Skilled laborers would have to be paid thousands more. Thousands of dollars Mortenson no longer had.

Mortenson told them he'd spent most of his money already on the school and he'd have to return to America and try to raise more money for the bridge. He expected the Korphe men to act as crushed as he felt. But waiting was as much a part of their makeup as breathing the thin air at ten thousand feet. They waited half of each year, in rooms choked with smoke from yak dung fires, for the weather to become hospitable enough for them to return outdoors. A Balti hunter would stalk a single ibex for days, maneuvering hour by hour to get close enough to risk a shot with the single expensive bullet he could afford to spend. A Balti groom might wait years for his marriage, until the twelve-year-old girl his parents had selected for him grew old enough to leave her family. The people of the Braldu had been promised schools by the distant Pakistani government for decades, and they were waiting still. Patience was their greatest skill.

"Thanyouvermuch," Haji Ali said, trying to speak English for Mortenson's benefit. Being thanked for botching the job so badly was almost more than Mortenson could bear. He crushed the old man against his chest, breathing in his blend of woodsmoke and wet wool. Haji Ali beamed and summoned Sakina from the cooking fire to pour his guest a fresh cup of the butter tea that Mortenson was enjoying more each time he tasted it.

Mortenson ordered Changazi to return to Skardu without him and took satisfaction in the shocked expression that flitted across his face before he swiftly reined it in. Mortenson was going to learn everything he needed to know about building the bridge before he returned home.

With Haji Ali he rode downriver in a jeep to study the bridges of the lower Braldu Valley. Back in Korphe, Mortenson sketched the sort of bridge that the people of the village had asked him to construct in his notebook. And he met with the elders of Korphe to discuss what plot of land he might build the school on, when, *Inshallah,* he returned from America.

When the wind blowing down the Baltoro began to carry snow crystals, which blanketed Korphe, signifying the onset of the long indoor months, Mortenson began to say his good-byes. By mid-December, more than two months after he'd arrived with Changazi, he couldn't avoid leaving any longer. After visiting half the homes in Korphe for a farewell cup of tea, Mortenson bounced back down the south bank of the Braldu in an overloaded jeep carrying the eleven Korphe men who insisted on seeing him off at Skardu. They were packed so tight that every time the jeep shuddered over an obstacle, the men would all rock together, leaning on each other for both balance and warmth.

Walking home after his hospital shift toward his bare room in Dudzinski's smoke-fouled flat, in that shadowland between night and morning when the world seems depopulated, Mortenson felt fatigued by loneliness. He seemed irretrievably far from the camaraderie of village life in Korphe. And calling Jean Hoerni, the one person who might be able to fund his return, seemed too intimidating to seriously consider.

All that winter, Mortenson worked out on the wall at the City Rock climbing gym, in a warehouse district between Berkeley and Oakland. It was more difficult to reach than when he'd had La Bamba, but he took the bus there as much for the company as the exercise. Preparing for K2, honing himself into shape, he'd been a hero to the members of City Rock. But now, every time he opened his mouth, his stories were about failures: a summit not reached, a woman lost, a bridge, and a school, not built.

One night, walking home very late after work, Mortenson was mugged across the street from his house by four boys who couldn't have been older than fourteen. While one held a pistol aimed shakily at Mortenson's chest, his accomplice emptied Mortenson's pockets. "Sheeyit. Bitch ain't got but two dollars," the boy said, pocketing the bills and handing Mortenson back his empty wallet. "Why we got to jump the most broke-down white dude in Berkeley?"

Broke. Broke down. Broken. Into the spring, Mortenson wallowed in his depression. He pictured the hopeful faces of the Korphe men when they'd put him on a bus to Islamabad, sure, *Inshallah*, that he'd be back soon with money. How could they have so much faith in him when he had so little in himself?

Late one afternoon in May, Mortenson was lying on his sleeping bag, thinking how badly it needed a wash, and debating whether he could bear the trip to a Laundromat, when the phone rang. It was Dr. Louis Reichardt. In 1978, Reichardt and his climbing partner Jim Wickwire had been the first Americans to reach the summit of K2. Mortenson had called him before setting out for K2, to ask Reichardt for advice, and they'd talked infrequently, but warmly, ever since. "Jean told me what you're trying to do with your school," Reichardt said. "How's it going?"

Mortenson told him everything, from the 580 letters to the bottleneck he'd reached with the bridge. He also found himself telling the fatherly older man his troubles, from losing his woman, to losing his job, to what he feared most—losing his way.

"Pull yourself together, Greg. Of course you've hit a few speed bumps," Reichardt said. "But what you're trying to do is much more difficult than climbing K2."

"Coming from Lou Reichardt, those words meant a lot," Mortenson says. "He was one of my heroes." The hardships Reichardt and Wickwire had endured to reach the summit were legendary in mountain lore. Wickwire had tried, at first, to summit in 1975. And the photographer Galen Rowell, a member of the expedition, wrote a book about the group's travails, documenting one of the most rancorous high-altitude failures in history.

Three years later, Reichardt and Wickwire returned and climbed to within three thousand feet of the summit on the fearsome West Ridge, where they were turned back by avalanche. Rather than retreating, they traversed across K2 at twenty-five thousand feet to the traditional route most climbers had tried, the Abruzzi Ridge, and, remarkably, made it to the top. Reichardt, his oxygen running low, wisely hurried down. But Wickwire lingered on the summit, attempting to unfog his camera lens to take pictures and savor the achievement of his lifelong goal. The miscalculation nearly cost him his life.

Without a headlamp, he couldn't make the technical descent in the dark and Wickwire was forced to endure one of the highest bivouacs ever recorded. His oxygen ran out and he suffered severe frostbite, pneumonia, pleurisy, and a cluster of potentially fatal clots in his lungs. Reichardt and the rest of the team struggled to keep him alive with constant medical care, until Wickwire could be evacuated by helicopter to a hospital, then home to Seattle where he underwent major chest surgery to repair the clots.

Lou Reichardt knew something about suffering for and reaching difficult goals. His acknowledgment of how tough a path Mortenson was trying to walk made Mortenson feel that he hadn't failed. He just hadn't completed the climb. Yet.

"Call Jean and tell him everything you told me," Reichardt said. "Ask him to pay for the bridge. Believe me, he can afford it."

Mortenson felt, for the first time since coming home, like a semblance of his old self. He hung up and rifled through the Ziploc bag that served as his address book until he found the scrap of graph paper with Hoerni's name and number. "Don't screw up," the paper said. Well, maybe he had. Maybe he hadn't. It depended who you talked to. But there were his fingers dialing the numbers anyway. And then the phone was ringing.

CHAPTER 10

BUILDING BRIDGES

*In the immensity of these ranges, at the limit of existence
where men may visit but cannot dwell, life has a new importance . . . but
Mountains are not chivalrous; one forgets their violence. Indifferently
they lash those who venture among them with snow, rock, wind, cold.*

—George Schaller, *Stones of Silence*

THE MAN'S VOICE on the other end of the line sounded like it was sputtering halfway across the Earth, even though Mortenson knew he couldn't be much more than two hundred kilometers away. "Say again?" the voice said.

Salaam Alaaikum, Mortenson shouted through the static. "I want to buy five four-hundred-foot spools of steel cable. Triple braid. Do you have that, sir?"

"Certainly," he said, and suddenly the line was clear. "One half *lakh* rupees one cable. Is that acceptable?"

"Do I have any choice?"

"No." The contractor laughed. "I am the only person in all the Northern Areas to possess so much cable. May I ask your good name?"

"Mortenson, Greg Mortenson."

"Where are you calling from, Mister Greg? Are you also in Gilgit?"

"I'm in Skardu."

"And may I know what you want with so much cable?"

"My friends' village in the upper Braldu Valley has no bridge. I'm going to help them build one."

"Ah, you are American, yes?"

"Yes, sir."

"I've heard about your bridge. Are the byways to your village jeepable?

"If it doesn't start raining. Can you deliver the cable?"

"*Inshallah.*"

Allah willing. Not "no." It was a wonderful response for Mortenson to hear after a dozen unsuccessful calls, and the only realistic way to answer any question involving transportion in the Northern Areas. He had his cable, the final and most difficult piece he needed to begin building the bridge. It was only early June 1995. And without any unconquerable setbacks, the bridge would be finished before winter, and work on the school could start the following spring.

For all Mortenson's anxiety about calling him, Jean Hoerni had been surprisingly kind about writing him a check for an additional ten thousand dollars. "You know, some of my ex-wives could spend more fund than that in a weekend," he said. He did, however, extract a promise. "Get the school built as quickly as you can. And when you finish, bring me a photo," Hoerni demanded, "I'm not getting any younger." Mortenson was more than happy to assure him that he would.

"This man has the cable?" Changazi asked.

"He does."

"And what will it cost?"

"The same as you said, eight hundred dollars each spool."

"He will deliver it upside?"

"*Inshallah,*" Mortenson said, replacing Changazi's phone in the cradle on the desk in his office. Flush with Hoerni's money and back on track, Mortenson was glad of Changazi's company once again. The price he paid in the rupees Changazi skimmed off every transaction was more than compensated for by the man's vast network of contacts. He had once been a policeman and seemed to know everyone in town. And after Changazi had written him an invoice for all the building materials he was storing for Mortenson's school, there seemed no reason not to take advantage of Changazi's skills.

During the week Mortenson had spent sleeping on the *charpoy* in Changazi's office, under the aged wall map of the world that he was nostalgically pleased to see still identified Tanzania as Tanganyika, he'd been entertained by Changazi's tales of roguery. The weather had been unusually fine all summer and business was good. Changazi had helped to outfit several expeditions, a German and a Japanese attempt at K2 and an Italian group trying for the second ascent of Gasherbrum IV. Consequently, Changazi had protein bars with German labels tucked into every crevice of his office, like a squirrel's winter hoard of nuts. And behind his desk, a case of a Japanese sports drink called Pokhari Sweat propped up half a dozen boxes of biscotti.

But the foreign delicacies Changazi savored most had names like Hildegund and Isabella. Despite that fact that the man had a wife and five children stashed at his home in distant 'Pindi and a second wife tucked away in a rented house near the superintendent of police's office in Skardu, Changazi had spent the tourist season tucking into a smorgasbord of the female tourists and trekkers who were arriving in Skardu in ever greater numbers.

Changazi told Mortenson how he squared his dalliances with his devotion to Islam. Heading to his mosque soon after another Inge or Aiko wandered into his sights, Changazi petitioned his mullah for permission to make a *muthaa,* or temporary marriage. The custom was still common in parts of Shiite Pakistan, for married men who might face intervals without the comfort of their wives, fighting in distant wars, or traveling on an extended trip. But Changazi had been granted a handful of *muthaa* already since the climbing season began in May. Better to sanctify the union, however short-lived, in Allah's sight, Changazi cheerfully explained to Mortenson, than simply to have sex.

Mortenson asked if Balti women whose husbands were away could also be granted *muthaa.*

"No, of course not," Changazi said, waggling his head at the naïveté of Mortenson's question, before offering him a biscotti to dunk in his tea.

Now that the cable was ordered and on its way, Mortenson hired a place on a jeep to Askole. All up the Shigar Valley, they tunneled through ripening apple and apricot trees. The air was so clear that the serrated rust and ochre ridges of the Karakoram's eighteen-thousand-foot foothills seemed close enough to touch. And the road seemed as passable as a boulder-strewn dirt track carved out of the edge of a cliff could ever be.

But as they turned up the Braldu Valley, low clouds pursued and overtook their jeep, moving fast from the south. That could only mean the monsoon, blowing in from India. And by the time they arrived in Askole, everyone in the windowless jeep was wet and spattered with gouts of gray mud.

Mortenson climbed out at the last stop, before the village of Askole, in a dense rain that raised welts in the muddy road. Korphe was still hours farther on by foot, and the driver couldn't be convinced to continue up the track in darkness, so Mortenson reluctantly spent the night, sprawled on bags of rice in a shop attached to the home of Askole's *nurmadhar,* Haji Mehdi, fending off rats that tried to climb up from the flooded floor.

In the morning, it was still raining in an apocalyptic fashion and the jeep driver had already contracted to carry a load back to Skardu. Mortenson set off on foot. He was still trying to warm to Askole. As the trailhead for all expeditions heading northeast up the Baltoro, it had been contaminated by repeated contact of the worst kind between Western trekkers needing to hire porters or purchase some staple they'd forgotten and hustlers hoping to take advantage of them. As in many last places, Askole merchants tended to inflate prices and ruthlessly refuse to bargain.

Wading through an alley running two feet deep with runoff, between the rounded walls of stone-and-mud huts, Mortenson felt his *shalwar* clutched from behind. He turned to see a boy, his head swarming with lice, his hand extended toward the *Angrezi.* He didn't have the English to ask for money or a pen, but his meaning couldn't have been clearer. Mortenson took an apple out of his rucksack and handed it to the boy, who threw it in the gutter.

Passing a field north of Askole, Mortenson had to hold the shirttail of his *shalwar* over his nose against the stench. The field, a campsite used by dozens of expeditions on their way up the Baltoro, was befouled by hundreds of piles of human waste.

A book he'd recently read, *Ancient Futures,* by Helena Norberg-Hodge, was much on Mortenson's mind. Norberg-Hodge had spent seventeen years living just south of these mountains, in Ladakh, a region much like Baltistan, but cut off from Pakistan by the arbitrary borders colonial powers drew across the Himalaya. After almost two decades studying Ladakhi culture, Norberg-Hodge had come to believe that preserving a traditional way of life in Ladakh—extended families living in harmony with the land—would bring about more happiness than "improving" Ladakhis' standard of living with unchecked development.

"I used to assume that the direction of 'progress' was somehow inevitable, not to be questioned," she writes. "I passively accepted a new road through the middle of the park, a steel-and-glass bank where a 200-year-old church had stood . . . and the fact that life seemed to get harder and faster with each day. I do not anymore. In Ladakh I have learned that there is more than one path into the future and I have had the privilege to witness another, saner, way of life—a pattern of existence based on the coevolution between human beings and the earth."

Norberg-Hodge continues to argue not only that Western development workers should not blindly impose modern "improvements" on ancient cultures, but that industrialized countries had lessons to learn from people like Ladakhis about building sustainable societies. "I have seen," she writes, "that community and a close relationship with the land can enrich human life beyond all comparison with material wealth or technological sophistication. I have learned that another way is possible."

As he walked up the rain-slick gorge to Korphe, keeping the rushing Braldu on his right, Mortenson fretted about the effect his bridge would have on the isolated village. "The people of Korphe had a hard life, but they also lived with a rare kind of purity," Mortenson says. "I knew the bridge would help them get to a hospital in hours instead of days, and would make it easier to sell their crops. But I couldn't help worrying about what the outside world, coming in over the bridge, would do to Korphe."

The men of Korphe met Mortenson at the riverbank and ushered him over in the hanging basket. On both sides of the river, where the two towers of the bridge would stand, hundreds of slabs of roughhewn granite were stacked, awaiting construction. Rather than having to haul rocks across the river and depend on the vagaries of transport up rutted roads, Haji Ali, in the end, had convinced Mortenson to use rock cut on hillsides only a few hundred yards distant from both banks. Korphe was poor in every material thing but its endless supply of rock.

Up through the rain-soaked village, Mortenson led a procession toward Haji Ali's house, to convene a meeting about how to proceed with the bridge. A long-haired black yak stood blocking their progress between two homes, while Tahira, the ten-year-old daughter of Hussein, Korphe's most educated man, pulled the yak by a bridle attached to the animal's nose ring and tried to coax him out of the way. The yak had other ideas. Leisurely, he voided a great steaming mound onto the mud, then walked off toward Tahira's home. Tahira swept her white headscarf out of the way and bent frantically to make patties out of the yak dung. She slapped them against the stone wall of the nearest home to dry, under the eaves, before the precious fuel could be washed away by the rain.

At Haji Ali's, Sakina took Mortenson's hand in welcome, and he realized it was the first time a Balti woman had touched him. She grinned boldly up into his face, as if daring him to be surprised. In answer, he crossed a threshold, too, and entered her "kitchen," just a fire ring of rocks, a few shelves, and a length of warped wood board on the packed dirt floor for chopping. Mortenson bent to a pile of kindling and said hello to Sakina's granddaughter Jahan, who smiled shyly, tucked her burgundy headscarf between her teeth, and hid behind it.

Sakina, giggling, tried to shoo Mortenson from her kitchen. But he took a handful of *tamburok*, an herbal-tasting green mountain tea, from a tarnished brass urn and filled the blackened teapot from a ten-gallon plastic gasoline container of river water. Mortenson added a few slivers of kindling to the smoldering fire, and put the tea on to boil.

He poured the bitter green tea for Korphe's council of elders himself, then took a cup and sat on a cushion between Haji Ali and the hearth, where burning yak dung filled the room with eye-smarting smoke.

"My grandmother was very shocked when Doctor Greg went into her kitchen," Jahan says. "But she already thought of him as her own child, so she accepted it. Soon, her ideas changed, and she began to tease my grandfather that he should learn how to be more helpful like his American son."

When overseeing the interests of Korphe, however, Haji Ali rarely relaxed his vigilance. "I was always amazed how, without a telephone, electricity, or a radio, Haji Ali kept himself informed about everything happening in the Braldu Valley and beyond," Mortenson says. Two jeeps carrying the cable for the bridge had made it to within eighteen miles of Korphe, Haji Ali told the group, before a rockslide blocked the road. Since the road might remain blocked for weeks, and heavy earth-moving equipment was unlikely to be dispatched from Skardu in bad weather, Haji Ali proposed that every able-bodied man in the village pitch in to carry the cable to Korphe so they could begin work on the bridge at once.

With a cheerfulness that Mortenson found surprising among men setting out on such a grueling mission, thirty-five Balti, ranging from teenagers to Haji Ali and his silver-bearded peers, walked all the next day in the rain, turned around, and spent twelve more hours carrying the cable up to Korphe. Each of the coils of cable weighed eight hundred pounds, and it took ten men at a time to carry the thick wood poles they threaded through the center of the spools.

More than a foot taller than all the Korphe men, Mortenson tried to carry his share, but tilted the load so steeply that he could only watch the other men work. No one minded. Most of them had served as porters for Western expeditions, carrying equally brutal loads up the Baltoro.

The men marched cheerfully, chewing *naswar,* the strong tobacco that Haji Ali distributed from the seemingly endless supply stashed in his vest pockets. Working this hard to improve life in their village, rather than chasing the inscrutable goals of foreign climbers, was a pleasure, Twaha told Mortenson, grinning up from under the yoke beside his father.

In Korphe, the men dug foundations deep into both muddy riverbanks. But the monsoon lingered, and the concrete wouldn't set in the wet weather. Twaha and a group of younger men proposed a trip to hunt for ibex while the rain persisted, and invited Mortenson to accompany them.

In only his running shoes, raincoat, *shalwar kamiz,* and a cheap Chinese acrylic sweater he'd purchased in Skardu's bazaar, Mortenson felt poorly prepared for a high-altitude trek. But none of the six other men were better equipped. Twaha, the *nurmadhar's* son, wore a sturdy pair of brown leather dress shoes given to him by a passing trekker. Two of the men's feet were wrapped in tightly lashed hides, and the others wore plastic sandals.

They walked north out of Korphe in a steady rain, through ripening buckwheat fields clinging to every surface where irrigation water could be coaxed. The well-developed wheat kernels looked like miniature ears of corn. Under the onslaught of thick raindrops, the kernels bobbed on the end of their swaying stalks. Twaha proudly carried the group's only gun over his shoulder, a British musket from the early colonial era. And Mortenson found it hard to believe they were hoping to bring down an ibex with such a museum piece.

Mortenson spotted the bridge he'd missed on his way back from K2, a sagging yak-hair *zamba*, lashed between enormous boulders on either side of the Braldu. He was cheered by the sight. It led to Askole and skirted the place he was coming to consider his second home. It was like looking at the less-interesting path his life might have taken had he not detoured down the trail to Korphe.

As they climbed, the canyon walls closed in and both rain and spray from the Braldu soaked them with equal thoroughness. The trail clung to the vertiginously sloping side of the canyon. Generations of Balti had buttressed it against washing away by wedging flat rocks together into a flimsy shelf. The Korphe men, carrying only light loads in woven baskets, walked along the shifting two-foot ledge as surely as if they were still strolling through level fields. Mortenson placed each foot carefully, leaning into the canyon wall, which he traced with trailing fingertips. He was all too conscious of the two-hundred-foot plunge to the Braldu.

Here the river was as ugly as the ice peaks that birthed it were beautiful. Snarling through a catacomb of sculpted black and brown boulders, down in the dank recesses where sunlight rarely reached, the mud-brown Braldu looked like a writhing serpent. It was difficult to believe that this grim torrent was the source of life for those golden buckwheat kernels, and all the crops of Korphe.

By the snout of the Biafo Glacier, the rain stopped. A shaft of stormlight skewered the cloud cover and picked out Bakhor Das, a peak to the east, in a burst of lemony light. These men knew the nineteen-thousand-foot pyramid as Korphe K2, since its purity of form echoed its big brother up the Baltoro, and it loomed over their homes like a protective deity. In valleys like the Upper Braldu, Islam has never completely vanquished older, animist beliefs. And the Korphe men seized this vision of their mountain as a good omen for the hunt. Led by Twaha, together the men chanted a placation of the Karakoram's deities, promising that they would take only one ibex.

To find ibex, they'd have to climb high. The celebrated field biologist George Schaller had pursued the ibex and their cousins all over the Himalaya. A 1973 trek with Schaller through western Nepal to study the bharal, or blue sheep, became the basis of Peter Matthiessen's stark masterpiece *The Snow Leopard*. Matthiessen anointed his account of their long walk through high mountains with a sense of pilgrimage.

The world's great mountains demand more than mere physical appreciation. In Schaller's own book, *Stones of Silence*, he confesses that his treks through the Karakoram, which he called "the most rugged range on earth," were, for him, spiritual odysseys as well as scientific expeditions. "Hardship and disappointment marked these journeys," Schaller writes, but, "mountains become an appetite. I wanted more of the Karakoram."

Schaller had trekked up this same gorge two decades earlier, gathering data on the ibex, Marco Polo sheep, and scouting sites he hoped the Pakistani government might preserve as the Karakoram National Park. But for long days hunched over his spotting scope, Schaller found himself simply admiring how magnificently the ibex had adapted to this harshest of all environments.

The alpine ibex is a large, well-muscled mountain goat easily distinguished by its long scimitar-shaped horns, which the Balti prize almost as much as they savor ibex meat. Schaller found that the ibex grazed higher than any animal in the Karakoram. Their sureness of foot allowed them to range over narrow ledges at altitudes up to seventeen thousand feet, high above their predators, the wolves and snow leopards. At the very limit where vegetation could exist, they mowed alpine shoots and grasses to the nub and had to forage ten to twelve hours every day to maintain their mass.

Twaha paused by the tongue of soiled ice that marked the leading edge of the Biafo Glacier and took a small circular object from the pocket of the wine-colored fleece jacket Mortenson had given him during his first visit to Korphe. It was a *tomar*, or "badge of courage." Balti hang a *tomar* around the neck of every newborn to ward off the evil spirits they blame for their communities' painfully high rates of infant mortality. And they wouldn't think of traveling over something as dangerous as a shifting river of ice without taking similar precautions. Twaha tied the intricate medallion woven of maroon and vermilion wool to the zipper of Mortenson's jacket. Each of the men fixed his own *tomar* in place, then stepped onto the glacier.

Traveling with a party of men hunting to eat, rather than Westerners aiming for summits with more complicated motives, Mortenson saw this wilderness of ice with new eyes. It was no wonder the great peaks of the Himalaya had remained unconquered until the mid-twentieth century. For millennia, the people who lived closest to the mountains never considered attempting such a thing. Scratching out enough food and warmth to survive on the roof of the world took all of one's energy.

In this sense, Balti men weren't so different from the ibex they pursued.

They climbed west, picking a path through shifting slabs of ice and deep pools tinted tropical blue. Water echoed from the depths of cre-vasses and rockfalls shattered the silence as the weather's constant warm-ing and cooling pried boulders loose. Near, to their north, somewhere within the wall of low clouds, was the Ogre, a sheer 23,900-foot wall that had only been conquered in 1977, by British climbers Chris Bon-ington and Doug Scott. But the Ogre exacted revenge during the de-scent, and Scott was forced to crawl back to base camp with two broken legs.

The Biafo rises to 16,600 feet at Snow Lake before joining with the Hispar Glacier, which descends into the Hunza Valley. At seventy-six miles from snout to snout, it forms the longest contiguous glacier sys-tem outside the Earth's poles. This natural highway was also the path Hunza raiding parties historically took to plunder the Braldu Valley. But the hunting party had this high traverse to themselves, except for the occasional tracks of the snow leopard Twaha pointed out excitedly, and two mournful lammergeiers, vultures that circled curiously on a thermal high above the hunters.

Walking for hours over the brittle ice in his running shoes, Mortenson's feet were soon freezing. But Hussein, Tahira's father, took hay out of his pack and lined Mortenson's Nikes with handfuls of folded stalks. With this, the cold was tolerable. Just. Mortenson wondered, without tents or sleeping bags, how they would pass the bitter nights. But the Balti had been hunting on the Biafo long before Westerners started arriving with the latest gear.

Each night, they slept in a series of caves along the lateral moraine, as well-known to the Balti as a string of watering holes would be to a caravan of Bedouin. Every cave was stocked with dry brush and bits of sage and juniper for fires. From under heavy piles of rocks, the men retrieved sacks of lentils and rice they'd placed there on previous visits. And with the loaves of skull-shaped *kurba* bread they baked over fire stones, they had all the fuel they needed to continue the hunt.

After four days they spotted their first ibex. It was a carcass lying on a flat rock, picked clean as snow by lammergeier and leopard. High on a ledge above the bones, Twaha spotted a herd of sixteen ibex grazing, shouting *skiin! skiin!* their name in Balti. Their great curving horns were silhouetted against a changeable sky, but too far above the men to hunt. Twaha guessed that a *rdo-rut,* an avalanche, had brought the dead ibex down, since he was so far below his grazing ground. He tore the bleached head and horns loose from the spine and lashed it to Mortenson's pack. A present.

The Biafo bores a trench through high peaks deeper than that of the Grand Canyon. They trekked up to where it met the long north ridge of Latok, which has repelled more than a dozen expeditions' attempts. Twice they worked their way stealthily downwind of ibex herds, but the animals sensed them with a cunning Mortenson couldn't help admiring, before they were close enough to attempt a shot.

Just before dusk on the seventh day, it was Twaha who sighted the big stag on an outcropping sixty feet above them. He tilted a tin of gunpowder into his musket, added a steel slug, and tamped it down. Mortenson and the others crawled behind him, pressing against the base of a cliff, which they hoped would conceal them. Twaha folded down two legs from the barrel of the gun, steadied them atop a boulder, and cocked back the hammer quietly, but not quietly enough. The ibex whirled toward them. They were close enough to see his long beard bristle with alarm. Mortenson saw Twaha's mouth moving in prayer as he pulled the trigger.

The report was deafening, and brought a rain of pebbles bouncing down from the heights. A spray of gunpowder painted Twaha's face black as a coal miner's. Mortenson was sure Twaha had missed because the ibex was still standing. Then the buck's front legs buckled, and Mortenson saw steam venting into the chill air from a wound in the animal's neck. The ibex struggled twice to get his legs back beneath him, quieted, and pitched over on his side. *"Allah-u-Akbhar!"* all the Korphe men shouted in a single voice.

The butchering began in the dark. Then they carried pieces of the carcass into a cave and lit a fire. Hussein expertly wielded a curved knife the length of his forearm. His long, mournfully intelligent face frowned with concentration as he filleted the liver and shared it out among the men. Mortenson was glad of the food's warmth, if nothing else. Alone among all the residents of Korphe, Hussein had left the Braldu and been educated through the twelfth grade in distant, lowland Lahore. Bent over the carcass in this cave, his forearms slick with blood, Hussein seemed to Mortenson immeasurably removed from his days of scholarship on the sweltering plains of the Punjab. He would be the perfect teacher for Korphe's school, Mortenson realized. He'd be able to bridge both worlds.

By the time the hunting party arrived back in Korphe, the monsoon had retreated and the weather had turned crisp and clear. They marched into the village to a heroes' welcome. Twaha led the way holding the fresh ibex head aloft. Mortenson, still carrying his present, brought up the back, with the horns of the avalanche victim bristling above his head like his own antlers.

The men passed out handfuls of cubed ibex fat to children who crowded around them, sucking on the tidbits like candy. The several hundred pounds of meat they carried in their baskets were shared evenly among the hunters' families. And after the meat had been boiled away, and the brains served in a stew with potatoes and onions, Haji Ali added the horns his son had brought back to a row of trophies nailed over the entrance of his home, proud evidence from the days when he was vigorous enough to hunt himself.

Mortenson had taken his sketches of the bridges spanning the lower Braldu to a Pakistani army engineer in the regional capital of Gilgit. He examined Mortenson's drawings, suggested some revisions to strengthen the structure, and drew a detailed blueprint for Korphe's bridge, indicating the precise placement of cables. His plan called for twin sixty-four-foot stone towers, topped with poured concrete arches wide enough for yak carts to pass through, and a 284-foot suspension span sixty feet above the high-water mark.

Mortenson hired an experienced crew of masons from Skardu to supervise the construction of the towers. Four Korphe men at a time lifted the blocks of quarried stone and attempted to place them squarely on top of the layer of cement the masons had troweled into place. Children turned out to watch the entertainment and shouted encouragement as their fathers' and uncles' faces reddened with the effort of holding the stones steady. Block by block, two three-tiered towers rose on either side of the river, narrowing as they tapered toward the top.

The clear fall weather made the long days of work pleasant and Mortenson reveled in the tangible results every evening as he measured how many blocks they'd managed to set that day. For most of July, as the men built the bridge, women tended the crops. As the sturdy twin towers rose above the river, women and children watched them rise from their roofs.

Before the claustrophobia of winter closed in, Korphe's people lived as much as possible outdoors. Most families took their two daily meals on their roof. And washing down a bowl of *dal* and rice with strong *tamburok* tea, after a satisfying day's work, Mortenson loved basking in the last of the sunlight with Haji Ali's family, and chatting across the rooftops to the dozens of families doing the same.

Norberg-Hodge admiringly quotes the king of another Himalayan country, Bhutan, who says the true measure of a nation's success is not gross national product, but "gross national happiness." On their warm, dry roofs, among the fruits of their successful harvest, eating, smoking, and gossiping with the same sense of leisure as Parisians on the terrace of a sidewalk café, Mortenson felt sure that, despite all that they lacked, the Balti still held the key to a kind of uncomplicated happiness that was disappearing in the developing world as fast as old-growth forests.

At night, bachelors like Twaha and Mortenson took advantage of the mild weather to sleep under the stars. By this time, Mortenson's Balti had become fluent, and he and Twaha sat up long after most of Korphe slept to talk. Their great subject was women. Mortenson was fast approaching forty, Twaha, about to turn thirty-five.

He told Mortenson how much he missed his wife, Rhokia. It had been nine years since he lost her in gaining their only child, Jahan. "She was very beautiful," he said, as they lay looking at a Milky Way that was so dense it covered them like a shawl. "Her face was small, like Jahan's, and she was always popping up laughing and singing, like a marmot."

"Will you marry again?" Mortenson asked.

"Oh, for me this is very easy," Twaha explained. One day I will be *nurmadhar* and already I have a lot of land. So far I don't love any other woman." He lowered his voice slyly. "But sometimes I . . . enjoy."

"Can you do that without marrying?" Mortenson said. It was something he'd been curious about since coming to Korphe, but had never felt confident enough to ask.

"Yes, of course," Twaha said. "With widows. We have many widows in Korphe."

Mortenson thought of the cramped quarters below, where dozens of family members were sleeping sprawled side by side on cushions. "Where can you, you know?"

"In the *handhok*, of course" Twaha said. Every Korphe home had a *handhok*, a small thatched hut on the roof where they stored grain. "You want me to find you a widow? I think a few love Doctor Greg already."

"Thank you," Mortenson said. "I don't think that would be a good idea."

"You have a sweetheart in your village?" Twaha asked. So Mortenson summarized his major dating failures of the last decade, concluding with Marina, and he couldn't help noticing, as he talked, that the wound felt far less raw.

"Ah, she left you because you had no house," Twaha said. "This thing happens often in Baltistan. But now you can tell her you have a house and almost a bridge in Korphe."

"She's not the one I want," Mortenson said, and realized he meant it.

"Then you better quickly find your woman," Twaha said, "before you grow too old and fat."

The day they strung the first cable between the towers, news traveled down the trail with porters returning from the Baltoro that a party of Americans was approaching. Mortenson sat on a boulder by the north bank of the Braldu with the engineer's blueprints. He supervised as two groups stretched the main cables with teams of yaks and tied them to the towers as tightly as they could manage without power tools. Then the nimblest among them tightroped back and forth, looping support cables through the lash points the engineer had outlined and screwing them tightly in place with clamps.

Down the north bank of the Braldu, a formidable-looking American man wearing a white baseball cap approached, leaning on a walking stick. At his side, a handsome, heavily muscled local guide hovered protectively.

"My first thought was, 'That's a big guy sitting on that rock,' " says George McCown, "and I couldn't figure out what the deal with him was. He had long hair. He was wearing local clothes. But it was obvious he was no Pakistani."

Mortenson slid down off the boulder and held out his hand. "Are you George McCown?" he asked. McCown took Mortenson's hand and nodded incredulously. "Then happy birthday," Mortenson said, grinning, and handed the man a sealed envelope.

George McCown served on the board of the American Himalayan Foundation, along with Lou Reichardt and Sir Edmund Hillary. He had spent his sixtieth birthday trekking to K2 with two of his children, Dan and Amy, to visit the base camp of an expedition he was helping to sponsor. The birthday card from the AHF's board of directors had arrived in Askole, then been passed on to Mortenson by mystified local authorities who figured one American would know how to locate another.

McCown had been President/CEO of Boise Cascade Home and Land Corporation and built the corporation's business from $100 million to $6 billion in six years, before it splintered and split apart. He learned his lesson well. In the 1980s, he founded his own venture capital firm in Menlo Park, California, and began buying up pieces of other companies that had grown too large and unwieldy. McCown was still recovering from knee surgery, and after weeks walking on the glacier and wondering if his knee would carry him back to civilization, the sight of Mortenson cheered him immeasurably.

"After a month away, I was suddenly talking with someone very competent in what can be a very hostile place," McCown says. "I couldn't have been happier to meet Greg Mortenson."

Mortenson told McCown how the funds for the bridge and the school had been raised only after the blurb Tom Vaughan had written for the AHF's newsletter. Both men were delighted by their coincidental meeting. "Greg's a guy you immediately like and trust," McCown says. "He has no guile. He's a gentle giant. Watching all those people work with him to build that bridge, it was obvious they loved him. He operated as one of them, and I wondered how in the hell an American had managed that."

Mortenson introduced himself to McCown's chaperone in Balti, and when he answered in Urdu, Mortenson learned that he was not Balti but a Wakhi tribesman from the remote Charpurson Valley, on the Afghanistan border, and his name was Faisal Baig.

Mortenson asked his countryman if he would consider doing him a favor. "I was feeling out on a limb in Korphe, operating all by myself," Mortenson says. "And I wanted these people to feel like it wasn't just me, that there were a bunch of other Americans back home concerned about helping them."

"He slipped me a big roll of rupees," McCown says, "and asked me to act like a big boss from America. So I hammed it up. I walked around like a chief, paying everyone their wages, telling them they were doing a great job, and to really throw themselves into it, and finish as fast as they could."

McCown walked on, following his family. But this day of stringing cables between two towers would connect more than the north and south banks of the Braldu. As life for foreigners in Pakistan would become progressively more dangerous, Baig would volunteer to serve as Mortenson's bodyguard. And from his perch in Menlo Park, McCown would become one of Mortenson's most powerful advocates.

In late August, ten weeks after breaking the then-muddy ground, Mortenson stood in the middle of the swaying 284-foot span, admiring the neat concrete arches on either end, the sturdy three-tiered stone foundations, and the webwork of cables that anchored it all together. Haji Ali offered him the last plank and asked him to lay it in place. But Mortenson insisted Korphe's chief complete Korphe's bridge. Haji Ali raised the board above his head and thanked all-merciful Allah for the foreigner he'd been kind enough to send to his village, then knelt and plugged the final gap over the foaming Braldu. From their lookout high above the south riverbank, the women and children of Korphe shouted their approval.

Broke again, and anxious not to dip into what funds still remained for the school, Mortenson prepared to head back to Berkeley and spend the winter and spring earning enough money to return. His last night in Korphe, he sat on the roof with Twaha, Hussein, and Haji Ali and firmed up plans for breaking ground on the school in the summer.

Hussein had offered to donate a level field that his wife Hawa owned for the school. It had an unimpeded view of Korphe K2, the kind of view that Mortenson thought would encourage students to aim high. He accepted on the condition that Hussein become the Korphe School's first teacher.

They sealed the deal over tea extravagantly sweetened for the occasion and handshakes, and talked excitedly about the school until well after dark.

Eight hundred feet below, lantern lights flickered from the middle of the Braldu, as the people of Korphe strolled curiously back and forth across the barrier that had once cut them off so completely from the wider world, the world to which Mortenson reluctantly prepared to return.

CHAPTER 11

Six Days

There is a candle in your heart, ready to be kindled.
There is a void in your soul, ready to be filled.
You feel it, don't you?

—Rumi

AT THE ALTA Bates Burn Unit, a constellation of red and green LEDs blinked across a bank of monitors. Though it was 4:00 A.M., and he was slumped behind the nurse's station, trying and failing to find a comfortable position in a plastic chair designed for a much smaller person, Mortenson felt something that had been in short supply ever since that evening he'd dropped the bottle of Baileys liqueur into the trash can at the Beach Motel—happiness.

Earlier, Mortenson had smoothed antibiotic cream into the hands of a twelve-year-old boy whose stepfather had pressed them to a stove, then redressed his bandages. Physically, at least, the boy was healing well. Otherwise, it had been a quiet night. He didn't need to travel to the other side of the world to be useful, Mortenson thought. He was helping here. But each shift, and the dollars accruing in his Bank of America account, brought Mortenson closer to the day he could resume construction of the Korphe School.

He was again living in his rented room at Witold Dudzinski's, and here in the half-empty ward, he was glad of a peaceful night away from the smoke and vodka fumes. Mortenson's cranberry-colored surgical scrubs were practically pajamas, and the light was dim enough for him to doze. If only the chair would allow it.

Groggily, Mortenson walked home after his shift. The black sky was bluing behind the ridgeline of the Berkeley Hills as he sipped thick coffee between bites of a glazed pastry from the Cambodian doughnut shop. Double-parked in front of Dudzinski's pickup truck, a black Saab sat in front of Mortenson's home. And slumped back in the reclined driver's seat, all but her lips obscured by a cascade of dark hair, lay Dr. Marina Villard. Mortenson licked the sugar from his fingers, then pulled open the driver's door.

Marina sat up, stretched, and hugged herself awake. "You wouldn't answer your phone," she said.

"I was working,"

"I left a lot of messages," she said. "Just erase them."

"What are you doing here?" Mortenson said.

"Aren't you glad to see me?"

Mortenson decided he wasn't. "Sure," he said. "How are you?"

"To tell the truth, not too great." She pulled down the visor and studied herself in the mirror, before reapplying red lipstick.

"What happened with Mario?"

"A mistake," she said.

Mortenson didn't know what to do with his hands. He put his coffee cup down on the roof of her Saab, then held them stiffly at his side.

"I miss you," Marina said. She pulled the lever at her hip to raise the seatback and the headrest smacked up against the back of her head. "Ow. Do you miss me?"

Mortenson felt something more potent than caffeine from the doughnut shop coursing through him. To just show up, after all this time. All those nights thrashing in the sleeping bag on Dudzinski's dusty floor, trying to banish her and the sense of family found and then lost so sleep could come. "The door is closed," Mortenson said, closing the driver's door on Marina Villard, and climbing up into the reek of stale smoke and spilled vodka to fall flat asleep.

Now that a bridge spanned the Upper Braldu, and the materials he'd made Changazi produce a signed inventory for were on the verge of turning into a school, now that he didn't feel like he was hiding out at Dudzinski's, but just economizing until returning to complete his work in Pakistan, Mortenson was glad to speak with anyone connected with the Karakoram.

He called Jean Hoerni, who sent him a plane ticket to Seattle and asked him to bring along pictures of the bridge. In Hoerni's penthouse apartment, with a sweeping view of Lake Washington, and the Cascades beyond, Mortenson met the man he'd found so intimidating on the phone. The scientist was slight, with a drooping mustache and dark eyes that measured Mortenson through his oversized glasses. Even at seventy, he had the wiry vigor of a lifelong mountaineer. "I was afraid of Jean, at first," Mortenson says. "He had a reputation as a real bastard, but he couldn't have been any kinder to me."

Mortenson unpacked his duffel bag, and soon he and Hoerni were bent over a coffee table studying the photos, architectural drawings, and maps that spilled over onto the deep cream-colored carpet. Hoerni, who'd trekked twice to K2 base camp, discussed with Mortenson all the villages, like Korphe, that didn't appear on the maps. And he took great pleasure in making an addition to one map, in black marker—the new bridge that spanned the Upper Braldu.

"Jean really responded to Greg right away," says Hoerni's widow, Jennifer Wilson, who later became a member of the Central Asia Institute's board of directors. "He appreciated how goofy and unbusinesslike Greg was. He liked the fact that Greg was a free agent. You see, Jean was an entrepreneur and he respected an individual trying to do something difficult. When he first read about Greg in the AHF newsletter, he told me, 'Americans care about Buddhists, not Muslims. This guy's not going to get any help. I'm going to have to make this happen.'

"Jean had accomplished a lot in his life." Wilson says, "But the challenge of building the Korphe School excited him just as much as his scientific work. He really felt a connection to the region. After Greg left, he told me, 'I think this young guy has a fifty-fifty chance of getting the job done. And if he does, more power to him.'"

Back in the Bay Area, Mortenson called George McCown, and the two reminisced about the twist of fortune that brought them together on the other side of the Earth, on a trail through the Upper Braldu. McCown invited him to an American Himalayan Association event in early September, where Sir Edmund Hillary was scheduled to deliver a speech. Mortenson said he'd see him there.

On Wednesday, September 13, 1995, Mortenson, in a brown wool sport coat that had been his father's, khakis, and beat-up leather boat shoes he wore without socks, arrived at the Fairmont Hotel. Atop Nob Hill, the posh Fairmont sits at the only intersection where all the city's cable car lines converge, an apt location for the evening that would tie together so many strands of Mortenson's life.

In 1945, diplomats from forty countries met at the Fairmont to draft the charter of the United Nations. Fifty years later, the crowd gathered in the gilded Venetian ballroom for the American Himalayan Foundation's annual fundraising dinner featured the same multiplicity of cultures. Suavely suited venture capitalists and fund managers crowded the bar, elbow to elbow with mountaineers, fidgeting in uncharacteristic jackets and ties. San Francisco society women wearing black velvet giggled at jokes told by Tibetan Buddhist monks draped in cinnamon-colored robes.

Mortenson stooped as he entered the room, to accept a *kata*, the white silk prayer scarves greeters were draping around all the guests' necks. He straightened up, fingering his scarf, and let the tide of nearly a thousand animated voices wash over him while he got his bearings. This was a room full of insiders, the sort of place he never found himself, and Mortenson felt very much on the margin. Then George McCown waved from the bar, where he was bending to listen to something a shorter man was saying, a man Mortenson recognized as Jean Hoerni. He walked over and hugged both of them.

"I just tell George he needs to give you some fund," Hoerni said.

"Well, I should have enough already to finish the school, if I can keep expenses down," Mortenson said.

"Not for the school," Hoerni said. "For you. What are you suppose to live on until you get this place built?"

"How does twenty thousand sound?" McCown said.

Mortenson couldn't think of any way to reply. He felt the blood filling his cheeks.

"Shall I take that as an okay?" McCown said.

"Bring him a cocktail," Hoerni said, grinning. "I think Greg is about to faint."

During dinner, a dapper photojournalist seated at Mortenson's table was so appalled by his bare ankles at a formal banquet that he left to purchase a pair of socks for him in the hotel gift shop. Other than that, Mortenson remembers little about the meal that evening, other than eating in a stupor, marveling at how his financial problems seemed to have been wiped out with one flourish.

But listening to one of his personal heroes speak after dinner was an indelible experience for him. Sir Edmund Hillary shambled on stage, looking more like the beekeeper he'd once been than a celebrity knighted by Britain's queen. "Ed from the Edge," as Hillary often referred to himself, had shaggy eyebrows under a mop of flyaway hair and terrible teeth. At seventy-five, New Zealand's most famous citizen had developed a slight paunch and no longer looked like he could stride straight up an eight-thousand-meter peak. But to this gathering of Himalayan enthusiasts, he was a living treasure.

Hillary began by showing slides of his pioneering 1953 Everest expedition. They were tinted with the bright, unreal tones of early Kodachrome, and in them he was preserved in perpetual youth, sunburned and squinting. Hillary downplayed his first ascent, saying many others might have beaten him and Tenzing Norgay to Everest's summit. "I was just an enthusiastic mountaineer of modest abilities who was willing to work quite hard and had the necessary imagination and determination," he told the hushed crowd. "I was just an average bloke. It was the media that tried to transform me into a heroic figure. But I've learned through the years, as long as you don't believe all that rubbish about yourself, you can't come to too much harm."

Past the obligatory images of Everest, Hillary lingered on frames taken in the 1960s and 1970s, of strapping Western men and slight Sherpas, working together to build schools and clinics in Nepal. In one picture taken during the construction of his first humanitarian project, a three-room school completed in 1961, a shirtless Hillary strode catlike across a roof beam, hammer in hand. In the four decades after reaching the top of the world, Hillary, rather than resting on his reputation, returned often to the Everest area, and with his younger brother Rex, constructed twenty-seven schools, twelve clinics, and two airfields so supplies could more easily reach the Khumbu region.

Mortenson felt so fired up he couldn't sit still. Excusing himself from the table, he strode to the rear of the room and paced back and forth to Hillary's presentation, burning between his desires to absorb every word and to get on the next plane that could take him toward Korphe so he could get right to work.

"I don't know if I particularly want to be remembered for anything," he heard Hillary say. "I have enjoyed great satisfaction from my climb of Everest. But my most worthwhile things have been the building of schools and medical clinics. That has given me more satisfaction than a footprint on a mountain."

Mortenson felt a tap on his shoulder and turned around. A pretty woman in a black dress was smiling up at him. She had short red hair and seemed familiar in a way Mortenson couldn't quite place.

"I knew who Greg was," says Tara Bishop. "I'd heard about what he was trying to do and I thought he had a great smile so I sort of sidled up to him." Together, the two began the kind of conversation that flows seamlessly, unstoppably, each fork begetting another branch of common interest, a conversation that continues until this day.

Whispering in each other's ear, so as not to intrude upon others still listening to Hillary, they held their heads close. "Greg swears that I was actually laying my head on his shoulder," Tara says. "I don't remember that, but it's possible. I was very taken with him. I remember staring at his hands. At how huge and strong they looked, and wanting to hold them."

Tara's father, Barry Bishop, a *National Geographic* photographer, reached the top of Everest on May 22, 1963, part of the first American expedition to summit. He chose his path up the summit ridge by studying photos of the route provided by his friend Sir Edmund Hillary. Bishop documented his grueling climb for *National Geographic*. "What do we do when we finally reach the summit and flop down?" Bishop wrote. "We weep. All inhibitions stripped away, we cry like babies. With joy for having scaled the mightiest of mountains; with relief that the long torture of the climb has ended."

His relief had been premature. On his descent, Bishop would nearly slide off a ledge all the way to Tibet. He would run out of oxygen, fall into a crevasse, and suffer frostbite so severe that he had to be carried down to the village of Namche Bazaar by tag-teams of Sherpa, before being evacuated by helicopter to a hospital in Katmandu. At expedition's end, Bishop had lost the tips of his little fingers, all of his toes, and none of his respect for the pioneers like Hillary who had preceded him to Everest's summit. "In the quiet of the hospital, I [pondered] the lessons we have learned," he wrote. "Everest is a harsh and hostile immensity. Whoever challenges it declares war. He must mount his assault with the skill and ruthlessness of a military operation. And when the battle ends, the mountain remains unvanquished. There are no true victors, only survivors."

Barry Bishop survived to return home to Washington where President Kennedy gave him and his fellow climbers a heroes' welcome in the White House Rose Garden. In 1968, he packed his wife, Lila, son Brent, and daughter Tara into an Airstream camper and drove from Amsterdam to Katmandu. They moved to Jumla, in western Nepal, for two years, while Bishop completed research for his doctorate on ancient trade routes. George Schaller visited their home, on his way to and from treks to survey disappearing Nepali wildlife.

Bishop survived to bring his family back to Washington, D.C., where he became chairman of *National Geographic*'s Committee for Research and Exploration. In Washington, Tara remembers, her father's friend Ed Hillary would drop over for visits, and the two indefatigable climbers would spend lazy evenings sprawled in front of the television, drinking cheap beer, reminiscing about Everest, and working their way through rented piles of the old western movies they both adored. He survived to move in 1994 with his wife to Bozeman, Montana, and build one of the world's finest private libraries of Himalayana in his basement.

But Barry Bishop didn't survive his drive to San Francisco. A year earlier, with his wife, Lila, on his way to speak at this same event, the annual American Himalayan Foundation fundraising dinner, Bishop's Ford Explorer, traveling eighty-five miles an hour, had swerved off the road in Pocatello, Idaho, and rolled four times before coming to a stop in a sandy ditch. Tara's mother was wearing her seatbelt and survived with minor injuries. But Tara's father wasn't wearing his. He was thrown clear of the wreck and died of head injuries.

Tara Bishop found herself telling the entire story to the perfect stranger standing beside her in the darkened ballroom: How the Explorer had been full of Tara's childhood artwork and journals that her father was bringing to her. How strangers at the crash site had gathered all of her treasured mementos, where they'd been scattered across the highway, and returned them to her. How she and her brother Brent had visited the spot, to hang prayer flags from the roadside shrubs and pour a bottle of their father's favorite Bombay Gin over the blood still staining the sand. "The weirdest thing about it was it didn't feel at all strange," Tara says. "Pouring out my heart to Greg made more sense than anything I'd done in the year since my father had died."

When the lights came up in the Venetian Room, where Tony Bennett had once debuted his signature song "I Left My Heart in San

Francisco," Mortenson felt his heart tugging him toward the woman he'd just met. "Tara had been wearing high heels, which I've never really liked," Mortenson remembers. "At the end of the night her feet hurt and she changed into a pair of combat boots. I don't know why that killed me but it did. I felt like a teenager. Looking at her in that little black dress and those big boots I was positive she was the woman for me."

Together, they paid their respects to Hillary, who told Tara how sorry he'd been to hear of her father's death. "It was incredible," Mortenson says. "I was more excited about meeting Tara than about getting to speak with a man I'd idolized for years." Mortenson introduced Tara to Jean Hoerni and George McCown, then joined the crowd filing out into the lobby. "By then Tara knew I didn't have a car and offered me a ride home," Mortenson says. "I'd already arranged a ride with friends, but I pretended I hadn't and blew them off to be with her." Mortenson had arrived at the Fairmont Hotel in what had become his customary state, broke and lonely. He was leaving with the promise of a year's salary, and his future wife on his arm.

Weaving through San Francisco's financial district in Tara's gray Volvo, through jammed traffic on the 101 freeway, and across the Bay Bridge, Mortenson told Tara his stories. About his childhood in Moshi. About the pepper tree, his father's hospital, and his mother's school. About Christa's death. And then Dempsey's. High above the black waters of San Francisco Bay, navigating toward the lights of the Oakland Hills, which beckoned like undiscovered constellations, Mortenson was building another bridge, spinning out events to bind two lives together.

They parked in front of Dudzinski's apartment. "I'd invite you in," Mortenson says, "but it's a nightmare in there." They sat in the ticking sedan and talked for two more hours, about Baltistan, and the obstacles he faced building the Korphe School. About Tara's brother Brent, who was planning his own expedition to Everest. "Sitting in the car beside him I remember having a very deliberate thought," Tara Bishop says. "We hadn't even touched yet, but I remember thinking, 'I'm going to be with this person for the rest of my life.' It was a very calm, lovely feeling."

"Would you mind if I kidnapped you?" she said. At her studio apartment, a converted garage in Oakland's charming Rockridge neighborhood, Tara Bishop poured two glasses of wine and gave Greg Mortenson a first, lingering kiss. Tashi, her Tibetan terrier, ran between their feet, barking wildly at the stranger.

"Welcome to my life," Tara said, pulling back to look Mortenson in the face.

"Welcome to my heart," he said, and wrapped her in his arms.

The following morning, a Thursday, they drove back over the Bay Bridge, to San Francisco International Airport. Mortenson was booked on a British Airways flight to Pakistan that was due to depart on Sunday. But together they told their story to an agent at the ticket counter, and charmed her into rebooking the flight for the following Sunday and waiving the charge.

Tara was a graduate student at the time, finishing a doctorate at the California School of Professional Psychology, before embarking on her planned career as a clinical psychologist. With classes completed, her schedule was largely her own. And Mortenson had no more hospital shifts booked so they spent every moment of every day together, giddy at their good fortune. In Tara's aging Volvo, they drove three hours south to Santa Cruz and stayed with Mortenson's relatives by the beach. "Greg was amazing," Tara says. "He was so comfortable sharing his life and his family with me. I'd been in some pretty awful relationships before and I realized, 'Oh, this is what it's like to be with the right person.'"

On the Sunday Mortenson's original flight for Pakistan left without him, they were driving back to the Bay Area, through tawny hills topped with green groves of intertwining oak. "So when are we getting married?" Tara Bishop asked, and turned to look at the passenger beside her, a man she'd met only four days earlier.

"How's Tuesday?" Mortenson said.

On Tuesday the nineteenth of September, Greg Mortenson, wearing khakis, an ivory raw-silk shirt, and an embroidered Tibetan vest, walked hand in hand up the steps of the Oakland City Hall with his fiancée, Tara Bishop. The bride wore a linen blazer and a floral miniskirt. And in deference to the taste of the man who would soon be her husband, she left her pumps at home and walked to her wedding in low-heeled sandals.

"We just thought we'd sign some papers, get a license, and have a ceremony with our families when Greg got back from Pakistan," Tara says. But Oakland City Hall provided full-service weddings. For eighty-three dollars, the couple was escorted by a city judge to a meeting room and instructed to stand against a wall, under an archway of white plastic flowers that had been stapled to a bulletin board. A middle-aged Hispanic woman named Margarita, who was working in the judge's secretarial pool, volunteered to serve as witness and cried throughout the ceremony.

Six days after whispering to each other in the darkened Fairmont Hotel ballroom, Greg Mortenson and Tara Bishop took their wedding vows. "When the judge got to the part about 'for richer or poorer' Greg and I both laughed out loud," Tara says. "By then I'd seen where he lived at Witold's, and how he took the cushions off the couch each night so he'd have a soft place to put his sleeping bag. I remember thinking two things at the same time: 'I'm marrying a man without a bed. And God I love him.'"

The newlyweds telephoned several shocked friends and asked them to meet at an Italian restaurant in San Francisco to celebrate. One of Mortenson's friends, James Bullock, was a cable-car operator. He insisted that they meet him on the San Francisco waterfront, at the cable-car roundabout by the Embarcadero. At rush hour, Bullock ushered them onto his crowded crimson-and-gold car, then rang his bell and announced their marriage to the other passengers. As the car clanked through the financial district, San Franciscans showered them with cigars, money, and congratulations.

After his last stop, Bullock locked the doors and took the newlyweds on a private tour of San Francisco, ringing his bell the whole way. The car rose magically on its unseen cable, and crested Nob Hill, past the Fairmont Hotel, to the tony and vertiginous streets where San Francisco's most mesmerizing view falls away to the north. Arm in arm with his wife, Greg Mortenson watched the setting sun kiss the Pacific beyond the Golden Gate Bridge, and paint Angel Island a rose color that he would forever after consider the exact hue of happiness. Feeling an unfamiliar fatigue in his cheeks, he realized he hadn't stopped smiling for six days.

"When people hear how I married Tara, they're always shocked," Mortenson says. "But marrying her after six days doesn't seem strange to me. It's the kind of thing my parents did and it worked for them.

What's amazing to me is that I met Tara at all. I found the one person in the world I was meant to be with."

The following Sunday, Mortenson packed his duffel bag, tucked his pouch of hundred-dollar bills into his jacket pocket, and drove to the airport. After parking on the departures ramp, he couldn't make himself leave the car. Mortenson turned toward his wife, who was grinning under the spell of the same thought. "I'll ask," Mortenson said. "But I don't know if they'll let me do it again."

Mortenson postponed his flight two more times, in each instance bringing his baggage to the airport in case they wouldn't let him reschedule. But he needn't have worried. Greg and Tara's story had become the stuff of romantic legend at the British Airways ticket counter, and agents repeatedly bent the rules to give Mortenson more time to get to know his new wife. "It was a very special two weeks, a secret time," Mortenson says. "No one knew I was still in town and we just barricaded ourselves inside Tara's apartment, trying to make up for all the years we hadn't known each other."

"Finally I came up for air and called my mother," Tara says. "She was in Nepal about to leave on a trek."

"After Tara reached me in Katmandu she told me to sit down. You don't forget a phone call like that," Lila Bishop says. "My daughter kept using the word 'wonderful' over and over, but all I could hear was 'six days.'"

"I told her, 'Mom, I just married the most wonderful man.' She sounded shocked. And I could tell she was skeptical, but she gathered herself up and tried her best to be happy for me. She said, 'Well, you're thirty-one and you've kissed a lot of toads. If you think he's your prince, then I'm sure he is.'"

The fourth time the gray Volvo pulled up in front of British Airways, Mortenson kissed the woman he felt like he'd already known his whole life good-bye and dragged his duffel bag to the ticket counter.

"You really want to go this time?" A female ticket agent teased. "You sure you're doing the right thing?"

"Oh, I'm doing the right thing," Mortenson said, and turned to wave one last time through the glass at his waving wife. "I've never been this sure of anything."

CHAPTER 12

HAJI ALI'S LESSON

It may seem absurd to believe that a "primitive" culture in the
Himalaya has anything to teach our industrialized society.
But our search for a future that works keeps spiraling back to an
ancient connection between ourselves and the earth,
an interconnectedness that ancient cultures have never abandoned.

—Helena Norberg-Hodge

AT THE DOOR to Changazi's compound in Skardu, Mortenson was
denied entrance by a gatekeeper small even by Balti standards.
Changazi's assistant Yakub had the hairless chin and the slight build
of a boy of twelve. But Yakub was a grown man in his mid-thirties. He
planted his ninety pounds squarely in Mortenson's path.

Mortenson pulled the worn Ziploc bag where he kept all his important documents from his rucksack and fished through it until he
produced the inventory of school supplies Changazi had prepared on
Mortenson's previous trip. "I need to pick these up," Mortenson said,
holding the list up for Yakub to study.

"Changazi Sahib is in 'Pindi," Yakub said.

"When will he come back to Skardu?" Mortenson asked.

"One or two month, maximum," Yakub said, trying to close the
door. "You come back then."

Mortenson put his arm against the door. "Let's telephone him now."

"Can not," Yakub said. "The line to 'Pindi is cut."

Mortenson reminded himself not to let his anger show. Did everyone working for Changazi have access to their boss's bottomless supply of excuses? Mortenson was weighing whether to press Yakub
further, or return with a policeman, when a dignified-looking older
man wearing a brown wool *topi* woven of unusually fine wool and a

carefully trimmed mustache appeared behind Yakub. This was Ghulam Parvi, an accountant Changazi had turned to for help unscram-
bling his books. Parvi had obtained a business degree from one of
Pakistan's finest graduate schools, the University of Karachi. His academic accomplishment was rare for a Balti, and he was known and respected throughout Skardu as a devout Shiite scholar. Yakub edged
deferentially out of the older man's way. "Can I be of some assistance,
sir?" Parvi said, in the most cultivated English Mortenson had ever
heard spoken in Skardu.

Mortenson introduced himself and his problem and handed Parvi
the receipt to inspect. "This is a most curious matter," Parvi said. "You
are striving to build a school for Balti children and yet, though he
knew I would take keen interest in your project, Changazi related
nothing of this to me," he said, shaking his head. "Most curious."

For a time, Ghulam Parvi had served as the director of an organization called SWAB, Social Welfare Association Baltistan. Under his
leadership SWAB had managed to build two primary schools on the
outskirts of Skardu, before the funds promised by the Pakistani government dried up and he was forced to take odd accounting jobs. On
one side of a green wooden doorway stood a foreigner with the money
to make Korphe's school a reality. On the other stood the man most
qualified in all of northern Pakistan to assist him, a man who shared
his goals.

"I could waste my time with Changazi's ledgers for the next two
weeks and still they would make no sense," Parvi said, winding a
camel-colored scarf around his neck. "Shall we see what has become
of your materials?"

Cowed by Parvi, Yakub drove them in Changazi's Land Cruiser to
a squalid building site near the bank of the Indus, a mile to the southwest of town. This was the husk of a hotel Changazi had begun constructing, before he'd run out of money. The low-slung mud-block
building stood roofless, amid a sea of trash that had been tossed over a
ten-foot fence topped with rolls of razor wire. Through glassless windows, they could see mounds of materials covered by blue plastic
tarps. Mortenson rattled the thick padlock on the fence and turned
to Yakub. "Only Changazi Sahib have the key," he said, avoiding
Mortenson's eyes.

The following afternoon, Mortenson returned with Parvi, who

produced a bolt-cutter from the trunk of their taxi and brandished it as they walked toward the gate. An armed guard hoisted himself off the boulder where he'd been dozing and unslung a rusty hunting rifle that looked more prop than weapon. Apparently phoning 'Pindi had been possible after all, Mortenson thought. "You can't go in," the guard said in Balti. "This building has been sold."

"This Changazi may wear white robes, but I think he is an exceedingly black-souled man," Parvi said to Mortenson, apologetically.

There was nothing apologetic in his tone when Parvi turned to confront the hireling guarding the gate. Spoken Balti can have a harsh, guttural quality. Parvi's speech hammered against the guard like chisel blows to a boulder, chipping away at his will to block their path. When Parvi finally fell silent, and raised his bolt-cutter to the lock, the guard put down his rifle, produced a key from his pocket and escorted them inside.

Within the damp rooms of the abandoned hotel, Mortenson lifted the blue tarps and found about two-thirds of his cement, wood, and corrugated sheets of roofing. Mortenson would never manage to account for the entire load he'd trucked up the Karakoram Highway, but this was enough to start building. With Parvi's help, he arranged to have the remaining supplies sent to Korphe by jeep.

"Without Ghulam Parvi, I never would have accomplished anything in Pakistan," Mortenson says. "My father was able to build his hospital because he had John Moshi, a smart, capable Tanzanian partner. Parvi is my John Moshi. When I was trying to build the first school, I really had no idea what I was doing. Parvi showed me how to get things done."

Before setting out for Korphe on a jeep himself, Mortenson shook Parvi's hand warmly and thanked him for his help. "Let me know if I can be of further assistance," Parvi said, with a slight bow. "What you're doing for the students of Baltistan is most laudable."

The rocks looked more like an ancient ruin than the building blocks of a new school. Though he stood on a plateau high above the Braldu River, in perfect fall weather that made the pyramid of Korphe K2 bristle, Mortenson was disheartened by the prospect before him.

The previous winter, before leaving Korphe, Mortenson had driven tent pegs into the frozen soil and tied red and blue braided nylon cord to them, marking out a floor plan of five rooms he imagined for the school. He'd left Haji Ali enough cash to hire laborers from villages downriver to help quarry and carry the stone. And when he arrived, he expected to find at least a foundation for the school excavated. Instead, he saw two mounds of stones standing in a field.

Inspecting the site with Haji Ali, Mortenson struggled to hide his disappointment. Between his four trips to the airport with his wife, and his tussle to reclaim his building materials, he had arrived here in mid-October, nearly a month after he'd told Haji Ali to expect him. They should be building the walls this week, he thought. Mortenson turned his anger inward, blaming himself. He couldn't keep returning to Pakistan forever. Now that he was married, he needed a career. He wanted to get the school finished so he could set about figuring out what his life's work would be. And now winter would delay construction once again. Mortenson kicked a stone angrily.

"What's the matter," Haji Ali said in Balti. "You look like the young ram at the time of butting."

Mortenson took a deep breath. "Why haven't you started?" he asked.

"Doctor Greg, we discussed your plan after you returned to your village," Haji Ali said. "And we decided it was foolish to waste your money paying the lazy men of Munjung and Askole. They know the school is being built by a rich foreigner, so they will work little and argue much. So we cut the stones ourselves. It took all summer, because many of the men had to leave for porter work. But don't worry. I have your money locked safely in my home."

"I'm not worried about the money." Mortenson said. "But I wanted to get a roof up before winter so the children would have some place to study."

Haji Ali put his hand on Mortenson's shoulder, and gave his impatient American a fatherly squeeze. "I thank all-merciful Allah for all you have done. But the people of Korphe have been here without a school for six hundred years," he said, smiling. "What is one winter more?"

Walking back to Haji Ali's home, through a corridor of wheat sheaves waiting to be threshed, Mortenson stopped every few yards to greet villagers who dropped their loads to welcome him back. Women, returning from the fields, bent forward to pour stalks of wheat out from the baskets they wore on their backs, before returning to harvest another load with scythes. Woven into the *urdwas* they wore on their heads, winking brightly among the dull wheat chaff that clung to the wool, Mortenson noticed blue and red strands of his nylon cord. Nothing in Korphe ever went to waste.

That night, lying under the stars on Haji Ali's roof next to Twaha, Mortenson thought of how lonely he'd been the last time he'd slept on this spot. He pictured Tara, remembering the lovely way she had waved at him through the glass at SFO, and a bubble of happiness rose up so forcefully that he couldn't keep it to himself.

"Twaha, you awake?" Mortenson asked.

"Yes, awake."

"I have something to tell you. I got married."

Mortenson heard a click, then squinted into the beam of the flashlight he'd just brought from America for his friend. Twaha sat up next to him, studying his face under the novel electric light to see if he was joking.

Then the flashlight fell to the ground and Mortenson felt a sharp flurry of fists pummeling his arms and shoulders in congratulations. Twaha collapsed on his pile of bedding with a happy sigh. "Haji Ali say Doctor Greg look different this time," Twaha said, laughing. "He really know everything." He switched the flashlight experimentally off and on. "Can I know her good name?"

"Tara."

"Ta . . . ra," Twaha said, weighing the name, the Urdu word for star, on his tongue. "She is lovely, your Tara?"

"Yes," Mortenson said, feeling himself blush. "Lovely."

"How many goat and ram you must give her father?" Twaha asked.

"Her father is dead, like mine," Mortenson said. "And in America, we don't pay a bride price."

"Did she cry when she left her mother?"

"She only told her mother about me after we were married."

Twaha fell silent for a moment, considering the exotic matrimonial customs of Americans.

Mortenson had been invited to dozens of weddings since he'd first arrived in Pakistan. The details of Balti nuptials varied from village to village, but the central feature of each ceremony he'd witnessed remained much the same—the anguish of the bride at leaving her family forever.

"Usually at a wedding, there's a solemn point when you'll see the bride and her mother clinging to each other, crying," Mortenson says. "The groom's father piles up sacks of flour and bags of sugar, and promises of goats and rams, while the bride's father folds his arms and turns his back, demanding more. When he considers the price fair, he turns around and nods. Then all hell breaks loose. I've seen men in the groom's family literally trying to pry the bride and her mother apart with all their strength, while the women scream and wail. If a bride leaves an isolated village like Korphe, she knows she may never see her family again."

The next morning, Mortenson found a precious boiled egg on his plate, next to his usual breakfast of *chapatti* and *lassi*. Sakina grinned proudly at him from the doorway to her kitchen. Haji Ali peeled the egg for Mortenson and explained. "So you'll be strong enough to make many children," he said, while Sakina giggled behind her shawl.

Haji Ali sat patiently at his side until Mortenson finished a second cup of milk tea. A grin smoldered, then ignited at the center of his thick beard. "Let's go build a school," he said.

Haji Ali climbed to his roof and called for all the men of Korphe to assemble at the local mosque. Mortenson, carrying five shovels he had recovered from Changazi's derelict hotel, followed Haji Ali down muddy alleys toward the mosque, as men streamed out of every doorway.

Korphe's mosque had adapted to a changing environment over the centuries, much like the people who filled it with their faith. The Balti, lacking a written language, compensated by passing down exacting oral history. Every Balti could recite their ancestry, stretching back ten to twenty generations. And everyone in Korphe knew the legend of this listing wooden building buttressed with earthern walls. It had stood for nearly five hundred years, and had served as a Buddhist temple before Islam had established a foothold in Baltistan.

For the first time since he'd arrived in Korphe, Mortenson stepped through the gate and set foot inside. During his visits he had kept respectful distance from the mosque, and Korphe's religious leader, Sher

Takhi. Mortenson was unsure how the mullah felt about having an infidel in the village, an infidel who proposed to educate Korphe's girls. Sher Takhi smiled at Mortenson and led him to a prayer mat at the rear of the room. He was thin and his beard was peppered with gray. Like most Balti living in the mountains, he looked decades older than his forty-odd years.

Sher Takhi, who called Korphe's widely dispersed faithful to prayer five times a day without the benefit of amplification, filled the small room with his booming voice. He led the men in a special *dua*, asking Allah's blessing and guidance as they began work on the school. Mortenson prayed as the tailor had taught him, folding his arms and bending at the waist. Korphe's men held their arms stiffly at their sides and pressed themselves almost prone against the ground. The tailor had instructed him in the Sunni way of prayer, Mortenson realized.

A few months earlier, Mortenson had read in the Islamabad papers about Pakistan's latest wave of Sunni-Shiite violence. A Skardu-bound bus had passed through the Indus Gorge on its way up the Karakoram Highway. Just past Chilas, a Sunni-dominated region, a dozen masked men armed with Kalashnikovs blocked the road and forced the passengers out. They separated the Shia from the Sunni and cut the throats of eighteen Shia men while their wives and children were made to watch. Now he was praying like a Sunni at the heart of Shiite Pakistan. Among the warring sects of Islam, Mortenson knew, men had been killed for less.

"I was torn between trying quickly to learn how to pray like a Shia and making the most of my opportunity to study the ancient Buddhist woodcarvings on the walls," Mortenson says. If the Balti respected Buddhism enough to practice their austere faith alongside extravagant Buddhist swastikas and wheels of life, Mortenson decided, as his eyes lingered on the carvings, they were probably tolerant enough to endure an infidel praying as a tailor had taught him.

Haji Ali provided the string this time. It was locally woven twine, not blue and red braided cord. With Mortenson, he measured out the correct lengths, dipped the twine in a mixture of calcium and lime, then used the village's time-tested method to mark the dimensions of a construction site. Haji Ali and Twaha pulled the cord taut and whipped it against the ground, leaving white lines on the packed earth where the walls of the school would stand. Mortenson passed out the five shovels and he and fifty other men took turns digging steadily all afternoon until they had hollowed out a trench, three feet wide and three feet deep, around the school's perimeter.

When the trench was done, Haji Ali nodded toward two large stones that had been carved for this purpose, and six men lifted them, shuffled agonizingly toward the trench, and lowered them into the corner of the foundation facing Korphe K2. Then he called for the *chogo rabak.*

Twaha strode seriously away and returned with a massive ash-colored animal with nobly curving horns. "Usually you have to drag a ram to make it move," Mortenson says. "But this was the village's number-one ram. It was so big that it was dragging Twaha, who was doing his best just to hold on as the animal led him to its own execution."

Twaha halted the *rabak* over the cornerstone and grasped its horns. Gently, he turned the animal's head toward Mecca as Sher Takhi chanted the story of Allah asking Abraham to sacrifice his son, before allowing him to substitute a ram after he passed his test of loyalty. In the Koran, the story appears in much the same manner as the covenant of Abraham and Isaac does in the Torah and the Bible. "Watching this scene straight out of the Bible stories I'd learned in Sunday school," Mortenson says, "I thought how much the different faiths had in common, how you could trace so many of their traditions back to the same root."

Hussain, an accomplished climbing porter with the build of a Balti-sized sumo wrestler, served as the village executioner. Baltoro porters were paid per twenty-five-kilogram load. Hussain was famous for hauling triple loads on expeditions, never carrying fewer than seventy kilograms, or nearly 150 pounds, at a time. He drew a sixteen-inch knife from its sheath and laid it lightly against the hair bristling on the ram's throat. Sher Takhi raised his hands, palms up, over the *rabak*'s head and requested Allah's permission to take its life. Then he nodded to the man holding the quivering knife.

Hussain braced his feet and drove the blade cleanly through the ram's windpipe, then on into the jugular vein. Hot blood fountained out, spattering the cornerstones, then tapered to pulses that slowed with the final thrusts of the animal's heart. Grunting with effort, Hussain sawed through the spinal cord, and Twaha held the head aloft by its horns. Mortenson stared at the animal's eyes, and they stared back, no less lifeless than they had been before Hussain wielded his knife.

The women prepared rice and *dal* while the men skinned and butchered the ram. "We didn't get anything else done that day," Mortenson says. "In fact we hardly got anything else done that fall. Haji Ali was in a hurry to sanctify the school, but not to build it. We just had a massive feast. For people who may only get meat a few times a year, that meal was a much more serious business than a school."

Every resident of Korphe got a share of the meat. After the last bone had been beaten and the last strip of marrow sucked dry, Mortenson joined a group of men who built a fire by what would one day soon, he hoped, become the courtyard of a completed school. As the moon rose over Korphe K2, they danced around the fire and taught Mortenson verses from the great Himalayan Epic of Gezar, beloved across much of the roof of the world, and introduced him to their inexhaustible supply of Balti folk songs.

Together, the Balti and the big American danced like dervishes and sang of feuding alpine kingdoms, of the savagery of Pathan warriors pouring in from Afghanistan, and battles between the Balti rajas and the strange European conquerors who came first from the West in the time of Alexander, and then, attended by their Gurkha hirelings, from British India to the south and east. Korphe's women, accustomed by now to the infidel among them, stood at the edge of the firelight, their faces glowing, as they clapped and sang along with their men.

The Balti had a history, a rich tradition, Mortenson realized. The fact that it wasn't written down didn't make it any less real. These faces ringing the fire didn't need to be taught so much as they needed help. And the school was a place where they could help themselves. Mortenson studied the construction site. It was little more than a shallow ditch spattered with ram's blood. He might not accomplish much more before returning home to Tara, but during that night of dancing, the school reached critical mass in his mind—it became real to him. He could see the completed building standing before him as clearly as Korphe K2, lit by the waxing moon. Mortenson turned back to face the fire.

Tara Bishop's landlord refused to let the couple move into her comfortable converted garage apartment, so Mortenson hauled the few of his wife's possessions that would fit to his rented room at Dudzinski's and filled his storage space with the rest of them. Seeing her books and lamps nestling against his father's carved ebony elephants, Mortenson felt their lives intertwining as the elephants did—tusk to tail, lamp cord to milk crate.

Tara withdrew enough from the small inheritance her father had left her to buy a queen-sized futon, which swallowed much of the floor space in their small bedroom. Mortenson marveled at the positive effects marriage had on his life. For the first time since coming to California, he moved out of his sleeping bag and into a bed. And for the first time in years, he had someone with whom he could discuss the odyssey he'd been on since he first set foot in Korphe.

"The more Greg talked about his work, the more I realized how lucky I was," Tara says. "He was so passionate about Pakistan, and that passion spilled over into everything else he did."

Jean Hoerni marveled at Mortenson's passion for the people of the Karakoram, too. He invited Mortenson and Bishop to spend Thanksgiving in Seattle. Hoerni and his wife, Jennifer Wilson, served a meal so extravagant that it reminded Mortenson of the banquets he'd been fed in Baltistan, during the tug-of war for the school. Hoerni was keen to hear every detail and Mortenson described the abductions by jeep, the duplicate dinner in Khane, the entire yak Changazi had served in Kuardu, and then brought him up to the present. He left his own food untouched, describing the groundbreaking at the Korphe School, the slaughter of the *chogo rabak,* and the long night of fire and dancing.

That Thanksgiving, Mortenson had much to be thankful for. "Listen," Hoerni said, as they settled before a fire with oversized goblets of red wine. "You love what you're doing in the Himalaya and it doesn't sound like you're too bad at it. Why don't you make a career? The children of those other village that try to bribe you need schools, too. And no one in the mountaineering world is going to lift a finger to help the Muslims. They have too many Sherpa and Tibetans, too many Buddhists, on the brain. What if I endowed a foundation and made you the director? You could build a school every year. What do you say?"

Mortenson squeezed his wife's hand. The idea felt so right that he was afraid to say anything. Afraid Hoerni might change his mind. He sipped his wine.

That winter, Tara Bishop became pregnant. With a child on the way, Witold Dudzinski's smoke-filled apartment looked increasingly unsuitable. Tara's mother, Lila Bishop, heard glowing reports about Mortenson's character from her contacts in the mountaineering world and invited the couple to visit her graceful arts and crafts home in the historic heart of Bozeman, Montana. Mortenson took immediately to the rustic town, at the foot of the wild Gallatin Range. He felt that Berkeley belonged to the climbing life he'd already left behind. Lila Bishop offered to loan them enough money for a down payment to buy a small house nearby.

In early spring, Mortenson closed the door on Berkeley Self-Storage stall 114 for the last time and drove to Montana with his wife in a U-Haul truck. They moved into a neat bungalow two blocks from Bishop's mother. It had a deep, fenced yard where children could play, far from the secondhand smoke of Polish handymen and gangs of fourteen-year-olds wielding guns.

In May 1996, when Mortenson filled out his arrival forms at the Islamabad airport, his pen hovered unfamiliarly over the box for "occupation." For years he'd written "climber." This time he scrawled in his messy block printing "Director, Central Asia Institute." Hoerni had suggested the name. The scientist envisioned an operation that could grow as fast as one of his semiconductor companies, spreading to build schools and other humanitarian projects beyond Pakistan, across the multitude of " 'stans" that spilled across the unraveling routes of the Silk Road. Mortenson wasn't so sure. He'd had too much trouble getting one school off the ground to think on Hoerni's scale. But he had a yearly salary of $21,798 he could count on and a mandate to start thinking long-term.

From Skardu, Mortenson sent a message to Mouzafer's village offering him steady wages if he'd come to Korphe and help with the school. He also visited Ghulam Parvi before he set off "upside." Parvi lived in a lushly planted neighborhood in Skardu's southern hills. His walled compound sat next to an ornate mosque he had helped to build on land his father had donated. Over tea in Parvi's courtyard, surrounded by blooming apple and apricot trees, Mortenson laid out his modest plan for the future—finish the Korphe School and build another school somewhere in Baltistan the following year—and asked Parvi to be part of it. As authorized by Hoerni, he offered Parvi a small salary to supplement his income as an accountant. "I could see the greatness of Greg's heart right away," Parvi says. "We both wanted the same things for Baltistan's children. How could I refuse such a man?"

With Makhmal, a skilled mason whom Parvi introduced him to in Skardu, Mortenson arrived at Korphe on a Friday afternoon. Walking over the new bridge to the village, Mortenson was surprised to see a dozen Korphe women strolling toward him turned out in their finest shawls and the dress shoes they wore only on special occasions. They bowed to him in welcome, before hurrying on to visit their families in neighboring villages for *Juma*, the holy day. "Now that they could be back in the same afternoon, Korphe's women started regular Friday visits to their families," Mortenson explains. "The bridge strengthened the village's maternal ties, and made the women feel a whole lot happier and less isolated. Who knew that something as simple as a bridge could empower women?"

On the far bank of the Braldu, Haji Ali stood, sculpted as always, to the highest point on the precipice. Flanked by Twaha and Jahan, he welcomed his American son back with a bear hug and warmly greeted the guest he'd brought from the big city.

Mortenson was delighted to see his old friend Mouzafer standing shyly behind Haji Ali. He too hugged Mortenson, then held his hand to his heart in respect as they pulled apart to look at each other. Mouzafer appeared to have aged dramatically since Mortenson had seen him last and looked unwell.

"*Yong chiina yot?*" Mortenson said, concerned, offering the traditional Balti greeting. "How are you?"

"I was fine that day, all thanks to Allah," Mouzafer says, speaking a decade later, in the soft cadences of an old man going deaf. "Just a little tired." As Mortenson learned that night over a meal of *dal* and rice at Haji Ali's, Mouzafer had just completed a heroic eighteen days. A landslide had once again blocked the only track from Skardu to Korphe, and Mouzafer, freshly returned from a 130-mile round trip on the Baltoro with a Japanese expedition, had led a small party of porters, carrying ninety-pound bags of cement eighteen miles upriver to Korphe. A slight man then in his mid-sixties, Mouzafer had made more than twenty trips bearing his heavy load, skipping meals and walking day and night so that the cement would be at the building site in time for Mortenson's arrival.

"When I first met Mr. Greg Mortenson on the Baltoro, he was a very friendly talking lad," Mouzafer says, "always joking and sharing his heart with the poor person like the porters. When I lost him and thought he might die out on the ice, I was awake all night, praying to Allah that I might be allowed to save him. And when I found him again, I promised to protect him forever with all my strength. Since then he has given much to the Balti. I am poor, and can only offer him my prayer. Also the strength of my back. This I gladly gave so he could build his school. Later, when I returned to my home village after the time carrying concrete, my wife looked at my small face and said, 'What happened to you? Were you in prison?' " Mouzafer says with a rasping laugh.

The next morning, before first light, Mortenson paced back and forth on Haji Ali's roof. He was here as the director of an organization now. He had wider responsibilities than just one school in one isolated village. The faith Jean Hoerni had invested in him lay heavy on his broad shoulders, and he was determined that there would be no more interminable meetings and banquets; he would drive the construction swiftly to completion.

When the village gathered by the construction site, Mortenson met them, plumb line, level, and ledger in hand. "Getting the construction going was like conducting an orchestra," Mortenson says. "First we used dynamite to blast the large boulders into smaller stones. Then we had dozens of people snaking through the chaos like a melody, carrying the stones to the masons. Then Makhmal the mason would form the stones into amazingly regular bricks with just a few blows from his chisel. Groups of women carried water from the river, which they mixed with cement in large holes we'd dug in the ground. Then masons would trowel on cement, and lay the bricks in slowly rising rows. Finally, dozens of village children would dart in, wedging slivers of stone into the chinks between bricks."

"We were all very excited to help," says Hussein the teacher's daughter Tahira, who was then ten years old. "My father told me the school would be something very special, but I had no idea then what a school was, so I came to see what everyone was so excited about, and to help. Everyone in my family helped."

"Doctor Greg brought books from his country," says Haji Ali's granddaughter Jahan, then nine, who would one day graduate with Tahira in the Korphe School's first class. "And they had pictures of schools in them, so I had some idea what we were hoping to build. I thought Doctor Greg was very distinguished with his clean clothes. And the children in the pictures looked very clean also. And I remember thinking, if I go to his school, maybe one day I can become distinguished, too."

All through June, the school walls rose steadily, but with half the construction crew missing on any given day as they left to tend their crops and animals, it progressed too slowly for Mortenson's liking. "I tried to be a tough but fair taskmaster," Mortenson says. "I spent all day at the construction site, from sunrise to sunset, using my level to make sure the walls were even and my plumb line to check that they were standing straight. I always had my notebook in my hand, and kept my eyes on everyone, anxious to account for every rupee. I didn't want to disappoint Jean Hoerni, so I drove people hard."

One clear afternoon at the beginning of August, Haji Ali tapped Mortenson on the shoulder at the construction site and asked him to take a walk. The old man led the former climber uphill for an hour, on legs still strong enough to humble the much younger man. Mortenson felt precious time slipping away, and by the time Haji Ali halted on a narrow ledge high above the village, Mortenson was panting, as much from the thought of all the tasks he was failing to supervise as from his exertion.

Haji Ali waited until Mortenson caught his breath, then instructed him to look at the view. The air had the fresh-scrubbed clarity that only comes with altitude. Beyond Korphe K2, the ice peaks of the inner Karakoram knifed relentlessly into a defenseless blue sky. A thousand feet below, Korphe, green with ripening barley fields, looked small and vulnerable, a life raft adrift on a sea of stone.

Haji Ali reached up and laid his hand on Mortenson's shoulder. "These mountains have been here a long time," he said. "And so have we." He reached for his rich brown lambswool *topi*, the only symbol of authority Korphe's *nurmadhar* ever wore, and centered it on his silver hair. "You can't tell the mountains what to do," he said, with an air of gravity that transfixed Mortenson as much as the view. "You must learn to listen to them. So now I am asking you to listen to me. By the mercy of Almighty Allah, you have done much for my people, and we appreciate it. But now you must do one more thing for me."

"Anything," Mortenson said.

"Sit down. And shut your mouth," Haji Ali said. "You're making everyone crazy."

"Then he reached out and took my plumb line, and my level and my account book, and he walked back down to Korphe," Mortenson says. "I followed him all the way to his house, worrying about what he was doing. He took the key he always kept around his neck on a leather thong, opened a cabinet decorated with faded Buddhist wood carvings, and locked my things in there, alongside a shank of curing ibex, his prayer beads, and his old British musket gun. Then he asked Sakina to bring us tea."

Mortenson waited nervously for half an hour while Sakina brewed the *paiyu cha*. Haji Ali ran his fingers along the text of the Koran that he cherished above all his belongings, turning pages randomly and mouthing almost silent Arabic prayer as he stared out into inward space.

When the porcelain bowls of scalding butter tea steamed in their hands, Haji Ali spoke. "If you want to thrive in Baltistan, you must respect our ways," Haji Ali said, blowing on his bowl. "The first time you share tea with a Balti, you are a stranger. The second time you take tea, you are an honored guest. The third time you share a cup of tea, you become family, and for our family, we are prepared to do anything, even die," he said, laying his hand warmly on Mortenson's own. "Doctor Greg, you must make time to share three cups of tea. We may be uneducated. But we are not stupid. We have lived and survived here for a long time."

"That day, Haji Ali taught me the most important lesson I've ever learned in my life," Mortenson says. "We Americans think you have to accomplish everything quickly. We're the country of thirty-minute power lunches and two-minute football drills. Our leaders thought their 'shock and awe' campaign could end the war in Iraq before it even started. Haji Ali taught me to share three cups of tea, to slow down and make building relationships as important as building projects. He taught me that I had more to learn from the people I work with than I could ever hope to teach them."

Three weeks later, with Mortenson demoted from foreman to spectator, the walls of the school had risen higher than the American's head and all that remained was putting on the roof. The roof beams Changazi pilfered were never recovered, and Mortenson returned to Skardu, where he and Parvi supervised the purchase and construction of wood beams strong enough to support the snows that mummified Korphe throughout deepest winter.

Predictably, the jeeps carrying the wood up to Korphe were halted by another landslide that cut the track, eighteen miles shy of their destination. "The next morning, while Parvi and I were discussing what to do, we saw this great big dust cloud coming down the valley," Mortenson says. "Haji Ali somehow heard about our problem, and the men of Korphe had walked all night. They arrived clapping and singing and in incredible spirits for people who hadn't slept. And then the most amazing thing of all happened. Sher Takhi had come with them and he insisted on carrying the first load.

"The holy men of the villages aren't supposed to degrade themselves with physical labor. But he wouldn't back down, and he led our column of thirty-five men carrying roof beams all the way, all eighteen miles to Korphe. Sher Takhi had polio as a child, and he walked with a limp, so it must have been agony for him. But he led us up the Braldu Valley, grinning under his load. It was this conservative mullah's way of showing his support for educating all the children of Korphe, even the girls."

Not all the people of the Braldu shared Sher Takhi's view. A week later, Mortenson stood with his arm over Twaha's shoulder, admiring the skillful way Makhmal and his crew were fitting the roof beams into place, when a cry went up from the boys scattered across Korphe's rooftops. A band of strangers was crossing the bridge, they warned, and on their way up to the village.

Mortenson followed Haji Ali to his lookout on the bluff high over the bridge. He saw five men approaching. One, who appeared to be the leader, walked at the head of the procession. The four burly men walking behind carried clubs made of poplar branches that they smacked against their palms in time with their steps. The leader was a thin, unhealthy looking older man who leaned on his cane as he climbed to Korphe. He stopped, rudely, fifty yards from Haji Ali, and made Korphe's *nurmadhar* walk out to greet him.

Twaha leaned toward Mortenson. "This man Haji Mehdi. No good," he whispered.

Mortenson was already acquainted with Haji Mehdi, the *nurmadhar* of Askole. "He made a show of being a devout Muslim," Mortenson says. "But he ran the economy of the whole Braldu Valley like a mafia boss. He took a percentage of every sheep, goat, or chicken the Balti sold, and he ripped off climbers, setting outrageous prices for supplies. If someone sold so much as an egg to an expedition without paying him his cut, Haji Mehdi sent his henchmen to beat them with clubs."

After Haji Ali embraced Mehdi, Askole's *nurmadhar* declined his invitation to tea. "I will speak out in the open, so you all can hear me," he said to the crowd assembled along the bluff. "I have heard that an infidel has come to poison Muslim children, boys as well as girls, with his teachings," Haji Mehdi barked. "Allah forbids the education of girls. And I forbid the construction of this school."

"We will finish our school," Haji Ali said evenly. "Whether you forbid it or not."

Mortenson stepped forward, hoping to defuse the violence gathering in the air. "Why don't we have tea and talk about this."

"I know who you are, *kafir*," Mehdi said, using the ugliest term for infidel. "And I have nothing to say to you."

"And you, are you not a Muslim?" Mehdi said, turning menacingly toward Haji Ali. "There is only one God. Do you worship Allah? Or this *kafir*?"

Haji Ali clapped his hand on Mortenson's shoulder. "No one else has ever come here to help my people. I've paid you money every year but you have done nothing for my village. This man is a better Muslim than you. He deserves my devotion more than you do."

Haji Mehdi's men fingered their clubs uneasily. He raised a hand to steady them. "If you insist on keeping your *kafir* school, you must pay a price," Mehdi said, the lids of his eyes lowering. "I demand twelve of your largest rams."

"As you wish," Haji Ali said, turning his back on Mehdi, to emphasize how he had degraded himself by demanding a bribe. "Bring the *chogo rabak*!" he ordered.

"You have to understand, in these villages, a ram is like a firstborn child, prize cow, and family pet all rolled into one," Mortenson explains. "The most sacred duty of each family's oldest boy was to care for their rams, and they were devastated."

Haji Ali kept his back turned to the visitors until twelve boys approached, dragging the thick-horned, heavy-hooved beasts. He accepted the bridles from them and tied the rams together. All the boys wept as they handed over their most cherished possessions to their *nurmadhar*. Haji Ali led the line of rams, lowing mournfully, to Haji Mehdi, and threw the lead to him without a word. Then he turned on his heel and herded his people toward the site of the school.

"It was one of the most humbling things I've ever seen," Mortenson says. "Haji Ali had just handed over half the wealth of the village to that crook, but he was smiling like he'd just won a lottery."

Haji Ali paused before the building everyone in the village had worked so hard to raise. It held its ground firmly before Korphe K2, with snugly built stone walls, plastered and painted yellow, and thick wooden doors to beat back the weather. Never again would Korphe's children kneel over their lessons on frozen ground. "Don't be sad," he told the shattered crowd. "Long after all those rams are dead and eaten this school will still stand. Haji Mehdi has food today. Now our children have education forever."

After dark, by the light of the fire that smoldered in his *balti*, Haji Ali beckoned Mortenson to sit beside him. He picked up his dog-eared, grease-spotted Koran and held it before the flames. "Do you see how beautiful this Koran is?" Haji Ali asked.

"Yes."

"I can't read it," he said. "I can't read anything. This is the greatest sadness in my life. I'll do anything so the children of my village never have to know this feeling. I'll pay any price so they have the education they deserve."

"Sitting there beside him," Mortenson says, "I realized that everything, all the difficulties I'd gone through, from the time I'd promised to build the school, through the long struggle to complete it, was nothing compared to the sacrifices he was prepared to make for his people. Here was this illiterate man, who'd hardly ever left his little village in the Karakoram," Mortenson says. "Yet he was the wisest man I've ever met."

CHAPTER 13

"A SMILE SHOULD BE MORE THAN A MEMORY"

> The Waziris are the largest tribe on the frontier, but their
> state of civilization is very low. They are a race of robbers and murderers,
> and the Waziri name is execrated even by the neighboring
> Mahommedan tribes. They have been described as being free-born and
> murderous, hotheaded and light-hearted, self-respecting but vain.
> Mahommedans from a settled district often regard them as utter barbarians.
>
> —from the 1911 edition of the *Encyclopedia Britannica*

FROM HIS SECOND-STORY hotel room in the decrepit *haveli*, Mortenson watched the progress of a legless boy, dragging himself through the chaos of the Khyber Bazaar on a wooden skid. He looked no older than ten, and the scar tissue on his stumps led Mortenson to believe he'd been the victim of a land mine. The boy made grueling progress past customers at a cart where an old turbaned man stirred a cauldron of cardamom tea, his head level with the exhaust pipes of passing taxis. Above the boy's field of vision, Mortenson saw a driver climb into a Datsun pickup truck loaded with artificial limbs and start the engine.

Mortenson was thinking how badly the boy needed a pair of the legs stacked like firewood in the pickup, and how unlikely it was that he'd ever receive them, because they'd probably been pilfered from a charity by some local Changazi, when he noticed the truck backing toward the boy. Mortenson didn't speak Pashto, the most common local language. "Look out!" he shouted in Urdu, hoping the boy would understand. But he needn't have worried. With the highly developed sense of self-preservation necessary to stay alive on Peshawar's streets, the boy sensed the danger and scuttled quickly crabwise to the curb.

Peshawar is the capital of Pakistan's wild west. And with the Korphe School all but completed, Mortenson had come to this frontier town straddling the old Grand Trunk Road in his new role as director of the Central Asia Institute.

At least that's what he told himself.

Peshawar is also the gateway to the Khyber Pass. Through this pipeline between Pakistan and Afghanistan historic forces were traveling. Students of Peshawar's *madrassas,* or Islamic theological schools, were trading in their books for Kalashnikovs and bandoliers and marching over the pass to join a movement that threatened to sweep Afghanistan's widely despised rulers from power.

That August of 1996, this mostly teenaged army, which called itself the *Taliban,* or "students of Islam," launched a surprise offensive and overran Jalalabad, a large city on the Afghan side of the Khyber Pass. Frontier Corps guards stood aside as thousands of bearded boys who wore turbans and lined their eyes with dark *surma* poured over the pass in hundreds of double-cab pickups, carrying Kalashnikovs and Korans.

Exhausted refugees, fleeing the fighting, were flowing east in equal numbers, and straining the capacity of muddy camps on the margin of Peshawar. Mortenson had planned to leave two days earlier, on a trip to scout sites for possible new schools, but the electricity in the air held him in Peshawar. The tea shops were abuzz with talk of lightning-quick Taliban victories. And rumors flew faster than bullets aimed skyward from the automatic weapons men fired randomly, at all hours, in celebration: Taliban battalions were massing on the outskirts of Kabul, the capital, or had already overrun it. President Najibullah, leader of Afghanistan's corrupt post-Soviet regime, had fled to France or been executed in a soccer stadium.

Into the storm, the seventeenth son of a wealthy Saudi family had flown in a privately chartered Ariana Airlines jet. When he touched down at a disused airbase outside Jalalabad, with attaché cases crammed with untraceable hundred-dollar bills, and a retinue of fighters, seasoned, as he was, by prior campaigns in Afghanistan to fight the Soviets, Osama Bin Laden was reportedly in a foul mood. Pressure from the United States and Egypt had led to his expulsion from a comfortable compound in Sudan. On the run, stripped of his Saudi citizenship, he'd chosen Afghanistan: Its chaos suited him perfectly.

But its lack of creature comforts didn't. After complaining to his Taliban hosts about the standard of quarters they found for him, he aimed his gathering fury at the people he considered responsible for his exile—Americans.

The same week Greg Mortenson lingered nearby in Peshawar, Bin Laden issued his first call for armed struggle against Americans. In his "Declaration of Open Jihad on the Americans Occupying the Country of the Two Sacred Places," meaning Saudi Arabia, where five thousand U.S. troops were then based, he exhorted his followers to attack Americans wherever they found them, and to "cause them as much harm as can be possibly achieved."

Like most Americans, Mortenson hadn't yet heard of Bin Laden. He felt he had a seat in the cockpit of history and was reluctant to leave town. There was also the problem of finding an appropriate escort. Before departing Korphe, Mortenson had discussed his plans with Haji Ali. "Promise me one thing," the old *nurmadhar* had said. "Don't go to any place alone. Find a host you trust, a village chief would be best, and wait until he invites you to his home to drink tea. Only in this way will you be safe."

Finding someone to trust in Peshawar was turning out to be harder than Mortenson had imagined. As a hub for Pakistan's black-market economy, the city was filled with unsavory characters. Opium, arms, and carpets were the town's lifeblood, and the men he'd met since arriving seemed as shabby and disreputable as his cheap hotel. The crumbling *haveli* where he'd slept for the last five nights had once been the home of a wealthy merchant. Mortenson's room had served as an observation post for the family's women. As it was open to the street through a latticework of carved sandstone, women could watch the activity in the bazaar below, without appearing in public and violating *purdah*.

Mortenson appreciated his vantage point behind the screen. That morning the hotel's *chokidar* had warned him that it was best for a foreigner to stay out of sight. Today was *Juma*, or Friday, the day mullahs unleashed their most fiery sermons to mosques packed with excitable young men. *Juma* fervor combined with the explosive news from Afghanistan could be a volatile combination for a foreigner caught in the crossfire.

From inside his room Mortenson heard a knock and answered the door. Badam Gul slipped past him with a cigarette dangling from his lip, a bundle under his arm, and a pot of tea on a tray. Mortenson had met the man, a fellow hotel guest, the evening before, by a radio in the lobby, where they'd both been listening to a BBC account of Taliban rebels rocketing Kabul.

Gul told him he was from Waziristan and had a lucrative career collecting rare butterflies all over Central Asia and supplying them to European museums. Mortenson presumed butterflies weren't all he transported as he criss-crossed the region's borders, but didn't press for details. When Gul learned Mortenson wanted to visit his tribal area south of Peshawar he volunteered his services as a guide to Ladha, his home village. Haji Ali wouldn't have approved, but Tara was due in a month, the clean-shaven Gul had a veneer of respectability, and Mortenson didn't have time to be choosy.

Gul poured tea before opening his bundle, which was wrapped in a newspaper splashed with pictures of bearded boys posing on their way to war. Mortenson held up a large white *shalwar kamiz*, collar-less, and decorated with fine silver embroidery on the chest and a dull gray vest. "Same as the *Wazir* man wear," Gul said, lighting a second cigarette off the stub of the first. "I get the bigger one in the whole bazaar. You can pay me now?"

Gul counted the rupees carefully before pocketing them. They agreed to leave at first light. Mortenson booked a three-minute call with the hotel operator and told Tara he was heading where there were no phones for a few days. And he promised to be back in time to welcome their child into the world.

The gray Toyota sedan was waiting when Mortenson came carefully down the stairs at dawn, afraid of splitting the seams on his clothes. The top of his *shalwar* was stretched taut across his shoulders and the pants came down only to the middle of his calves. Gul, smiling reassuringly, told him he'd been called suddenly to Afghanistan on business. The good news, however, was that the driver, a Mr. Khan, was a native of a small village near Ladha and had agreed to take him there. Mortenson briefly considered backing out, but climbed in gingerly.

Rolling south at sunrise, Mortenson pushed aside the white lace curtain that protected the rear seat from prying eyes. The great curving ramparts of the Bala Hisar Fort loomed over the receding town, glowing in the fiery light like a long-dormant volcano on the verge of awakening.

One hundred kilometers south of the city they passed into Waziristan, the most untamed of Pakistan's Northwest Frontier Provinces, fierce tribal territories that formed a buffer zone between Pakistan and Afghanistan. The Wazir were a people apart, and as such, they had captured Mortenson's imagination. "Part of what drew me to the Balti, I guess, was they were such obvious underdogs," Mortenson says. "Their resources and talents were exploited by the Pakistani government, who gave them very little in return, and didn't even allow them to vote."

The Wazir were also underdogs, Mortenson felt. Since Jean Hoerni had named him director of the new organization, Mortenson had vowed to become as expert as the unfamiliar title sounded to his ears—director of the Central Asia Institute. Over the winter, between trips to the midwife with Tara, and days of wallpapering and outfitting the upstairs bedroom where their child's life would be launched, he read every book he could find on Central Asia. He soon saw the region for what it was—bands of tribal powers, shunted into states created arbitrarily by Europeans, states that took little account of each tribe's primal alliance to its own people.

No tribe captured his imagination like the Wazir. Loyal to neither Pakistan nor Afghanistan, they were Pashtuns, and allied with their greater tribe above all else. Since the time of Alexander, foreigners had met fierce resistance every time they sent troops into the area. With each defeat of a larger, better equipped force that arrived in Waziristan, the region's infamy grew. After losing hundreds of his men to a small guerilla force, Alexander ordered that his troops thereafter skirt the lands of "these devils of the deserts." The British fared no better, losing two wars to the Wazir and the greater Pashtun tribe.

In 1893, bloodied British forces fell back from Waziristan to the Durand Line, the border they created between British India and Afghanistan. The Durand Line was drawn down the center of the Pashtun tribe, a British attempt to divide and conquer. But no one had ever conquered the Wazir. Though Waziristan has been nominally a part of Pakistan since 1947, the little influence Islamabad has ever had on the Wazir has been the product of bribes distributed to tribal leaders and fortresslike army garrisons with little control over anything out of sight of their gun slits.

Mortenson admired these people, who had so fiercely resisted the world's great powers. He'd read equally negative accounts of the Balti before climbing K2 and wondered if the Wazir were similarly misunderstood. Mortenson remembered hearing how the Balti treated outsiders harshly and were unfriendly to a fault. Now he believed nothing was further from the truth. Here were more outcasts he might serve.

The Toyota passed through six militia checkpoints before entering Waziristan proper. Mortenson felt sure he would be stopped and turned back. At each post, sentries pulled aside the sedan's curtains and studied the large, sweating foreigner in the ridiculous ill-fitting outfit, and each time, Khan reached into the pocket of the leather aviator jacket he wore despite the heat and counted out enough rupees to keep the car moving south.

Mortenson's first impression of Waziristan was admiration that people had managed to survive in such an environment. They drove down a gravel track, through a level, vegetationless valley carpeted with black pebbles. The stones gathered the desert sun and vibrated with it, lending the landscape the feeling of a fever dream.

Half of the brown, extinct-looking mountains ten miles to their west belonged, on paper, to Pakistan. Half were the property of Afghanistan. The British must have had a sense of humor to draw a border across such an indefensible wasteland, Mortenson thought. Five years later, American forces would learn the futility of trying to hunt down guerillas familiar with these hills. There were as many caves as there were mountains, each one known to the generations of smugglers who plied these passes. The labyrinth of Tora Bora, just across the border, would baffle American Special Forces who tried unsuccessfully, according to locals who claim to have protected him, to prevent Osama Bin Laden and his Al Qaeda comrades from slipping into Waziristan.

Past the gauntlet of black pebbles, Mortenson felt he had entered a medieval society of warring city states. Former British forts, now occupied by Pakistani soldiers serving a one-year tour of hardship duty, were battened down tight. Wazir tribal compounds rose out of the stony highlands on both sides of the road. Each was all but invisible, surrounded by twenty-foot-high packed-earth walls, and topped with gun towers. Mortenson mistook the lone figures on top of many of the towers for scarecrows, until they passed near enough to see one gunman tracking their progress along the valley floor through the scope of his rifle.

The Wazir practiced *purdah,* not just for their women, but from all outsiders. Since at least 600 B.C., Wazir have resisted the influence of the world outside their walls, preferring instead to keep all of Waziristan as pure and veiled as its women.

They passed squat gun factories, where Wazir craftsmen made skillful copies of many of the world's automatic weapons, and stopped for lunch in Bannu, Waziristan's biggest settlement, where they wove through dense traffic of donkey carts and double-cab pickups. At a tea shop, Mortenson stretched as much as his *shalwar* would allow, and tried to strike up a conversation with a table of men, the type of elders Haji Ali had advised him to seek out, while the driver went looking for a shop selling his brand of cigarettes. Mortenson's Urdu produced blank stares, and he promised himself he'd devote some of his time back in Bozeman to studying Pashto.

Across the dusty street, behind high walls, was the Saudi-built *Madrassa-I-Arabia,* where two years later, John Walker Lindh, the "American Taliban," would come to study a fundamentalist brand of Islam called "Wahhabism." Lindh, fresh from the crisp climate of Marin County, would reportedly wilt under the anvil of Waziristan's sun, and cross the passes into Afghanistan, to continue his education at a *madrassa* in the mountains with a more temperate climate, a *madrassa* financed by another Saudi, Osama Bin Laden.

All afternoon, they drove deeper into Waziristan, while Mortenson practiced a few polite Pashto greetings the driver taught him. "It was the most stark area you could imagine, but also beautifully serene," Mortenson says. "We were really getting to the heartland of the tribal areas and I was excited to have made it so far." Just south of Ladha, as the sun dropped into Afghanistan, they arrived at Kot Langarkhel, Khan's ancestral home. The village was just two general stores flanking a sandstone mosque and had the flyblown feel of end places the world over. A dusty piebald goat relaxed across the center of the road, its legs splayed so flat it looked like roadkill. Khan called out a greeting to men in a warehouse behind the bigger of the two shops and they told the driver to pull the car inside, where it would be safe overnight.

The scene inside the warehouse set Mortenson immediately on edge. Six Wazir men with bandoliers criss-crossed on their chests slumped on packing crates smoking hashish from a multinecked hookah. Piled against the walls, Mortenson saw stacks of bazookas, rocket-propelled grenade launchers, and crates of oily new AK-47s. He noticed the whip antennas of military-grade field radios sticking up behind boxes of powdered fruit-punch-flavored Gatorade and Oil of Olay and realized he'd blundered into the stronghold of a large and well-organized smuggling operation.

Wazir, like all Pashtuns, live by the code of *Pashtunwali*. *Badal*, revenging blood feuds and defense of *zan*, *zar*, and *zameen*, or family, treasure, and land, are central pillars of *Pashtunwali*. As is *nenawatay*, hospitality and asylum for guests who arrive seeking help. The trick was to arrive as a guest, rather than an invader. Mortenson climbed out of the car in his ridiculous costume and set about trying to become the former, since it was too dangerous to search for another place to stay after dark.

"I used everything I'd learned in Baltistan and greeted each of the men as respectfully as I knew how," Mortenson says. "With the few Pashto words Khan taught me on the drive down, I asked how were their families and if they were in good health." Many of the Wazir men had fought alongside American Special Forces in their crusade to drive the Soviets from Pashtun lands in Afghanistan. Five years before B52s would begin carpet-bombing these hills, they still greeted some Americans warmly.

The scruffiest of the smugglers, who smelled as if hashish oil was seeping from his pores, offered Mortenson a mouthpiece of the hookah, which he declined as politely as possible. "I probably should have smoked some just to make friends, but I didn't want to get any more paranoid than I already felt," Mortenson says.

Khan and the elder of the gang, a tall man with rose-colored aviator glasses and a thick black mustache that perched, batlike, on his upper lip, talked heatedly in Pashto about what to do with the outsider for the evening. After they'd finished, the driver took a long draw from the hookah and turned to Mortenson. "Haji Mirza please to invite you his house," he said, smoke dribbling through his teeth. The tension that had been holding Mortenson's shoulders bunched against his tight *shalwar* drained away. He'd be all right now. He was a guest.

They climbed uphill for half an hour in the dark, past ripening fig trees that smelled as sweet as the hash fumes wafting off the Wazir's clothes. The group walked silently except for the rhythmic clink of gunstock against ammunition belt. A blood-red line along the horizon was the last light fading over Afghanistan. At a hilltop compound, Haji Mirza called out, and massive wooden doors set into a twenty-foot earthen wall were unbolted from inside and swung slowly open. A wide-eyed guard studied Mortenson in the light of a kerosene lantern and looked like he'd prefer to empty his AK-47 into the foreigner, just to be on the safe side. After a harsh grunt from Haji Mirza, he stepped aside and let the entire party pass.

"Only a day's drive from the modern world, I really felt we'd arrived in the Middle Ages," Mortenson says. "There was no moat to cross, but I felt that way when I walked inside." The walls were massive, and the cavernous rooms were ineffectually lit by flickering lanterns. A gun tower rose fifty feet above the courtyard so snipers could pick off anyone approaching uninvited.

Mortenson and his driver were led to a room at the center of the compound piled with carpets. By the time the traditional *shin chai,* green tea flavored with cardamom, arrived, the driver had slumped against a cushion, flung his leather coat over his head, and set Mortenson's nerves rattling by settling into a phlegmy bout of snoring. Haji Mirza left to supervise the preparation of a meal, and Mortenson sipped tea in uncomfortable silence for two hours with four of his henchmen until dinner was served.

Mahnam do die, Haji Mirza announced, "dinner." The savory smell of lamb lured Khan out from under his coat. Urbanized as he appeared, the driver still drew a dagger at the sight of roasted meat with the dozen other Wazir at the feast. Haji Mirza's servant placed a steaming tray of *Kabuli pilau,* rice with carrots, cloves, and raisins, on the floor next to the lamb, but the men only had eyes for the animal. They attacked it with their long daggers, stripping tender meat from the bone and cramming it into their mouths with the blades of their knives. "I thought the Balti ate meat with gusto," Mortenson said, "but this was the most primal, barbaric meal I've ever been a part of. After ten minutes of tearing and grunting, the lamb was nothing but bones, and the men were burping and wiping the grease off their beards."

The Wazir lay groaning against pillows and lit hash pipes and cigarettes. Mortenson accepted a lamb-scented cigarette from one of the Wazir's hands and dutifully smoked it to a stub, as an honored guest should. By midnight, Mortenson's eyelids were leaden, and one of the men rolled out a mat for him to sleep on. He hadn't done so badly, he thought, as the tableau of turbaned men slipped in and out of focus. He'd made contact with at least one tribal elder, however hash-besotted, and tomorrow he'd press him for further introductions and begin to explore how the village felt about a school.

The shouting worked its way into Mortenson's dream. Just before abandoning sleep, he was back in Khane, listening to Janjungpa screaming at Akhmalu about why their village needed a climbing school instead of a school for children. Then he sat up and what he saw made no sense. A pressure lamp dangled in front of his face, sending shadows lurching grotesquely up the walls. Behind the lamp, Mortenson saw the barrel of an AK-47, aimed, he realized, his consciousness ratcheting up a notch with this information, at his chest.

Behind the gun, a wild man with a matted beard and gray turban was shouting in a language he didn't understand. It was 2:00 A.M. Mortenson had only slept for two hours, and as he struggled to understand what was happening to him, being deprived of the sleep he so badly needed bothered him more than the eight unfamiliar men pointing weapons at him and pulling him up by the arms.

They jerked him roughly to his feet and dragged him toward the door. Mortenson searched the dim room for Khan or Haji Mirza's men, but he was quite alone with the armed strangers. Calloused hands gripped his biceps on both sides and led him out the unbolted compound doors.

Someone slipped an unrolled turban over Mortenson's head from behind and tied it tight. "I remember thinking, 'It's so dark out here what could I possibly see?'" Mortenson says. They led him down a trail in the doubled darkness, pressing him to walk fast and propping him up when he stumbled over rocks in his heelless sandals. At the trailhead, a phalanx of arms guided him up into the bed of a pickup and piled in after him.

"We drove for about forty-five minutes," Mortenson says. "I was finally fully awake and I was shivering, partly because it was cold in an open truck in the desert. And also because now I was really afraid." The men pressing against him argued violently in Pashto, and Mortenson assumed they were debating what to do with him. But why had they taken him in the first place? And where had Haji Mirza's armed guards been when this *lashkar*, or posse, had burst in without firing a shot? The thought that these men were Mirza's accomplices hit Mortenson like a blow to the face. Pressing against him, his abductors smelled smoky and unwashed, and each minute the pickup drove deeper into the night felt, to Mortenson, like a mile further from ever seeing his wife again.

The truck pulled off the highway, then bumped uphill along a rutted track. Mortenson felt the driver hit the brakes, and the truck turned sharply before stopping. Strong hands pulled him out onto the ground. He heard someone fumbling with a lock, then a large metal door swinging open. Mortenson stumbled over the doorframe, hands bruising his upper arms, down a hallway that echoed with their progress, and into a dark room. He heard the heavy outer door slamming shut. Then his blindfold was removed.

He was in spare, high-ceilinged room, ten feet wide and twenty long. A kerosene lantern burned on the sill of a single small window, shuttered from the outside. He turned toward the men who had brought him, telling himself not to panic, trying to marshal the presence of mind to produce some same small pleasantry, anything to start trying to win their sympathy, and saw a heavy door clicking closed behind them. Through the thick wood, he heard the dispiriting sound of a padlock snapping shut.

In a pool of darkness at the far end of the room, Mortenson saw a blanket and pad on the dirt floor. Something elemental told him sleep was a better option than pacing the room, worrying about what was to come. So he lay down on the thin pad, his feet dangling a foot over the edge, pulled a musty wool blanket over his chest, and dropped into dreamless, uninterrupted sleep.

When he opened his eyes he saw two of his abductors squatting on their heels beside his bed and daylight trickling through the slatted window. "*Chai,*" the nearest one said, pouring him a cup of tepid plain green tea. He sipped from a plastic mug with a show of enthusiasm, smiling at the men, while he studied them. They had the hard, winnowed look of men who've spent much of their life outdoors, suffering privation. Both were well into their fifties, he guessed, with beards as matted and dense as wolves' winter coats. A deep red welt ran the width of the forehead of the one who'd served him tea. And Mortenson took it for a shrapnel wound, or the crease that marked the transit of a nearly fatal bullet. They had been *mujahadeen*, he decided, veterans of the Afghan guerilla war against the Soviets. But what were they now? And what were they planning to do with him?

Mortenson drained his mug of tea and mimed his desire to visit a toilet. The guards slung Kalashnikovs over their shoulders and led him out into a courtyard. The twenty-foot walls were too high for Mortenson to see any of the countryside, and he noted a guard manning the gun tower high above the far corner of the compound. The scarred man motioned toward a door with the barrel of his Kalashnikov, and Mortenson entered a stall with a squat toilet. He put his hand on the door to pull it shut, but the scarless guard held it open with his foot and walked inside with him while the other stared in from outside. "I use squat toilets with buckets of water all the time," Mortenson says. "But to do it with two men watching. To have to, you know, clean yourself afterward while they stare at you, was nerve-wracking."

After he'd finished, the guards jerked the barrels of their guns back the way they'd come and prodded Mortenson toward the room. He sat cross-legged on his sleeping mat and tried to make conversation. But the guards weren't interested in trying to decode his gestures and hand signals. They took up positions by the door, smoked bowl after bowl of hashish, and ignored him.

"I began to get really depressed," Mortenson says. "I thought, 'This could go on for a very long time.' And that seemed worse than just, you know, getting it over with." With the single small window shuttered, and the lamp guttering low, the room was night-dim. Mortenson's depression outweighed his fear and he dozed, slipping in and out of half sleep as the hours passed.

Bobbing up into consciousness, he noticed something on the floor by the end of his mat. He picked it up. It was a tattered *Time* magazine dated November 1979, then seventeen years out of date. Under a coverline that read "The Test of Wills," a garish painting of a scowling Ayatollah Khomeini loomed like a banshee over an inset photograph of a defeated-looking Jimmy Carter.

Mortenson flipped through pages, limp with age, detailing the early days of the Iran Hostage Crisis. With a jolt that jarred his stomach, he confronted photos of helpless blindfolded Americans at the mercy of fanatical, taunting crowds. Had this particular *Time* magazine been put here as a message of some sort? Or was it a hospitable gesture, the only English reading material his hosts had on hand? He snuck a glance at the guards to see if their faces were ripe with any new meaning, but they continued talking quietly together over their hashish, still seemingly uninterested in him.

There was nothing else to do but read. Angling the pages toward the kerosene lantern, he studied a special report, in *Time*'s stentorian style, on the ordeal of the American hostages in Teheran. Details were provided by five female embassy secretaries and by seven black Marine guards, who were released soon after the embassy was taken. Mortenson learned that the black hostages were released at a press conference under a banner that read "Oppressed Blacks, The U.S. Government is our Common Enemy."

Marine Sergeant Ladell Maples reported that he was forced to record statements praising the Iranian revolution and told he'd be shot if he misspoke.

Kathy Jean Gross, who spoke some Farsi, said she struck up a tenuous relationship with one of her female guards and wondered whether that led to her release.

Mortenson read how the hostages were forced to sleep on the floor with their hands and feet tied. They were untied for meals, to use the toilet, and for the smokers among them to indulge their habit. "Some of us were so desperate to be untied longer that the nonsmokers started to smoke," *Time* quoted one woman, named Elizabeth Montagne.

The special report ended on what *Time*'s team of writers considered a powerfully ominous note: "The White House was prepared for the chilling but very real possibility that the hostages would spend their Christmas with Khomeini's militants in the Teheran Embassy." With the benefit of seventeen years of hindsight, Mortenson knew what journalists never suspected in November 1979—that more than two Christmases would pass before the hostages' 444-day ordeal came to an end.

Mortenson put down the magazine. At least no one had tied him up or threatened to shoot him. Yet. Things could be worse, Mortenson thought. But 444 days in this dim room was too terrible to contemplate. He might not be able to speak Pashto, but he'd find a way to follow Kathy Jean Gross's lead, Mortenson decided. He'd manufacture some way to communicate with these men.

After picking at a meal of *dal* and *Kabuli pilau*, Mortenson lay awake much of the second night, test-driving and rejecting various strategies. His *Time* magazine talked about the Iranian captors' suspicion that some of their hostages were employed by the CIA. Could that be why he was kidnapped? Did they suspect him of being an agent sent to spy on this relatively unknown new phenomenon, the Taliban? It was possible, but with his limited language skills there was no way he could explain the work he did for Pakistan's children, so he put persuasion aside.

Was he being held for ransom? Despite the fact that he still clung to the hope that the Wazir were simply well meaning and misunderstood, he had to admit that money might be a motive. But again, he hadn't the Pashto to convince them how comically little cash he had. Was he abducted because he was an infidel trespassing in a fundamentalist land? Turning this over as the guards enjoyed their chemically enhanced sleep, he thought it might be likely. And thanks to a tailor, he might be able to influence his captors without speaking their language.

His second morning in the room, when the guards roused him with tea, he was ready. "El Koran?" he said, miming a man of faith paging through a holy book. The guards understood at once, since Arabic is the language of worship for Muslims the world over. The one with the forehead scar said something in Pashto that Mortenson couldn't decipher, but he chose to interpret that his request had been noted.

It wasn't until the afternoon of the third day that an older man, whom Mortenson took to be the village mullah, arrived holding a dusty Koran, covered in green velvet. Mortenson thanked him in Urdu, just in case, but nothing flickered in the old man's hooded eyes. Mortenson brought the book to his mat on the floor and performed *wudu*, the ritual washing when water isn't available, before he opened it reverently.

Mortenson bent over the sacred book, pretending he was reading, quietly speaking the Koranic verses he'd learned under the eyeless gaze of a dressmaker's dummy in Rawalpindi. The grizzled mullah nodded once, as if satisfied, and left Mortenson alone with the guards. Mortenson thought of Haji Ali, likewise illiterate in Arabic, but tenderly turning the pages of his Koran just the same, and smiled, warming himself over this ember of feeling.

He prayed five times a day when he heard the call from a nearby mosque, worshipping in the Sunni way in this Sunni land, and poring over the Koran. But if his plan was having any effect, he noted no change in the demeanor of his guards. When he wasn't pretending to read the Koran, Mortenson turned to his *Time* magazine for comfort.

He'd decided to avoid the stories about the hostage crisis, noting how his head spun with anxiety after each rereading. He blotted out his surroundings for thirty minutes at a time with a fawning profile of the famous candidate who'd just declared his desire to run for president—Ronald Reagan. "It is time to stop worrying about whether someone likes us and decide we are going to be respected again in the world," Reagan told *Time*'s editors, "So no dictator would ever again seize our embassy and take our people." Under President Clinton, America's respect in the world had steadily climbed, Mortenson thought. But how, exactly, could that help him? Even if an American diplomat could trade on that prestige to try to free him, no one even knew where he was.

The fourth and fifth days trickled past, marked only by changes in the quality of light leaking in through the shutters. At night, short, fierce bursts of automatic weapons fire echoed outside the compound and were answered with stuttering retorts from the gun tower.

During daylight, Mortenson snuck glances through the window's slats. But the view—of the blank face of the compound's outer wall—provided no relief from the tedium of the room. Mortenson was desperate to distract himself. But there were only so many times he could read *Time*'s withering critique of the cultural bias of the Stanford-Binet IQ Test, or the breathless account of how sunflowers were becoming North Dakota's newest cash crop.

The ads were the answer. They were windows home.

At what he judged to be the middle of the fifth night, Mortenson felt a wave of blackness lapping at his feet, surging up to his knees, threatening to drown him in despair. He missed Tara like a limb. He'd told her he'd be back in a day or two and it crushed him that there was no way to comfort her. He would give anything, he thought, to see the picture he'd taken with Tara on their wedding day. In the photo, he held her in his arms in front of the streetcar that had taken them on that enchanted ride. Tara beamed at the camera, looking as happy as he'd ever seen her. He cursed himself for leaving his wallet in his duffel bag at his Peshawar hotel.

Through force of will, Mortenson held the black water at bay, and

Greg Mortenson

K2 photographed by Mortenson during his failed 1993 attempt at the summit.

Mortenson (third from right in cap) with Scott Darsney (far right) and expedition leaders Daniel Mazur (second from right) and Jonathan Pratt (far left) before taking on K2's challenging West Ridge route.

Mouzafer Ali,
the renowned Balti porter
who led Mortenson safely
off the Baltoro Glacier.

Haji Ali, the *nurmadhar*
of Korphe village, and
Mortenson's mentor.

Mortenson in Tanzania with sisters Kari (standing), Sonja, and family friend John Haule.

Mortenson, with Sir Edmund Hillary (center) and Jean Hoerni, whose donation established the Central Asia Institute, at the American Himalayan Foundation dinner where Mortenson met his wife, Tara Bishop.

Led by Sher Takhi, the men of Korphe carry roof beams for their school eighteen miles, after landslides close the only road up the Braldu Valley.

The Korphe School under construction.

Mortenson with students of the Khanday School.

Inauguration of the Hushe School.

Mortenson with supporters and members of CAI's staff in Skardu. Front row, kneeling: Saidullah Baig (left), Sarfraz Khan; back row, standing (left to right): Mohammed Nazir, Faisal Baig, Ghulam Parvi, Greg Mortenson, Apo Mohammed, Mehdi Ali, Suleman Minhas.

Mortenson with wife, Tara Bishop, and daughter, Amira, age nine months, at the Khyber Pass. This image was used for a family Christmas card, with the caption "Peace on Earth."

Syed Abbas, supreme leader of northern Pakistan's Shia,
and key supporter of Mortenson's mission.

Mortenson and Twaha in Korphe, at the grave of Twaha's father, Haji Ali.

Mortenson with Korphe's children.

The Lower Hushe Valley.

Aslam, *nurmadhar* of Hushe village, with his daughter Shakeela,
the Hushe Valley's first educated woman.

David Oliver Relin

Relin with Ibrahim, an elder of Hushe village.

Jahan, the first educated woman of the Braldu Valley, in Skardu,
where she is continuing her studies.

Mortenson briefing
U.S. representative
Mary Bono on the
latest developments
in Afghanistan.

Relin, at President Musharraf's personal helipad in Islamabad, preparing to leave
for a visit to the Northern Areas in a Vietnam-era Alouette.

Mortenson with Sadhar Khan, *commandhan* of Badakshan.

turned the pages of the magazine, searching for a foothold in the warm dry world he'd left behind. He lingered at an ad for the Chevrolet Classic Estate Wagon, at the pretty suburban mother smiling, from the passenger seat, at something the two adorable children in the back of the safe, fuel-efficient, wood-paneled vehicle were saying to her.

For almost two hours, he pored over a spread selling Kodak Instamatic Cameras. On the branches of a Christmas tree, hung like ornaments, were photos of an indisputably contented family. A distinguished grandfather, warmly wrapped in a cozy red bathrobe, taught an idealized blond boy how to use his new gift—a fishing pole. A beaming mom looked on while apple-cheeked children unwrapped football helmets and roughhoused with fledgling puppies. Despite the fact that Mortenson's own childhood Christmases had been spent in Africa, and the closest he had ever come to a traditional tree had been a small artificial pine they dusted off each year, he clung to this lifesaver flung from the world he knew, the world that wasn't this kerosene-smelling room and these malevolent men.

Dawn of his sixth morning in captivity found Mortenson's eyes tearing up over an ad for a WaterPik Oral Hygiene Appliance. The tagline read, "A smile should be more than a memory," and the text expressed unemotional information about a "bacteria called plaque that grows and thrives below the gumline," but Mortenson was far beyond language. The photo of three generations of a stable American family standing on the porch of a solid brick home was almost more than he could bear. The way they all flashed dazzling smiles and leaned into each other implied levels of love and concern, the feelings he had for his Tara, the feelings no one here had for him.

He sensed, before he saw, someone standing over his bundle of bedding. Mortenson looked up, into the eyes of a large man. His silvery beard was trimmed in a scholarly fashion, and he smiled kindly as he greeted Mortenson in Pashto, then said, "So you must be the American." In English.

Mortenson stood up to shake his hand and the room spun uncontrollably. For four days, as he'd become increasingly depressed, he'd refused everything but rice and tea. The man grabbed his shoulders, steadying him, and called for breakfast.

Between mouthfuls of warm *chapatti*, Mortenson made up for six days without speaking. When he asked the kindly man's name he paused significantly before saying, "Just call me Khan," Waziristan's equivalent of "Smith."

Though he was Wazir, "Khan" had been educated in a British school in Peshawar and spoke with the clipped cadences of his school days. He didn't explain why he had come, but it was understood he had been summoned to take stock of the American. Mortenson told him about his work in Baltistan, spinning the tale out over pots of green tea. He explained that he planned to build many more schools for Pakistan's most neglected children, and he'd come to Waziristan to see if his services were wanted here.

He waited anxiously for Khan's response, hoping his detention would be declared a misunderstanding and he'd soon be on his way back to Peshawar. But he got no such comfort from the bearlike man before him. Khan picked up the *Time* magazine and paged through it distractedly, his mind obviously elsewhere. He paused at an ad for the U.S. Army and Mortenson sensed danger. Pointing to a picture of a woman in camouflage operating a field radio, Khan asked, "Your American military sends women into battle nowadays, does it?"

"Not usually," Mortenson said, searching for diplomacy, "but women in our culture are free to choose any career." He felt even that response contained the kernel of an offense. His mind raced through subjects where they might find common ground.

"My wife is about to give birth to our first child, a *zoi*, a son," Mortenson said. "And I need to get home for his arrival."

Several months earlier Tara had had an ultrasound done, and Mortenson had seen the fuzzy aquatic image of his new daughter. "But I knew that for a Muslim the birth of a son is a really big deal," Mortenson says. "I felt bad about lying, but I thought the birth of a son might make them let me go."

Khan continued frowning over the army ad as if he'd heard nothing. "I told my wife I'd be home already," Mortenson prodded. "And I'm sure she's really worried. Can I telephone her to tell her I'm all right?"

"There are no telephones here," the man who called himself Khan said.

"What if you took me to one of the Pakistani army posts? I could call from there?"

Khan sighed. "I'm afraid that's not possible," he said. Then he looked Mortenson in the eye, a lingering look that hinted at sympathies he wasn't free to extend. "Don't worry," he said, gathering the tea things and taking his leave. "You'll be just fine."

On the afternoon of the eighth day, Khan called on Mortenson again. "Are you a fan of football?" he asked.

Mortenson probed the question for dangerous hidden depths and decided there were none. "Sure," he said. "I played football in col, uh, university," he said, and as he translated from American to British English he realized Khan meant soccer.

"Then we will entertain you with a match," Khan said, beckoning Mortenson toward the door. "Come."

He followed Khan's broad back out the unbolted front gate and, dizzy in the wide open space, had his first glimpse of his surroundings in a week. At the bottom of a sloping gravel road, by the minarets of a crumbling mosque, he could see a highway bisecting the valley. And on the far side, not a mile distant, he saw the fortified towers of a Pakistani army post. Mortenson considered making a run for it, then remembered the sniper in his captors' gun tower. So he followed Khan uphill, to a wide stony field where two dozen young, bearded men he'd never seen were playing a surprisingly accomplished game of soccer, trying to thread a ball through goalposts of empty stacked ammunition crates.

Khan led him to a white plastic chair that had been set by the side of the field in his honor. And Mortenson dutifully watched the players kicking up clouds of dust that adhered to their sweaty *shalwar kamiz*, before a cry came out from the gun tower. The sentry had spotted movement at the army post. "Terribly sorry," Khan said, herding Mortenson quickly back behind the compound's high earthen walls.

That night, Mortenson fought for sleep and lost. By his bearing and the respect others showed him, Mortenson realized, Khan was most likely an emerging Taliban commander. But what did that mean for him? Was the soccer match a sign that he'd soon be released? Or the equivalent of a last cigarette?

At 4:00 A.M., when they came for him, he had his answer. Khan put on the blindfold himself, draped a blanket over Mortenson's shoulders, and led him gently by the arm out to the bed of the pickup truck full of men. "Back then, before 9/11, beheading foreigners wasn't in fashion," Mortenson says. "And I didn't think being shot was such a bad way to die. But the idea that Tara would have to raise our child on her own and would probably never find out what happened to me made me crazy. I could picture her pain and uncertainty going on and on and that seemed like the most horrible thing of all."

In the windy bed of the pickup, someone offered Mortenson a cigarette, but he declined. He had no need to make a hospitable impression anymore, and a cigarette wasn't the last taste he wanted to have in his mouth. For the half hour that they drove, he pulled the blanket tightly around his shoulders, but couldn't stop shivering. But when the pickup turned down a dirt road, toward the sound of intense automatic weapons fire, Mortenson broke out in a sweat.

The driver locked up the brakes and the truck slid to a stop amid the deafening cacophony of dozens of AK-47s firing on full automatic. Khan unwrapped Mortenson's blindfold and squeezed him to his chest. "You see," he said. "I told you everything would work out for the best." Over Khan's shoulder Mortenson saw hundreds of big, bearded Wazir, dancing around bonfires, shooting their weapons in the air. On their firelit faces, Mortenson was amazed to see not bloodlust, but rapture.

The *lashkar* he'd come with jumped out of the pickup whooping with glee and added fire from their weapons to the fusillade. It had to be almost dawn, but Mortenson saw pots boiling and goats roasting over the flames.

"What is this?" he yelled, following Khan into the frenzy of dancing men, not trusting that his eight days of danger had finally passed. "Why am I here?"

"It is best if I don't tell you too much," Khan shouted over the gunfire. "Let's just say we considered other . . . contingencies. There was a dispute and we might have had a big big problem. But now everything is settled by *jirga* and we're throwing a party. A party before we take you back to Peshawar."

Mortenson still didn't believe him, but the first handful of rupees helped to convince him his ordeal was finally over. The guard with the bullet-creased forehead stumbled toward him, his grinning face lit by both flames and hashish. In his hand he waved a wad of pink hundred-rupee notes, as filthy and tattered as he was, before stuffing them into the chest pocket of Mortenson's *shalwar*.

Mortenson, speechless, turned to Khan for an explanation. "For your schools!" he shouted in Mortenson's ear. "So, *Inshallah,* you'll build many more!"

Dozens of other Wazir ceased firing their weapons long enough to embrace Mortenson, bring him steaming slivers of goat, and make similar donations. As the day dawned, and his stomach and *shalwar* pocket swelled, Mortenson felt the fear he'd carried pressed to his chest for eight days deflate.

Giddily, he joined in the celebration, goat grease trickling down his eight-day beard, performing the old Tanzanian steps he thought he'd forgotten to shouts of encouragement from the Wazir, dancing with the absolute bliss, with the wild abandon, bequeathed by freedom.

CHAPTER 14

EQUILIBRIUM

The seeming opposition between life and death is now cut through.
Do not thrash or lunge or flee. There is no longer a container or anything
to be contained. All is resolved in dazzling measureless freedom.

—from the *Warrior Song of King Gezar*

THE STRANGE SUBCOMPACT parked in Mortenson's Montana driveway displayed more mud than paint. The custom license plate said "BABY CATCHER."

Mortenson walked into his snug home, amazed, as he was each time he entered it, that the quaint old house belonged to him. He put the grocery bags filled with things Tara had been craving—fresh fruit and half a dozen different pints of Häagen-Dazs—down on the kitchen table and went to look for his wife.

He found her in their small upstairs bedroom, in the company of a large woman. "Roberta's here, sweetie," Tara said from her prone position on the bed. Mortenson, in Bozeman only a week, had been in Pakistan for three months, and was still getting used to the sight of his small wife looking like an overripe fruit. Mortenson nodded at the midwife sitting on the end of her bed.

"Hi."

"Howdy," Roberta said, in her Montana twang, then turned to Tara. "I'll just fill him in on what we were dialoguing about. We were discussing where the birthing should take place, and Tara told me she'd like to bring your baby girl into the world right here, in bed. And I agreed. This room has a very peaceful energy."

"That's fine by me," Mortenson said, taking Tara's hand. And it was. As a former nurse he was happy to keep his wife away from hospitals. Roberta gave them a phone number and told them to call her

174

log cabin in the mountains outside Bozeman any time, day or night, whenever the contractions began.

For the rest of the week, Mortenson hovered so protectively over Tara that she felt suffocated by his attention and sent him out walking so she could nap. After Waziristan, Bozeman's leafy fall perfection felt too good to be true. These long walks through the charming wooded streets around his home, past Montana State students throwing Frisbees to their dogs in well-tended parks, was the antidote he needed to eight days in an airless room.

After he'd been returned safely to his Peshawar hotel, pockets crammed full of nearly four hundred dollars in pink hundred-rupee notes donated by the Wazir, Mortenson had taken Tara's photo with him to a government telephone office and held it before him as he phoned his wife in the middle of Sunday night in America.

Tara was already awake.

"Hi, sweetie, I'm okay," he said through a crackling connection.

"Where were you, what happened?"

"I was detained."

"What do you mean detained? By the government?" He heard the tight fear in Tara's voice.

"It's hard to explain," he said, trying not to frighten his wife any further. "But I'm coming home. I'll see you in a few days." On the three long flights home, he repeatedly pulled Tara's picture out of his wallet, letting his eyes linger on it, taking long sips of medicine.

In Montana, Tara was recovering, too. "The first few days I didn't hear from him, I figured, you know, that's just Greg, losing track of time. But after a week I was a mess. I considered calling the State Department and talked it over with my mother, but I knew Greg was in a closed area and we could create an international incident. I felt very vulnerable, alone and pregnant, and whatever kind of panic you can imagine, I probably felt. When he finally called from Peshawar, I'd started forcing myself to face the fact that he could be dead."

At seven in the morning on September 13, 1996, exactly a year since the fateful evening at the Fairmont Hotel, Tara felt her first contraction.

At 7:12 P.M., accompanied by a tape of chanting Tibetan monks that her father had chosen, Amira Eliana Mortenson made her first official appearance on the planet. "Amira," because it meant "female leader" in

Persian. And "Eliana," which means "gift of God," in Chagga, the tribal language of the Kilimanjaro region, after Mortenson's late beloved sister Christa Eliana Mortenson.

After the midwife left, Mortenson lay in bed, cocooning with his wife and daughter. He placed a multicolored *tomar* Haji Ali had given him around his daughter's neck. Then he struggled with the cork on the first bottle of champagne he'd ever purchased.

"Give it to me," Tara said, laughing, and traded Mortenson the baby for the bottle. As his wife popped the cork, Mortenson covered his daughter's small soft head with his large hand. He felt a happiness so expansive it made his eyes swim. It just wasn't possible, he thought, that those eight days in that kerosene-smelling room and this moment, in this cozy upstairs bedroom in a house on a tree-lined street, snug in the embrace of his family, were part of the same world.

"What is it?" Tara asked.

"Shhh," he said, smoothing the furrow from her forehead with his free hand before accepting a glass of champagne, "Shhh."

The phone call from Seattle demonstrated the planet's relentless march toward equilibrium. Jean Hoerni wanted to know exactly when he could see a photograph of a completed Korphe School. Mortenson told him about the kidnapping and his plans to return to Pakistan after spending a few weeks getting to know his new daughter.

Hoerni was so shrill and impatient about the progress of the school that Mortenson asked what was troubling him. Hoerni bristled, before admitting that he'd been diagnosed with myelofibrosis, a fatal form of leukemia. His doctors told him he could be dead in a matter of months. "I must see that school before I die," Hoerni said. "Promise me you'll bring me a picture as soon as possible."

"I promise," Mortenson said, through the knot of grief that had formed in his throat for this ornery old man, this contrarian who had for some reason chosen to fasten his hopes on the unlikeliest of heroes—him.

In Korphe that fall it was clear but unseasonably cold. The weather drove the village families off their roofs early to huddle around smoky fires. Mortenson had torn himself away from his new family after only a few weeks, trying to keep his promise to Hoerni. Each day Mortenson and the village men would bundle blankets over their *shalwars* and climb on top of the school to fit the final beams in place. Mortenson kept a nervous eye trained on the sky, worried that snow would shut them down once again.

Twaha remembers being surprised by how easily Mortenson adapted to cold weather in Korphe. "We were all worried about Dr. Greg sleeping inside with the smoke and the animals, but he seemed to take no notice of these things," Twaha says. "We saw he had peculiar habits, very different from other Europeans. He made no demands for good food and environment. He ate whatever my mother put before him and slept together with us in the smoke like a Balti. Due to Dr. Greg's excellent manners and he never tells a lie, my parents and I came to love him very much."

One evening, sheepishly, Mortenson confessed the story of his kidnapping to Haji Ali just after the chief had taken his mouthful of after-dinner *naswar*. The *nurmadhar* spat the plug of tobacco he'd been chewing into the fire so he could speak more clearly.

"You went alone!" Haji Ali accused him. "You didn't seek the hospitality of a village chief! If you learn only one thing from me, learn this lesson well: Never go anywhere in Pakistan alone. Promise me that."

"I promise," Mortenson said, adding the burden of another vow to the weighty collection of oaths old men kept making him take.

Haji Ali tore off a fresh plug of *naswar*, and softened it inside his cheek, thinking. "Where will you build your next school," he asked.

"I thought I'd travel to the Hushe Valley," Mortenson said. "Visit a few villages and see who—"

"Can I give you some more advice," Haji Ali interrupted.

"Sure."

"Why don't you leave it to us? I'll call a meeting of all the elders of the Braldu and see what village is ready to donate free land and labor for a school. That way you don't have to flap all over Baltistan like a crow again, eating here and there," Haji Ali said, laughing.

"So once again, an illiterate old Balti taught a Westerner how to best go about developing his 'backward' area," Mortenson says. "Ever since then, with all the schools I've built, I've remembered Haji Ali's advice and expanded slowly, from village to village and valley to valley, going where we'd already built relationships, instead of trying to hopscotch to places I had no contacts, like Waziristan."

By early December, all the Korphe School's windows had been calked and blackboards had been installed in each of the four classrooms. All that remained was nailing the sheets of corrugated metal roofing in place. The aluminum sheets were sharp-edged and could be dangerous when the wind whistling down the gorge whipped them about like saw blades. Mortenson kept his medical kit close by as he worked, having already treated half a dozen wounds inflicted by flying metal.

Ibrahim, one of the construction crew, called Mortenson down from the roof with an urgent request for medical attention. Mortenson studied this large, handsome porter, looking for slash marks, but Ibrahim clutched Mortenson's wrist and led him toward his home. "It's my wife, Doctor Sahib," he said, nervously. "Her baby is not good."

Ibrahim kept Korphe's only store, a spare room in his house where villagers could buy tea, soap, cigarettes, and other necessities. In the ground-floor stable beneath Ibrahim's living quarters, Mortenson found the man's wife, Rhokia, surrounded by restless sheep and frantic family members. Rhokia had given birth to a baby girl two days earlier, Mortenson learned, and had never recovered. "The smell of putrid flesh was overwhelming," Mortenson says. By the light of an oil lantern, he examined Rhokia, who lay on a blood-slick bed of hay. With Ibrahim's permission he took Rhokia's pulse, which was alarmingly high. "She was gray-faced and unconscious," Mortenson says. "Her placenta hadn't come out after the birth and she was in danger of dying from septic shock."

Rhokia's grief-stricken sister held the barely conscious baby girl. The infant, too, was near death, Mortenson realized. Since the family believed Rhokia had been poisoned, they hadn't given the baby to its mother to nurse. "Nursing stimulates the uterus, triggering it to expel the placenta," Mortenson says. "So I insisted they let the baby nurse, and I gave Rhokia an antibiotic to treat the shock." But all day, even as the infant began to regain her strength, Rhokia lay on the straw, moaning in pain when she slipped into consciousness.

"I knew what I had to do," Mortenson says. "But I was very worried about how Ibrahim would take it." Mortenson pulled the porter aside. Ibrahim was among the most worldly of Korphe's men. He wore his hair long and shaved his face smooth, styling himself after the foreign mountaineers whose loads he carried. But he was still a Balti. Mortenson explained, quietly, that he needed to reach inside Ibrahim's wife and remove the substance that was making her sick.

Ibrahim clapped his hands warmly on Mortenson's shoulders and told him to do what he must. While Ibrahim held a kerosene lantern, Mortenson washed his hands with a kettle of hot water, then reached into Rhokia's uterus and pulled the decomposing placenta out.

The next day, from the roof of the school, Mortenson saw Rhokia up and walking around the village, cooing to the healthy baby girl she carried bundled in a blanket. "I was happy that I'd been able to help Ibrahim's family," Mortenson says. "For a Balti to let a foreign man, an infidel, have that kind of intimate contact with your wife took an incredible leap of faith. I felt humbled by how much they'd come to trust me."

From that day on, Mortenson noticed the women of Korphe describing circles in the air with their outstretched hands as he walked by their homes, blessing his passage.

On the afternoon of December 10, 1996, Greg Mortenson crouched on the roof of the Korphe School with Twaha, Hussein, and a gleeful construction crew, and pounded the final nail into the completed building just as the season's first snowflakes swirled around his raw, red hands. Haji Ali cheered the accomplishment from the courtyard. "I asked Almighty Allah to delay the snow until you were done," he said, grinning, "and in his infinite wisdom he did. Now come down and take some tea!"

That evening, by the light of a fire that burned in his *balti*, Haji Ali unlocked his cupboard and returned Mortenson's level, plumb line, and account book. Then he handed him a ledger. Mortenson leafed through it and was amazed to see neat columns of figures spanning page after page. It was something he could display proudly to Jean Hoerni. "The village had accounted for every rupee spent on the school, adding up the cost of every brick, nail, and board, and the wages paid to put them together. They used the old British colonial accounting method," he says. "And they did a much better job of it than I ever could have."

Down the Braldu Valley, heading for Skardu, Islamabad, and home, Mortenson's jeep crawled through a snowstorm that announced winter had hit the Karakoram full force. The driver, an elderly man with one opaque eye, reached out the window every few minutes to knock loose the ice obscuring the wiperless windshield. As the jeep skidded along an icy ledge, high over the ravine where the Braldu was whited out, the passengers clung to each other for comfort every time the driver took his hands off the wheel and raised them up, offering panicky prayers to Allah that he help them survive the storm.

Snow blowing sideways at fifty miles an hour obscured the road. Mortenson squeezed the wheel between his big hands and tried to keep the Volvo on the invisible pavement. The drive from Bozeman to the hospital where Jean Hoerni had been admitted in Hailey, Idaho, should have taken no more than seven hours. They had left home twelve hours earlier, with a few gentle flakes drifting down through Bozeman's bare branches. And now, at 10:00 P.M., in the full fury of the blizzard, they were still seventy miles from their destination.

Mortenson stole a glance from the snow to the child seat behind him where Amira slept. Driving through a storm by himself in Baltistan was an acceptable risk, Mortenson thought. But dragging his wife and child through this desolate, snowswept place just so he could deliver a photo to a dying man was unforgivable, especially since they were only a few miles from the site of the car crash that had killed Tara's father.

In the shelter of a billboard announcing they were entering Craters of the Moon National Park, where he could see the shoulder, Mortenson backed the old Volvo off the road and parked with the rear of the vehicle facing the wind to wait out the whiteout. In his rush to reach Hoerni, Mortenson had forgotten to put antifreeze in the radiator, and if he turned the Volvo off he was afraid it wouldn't start. For two hours, he watched Tara and Amira sleep, keeping his eye on the dipping gas gauge, before the storm calmed enough for them to continue.

After dropping his drowsy wife and daughter at Hoerni's home in Hailey, Mortenson found the Blaine County Medical Center. The hospital, constructed to treat the orthopedic injuries of visitors to the nearby Sun Valley ski resort, had only eight rooms and this early in the ski season seven of them were vacant. Mortenson tiptoed past a night nurse sleeping behind the reception desk and walked toward the light spilling into the hall from the last doorway on the right.

He found Hoerni sitting up in bed. It was 2:00 A.M.

"You're late," Hoerni said. "Again."

Mortenson shifted awkwardly in the doorway. He was shocked by how quickly Hoerni's illness had progressed. The lean intensity of his face had been winnowed down to bone. And Mortenson felt he was speaking with a skull. "How are you feeling, Jean?" he said, stepping in to rest his hand on Hoerni's shoulder.

"Do you have this damn picture?" Hoerni said.

Mortenson put his pack down on the bed, careful not to jar Hoerni's brittle-looking legs, mountaineer's legs that had carried him on a circuit around Mount Kailash in Tibet only a year earlier. He placed a manila envelope into a pair of gnarled hands and watched Hoerni's face as he opened it.

Jean Hoerni pulled out the eight-by-ten print Mortenson had made in Bozeman and held it up tremblingly. He squinted to study the picture of the Korphe School Mortenson had taken the morning he left. *"Magnifique!"* Hoerni said, nodding approvingly at the sturdy butter-colored structure, at the freshly painted crimson trim, and traced his finger along a line of seventy raggedy, smiling students who were about to begin their formal education in the building.

Hoerni picked up the phone by his bed and summoned the night nurse. When she stood in the doorway, he asked her to bring a hammer and nail.

"What for, honey?" she asked sleepily.

"So I can put up a picture of the school I am building in Pakistan."

"I'm afraid I can't do that," she said with a soothing voice meant to placate the overmedicated. "Regulations."

"I'll buy this whole hospital if I have to!" Hoerni barked, sitting up in bed and scaring her into action. "Bring me a damn hammer!"

The nurse returned a moment later carrying a stapler. "This is the heaviest thing I could find," she said.

"Take that off the wall and put this up," Hoerni ordered. Mortenson pulled a watercolor of two kittens playing with a ball of yarn from its hook, pried loose the nail it hung from, and pounded the picture of the Korphe School into Hoerni's line of sight with the stapler, scattering plaster with each blow.

He turned back to Hoerni and saw him hunched over the phone, ordering an overseas operator to locate a certain number for him in Switzerland. *"Salut,"* Hoerni said finally, to a childhood friend from

Geneva. *"C'est moi, Jean. I built a school in the Karakoram Himalaya,"* he boasted. *"What have you done for the last fifty years?"*

Hoerni had homes in Switzerland and Sun Valley. But he chose to die in Seattle. By Christmas, Hoerni had been moved to the Virginia Mason Hospital, high atop Seattle's Pill Hill. From his private room, when the weather was clear, Hoerni had a view of Elliot Bay and the sharp peaks of the Olympic Peninsula. But Hoerni, his health rapidly fading, spent most of his time staring at the legal document he kept continually at hand on his bedside table.

"Jean spent the last weeks of his life revising his will," Mortenson says. "Whenever he got angry at someone, and there was usually someone Jean was mad at, he'd take this big black magic marker and cross them out of the will. Then he'd call his estate attorney, Franklin Montgomery, at any time, day or night, and make sure he cut off their inheritance."

For the last time in his life, Mortenson served as a night nurse. He left his family in Montana and stayed with Hoerni round the clock, bathing him, changing his bedpans, and adjusting his catheter, glad he had the skills to make Hoerni's last days comfortable.

Mortenson had another eight-by-ten of the Korphe School framed and hung it over the hospital bed. And he hooked the video camera Hoerni had given him before the last trip to Pakistan to the hospital television and showed him footage he'd taken of village life in Korphe. "Jean didn't go quietly. He was angry about dying," Mortenson says. But lying in bed, holding Mortenson's hand, watching a video of Korphe's children sweetly singing, "Mary, Mary, had a, had a, little lamb, little lamb," in their imperfect English, his fury drained away.

Hoerni squeezed Mortenson's hand with the surprising strength of the dying. "He told me, 'I love you like a son,'" Mortenson says. "Jean's breath had the sweet ketone smell people often get when they're about to die, and I knew he didn't have long."

"Jean was known for his scientific accomplishments," his widow, Jennifer Wilson, says. "But I think he cared just as much about that little school in Korphe. He felt he was really leaving something behind."

Hoerni also wanted to insure that the Central Asia Institute was on ground as solid as the Korphe School. He endowed the CAI with a million dollars before entering the hospital.

On New Year's Day 1997, Mortenson came back from the cafeteria to find Hoerni wearing a cashmere blazer and trousers and tugging at the IV in his arm. "I need to go to my apartment for a few hours," he said. "Call a limousine."

Mortenson convinced a startled staff physician to release Hoerni into his care, and ordered a black Lincoln that drove them to the penthouse apartment on the shore of Lake Washington. Too weak to hold a phone, Hoerni leafed through a leather-bound address book and asked, Mortenson says, to have flowers sent to several long-lost friends.

"*Bon,*" he said, after the final bouquet was ordered. "Now I can die. Take me back to hospital."

On January 12, 1997, the long and controversial life of the visionary who helped found the semiconductor industry, and the Central Asia Institute, came to an end. The following month, Greg Mortenson purchased the first good suit he'd ever owned in his life and gave a eulogy to a crowd of Hoerni's family and former colleagues gathered for a memorial service at the Stanford University Chapel, at the heart of the Silicon Valley culture Hoerni helped to create. "Jean Hoerni had the foresight to lead us to the twenty-first century with cutting-edge technology," Mortenson told the assembled mourners. "But he also had the rare vision to look behind and reach out to people living as they have for centuries."

CHAPTER 15

MORTENSON IN MOTION

Not hammer-strokes, but dance of the water,
sings the pebbles into perfection.

—Rabindranath Tagore

AT 3:00 A.M., in the Central Asia Institute's Bozeman "office," a converted laundry room in the basement of his home, Greg Mortenson learned that the *sher* of Chakpo, a village in the Braldu Valley, had declared a *fatwa* against him. It was midafternoon in Skardu, where Ghulam Parvi shouted into the phone that Mortenson had paid to have installed in his home.

"This mullah is not about Islam!" Parvi bellowed. "He is a crook concerned with money! He has no business pronouncing a *fatwa!*"

Mortenson knew from the venom in Parvi's voice how serious a problem the *fatwa* presented. But home in his pajamas, half a world away, half awake, with his bare feet propped comfortably over a heating vent, it was difficult to summon the alarm the development apparently deserved.

"Can you go talk to him, see if you can work it out?" Mortenson asked.

"You need to come here. He won't agree to meet me unless I bring a valise stuffed with rupees. Do you want me to do that?"

"We don't pay bribes and we're not going to start," Mortenson said, stifling a yawn so as not to offend Parvi. "We need to talk to a mullah more powerful than him. Do you know someone?"

"Maybe," Parvi said. "Same program tomorrow? Call the same time?"

"Yes, the same time," Mortenson said. *"Khuda hafiz."*

"Allah be with you also, sir," Parvi signed off.

Mortenson had fallen into the daily routine he would adhere to for the next decade, dictated by the thirteen-hour time difference between Bozeman and Baltistan. He went to bed by 9:00 P.M., after making "morning" calls to Pakistan. He woke up at 2:00 or 3:00 A.M., in time to contact Pakistanis before the close of business. Consumed with leading the Central Asia Institute, he rarely slept more than five hours a night.

Mortenson padded up to the kitchen to make a pot of coffee, then returned to the basement to compose the first e-mail of the day: "To: All CAI Board Members," Mortenson typed. "Subject: *fatwa* declared on Greg Mortenson, text: Greetings from Bozeman! Just got off the phone with new CAI Pakistan Project Manager Ghulam Parvi. (He says thank you, his phone is working well!) Parvi said that a local *sher,* a religious leader who doesn't like the idea of us educating girls, just declared a *fatwa* on me, trying to prevent CAI from building any more schools in Pakistan. FYI: a *fatwa* is a religious ruling. And Pakistan is ruled by civil law, but also by Shariat, which is a system of Islamic law like they have in Iran.

"In the small mountain villages where we work, a local mullah, even a crooked one, has more power than the Pakistani government. Parvi asked if I wanted to bribe him. (I said no way Jose.) Anyway, this guy can cause a lot of problems for us. I asked Parvi to see if some bigshot mullah might be able to overrule him and I'll let you know what he finds out. But this means I'll probably have to go back over there soon to sort it out, *Inshallah*. Peace, Greg."

Jean Hoerni had left Mortenson $22,315 in his will, the amount of Mortenson's own money the old scientist judged his young friend had spent in Pakistan. And he left Mortenson in an unfamiliar position— in charge of a charitable organization with an endowment of nearly a million dollars. Mortenson asked Hoerni's widow, Jennifer Wilson, to serve on a newly formed board of directors, along with his old friend Tom Vaughan, the pulmonologist and climber from Marin County who'd helped talk Mortenson through his darkest days in Berkeley. Dr. Andrew Marcus, the chairman of Montana State's Earth Sciences Department, agreed to serve as well. But the most surprising addition to the board came in the form of Jennifer Wilson's cousin, Julia Bergman.

In October 1996, Bergman had been traveling in Pakistan with a group of friends who chartered a huge Russian MI-17 helicopter out of Skardu in hopes of getting a glimpse of K2. On the way back the pilot asked if they wanted to visit a typical village. They happened to land just below Korphe, and when local boys learned Bergman was American they took her hand and led her to see a curious new tourist attraction— a sturdy yellow school built by another American, which stood where none had ever been before, in a small village called Korphe.

"I looked at a sign in front of the school and saw that it had been donated by Jean Hoerni, my cousin Jennifer's husband," Bergman says. "Jennifer told me Jean had been trying to build a school some-where in the Himalaya, but to land in that exact spot in a range that stretches thousands of miles felt like more than a coincidence. I'm not a religious person," Bergman says, "but I felt I'd been brought there for a reason and I couldn't stop crying."

A few months later, at Hoerni's memorial service, Bergman introduced herself to Mortenson. "I was there!" she said, wrapping the startled man she'd just met in a bruising hug. "I saw the school!"

"You're the blonde in the helicopter," Mortenson said, shaking his head in amazement. "I heard a foreign woman had been in the village but I didn't believe it!"

"There's a message here. This is meant to be," Julia Bergman said. "I want to help. Is there anything I can do?"

"Well, I want to collect books and create a library for the Korphe School," Mortenson said.

Bergman felt the same sense of predestination she'd encountered that day in Korphe. "I'm a librarian," she said.

After sending his e-mail to Bergman and the other board members, Mortenson wrote letters to a helpful government minister he'd met on his last trip and to Mohammed Niaz, Skardu's director of education, asking for advice about the *sher* of Chakpo. Then he knelt in the dim light from his desk lamp and searched through the towering stacks of books leaning against the walls, before he found what he was looking for, a *fakhir*—a scholarly treatise on the application of Islamic law in modern society, translated from the Farsi. He demolished four cups of coffee, reading intently, until he heard Tara's feet on the kitchen floor above his head.

Tara sat at the kitchen table, nursing Amira and a tall mug of latte. Mortenson didn't want to disturb the tranquil scene with what he had to say. He kissed his wife good morning before breaking the news. "I have to go over there sooner than we planned," he said.

On a frosty March morning in Skardu, Mortenson's supporters met for tea at his informal headquarters, the lobby of the Indus Hotel. The Indus suited Mortenson perfectly. Unlike Skardu's handful of tourist resorts, which were hidden away among idyllic landscaped grounds, this clean and inexpensive hotel sat on Skardu's main road without pretension, between Changazi's compound and a PSO gas station, mere feet from the Bedfords rumbling by on their way back to Islamabad.

In the lobby, under a bulletin board where climbers posted pictures from recent expeditions, two long wood plank tables were perfect for accommodating the lengthy tea parties it took to do any sort of business in town. This morning, eight of Mortenson's supporters sat around a table, spreading Chinese jam on the hotel's excellent *chapatti,* and sipping milk tea the way Parvi preferred it—painfully sweet.

Mortenson marveled at how efficiently he'd been able to summon these men from the far corners of northern Pakistan, even though their distant valleys didn't have phones. It might take a week from the time he sent a note with a jeep driver to the day the person he'd summoned arrived in Skardu, but in an era before satellite phones became common in this part of the world, there was no other way to defeat the rugged distance of these ranges.

From the Hushe Valley, a hundred miles east, Mouzafer had made his way to this convivial table with his friend, an old-time porter and base camp cook of wide renown known as "Apo," or "Old Man" Razak. Next to them, Haji Ali and Twaha wolfed their breakfast, glad of the excuse to leave the Braldu Valley to the north, which was still mired in snow of midwinter depth. And Faisal Baig had strolled into the lobby just that morning, after traveling more than two hundred miles from the rugged Charpurson Valley to the west, on the border of Afghanistan.

Mortenson had arrived two days earlier, after a forty-eight-hour bus trip up the Karakoram Highway, traveling with the newest addition to his odd band, a forty-year-old Rawalpindi taxi driver named Suleman Minhas. After Mortenson's kidnapping, Suleman had chanced to pick him up at the Islamabad airport.

On the drive to his hotel, Mortenson related the details of his recent detention in Waziristan, and Suleman, enraged that his countrymen had put a guest through such an inhospitable ordeal, had turned as protective as a mother hen. He convinced Mortenson to stay at an inexpensive guest house he knew in Islamabad, in a much safer location than his old standby, the Khyaban, where sectarian bomb blasts had begun terrorizing the neighborhood nearly every Friday after *Juma* prayers.

Suleman had returned each day to monitor Mortenson's recovery, bringing him bags of sweets and medicines for the parasites Mortenson had picked up in Waziristan and taking him out for meals at his favorite Kabuli sidewalk barbecue. After their taxi had been stopped by a police roadblock on the way to the airport for Mortenson's flight home, Suleman had talked his way past the police with such easygoing charm that Mortenson offered him a job as CAI's "fixer" in Islamabad before getting on his flight.

In the Indus lobby, Suleman sat like a smiling Buddha next to Mortenson, his arms crossed over the beginning of a pot belly, entertaining the whole table between puffs of the Marlboros Mortenson had brought him from America with tales of the life of a big-city taxi driver. A member of Pakistan's Punjabi majority, he had never been to the mountains before and rattled volubly on, relieved that these men who lived at the edge of the known world spoke Urdu in addition to their native tongues.

Mohammed Ali Changazi walked past in his white robes, visible through the glass walls of the lobby, and old Apo Razak, with a jester's leer blooming below his hooked nose, leaned forward and told the men a rumor about Changazi's successful conquest of two different German sisters who'd come to Skardu on the same expedition.

"Yes, I can see he's a very religious man," Suleman said in Urdu, waggling his head for emphasis, playing to the table. "He must pray six times a day. And wash this six times each day also," he said pointing to his lap. The roar of laughter all around the table told Mortenson his instincts had served him well in assembling this mismatched group.

Mouzafer and the Korphe men were Shiite Muslims, along with Skardu residents Ghulam Parvi, and Makhmal the mason. Apo Razak, a refugee from Indian-occupied Kashmir, was a Sunni, as was Suleman.

And the fiercely dignified bodyguard Faisal Baig belonged to the Ismaeli sect. "We all sat there laughing and sipping tea peacefully," Mortenson says. "An infidel and representatives from three warring sects of Islam. And I thought if we can get along this well, we can accomplish anything. The British policy was 'divide and conquer.' But I say 'unite and conquer.' "

Ghulam Parvi spoke calmly to the group about the *fatwa*, his anger having cooled to practicality. He told Mortenson he had arranged a meeting for him with Syed Abbas Risvi, the religious leader of northern Pakistan's Shia Muslims. "Abbas is a good man, but suspicious of foreigners," Parvi said. "When he sees that you respect Islam and our ways he can be of much help, *Inshallah.*"

Parvi also said that Sheikh Mohammed, a religious scholar and rival of the *sher* of Chakpo, had, along with his son, Mehdi Ali, petitioned for a CAI school to be built in his village of Hemasil and written a letter to the Supreme Council of Ayatollahs in Qom, asking Iran's leading clerics, the ultimate authority to the world's Shia, to rule on whether the *fatwa* was justified.

Haji Ali announced he'd met with the elders of all the Braldu villages and they had selected Pakhora, an especially impoverished community in the Lower Braldu Valley, governed by his close friend Haji Mousin, as their choice for the site of the CAI's second school.

Makhmal the mason, who'd done such a professional job in Korphe, requested a school for his home village of Ranga, on the outskirts of Skardu, and said his extended family, all skilled construction workers, could be counted on to complete the project quickly.

Mortenson imagined how happy Hoerni would have been to sit at such a table. His advice about not holding grudges against the villages that competed in the tug-of-war for the first school rang clearly in Mortenson's ears: "The children of all those other villages that tried to bribe you need schools, too."

Mortenson thought of the goatherding children he'd taught the day he bolted out of Changazi's banquet, of the thirsty way they gulped down even his goofy lesson about the English name for "nose," and proposed building a school in Kuardu, Changazi's village, since the elders had already agreed to donate land.

"So, Dr. Greg," Ghulam Parvi said, his pen tip tapping at the tablet where he'd been taking notes. "Which school will we build this year?"

"All of them, *Inshallah*," Mortenson said.

Greg Mortenson felt that his life was speeding up. He had a house, a dog, a family, and before he'd left, he and Tara had discussed having more children. He'd built one school, been threatened by an enraged mullah, assembled an American board and a scruffy Pakistani staff. He had fifty thousand dollars of CAI's money in his rucksack and more in the bank. The neglect and suffering northern Pakistan's children endured towered as high as the mountains encircling Skardu. With the *fatwa* dangling over his head like a scimitar, who knew how long he would be allowed to work in Pakistan? Now was the time to act with all the energy he could summon.

For fifty-eight hundred dollars, Mortenson bought an army-green, twenty-year-old Toyota Land Cruiser with the low-end torque to rumble over any obstacle the Karakoram highways could throw at him. He hired a calm, experienced chain-smoking driver named Hussain, who promptly bought a box of dynamite and stowed it under the passenger seat, so they could blast their way through landslides without waiting for government road crews. And with Parvi and Makhmal bargaining ruthlessly by his side, Mortenson purchased enough construction supplies from the merchants of Skardu to break ground on three schools as soon as the soil thawed.

For the second time in Greg Mortenson's life, a gas station proved pivotal to his involvement with Islam. One warm April afternoon, standing in a fine drizzle by the pumps of the PSO petrol station, Mortenson met Syed Abbas Risvi. Parvi explained that it was best that they meet in a public place, until the mullah had made up his mind about the infidel, and suggested this busy lot near Mortenson's hotel.

Abbas arrived with two younger assistants, both lavishly bearded, who hovered protectively. He was tall and thin, with the trimmed beard of the Shia scholar who had outshone most of his peers at *madrassa* in Najaf, Iraq. He wore a severe black turban wrapped tightly around his high brow and studied the large American wearing Pakistani clothes through a set of square, old-fashioned spectacles, before offering his hand for a firm shake.

"*As-Salaam Alaaikum*," Mortenson said, bowing with his hand held respectfully over his heart. "It's a great honor to meet you, Syed Abbas," he continued in Balti. "Mr. Parvi has told me much about your wisdom and compassion for the poor."

"There are certain Europeans who come to Pakistan determined to tear Islam down," Syed Abbas says. "And I was worried, at first, that Dr. Greg was one of them. But I looked into his heart that day at the petrol pump and saw him for what he is—an infidel, but a noble man nonetheless, who dedicates his life to the education of children. I decided on the spot to help him in any way I could."

It had taken Mortenson more than three years, years of false steps, failures, and delays, to drive the Korphe School from promise to completion. Having taken his mistakes to heart, with the money finally to make his vision a reality and a staff and army of volunteers who were passionately dedicated to improving the lives of Balti children, Greg Mortenson's CAI built three more primary schools in only three months.

Makhmal was true to his word. He and his family of Kashmiri masons spearheaded the assault on the school in their village of Ranga, constructing a replica of the Korphe School in only ten weeks. In a place where schools often took years to complete, this pace was unprecedented. Though their village was only eight miles outside Skardu, Ranga's children had been offered no education by the government. Unless they could afford the cost of transportation to, and fees for, private schools in Skardu, the children of Ranga had remained uneducated. After one spring of furious labor, the fortunes of Ranga's children had been changed forever.

In Pakhora, Haji Ali's friend Haji Mousin made the most of the opportunity for his village. Convincing many of the Pakhora men not to take jobs as expedition porters until the school was built, Pakhora's *nurmadhar* assembled a large and enthusiastic crew of unskilled laborers. Zaman, a local contractor, turned down a construction job for the army and led the effort to build a beautiful U-shaped stone school, shaded by a grove of poplars. "Zaman did an incredible job," Mortenson says. "In one of the most remote villages of northern Pakistan, he built a school in twelve weeks that was vastly superior to anything the Pakistani government could have built, and at half the cost of a project that would have taken the government years to finish."

In Changazi's village of Kuardu, elders were so determined to make their school a success that they donated a plot for it at the very center of the settlement and demolished a two-story stone house so the school could sit on prime real estate. Like everything associated with Changazi, the Kuardu School's trappings were made to exceed the local standard. Kuardu's men built a solid stone foundation six feet deep and constructed the stone walls double-width, determined the school should stand proudly at the center of village life forever.

All spring and summer, Mortenson whirled around Baltistan like a dervish in a green Land Cruiser. He and his crew delivered bags of cement when the various construction sites fell short, drove Makhmal up the Braldu to adjust a set of ill-fitting roof beams at Pakhora, and buzzed over to the woodshop in Skardu to check on the progress of five hundred students' desks he was having constructed.

When it was clear all the school projects would be completed ahead of time, Mortenson launched an ambitious array of new initiatives. Parvi alerted Mortenson that more than fifty girls had been studying in cramped conditions in a one-room school on the south bank of the Indus, in the village of Torghu Balla. With supplies left over from the other building projects, Mortenson saw that a two-room extension was added to the school.

On a trip to visit Mouzafer's village, Halde, in the Hushe Valley, where he promised village elders he'd construct a school the following year, Mortenson learned of a crisis at an existing government school in nearby Khanday village. In Khanday, a dedicated local teacher named Ghulam was struggling to hold classes for ninety-two students, despite not having received a paycheck from the government for more than two years. An outraged Mortenson offered to pay Ghulam's salary, and hire two more teachers to reduce Khanday's student-teacher ratio to a reasonable level.

During his travels, Syed Abbas had heard hundreds of Balti praising Mortenson's character and speaking glowingly of the endless acts of *zakat* Mortenson had performed in his time among them. Syed Abbas sent a messenger to the Indus Hotel inviting Mortenson to his home.

Mortenson, Parvi, and the religious leader sat cross-legged on the floor of Syed Abbas's reception room, on especially fine Iranian carpets, while Abbas's son brought them green tea in pink porcelain cups and sugar cookies on a wayward Delft tray decorated with windmills.

"I've contacted the *sher* of Chakpo and asked him to withdraw his *fatwa*," Syed Abbas said, sighing, "but he refused. This man doesn't follow Islam. He follows his own mind. He wants you banished from Pakistan."

"If you think I'm doing anything against Islam, tell me to leave Pakistan forever and I will," Mortenson said.

"Continue your work," Syed Abbas said. "But stay away from Chakpo. I don't think you're in danger, but I can't be certain." Pakistan's supreme Shia cleric handed Mortenson an envelope. "I've prepared a letter for you stating my support. It may be helpful, *Inshallah*, with some of the other village mullahs."

Skirting Chakpo, Mortenson returned by Land Cruiser to Korphe, to arrange an inauguration ceremony for the school. While he held a meeting on the roof with Haji Ali, Twaha, and Hussein, Hussein's wife, Hawa, and Sakina sat boldly down with the men and asked if they could speak. "We appreciate everything you're doing for our children," Hawa said. "But the women want me to ask you for something more."

"Yes?" Mortenson said.

"Winter here is very hard. We sit all day like animals in the cold months, with nothing to do. Allah willing, we'd like a center for the women, a place to talk and sew."

Sakina tugged Haji Ali's beard teasingly. "And to get away from our husbands."

By August, with guests due to arrive for the school-opening ceremony, Hawa presided glowingly over the new Korphe Women's Vocational Center. In a disused room at the back of Haji Ali's home, Korphe's women gathered each afternoon, learning to use the four new Singer hand-crank sewing machines Mortenson purchased, under the tutelage of Fida, a master Skardu tailor who'd transported bales of fabric, boxes of thread, and the machines, tenderly, on their trip "upside."

"Balti already had a rich tradition of sewing and weaving," Mortenson says. "They just needed some help to revive the dying practice. Hawa's idea was such an easy way to empower women that I decided from that day on to put in vocational centers wherever we built schools."

In early August 1997, Greg Mortenson rode triumphantly up the Braldu Valley in a convoy of jeeps. In the green Land Cruiser sat Tara, and on her lap, Amira Mortenson, not yet one. Their entourage included police officers, army commanders, local politicians, and board members Jennifer Wilson and Julia Bergman, who'd spent months assembling a collection of culturally appropriate books to create a library for Korphe.

"It was incredible to finally see the place Greg had talked so passionately about for years," Tara says. "It made a whole part of my husband more real to me."

The jeeps parked by the bridge and, as the procession of Westerners crossed it, the people of Korphe cheered their arrival from the bluff above. The small yellow school, freshly painted for the occasion and festooned with banners and Pakistani flags, was clearly visible as the group climbed to Korphe.

Two years later, when Mortenson's mother, Jerene, visited Korphe, she remembers being overwhelmed by the sight of her son's labors. "After I saw the school way off in the distance, I cried all the way up," Jerene says. "I knew how much of his heart Greg had put into building it—how hard he worked and how much he cared. When your kids accomplish something it means much more than anything you've done."

"The day of the inauguration, we met Haji Ali and his wife, and the whole village competed to take turns holding Amira," Tara says. "She was in heaven, a little blonde toy everyone wanted to play with."

The school was buffed to perfection. Dozens of new wooden desks sat in each classroom, on carpets thick enough to shield students' feet from the cold. Colorful world maps and portraits of Pakistan's leaders decorated the walls. And in the courtyard, on a stage beneath a large hand-lettered banner proclaiming "Welcome Cherished Guests," the speeches went on for hours beneath an untempered sun, while sixty Korphe students squatted patiently on their heels.

"It was the most exciting day of my life," says schoolmaster Hussein's daughter, Tahira. "Mr. Parvi handed each of us new books and I didn't dare to open them, they were so beautiful. I'd never had my own books before."

Jennifer Wilson wrote a speech about how much her husband, Jean Hoerni, would have loved to see this day in person, and had Ghulam Parvi render it into phonetic Balti so she could directly address the crowd. Then she handed each student a crisp new school uniform, neatly folded inside its cellophane wrapper.

"I couldn't take my eyes off all the foreign ladies," says Jahan, who, along with Tahira, would one day become the first educated woman in the long history of the Braldu Valley. "They seemed so dignified. Whenever I'd seen people from downside before, I'd run away, ashamed of my dirty clothes. But that day I held the first set of clean, new clothes I'd ever owned," Jahan says. "And I remember thinking, 'Maybe I shouldn't feel so ashamed. Maybe, one day, Allah willing, I can become a great lady, too.' "

Master Hussein, and the two new teachers who'd come to work with him, made speeches, as did Haji Ali and each of the visiting dignitaries. Everyone except for Greg Mortenson. "While the speeches went on Greg stood in the background, against a wall," Tara says, "holding a baby someone had handed him. It was the most filthy baby I'd ever seen, but he didn't seem to notice. He just stood there happily, bouncing it in his arms. And I told myself, 'That's the essence of Greg right there. Always remember this moment.' "

For the first time in recorded history, the children of Korphe village began the daily task of learning to read and write in a building that kept the elements at bay. With Jennifer Wilson, Mortenson poured Jean Hoerni's ashes off the bridge the scientist had paid to build, into the rushing waters of the Braldu River. Then Mortenson returned to Skardu with his family. During the days he spent showing Tara around his adopted hometown, driving into Skardu's southern hills to share a meal at Parvi's house, or hiking up to crystalline Satpara Lake south of town, he became convinced he was being followed by an agent of Pakistan's feared intelligence service, the ISI.

"The guy they assigned to tail me must not have been very high up in the organization," Mortenson says, "because he was poor at his job. He had bright red hair and wobbled around on his red Suzuki motorcycle so it was impossible to miss him. And every time I'd turn around, there he would be, smoking, trying to look like he wasn't watching me. I had nothing to hide, so I decided I might as well let him figure that out and report back to his superiors."

Another Skardu resident paid uncomfortably close attention to Mortenson's family, too. One afternoon, Mortenson left Tara and Amira in the rear seat of his Land Cruiser while he stopped to buy bottles of mineral water in Skardu's bazaar. Tara took advantage of the time alone to nurse Amira discreetly. When Mortenson returned, he saw a young man pressing his face to the Land Cruiser's window, leering in at his wife. His bodyguard Faisal Baig saw the voyeur, too, and got to him before Mortenson could.

"Faisal dragged the guy around a corner, into an alley, so Tara wouldn't have to be degraded by watching, and beat him unconscious," Mortenson says. "I ran over and asked Faisal to stop. And I checked his pulse, making sure he hadn't killed him."

Mortenson wanted to take the man to a hospital. But Baig kicked and spat on the man's prone figure when Mortenson suggested helping him and insisted that he remain where he belonged, lying in the gutter. "This *shetan*, this devil, is lucky I didn't kill him," Baig said. "If I did, no one in Skardu would disagree." Years later, Mortenson learned that the man had been so ostracized in Skardu after word spread about how he had disrespected the wife of Dr. Greg that he was forced to move out of town.

After putting his wife and daughter safely on a plane home, Mortenson stayed on in Pakistan for two more months. The success of the Women's Vocational Center led the men of Korphe to ask if there wasn't something Mortenson could do to help them earn extra money, too.

With Tara's brother, Brent Bishop, Mortenson organized Pakistan's first porter-training program, the Karakoram Porter Training and Environmental Institute. Bishop, a successful Everest climber like his late father, convinced one of his sponsors, Nike, to donate funds and equipment for the effort. "Balti porters worked gallantly in some of the harshest alpine terrain on earth," Mortenson says. "But they had no mountaineering training." On an expedition led and organized by Mouzafer, Mortenson, Bishop, and eighty porters trekked up the Baltoro. Apo Razak, a veteran at feeding large groups in inhospitable places, worked as the head cook. On the glacier, the American mountaineers taught classes in first aid, crevasse rescue, and basic ropecraft.

They also focused on repairing the environmental damage done to the Baltoro each climbing season, constructing stone latrines at campsites along the glacier, which they hoped would eliminate the fields of frozen turds expeditions left in their wake.

And for the porters who returned after each trip up the glacier with empty baskets, they created an annual recycling program, which removed more than a ton of tin cans, glass, and plastic from K2, Broad Peak, and Gasherbrum base camps that first year. Mortenson arranged to have the recyclables transported to Skardu and saw that the porters were paid for their efforts by the pound.

When winter clasped the high valleys of the Karakoram in its annual lingering embrace, Mortenson returned home at the end of the busiest year of his life to his basement in Bozeman.

"When I look back at everything we accomplished that year, despite the *fatwa*, I have no idea how I did it, how I had that kind of energy." Mortenson says.

But his hyperactive efforts had only made him more aware of the ocean of need still awaiting him. With a nocturnal flurry of phone calls to Pakistan, e-mails to his board, and countless pots of coffee, he began planning his spring assault on Pakistan's poverty.

CHAPTER 16

RED VELVET BOX

No human, nor any living thing, survives long under the eternal sky. The
most beautiful women, the most learned men, even Mohammed,
who heard Allah's own voice, all did wither and die. All is temporary.
The sky outlives everything. Even suffering.

—Bowa Johar, Balti poet, and grandfather of Mouzafer Ali

MORTENSON IMAGINED THE messenger traveling inexorably to the
southeast. He envisioned the Supreme Council's ruling tucked into an
emissary's saddlebags as he rode from Iran into Afghanistan, pictured
a small mountain pony skirting the heavily mined Shomali Plain, before plodding up the high passes of the Hindu Kush and crossing into
Pakistan. In his mind, Mortenson tried to slow the messenger down,
planted rockslide and avalanche in his path. The messenger would take
years to arrive, he hoped. Because if he came bearing the worst news,
Mortenson might be banished from Pakistan forever.

In reality, the red velvet box containing the ruling was mailed from
Qom to Islamabad. It was flown in a PIA 737 to Skardu, and delivered
to the foremost Shia clerics in northern Pakistan for a public reading.

While the Supreme Council had pondered Mortenson's case, they
had dispatched spies to inquire into the affairs of the American working at the heart of Shia Pakistan, Parvi says. "From many, many
schools, I began to get reports that strange men had visited, asking
about each school's curriculum. Did the schools recruit for Christianity
or promote Western-style licentiousness? these men wanted to know.

"Finally, an Iranian mullah visited me, myself, at my home. And he
asked me directly, 'Have you ever seen this infidel drink alcohol, or try
to seduce Muslim ladies?' I told him truthfully that I had never seen
Dr. Greg take a drink, and that he was a married man, who respected his

wife and children and would never Eve-tease any Balti girls. I also told him that he was welcome to come and investigate any of our schools, and that I would arrange his transportation and pay his expenses if he wanted to set out right away. 'We have been to your schools,' he said, and thanked me most courteously for my time."

Early on an April morning in 1998, Parvi appeared at the door to Mortenson's room in the Indus Hotel and told him they'd both been summoned.

Mortenson shaved and changed into the cleanest of the five mud-colored *shalwar kamiz* he'd by then accumulated.

The Imam Bara Mosque, like much of Shia Pakistan, showed little of its face to the outside world. Its high earthern walls were un-adorned, and it focused its energies inward, except for a tall, green-and-blue-painted minaret mounted with loudspeakers to summon the faithful inside.

They were led through the courtyard, and into an arched doorway. Mortenson brushed aside a heavy chocolate-colored velvet curtain and approached the mosque's inner sanctum, a place no infidel had been invited before. Mortenson, making sure to step carefully over the threshold with his right foot, to avoid offense, entered.

Inside stood the eight imposing black-turbaned members of the Council of Mullahs. From the severity with which Syed Mohammed Abbas Risvi greeted him, Mortenson presumed the worst. With Parvi, he sank heavily down on an exquisite Isfahan carpet woven with a pat-tern of flowing vines. Syed Abbas motioned for the rest of the council to join them in a circle on the carpet, then sat himself, placing a small red velvet box on the plush wool before his knees.

With due ceremony, Syed Abbas tilted back the lid of the box, withdrew a scroll of parchment wrapped in red ribbon, unfurled it, and revealed Mortenson's future. "Dear Compassionate of the Poor," he translated from the elegant Farsi calligraphy, "our Holy Koran tells us all children should receive education, including our daughters and sisters. Your noble work follows the highest principles of Islam, to tend to the poor and sick. In the Holy Koran there is no law to pro-hibit an infidel from providing assistance to our Muslim brothers and sisters. Therefore," the decree concluded, "we direct all clerics in Paki-stan to not interfere with your noble intentions. You have our permis-sion, blessings, and prayers."

Syed Abbas rolled the scroll, stowed it in the red velvet box, and presented it to Mortenson, grinning. Then he offered his hand.

Mortenson shook the hand of each member of the council in turn, his head swimming. "Does this mean . . ." he tried to speak. "The *fatwa*, is it . . ."

"Forget all that small-minded, small-village nonsense," Parvi said, beaming. "We have the blessing of the highest *mufti* in Iran. No Shia will dare to interfere with our work now, *Inshallah*."

Syed Abbas called for tea. "I want to speak with you about another matter," he said, relaxing now that his formal duty had been discharged. "I'd like to propose a little collaboration."

That spring, word of the ruling in the red velvet box spread throughout Baltistan more thoroughly than the glacial meltwater trickling down to its valleys from the high Karakoram. Mortenson's peaceful morning gatherings over tea in the lobby of the Indus Hotel grew too large for the two tables and had to be moved to a banquet room upstairs, where the meetings became increasingly raucous. Each day he was in Skardu, emissaries from Baltistan's hundreds of remote villages sought him out with petitions for new projects, now that he had the Supreme Council of Ayatollahs' stamp of approval.

Mortenson began taking his meals in the hotel kitchen, where he could finish an omelette or a plate of vegetable curry without having to respond to a note, in tortured English, asking for a loan to kickstart a semiprecious-stone-mining venture, or funds to rebuild a neglected village mosque.

Though he didn't fully recognize it yet, a new phase in Mortenson's life had now begun. He no longer had the time to speak with everyone who came to him with a request, though, at first, he tried. He'd been busy before, but now each day seemed five or six hours too brief. He set himself the task of sifting through the flood of requests for the few worthy projects he had the means and ability to accomplish.

Syed Abbas, whose influence extended up dozens of wild mountain valleys, had an acute sense of each community's needs. He told Mortenson he agreed that education was the only long-term tactic to combat poverty. But he argued that the children of Baltistan faced a more immediate crisis. In villages like Chunda, in the lower Shigar Valley, Syed Abbas said, more than one child in three died before celebrating their first birthday. Poor hygiene and lack of clean drinking water were the culprits, he said.

Mortenson wove this new strand into his mission enthusiastically. One had to water a plant before it could be coaxed to grow; children had to survive long enough to benefit from school. With Syed Abbas, he visited the *nurmadhar* of Chunda, Haji Ibramin, and convinced him to put the men of his village at their disposal. Residents of four neighboring villages requested permission to join the project. And with hundreds of workers digging trenches ten hours a day they completed the project in one week. Through twelve thousand feet of pipe Mortenson provided, fresh spring water flowed to public taps in the five villages.

"I came to respect and depend on the vision of Syed Abbas," Mortenson says. "He's the type of religious leader I admire most. He is about compassion in action, not talk. He doesn't just lock himself up with his books. Syed Abbas believes in rolling up his sleeves and making the world a better place. Because of his work, the women of Chunda no longer had to walk long distances to find clean water. And overnight, the infant mortality rate of a community of two thousand people was cut in half."

At a meeting before Mortenson left for Pakistan, the board had approved the construction of three more schools in the spring and summer of 1998. Mouzafer's school was Mortenson's priority. During their last few visits, Mouzafer hadn't seemed himself. The oxlike strength of the man who led him off the Baltoro was less evident. He'd become increasingly deaf. And as with so many Balti men who've labored for years in the elements, the onset of old age stalked him as swiftly as a snow leopard.

Halde, Mouzafer's village, was in the lush Lower Hushe Valley. By the bank of the Shyok River, where it slows and widens before meeting the Indus, Halde was as perfect a place as Mortenson had seen in Pakistan. Irrigation channels trickled through neat patchwork fields that rolled down to the riverbank. The village pathways were shaded by mature apricot and mulberry trees. "Halde is my kind of Shangri-La. It's the kind of place I could see bringing a pile of books, taking my shoes off, and hiding out for a very long time," Mortenson says. He had no such luxury. But Mouzafer, his trekking days having come to an end, envisioned his last quiet years spent here in his small home surrounded by orchards and his children and their children, far below the land of eternal ice.

With the process he, Parvi, and Makhmal had now perfected, Mortenson obtained a plot of open land between two groves of apricot trees and, with the village's help, built a sturdy stone four-classroom school in three months, for just over twelve thousand dollars. Mouzafer's grandfather Bowa Johar had been a poet, renowned throughout Baltistan. Mouzafer had labored as a simple porter his whole adult life, and enjoyed no special standing in Halde. But his ability to bring a school to the village conferred a new level of respect on the kindly man who carried quarried rocks to the construction site and raised roof beams, though younger hands tried to shift the burden from his shoulders.

Standing with Mortenson before the finished school, watching Halde's children stretch on tiptoe to look through unfamiliar glass panes at the mysterious rooms where they would start class in the fall, Mouzafer took Mortenson's hand in both of his.

"My upside days are over, Greg Sahib," he said. "I'd like to work with you for many years more, but Allah, in his wisdom, has taken much of my strength."

Mortenson hugged this man who'd helped him so often to find his way. Despite Mouzafer's talk of weakness, his arms were still strong enough to squeeze the breath out of a large American. "What will you do?" Mortenson asked.

"My work now," Mouzafer said simply, "is to give water to the trees."

High up at the head of the Hushe Valley, in the shadow of Masherbrum's hanging glaciers, Mohammed Aslam Khan had been a boy in the time before roads. There was nothing wrong with life in the village of Hushe. It proceeded as it always had. In the summer, boys like Aslam led the sheep and goats to high pastures while the women made yoghurt and cheese. From the highest grazing grounds, the mountain they called Chogo Ri, or "Big Mountain," known to the wider world as K2, could be seen thrusting into the heavens over Masherbrum's broad shoulder.

In the fall, Aslam took turns with other village boys driving a team of six panting yak in circles around a pole, so their heavy hooves would thresh the newly harvested wheat. Throughout the long winter, he would huddle as near to the fire as he could creep, competing with his five brothers, three sisters, and the family's livestock to find the warmest spot on the coldest days.

This was life. It was how every boy in Hushe could expect to spend his days. But Aslam's father, Golowa Ali, was the *nurmadhar* of Hushe. Everyone said Aslam was the cleverest child in the family, and his father had other plans for him.

In late spring, when the worst of the weather had retreated, but the Shyok still ran fast with glacial melt, Golowa Ali woke his son up before first light and told him to prepare to leave the village. Aslam couldn't imagine what he meant. But when he saw that his father had packed luggage for him, wrapping a block of *churpa*, hard sheep cheese, into a bundle of clothes, he began to cry.

Questioning his father's will was not allowed, but Aslam challenged the village chief anyway.

"Why do I have to go?" he said, turning to his mother for support. By the light of a guttering oil lamp, Aslam was shocked to see that she, too, was crying.

"You're going to school," his father said.

Aslam walked downside with his father for two days. Like every Hushe boy, Aslam had roamed the narrow mountain paths that clung to the bare cliffsides like ivy tendrils to stone walls. But he had never been so far from home. Down here the earth was sandy and free of snow. Behind him, Masherbrum had lost the reassuring bulk that placed it at the center of the known universe. It was only one mountain among many.

When the trail ended at the bank of the Shyok, Golowa Ali hung a leather pouch containing two gold coins around his son's neck on a cord. "When, *Inshallah,* you get to the town of Khaplu, you will find a school. Give the Sahib who runs the school these coins to pay for your education."

"When will I come home?" Aslam asked, trying to control his trembling lips.

"You'll know when," his father said. Golowa Ali inflated six goat bladders and lashed them together into a *zaks,* or raft, the traditional Balti means of fording a river when it ran too deep to cross on foot. "Now hold on tight," he said.

Aslam couldn't swim.

"When my father put me in the water I couldn't control myself and I cried. He was a strong man, and proud, but as I floated away down the Shyok, I saw he had tears in his eyes, too."

Aslam clung to the *zaks* as the Shyok sucked him from his father's sight. He bobbed over rapids, sobbing openly now that no one was watching, shivering in the water's glacial chill. After a passage of blurred terror that might have taken ten minutes or two hours, Aslam noticed he was moving more slowly as the river widened. He saw some people on the far bank and kicked toward them, too afraid of losing the *zaks* to use his arms.

"An old man fished me out of the water and wrapped me in a warm yak-hair blanket," Aslam said. "I was still shivering and crying and he asked me why I had crossed the river, so I told him of my father's instructions."

"Don't be afraid," the old man counseled Aslam. "You're a brave boy to come so far from home. One day, you'll be honored by everyone when you return." He stuffed two wrinkled rupee notes into Aslam's hand and accompanied him down the path toward Khaplu, until he could hand him off to another elder.

In this fashion, Aslam and his story traveled down the Lower Hushe Valley. He was passed from hand to hand, and each man who accompanied him made a small contribution toward his education. "People were so kind that I was very encouraged," Aslam remembers. "And soon I was enrolled in a government school in Khaplu, and studying as hard as I was able."

Students in bustling Khaplu, the largest settlement Aslam had ever seen, were cosmopolitan by comparison. They teased Aslam about his appearance. "I wore yak-skin shoes and woolen clothes and all the students had fine uniforms," Aslam says. Teachers, taking pity, pooled their money and purchased a white shirt, maroon sweater, and black trousers for Aslam so he could blend in with the other boys. He wore the uniform every day and cleaned it as well as he could at night. And after his first year of school, when he walked back up the Hushe Valley to visit his family, he made the impression the old man who plucked him out of the Shyok had predicted.

"When I went upside," Aslam says. "I was clean and wearing my uniform. Everyone was gazing at me and saying I had changed. Everyone honored me. I realized I must live up to this honor."

In 1976, after Aslam graduated at the top of the Tenth Class in Khaplu, he was offered a post with the government of the Northern Areas. But he decided to return home to Hushe, and after his father's death, was elected *nurmadhar*. "I had seen how people live downside and it was my duty to work to improve the quality of life upside in my village," Aslam says.

Petitioning the government officials who had offered him a job, Aslam helped convince the Northern Areas Administration to bulldoze and blast a dirt road all the way up the valley to Hushe. He also pestered them into funding a small school he built in a drafty farm shed for twenty-five boys, but Aslam had trouble convincing the families of his village to send their sons to study in this poorly equipped building, rather than work in the fields. The men of Hushe waylaid Aslam as he walked, whispering bribes of butter and bags of flour if he'd exempt their sons from school.

As his own children reached school age, Aslam realized he needed help if he hoped to educate all of them. "I have been blessed nine times," Aslam says. "With five boys and four girls. But my daughter Shakeela is the most clever among them. There was nowhere for her to pursue her studies and she was too young to send away. Although many thousand climbers had passed through my village for many years not one had offered to help our children. I began to hear rumors about a big *Angrezi* who was building schools that welcomed both boys and girls all over Baltistan, and I decided to seek him out."

In the spring of 1997, Aslam traveled two days by jeep to Skardu and asked for Mortenson at the Indus Hotel, only to be told he had left for the Upper Braldu Valley and might be gone for weeks. "I left a letter for the *Angrezi*, inviting him to my village," Aslam says, "but I never heard from him." Then one June day in 1998, when he was home in Hushe, Aslam learned from a jeep driver that the *Angrezi* was only a few villages down the valley, in Khane.

"That spring I had come back to Khane," Mortenson says, "figuring I'd call a *jirga*, a big meeting, and get everyone to outvote Janjungpa so I could finally build a school there." But Janjungpa, not willing to relinquish his fantasy of a climbing school of his own, had contacted the local police, and told them the one thing certain to arouse suspicion about an outsider in this sensitive border region. "He said I was a spy, working for their archenemy," Mortenson says. "India."

205

As Mortenson struggled to placate a policeman demanding that he hand over his passport for inspection, Aslam arrived in a borrowed jeep and introduced himself. "I told him, 'I am the *nurmadhar* of Hushe and I've been trying to meet you for one year now,' " Aslam remembers. "I said, 'Please, in evening time, you come to Hushe and attend our tea party.' " Mortenson was coming to consider Khane a cursed village. He no longer wanted a full moon, tottering on the canyon's rim, to fall and crush it. But he was happy to have an excuse to leave.

An innovator educationally and otherwise, Aslam had painted the walls of his house with bold geometric designs in primary colors. To Mortenson, the house had a vaguely African flavor that made him feel instantly at home. On the roof, he sipped *paiyu cha* deep into the night with his new friend the *nurmadhar,* hearing the story of Aslam's odyssey. And by the time the rising sun iced the hanging glaciers of Masherbrum pale pink, like a gargantuan pastry dangling above them at breakfast time, Mortenson had agreed to shift the funds his board had approved for the doomed Khane school upside to this village whose headman had traveled so far downriver to educate himself.

"After seeking him all over Baltistan, I was very surprised when I finally met Dr. Greg," Aslam says. "I expected to have to plead with an *Angrezi Sahib* like a little man. But he spoke to me as a brother. I found Greg a very kind, soft-hearted, naturally pleasing man. When I first met him, I actually fell in love with his personality. Every year since we built our school this feeling gets stronger, and finally, that love has spread to all my children and all the families of Hushe."

The building Aslam and the other men of his village constructed in the summer of 1998, with funds and assistance from Mortenson's CAI, may be the most beautiful school in northern Pakistan. It is nothing if not a monument to the hope Aslam convinced his village to invest in its children. Mortenson turned the particulars of design over to the *nurmadhar,* and Aslam's vision is evident in the scarlet-painted finely turned wooden trim adorning every window, roofline, and doorway. Along the borders of the school's walled courtyard, sunflowers grow higher than even the oldest students throughout the warmer months. And the inspiring view that greets these students from every classroom—the roof of the world, represented by Masherbrum's soaring summit ridge—has already helped convince many of Hushe's children to aim high.

In a house he recently rented for her, near the Government Girl's High School she attends today in Khaplu, Aslam's eldest daughter, Shakeela, reflects on the path the Hushe School opened to her the year it first appeared in her village, when she was eight years old. Sitting cross-legged on a rough striped wool carpet next to her distinguished father, Shakeela, poised and pretty at fifteen, smiles confidently out from under a cream-colored shawl festooned with falling leaves as she speaks.

"At first, when I began to attend school, many people in my village told me a girl has no business doing such a thing," Shakeela says. "They said you will end up working in the field, like all women, so why fill your head with the foolishness found in books? But I knew how much my father valued education, so I tried to shut my mind to the talk and I persisted with my studies."

"I have tried to encourage all of my children," Aslam says, nodding toward two of Shakeela's older brothers, college students who live with her in Khaplu and act as chaperones. "But I saw a special attitude in this girl from an early age."

Shakeela covers her face with her shawl in embarrassment, then brushes it aside to speak. "I am not such a special student," she says. "But I was able to pass through school in Hushe with good marks."

Adjusting to cosmopolitan Khaplu has proven harder. "The environment here is very exceptional," Shakeela says. "Everything is quick. Everything is available." She shows her father a recent physics exam, on which she is ashamed to have scored only an 82. "My classes are very difficult here, but I am adjusting," she says. "In Hushe, I was the most advanced student. Here at least there is always a senior student or teacher available to help when I lose my way."

With a road in place now to take her all the way downside, Shakeela's route to higher education in Khaplu wasn't as physically dangerous as her father's. But in her own way, she has blazed just as dramatic a trail. "Shakeela is the first girl in all of the Hushe Valley to be granted the privilege of a higher education," Aslam says proudly. "And now, all the girls of Hushe look up to her."

Her father's praise drives Shakeela back, briefly, behind her shawl. "People's minds in Hushe are beginning to change," Shakeela says, emerging once again. "Now when I return to my village, I see all the families sending their girls to school. And they tell me, 'Shakeela, we were mistaken. You were right to read so many books and brave to study so far from home. You're bringing honor to the village.' "

If she can master difficult new subjects like physics, Shakeela says she wants to go as far as her education can take her—ideally to medical school. "I'd like to become a doctor and go to work wherever I am needed," she says. "I've learned the world is a very large place and so far, I've only seen a little of it."

Shakeela's academic success is influencing not only the women of Hushe Valley, but her elder brothers as well. Yakub, eighteen, attended university in Lahore for a year, but failed six of his eight classes. Enrolled now in a local college in Khaplu, he is rededicating himself to his studies in hopes of earning a government post. "I have no choice," Yakub says, sheepishly adjusting a baseball cap bearing a gold star, the kind of mark his sister earned frequently during her years at the Hushe School. "My sister is pushing me. She works hard, so I must, too."

Studying a sheaf of Shakeela's recent work, Aslam finds a test on which his daughter has scored a perfect 100—an Urdu exam. He holds the page tenderly, like a nugget of precious ore sifted from the Shyok. "For these blessings, I thank Almighty Allah," Aslam says, "and Mister Greg Mortenson."

Across northern Pakistan, thousands of people likewise sang Mortenson's praises throughout the summer and fall of 1998. Returning to Peshawar, the city that continued to fascinate him, Mortenson toured the refugee camps that strained to feed, shelter, and educate hundreds of thousands, now that the Taliban's ruthless brand of fundamentalist Islam had conquered most of Afghanistan. Constructing schools under such apocalyptic conditions was clearly out of the question. But at the Shamshatoo Refugee Camp, southwest of Peshawar, he organized eighty teachers, who held classes for four thousand Afghan students, and agreed to see that their salaries were paid as long as the refugees remained in Pakistan.

With eye disease rampant in northern Pakistan, Mortenson arranged for Dr. Geoff Tabin, an American cataract surgeon, to offer free surgery to sixty elderly patients in Skardu and Gilgit. And he sent Dr. Niaz Ali, the only eye doctor in Baltistan, to the renowned Tilanga Eye Hospital in Nepal for specialized training so he could perform the surgeries himself long after Dr. Tabin returned home to America.

After attending a conference of development experts in Bangladesh, Mortenson decided CAI schools should educate students only up through the fifth grade and focus on increasing the enrollment of girls. "Once you educate the boys, they tend to leave the villages and go search for work in the cities," Mortenson explains. "But the girls stay home, become leaders in the community, and pass on what they've learned. If you really want to change a culture, to empower women, improve basic hygiene and health care, and fight high rates of infant mortality, the answer is to educate girls."

Bumping up to each village where CAI operated in his green Land Cruiser, Mortenson held meetings with elders and insisted they sign pledges to increase the enrollment of girls at each school by 10 percent a year if they wanted CAI's continued support. "If the girls can just get to a fifth-grade level," Mortenson says, "everything changes."

The CAI's board of directors evolved along with its philosophy. George McCown's wife, Karen, who had founded a charter school in the Bay Area, joined, as did Abdul Jabbar, a Pakistani professor at the City College of San Francisco. The entire board was by now comprised of professional educators.

With a dozen schools now up and running, Julia Bergman, with the help of two teachers from the City College, Joy Durighello and Bob Irwin, organized a teacher-training workshop to be held in Skardu each summer and compiled a permanent resource library for all of CAI's teachers. In meetings that summer in Skardu, with Ghulam Parvi, the master teachers Bergman brought to Pakistan from America, and all the Pakistani instructors on CAI's payroll, Mortenson hammered out an educational philosophy.

CAI schools would teach the exact same curriculum as any good Pakistani government school. There would be none of the "comparative cultures" classes then so popular in the West, nothing conservative religious leaders could point to as "anti-Islamic" in an effort to shut the schools down. But neither would they let the schools preach the fiery brand of fundamentalist Islam taught in many of the country's *madrassas*.

"I don't want to teach Pakistan's children to think like Americans," Mortenson says. "I just want them to have a balanced, nonextremist education. That idea is at the very center of what we do."

Each successfully completed project added luster to Mortenson's reputation in northern Pakistan. His picture began to appear over the hearths of homes and on jeep drivers' dashboards. Bound by Islam's prohibition against false idols, Pakistanis don't embrace the endless pantheon of deities plastered across windshields in the Hindu country to the east. But as in India, certain public figures in Pakistan begin to transcend the merely mortal realm.

Cricket hero Imran Khan had become a sort of secular saint. And rippling out from Mortenson's headquarters in Skardu, over the parched dunes, through the twisting gorges, and up the weatherbound valleys of Baltistan, the legend of a gentle infidel called Dr. Greg was likewise growing.

CHAPTER 17

CHERRY TREES IN THE SAND

The most dangerous place in the world today, I think you could argue,
is the Indian Subcontinent and the Line of Control in Kashmir.

—President Bill Clinton, before leaving Washington on a diplomatic visit to,
and peacemaking mission between, India and Pakistan

FATIMA BATOOL REMEMBERS the first "whump," clearly audible from
the Indian artillery battery, just twelve kilometers across the mountains. She remembers the first shell whistling gracefully as it fell out
of the blameless blue sky, and the way she and her sister Aamina,
working together sowing buckwheat, looked at each other just before
the first explosion.

In Brolmo, their village in the Gultori Valley, a place that appeared
on maps carried by the Indian army across the nearby border as "Pak-
istani-Occupied Kashmir," nothing new ever happened. At least that's
the way it seemed to Fatima, at age ten. She remembers looking into
her older sister's face when the sky began singing its unfamiliar song,
and seeing her own surprise echoed there in Aamina's wide eyes, a
look that said, "Here is something new."

But after the firestorm of flying metal from the first 155-
millimeter shell, Fatima chooses to remember as little as she possibly
can. The images, like stones buried among coals to bake loaves of
kurba, are too hot to touch. There were bodies, and parts of bodies, in
the wheat field, as the whumps, whistles, and explosions came so
quickly, so close together, that they became a single scream.

Aamina grabbed Fatima's hand, and together, they joined the
stampede of panicked villagers, running as fast as their legs could take
them, but all too slowly all the same, toward caves where they could
escape the sky.

211

From her haven in the anxious dark, Fatima can't or won't remember how Aamina came to be back out in the storm of sound. Perhaps, she thinks, her older sister was shepherding the younger
children in. That would have been in Aamina's character, Fatima says.
About the shell that landed then, just outside the mouth of the cave,
Fatima has no memory at all. All she can say is that, after it exploded,
her sister's *hayaat*, or spirit, was broken, and neither of their lives was
ever the same.

On May 27, 1999, in his basement office, in the middle of the Montana
night, Mortenson scoured the wire services for details about the fighting that had suddenly flared in Kashmir. He'd never heard of anything
like it.

Ever since the violent partition that pulled India and Pakistan
apart, Kashmir had been combustible. India, with its superior military
force, was able to seize the majority of the former principality. And
though India promised to hold elections, and let Kashmiris determine
their own future, the overwhelmingly Muslim population of Kashmir
had never been extended that opportunity.

To the people of Pakistan, Kashmir became a symbol of all the oppression they felt Muslims had suffered as British India unraveled.
And to Indians, Kashmir represented a line drawn, if not in the sand,
then across a range of eighteen-thousand-foot peaks. It became the
territorial jewel that the Jammu-Kashmir Liberation Front (JKLF)
fighters they branded terrorists could not be allowed to wrest from India's crown. And to both sides, the line drawn over inhospitable glaciers at the behest of Britain's Lord Mountbatten remained a raw
wound reminding them of their colonial humiliations.

In 1971, after decades of skirmishing, both nations agreed to a
Line of Control (LOC), drawn across terrain so rugged and inhos-
pitable that it already formed an effective barrier to military incursion.
"The reports of heavy casualties shocked me," Mortenson remembers.
"For most of my first six years in Pakistan, the fighting along the
LOC was waged like an old-fashioned gentleman's agreement.

"The Indian and Pakistan military both built observation posts and
artillery batteries way up on the glaciers. Right after their morning *chai*,
the Indians would lob a shell or two toward Pakistan's posts with their
big Swedish-made Bofors guns. And Pakistan's forces would retort by

firing off a few rounds themselves after completing morning prayer. There were few casualties, and each September, when the cold weather started rolling in, with a wink, both sides would abandon their posts until spring."

But in April 1999, during an unusually early thaw, the government of Pakistan's prime minister Nawaz Sharif decided to test India's will to fight. A year earlier, Pakistan had stunned the world by conducting five successful tests of nuclear weapons. And achieving destructive parity with their Hindu neighbor provoked such an acute spike in national pride—and approval for Pakistan's government—that Sharif had a scale model of the peak in the Chagai Hills where the "Muslim Bomb" was detonated constructed next to a freeway overpass at Zero Point, the spot where 'Pindi and Islamabad intersect.

That month, about eight hundred heavily armed Islamic warriors crossed the LOC via the Gultori and took up positions along ridges inside Indian Kashmir. According to India, members of the Northern Light Infantry Brigade, the elite force assigned to protect much of Pakistan's Northern Areas, put on civilian clothes and managed the invasion alongside irregular *mujahadeen*. The combined troops moved into position so stealthily that they weren't discovered for nearly a month, until Indian army spotters realized the high ridges overlooking their positions in and around the town of Kargil were all occupied by Pakistan and its allies.

Indian prime minister Atal Bihari Vajpayee accused Sharif of invading India. Sharif responded that the invaders were "freedom fighters," operating independently of Pakistan's military, who had spontaneously decided to join the fight to free Kashmir's Muslims from their Hindu oppressors. Northern Light Infantry pay stubs and ID cards Indians later claimed to have found on dead soldiers insinuate a different story.

On May 26, 1999, Vajpayee ordered India's air force into action against Pakistan for the first time in more than twenty years. Wave after wave of Indian MiG and Mirage fighter jets bombed the entrenched positions. And the fighters holding the hilltops, armed with Stinger missiles the Americans had provided *mujahadeen* commanders in Afghanistan, to shoot down Soviet aircraft, blew a MiG and an MI-17 helicopter gunship out of the sky in the first days of what would come to be known as the "Kargil Conflict."

Undeclared wars, like the American "police action" in Vietnam, as it was officially known in its early years, are all too often sanitized by their official names. "Conflict" does not begin to describe the volume of high explosives Pakistan's and India's forces fired at each other in 1999. Pakistan's forces killed hundreds of Indian soldiers and, according to India, scores of civilians caught in the crossfire. The far more powerful Indian Army fired five thousand artillery shells, mortar rounds, and rockets a day.

Throughout the spring and summer of 1999, more than 250,000 Indian shells, bombs, and rockets rained down on Pakistan, according to GlobalSecurity.org. Such high rates of fire hadn't afflicted any place on Earth since World War II. And though the Indian military continues to deny it, civilian accounts suggest that many of those munitions were fired indiscriminately, onto villages unlucky enough to be located along the Line of Control, villages like Fatima Batool's.

Mortenson, feeling helpless, paced his basement between calls to his contacts in Pakistan's military. And the reports he heard robbed him of the few hours of sleep that he ordinarily managed. Streams of refugees from the fighting were crossing the high passes on foot and approaching Skardu, exhausted, injured, and badly in need of services no one in Baltistan was equipped to provide. The answers weren't in the stacks of books piling ever higher against the walls and spilling off shelves onto the floor. They were in Pakistan.

Mortenson booked his flight.

The Deosai Plateau in mid-June is one of the most beautiful wilderness areas on the planet, Mortenson thought, as his Land Cruiser climbed toward Baltistan. Patches of purple lupines had been applied to the high meadows between mountains with broad brush strokes. Herds of big-horned *bharal*, thriving far from human habitation, watched the vehicle's progress with impunity. And to the west, the Rupal Face of Nanga Parbat, the greatest single unbroken pitch of rock on Earth, mesmerized Mortenson seen from this unfamiliar angle.

Hussein, Apo, and Faisal had arrived in Islamabad to fetch Mortenson, and Apo had convinced him to attempt the thirty-six-hour drive to Skardu over the Deosai's often-impassible roads, since the Karakoram Highway was jammed with military convoys hauling supplies to the war zone and carrying truckloads of *shahids*, or martyrs, home for funerals.

Mortenson expected to be alone in the Deosai, since the high passes of this fourteen-thousand-foot plateau bordering India were still snow-covered. But both driving toward the Kargil Conflict and retreating from it, convoys of double-cab Toyota pickups, the war wagons of the Taliban, were wedged full of bearded fighters in black turbans. The warriors in pickups on their way northeast waved their Kalashnikovs and rocket-propelled grenade launchers as they passed. The wounded heading southwest brandished their bandages proudly.

"Apo!" Mortenson shouted over the engine, after four horn-honking convoys had forced the Land Cruiser to the side of the road in as many minutes, "have you ever seen so many Taliban?"

"The Kabulis always come," Apo said, using the local term for the outsiders he despised for the violence they brought to Baltistan. "But never in such numbers." Apo shook his head ruefully. "They must be in a big hurry," he said, spitting a long stream of the Copenhagen chewing tobacco Mortenson had brought him from Montana out the window, "to become martyrs."

Skardu was gripped in war fever when they arrived. Bedfords rumbled in from the front lines, filled with coffins solemnly draped in the Pakistani flag. Dull green helicopters buzzed overhead in numbers Mortenson had never seen. And nomadic Gojar shepherds, the gypsies of Pakistan, coaxed flocks of skittish goats through the heaving military traffic, herding them on the long march toward India, where they would feed Pakistan's troops.

Outside the Indus Hotel, two black Toyota double-cabs with distinctive light blue United Arab Emirates plates and the word SURF inexplicably stenciled on the doors were angled up to the entrance, their tailgates jutting out and blocking the progress of jeep drivers who wouldn't dare to honk their horns. And in the lobby, over their shoulders, as Mortenson hugged Ghulam the manager and his younger brother Nazir hello, he saw two large bearded men drinking tea at one of the plank tables. Their clothes, like Mortenson's, were covered with dust.

"The bigger guy looked up from his tea and said, 'Chai!' waving me over," Mortenson says. "I'd guess he was in his fifties and he must have been six-six, which stuck in my mind because I was used to being the biggest guy in Baltistan. He had, howdaya call it? Jowls. And a huge belly. I knew there was no way he had been climbing up eighteen-thousand-foot passes, so I figured he must be a commander."

With his back to the men, Ghulam the manager raised his eyebrows at Mortenson, warning him.

"I know," Mortenson said, walking over to join them.

He shook the hand of both the big man and his companion, who had a straggly beard that hung almost to his waist and forearms corded like weathered wood. As Mortenson sat down with the men, he saw a pair of well-oiled AK-47s on the floor between their feet.

"*Pe khayr raghie,*" the man said in Pashto, "Welcome."

"*Khayr ose,*" Mortenson replied, offering his respects in Pashto, which he'd been studying ever since his eight-day detention in Waziristan.

"*Kenastel!*" the commander ordered, "Sit."

Mortenson did, then switched to Urdu, so he could take care not to misspeak. He had a black-and-white-checked *kaffiyeh* wrapped around his head, the sort associated with Yasir Arafat. He'd worn it to keep the Deosai dust out of his teeth. But the men took it for political affiliation and offered him tea.

"The huge guy introduced himself as Gul Mohammed," Mortenson says. "Then he asked if I was an American. I figured they would find out anyway so I told them I was." Mortenson nodded almost imperceptibly at Faisal Baig, who stood a few feet from the table on full alert, and the bodyguard backed away and sat with Apo and Parvi.

"Okay Bill Clinton!" Gul Mohammed said in English, raising his thumb up enthusiastically. Clinton may have failed, ultimately, to forge peace between Israel and Palestine, but he had, however belatedly, sent American forces to Bosnia in 1994 to halt the slaughter of Muslims by the Christian Serbians, a fact *mujahadeen* like Gul would never forget.

The enormous man rested his hand appraisingly on the American's shoulder. Mortenson was hit by a wave of body odor and the aroma of roasted lamb. "You are a soldier," he said, rather than asked.

"I was," Mortenson replied. "A long time ago. Now I build schools for children."

"Do you know Lieutenant Colonel Samuel Smith, from Fort Worth, Texas?" the leaner man asked. "He was an American soldier also. Together we crushed Soviets like bugs in Spin Boldak," he said, grinding the heel of his combat boot into the floor.

"Sorry," Mortenson said. "America is big."

"Big and powerful. We had Allah on our side in Afghanistan," Gul said, grinning. "Also American Stinger missiles."

Mortenson asked the men if they'd come from the front and Gul Mohammed seemed almost relieved to describe what he'd seen there. He said the *mujahadeen* were fighting bravely, but the Indian air force was inflicting terrible carnage on the men trying to hold hilltop positions ever since they learned to drop their bombs from above the range of the *mujahadeen*'s missiles. "Also their Bofors artillery is very strong," Gul explained. "Sweden says it is a peaceful country, but they sell very deadly guns."

The men questioned Mortenson closely about his work and nodded in approval when they learned he was educating four thousand Sunni Afghan refugees in Peshawar as well as the Shia children of Baltistan. Gul said he lived in the Daryle Valley, not far from the bridge *mujahadeen* had blocked five years earlier, when Mortenson was riding the Korphe School up the Karakoram Highway on top of his rented Bedford. "We have a great need for schools in my valley," Gul said. "Why don't you come back with us and build ten or twenty there? Even for girls, no problem."

Mortenson explained that the CAI operated on a small budget and all the school projects had to be approved by his board. He suppressed a smile as he imagined making that particular request, then promised to bring the subject up at the next board meeting.

By 9:00 P.M., despite the charged air in the Indus's lobby, Mortenson felt his eyelids drooping. He'd had too little sleep during his dusty trip across the Deosai. With the hospitality dictated by *Pashtunwali*, the commanders asked Mortenson if he'd like to share their quarters for the evening. Ghulam and Nazir kept a small, quiet room at the rear of the hotel available, always, for Mortenson. He told the men as much and bowing, with his hand over his heart, took his leave.

Halfway down the hallway to his room, a skinny red-haired apparition with bulging blue eyes burst out the swinging kitchen door and clutched Mortenson's sleeve. Agha Ahmed, the Indus Hotel's unbalanced kitchen boy and baggage hauler, had been watching the lobby through the door's slats. "Doctor Greek!" he shouted in warning, loud enough for the entire hotel to hear, a bubble of saliva forming, as always, at the corner of his mouth. "Taliban!"

"I know," Mortenson said, smiling, and shuffled down the hall toward sleep.

Syed Abbas himself called on Mortenson in the morning. Mortenson had never seen him so upset. Ordinarily, the cleric carried himself with a grave dignity and released words with the same measured regularity with which he fingered his *tasbih,* or string of prayer beads. But this morning, Syed Abbas's speech poured out of him in a torrent. The war was a catastrophe for the civilians of the Gultori, Abbas said. No one knew how many villagers had been killed or maimed by Indian bombs and artillery, but already two thousand refugees had arrived in Skardu, and thousands of others were waiting out the worst of the fighting in caves, before coming to join them.

Syed Abbas said he had contacted the Northern Areas Administration and the United Nations' High Commission for Refugees and both had refused his pleas for help. The local government said they didn't have the resources to handle the crisis. And the UN said they couldn't come to the aid of the Gultori families fleeing the fighting since they were internally displaced refugees who hadn't fled across international borders.

"What do the people need?" Mortenson asked.

"Everything," Abbas said. "But above all, water."

West of Skardu, Syed Abbas drove Mortenson, Apo, and Parvi to see the new tent city of sun-faded plastic tarps that had sprung up in the sand dunes bordering the airport. They left the road, took their shoes off, and as the French-made Mirage fighters of Pakistan's air force screamed overhead on patrol, they walked over a dozen dunes toward the refugees. Ringing the airport, antiaircraft gunners sat in their sandbagged emplacements on high alert, tracing arabesques with the barrels of their guns in the sky over India.

The refugees had been shunted to the only land in Skardu no one wanted. Their encampment in the middle of the dunes had no natural water source, and they were more than an hour's walk away from the Indus River. Mortenson's head throbbed, and not just from the heat reflecting off the dunes; he contemplated the immensity of their task. "How can we bring water here?" he asked. "We're a long way uphill from the river."

"I know about some projects in Iran," Syed Abbas said. "They call them 'uplift water schemes.' We'll have to dig very deep to the ground-water and put in pumps, but with Allah's help, it is possible."

Syed Abbas, his black robes billowing, ran ahead over the bright sand, pointing out places where he thought they might probe for groundwater. "I wish Westerners who misunderstand Muslims could have seen Syed Abbas in action that day," Mortenson says. "They would see that most people who practice the true teachings of Islam, even conservative mullahs like Syed Abbas, believe in peace and justice, not in terror. Just as the Torah and Bible teach concern for those in distress, the Koran instructs all Muslims to make caring for widows, orphans, and refugees a priority."

The tent city appeared deserted at first because its inhabitants were huddling under their tarps, seeking mercy from the sun. Apo, himself a refugee whose ancestral home, Dras, abuts the Gultori, on the Indian side of the border, wandered from tent to tent, taking orders for urgently needed supplies.

Mortenson, Parvi, and Syed Abbas stood in a clearing at the center of the tents, discussing the logistics of the uplift water scheme. Parvi was sure he could convince his neighbor, the director of Skardu's Public Works Department (PWD), to lend them heavy earth-moving equipment if the CAI agreed to purchase the pipe and water pumps.

"How many people live here?" Mortenson asked.

"Just over fifteen hundred now," Syed Abbas said. "Mostly men. They have come to find work and set up shelter before sending for their women and children. Within a few months, we may have four or five thousand refugees to deal with."

Ducking out through the flap of a tent, Apo Razak bore down on the talking men. If there was one constant in Baltistan, it was the jester-like leer on the face of the old expedition cook who had spent his life providing food and comfort for large groups in inhospitable places. But his face, as he approached, was uncharacteristically grave, and his mouth was set like a vein of quartz in granite. Like Lear's Jester, he had no trouble pointing out hard truths to his so-called superiors.

"Doctor Greg," he said, taking Mortenson's hand and leading him toward the tents, "enough talking. How can you know what the people need if you don't ask them?"

* * *

Mullah Gulzar sat under a blue tarp in a black skullcap and struggled to his feet after Apo led Mortenson in. The elderly cleric of Brolmo village clasped Mortenson's hand and apologized that he didn't have the means to make tea. When they were all seated cross-legged on a plastic tablecloth that covered the warm sand, Apo prodded the mullah to tell his story.

The bright light filtering through the blue tarp reflected off the mullah's oversized glasses and obscured his eyes as he spoke, giving Mortenson the unsettling impression he was listening to a blind man wearing opaque blue lenses.

"We didn't want to come here," Mullah Gulzar said, stroking his long wispy beard. "Brolmo is a good place. Or it was. We stayed as long as we could, hiding in the caves by day, and working the fields at night. If we had worked by day none of us would have survived, because there were so many shells falling. Finally, all the irrigation channels were broken, the fields were ruined, and the houses were shattered. We knew our women and children would die if we didn't do something, so we walked over the mountains to Skardu. I'm not young and it was very difficult.

"When we came to the Skardu town, the army told us to make our home here," Mullah Gulzar said. "And when we saw this place, this sand, we decided to go home. But the army would not permit it. They said, 'You have no home to go back to. It is broken.' Still, we would return if we could, for this is not a life. And now our women and children will soon come to this wasteland and what can we tell them?"

Mortenson took the old mullah's hand in both of his. "We will help you bring water here for your families," he promised.

"Thanks to Allah Almighty for that," the mullah said. "But water is only a beginning. We need food, and medicine, and education for our children. This is our home now. I'm ashamed to ask for so much, but no one else has come."

The elderly cleric inclined his head toward the sky the blue tarp imperfectly sheltered him from, as if casting his lamentation directly up to the ears of Allah. From this new angle, the glare vanished from his glasses and Mortenson saw the mullah's eyes were moist.

"And we have nothing. For your *mal-la khwong*, for your kindness in fulfilling our prayers, I can offer you nothing," Mullah Gulzar said. "Not even tea."

* * *

The first uplift water scheme in the history of northern Pakistan took eight weeks to build. True to his word, Ghulam Parvi convinced his neighbor to donate the use of earth-moving equipment. The Director of Skardu's PWD also donated all the pipe the project required. And twelve tractors appeared on loan from the army to move stones. Mortenson patiently returned again and again to the Public Call Office until, finally, he reached San Francisco. He requested, and was granted, permission to spend six thousand dollars of CAI's funds on the project.

Mortenson ordered powerful pumps and Honda generators from Gilgit. With all the men of Brolmo village laboring around the clock, they constructed a huge concrete tank, capable of storing enough water to supply a settlement of five thousand people. And after drilling to a depth of 120 feet, they found the groundwater to draw up and fill it. Now the men of Brolmo could start building mud-block houses and transforming the desert wastes into a green new home for their families. But first their women and children had to survive the journey to Skardu.

During their time in the caves, Fatima Batool couldn't stop crying. And Aamina, who had always been the one to comfort her younger sister, wasn't capable of caring even for herself. Aamina's physical wounds from flying shrapnel were slight. But the damage had been driven deeper than the skin. Ever since the day the artillery shell had landed near her by the mouth of the cave, after she had screamed once in fear and pain and collapsed, Aamina had said nothing. Not a word. Some mornings, huddled in the cave with the others, when the shells fell with especially brutal regularity, she would tremble and produce a sort of pleading whimper. But it was an animal sound, not human speech at all, and it gave Fatima no comfort.

"Life was very cruel in the caves," says Fatima's friend Nargiz Ali. "Our village, Brolmo, was a very beautiful place, with apricot and even cherry trees, on a slope by the Indus River. But we could only glance out at it and watch it being destroyed. We couldn't go there. I was a little type of girl at the time and other relatives had to carry me quickly inside whenever the shells began to fall. I couldn't leave to play outside or care for the animals, or even to pick the fruit that we watched ripening and then rotting.

"During rainy days, or, for example, snowfall, it was very difficult to cook or sleep there. But we remained for a long time, because only over the *nullah* was India, and it was too dangerous out in the open."

One day, Nargiz says, returning to the caves after searching through the rubble of his home for supplies, her uncle Hawalda Abrahim was hit by a single shell that fell without accompaniment. "He was a very loving man and we wanted to go to him right away, but we had to wait until nighttime, until we were sure no more shells would fall, to carry my uncle inside," Nargiz says. "Normally, people would wash the body after death. But he was so shattered, we couldn't wash him. We could only gather him together in a cloth."

The few men remaining in Brolmo held a *jirga* and announced afterward, to all the children like Fatima and Nargiz, that the time had come to be brave. They must venture out into the open, and walk a long way with little food, because remaining in the caves could not be considered a life.

They packed what little they could scavenge from their homes and left in the middle of the night, walking to a neighboring village that they considered sufficiently distant from the Indian artillery to be safe. That morning, for the first time in months, they took pleasure in watching the sun rise outdoors, out in the open. But while they were baking *kurba* for the journey over a fire, shells began to fall, marching toward them up the valley floor. A spotter on the ridges to the south must have seen them, Fatima believes, and was directing fire their way.

"Every time a shell exploded Aamina would shake and cry and fall to the earth," Fatima says. "In that place there were no caves, so all we could do was run. I'm ashamed to say that I was so frightened that I stopped tugging at my sister and ran to save myself. I was fearful that she would be killed, but being alone must have been more frightening to my sister than the shelling, and she ran to join the rest of the village."

For three weeks, the survivors of Brolmo trekked to the northwest. "Often, we walked on paths that animals had made, paths that were not for people at all," Fatima says. "We had to leave all our *kurba* behind in the fire when the shells started to fall, so we were very hungry. The people cut the wild plants for food and ate the small berries to stay alive, even though they made our stomachs hurt."

After surviving their odyssey, the last residents of Brolmo village arrived, exhausted and emaciated, in Skardu, where the military directed them to their new home. Here in the dunes by the airport, Fatima and the other survivors would begin the long process of learning to forget what they had endured and starting over. All except Aamina Batool. "When we reached our new village, Aamina lay down and would not get up," Fatima says. "No one could revive her and not even being safe at last with our father and uncles seemed to cheer her. She died after a few days."

Speaking about her sister's death five years later, the anguish in Fatima's face looks as raw as it must have felt that day, as she allows the memory to bob to the surface briefly, before pushing it back down.

At her desk, in the fifth-grade classroom of the Gultori Girls Refugee School, which the Central Asia Institute constructed on sand dunes by the Skardu airport in the summer of 1999, at the height of the Kargil Conflict, Fatima Batool, fifteen, lets her white shawl fall over her face, taking refuge within the fabric from too many questions.

Her classmate Nargiz Ali, now fourteen, picks up the thread of the story, and explains how she came to be sitting at this desk, under a colorful relief map of the world, caressing her own brand-new notebook, pencil, and sharpener provided by a charitable organization headquartered in a place she has tried and failed to find on that map, Bozeman, Montana.

"When we arrived after our long walk, we were, of course, very happy to see all our family," Nargiz says. "But then I looked at the place where we were supposed to live and I felt frightened and unsure. There were no houses. No trees. No mosque. No facility of any kind. Then Syed Abbas brought a large *Angrezi* to talk with us. He told us that if we were willing to work hard, he would help us build a school. And do you know, he kept his *chat-ndo,* his promise."

Fifth-grade students at the Gultori Girls Refugee School, like Fatima and Nargiz, lag behind most of their peers. Because their formal education began only after they had fled from their ancestral villages, the average age of a fifth-grade student here is fifteen. Their brothers walk an hour each way to the government boys' schools in surrounding villages that took most of the male refugee students in. But for the 129 Gultori girls who might never have seen the inside of a school, this building is the lone bright spot at the end of a long tunnel of fear and flight.

That's why, despite how much talking about her ordeal has taken from her, Fatima Batool brushes aside her shawl and sits up straight at her desk, to tell her visitors one thing more. "I've heard some people say Americans are bad," she says softly. "But we love Americans. They are the most kind people for us. They are the only ones who cared to help us."

In recent years, some of the refugees have returned to the Gultori, to the two schools the Central Asia Institute has since established there, carved into caves, so that students will be safe from the shells that can still rain down from India whenever relations between the two countries chill. But Nargiz and Fatima are staying in the new village outside Skardu. It is their home now, they say.

Beyond the sandy courtyard of their ochre-colored five-room school, neat rows of mud-block homes now march toward the horizon, some equipped, even, with that ultimate symbol of luxury and permanent residence, the satellite dish. And shading these homes, where the unrelenting dunes once stood, cherry trees, nurtured by an uplift water scheme, grow thick and green and lush, blooming out of the sand as improbably as the students who walk home after school beneath their boughs, the girls of the Gultori.

CHAPTER 18

SHROUDED FIGURE

Let nothing perturb you, nothing frighten you. All things pass.
God does not change. Patience achieves everything.

—Mother Teresa

SETTING UP THE two hundred chairs was taking longer than Mortenson had expected. At most of the potlucks, outdoor stores, churches, and colleges where he gave his slide shows, someone was on hand to help. But here at Mr. Sports, in Apple Valley, Minnesota, all the staff members were sorting inventory for an after-Christmas sale, so Mortenson worked alone.

At 6:45 P.M., with his talk due to begin in fifteen minutes, Mortenson had unfolded just over one hundred tan metal chairs, arranging them in neat rows between the racks of unfurled subzero sleeping bags and a locked case displaying valuable electronic GPS devices, altimeters, and avalanche beacons. He pushed himself to work faster, jerking the chairs open and slapping them into place with the sense of urgency he'd felt while working on the Korphe bridge.

Mortenson was soon slick with sweat. He had become increasingly self-conscious about the weight he had gained since K2, and was reluctant to remove the heavy, shapeless green sweatshirt he wore, especially in a room that would soon be packed with fit outdoor types. He smacked the last chairs into place at 7:02 and strode breathlessly along the rows, placing a Central Asia Institute newsletter on each of the two hundred seats. At the back of every photocopied pamphlet, a donation envelope was stapled into place, addressed to CAI's post office box in Bozeman.

The harvest he reaped from these envelopes made the slide shows just bearable. With the CAI's finances dipping toward insolvency,

Mortenson was now averaging one talk every week he wasn't in Pakistan. There were few things he loathed more than getting up in front of a large group of people and speaking about himself, but the difference even one bad night's take, typically a few hundred dollars, could make for the children of Pakistan kept him hauling his overnight bag to the Bozeman airport.

He inspected the old slide projector he'd recently repaired with duct tape, to make sure the correct carousel was slotted, patted his pants pocket, checking that the laser pointer he used to highlight the peaks of the Karakoram was in place, and turned to face his audience. Mortenson was alone with two hundred empty chairs.

He'd put up posters on local college campuses, pleaded for publicity with the editors of local papers, and done a brief early-morning interview for the drivetime segment of an AM radio station's morning show, and he expected a full house, so Mortenson leaned against a rack of self-inflating sleeping pads, waiting for his audience to arrive.

He smiled broadly at a woman in an orange Gore-Tex parka with long gray braids coiled on top of her head as she approached. But she ducked her eyes apologetically, inspected the temperature rating on an eggplant-colored polarfill sleeping bag, and bundled it away toward the register.

By 7:30 Mortenson was still staring at a sea of empty chairs.

Over the store's loudspeaker, an employee pleaded for the bargain hunters sifting through the sale racks to occupy some of the two hundred empty seats. "People, we have, like, a world-class climber waiting to show you gnarly slides of K2! Go on, check him out!"

Two salespeople in green vests, having completed their inventory, took seats in the last row. "What should I do?" Mortenson said. "Should I still give my talk?"

"It's about climbing K2, right?" said a young, bearded employee, whose blond dreadlocks, stuffed up into a silver wool hat, made his head look like a cooked package of Jiffy Pop Popcorn.

"Sort of," Mortenson said.

"Sweet, Dude," Jiffy Pop said. "Go for it!"

After Mortenson showed the requisite images he'd taken of K2, and detailed his failed attempt of seven summers past, he segued awkwardly into the crux of his presentation: He told stories about and showed photos of the eighteen CAI-funded schools now operating, lingering on images of the latest: two schools in the Gul-tori Valley, built flush with the entrances of caves, so that the shells still falling—now that the Kargil "Conflict" had officially ended—couldn't prevent the thousands of villagers now returning to piece together their shattered homes from sending their children to study in safety.

As images he'd taken just a month earlier, of Fatima, Nargiz, and their classmates, smiling over their textbooks in the newly built Gultori Girls Refugee School, flashed across the screen, Mortenson noticed a professorial-looking middle-aged male customer leaning around a corner, trying to unobtrusively study a display of multifunc-tion digital watches. Mortenson paused to smile at him, and the man took a seat, letting his eyes rest on the screen.

Buoyed now that his audience had grown by 50 percent, Morten-son spoke passionately for thirty minutes more, detailing the crushing poverty children in the Karakoram faced every day, and unveiling his plans to begin constructing schools the following spring at the very edge of northern Pakistan, along Afghanistan's border.

"By building relationships, and getting a community to invest its own land and labor, we can construct and maintain a school for a gen-eration that will educate thousands of children for less than twenty thousand dollars. That's about half what it would cost the government of Pakistan to build the same school, and one-fifth of what the World Bank would spend on the same project."

Mortenson wrapped up the evening by paraphrasing one of his fa-vorite quotations from Mother Teresa. "What we are trying to do may be just a drop in the ocean," Mortenson said, smiling warmly at his au-dience of three. "But the ocean would be less because of that missing drop."

Mortenson appreciated the applause, even from six hands, almost as much as he was relieved to be done speaking. As he switched off the projector and began collecting CAI pamphlets from the empty seats, the two employees bent to help him, asking questions. "Do you, like, have any kind of volunteer deals over there?" Jiffy Pop's coworker asked. " 'Cause I've worked construction and I could, like, come over there and pound in some nails."

Mortenson explained that with CAI's limited budget ("more lim-ited than ever these days," he thought), it was too expensive to send

American volunteers to Pakistan, and directed him toward a few other NGOs working in Asia that accepted volunteers.

The bearded boy with the dreadlocks fished into his front pocket and handed Mortenson a ten-dollar bill. "I was going to go out for a couple beers after work," he said, shuffling from foot to foot, "but, you know . . ."

"Thanks," Mortenson said, sincerely, shaking his hand, before folding the bill and placing it into the empty manila envelope he'd brought along to collect contributions. Mortenson picked up the last few pamphlets and crammed them into his overnight bag with the others, sighing over the extra weight he'd carried halfway across the country for ten dollars, and would now have to carry home.

On the seat of the last chair in the last row, next to the display of digital watches, Mortenson found an envelope torn from the back of a CAI newsletter. Inside was a personal check for twenty thousand dollars.

Mortenson didn't face a sea of empty seats every week. In the Pacific Northwest particularly, the outdoor community had begun to embrace him, especially after the details of his story began to trickle out to the public. In February 1999, the *Oregonian* became the first major American newspaper to tell Mortenson's story. Outdoor writer Terry Richard drew his readers' attention to the former climber's unlikely success scaling a different sort of peak from the physical kind. "It's a part of the world where Americans are mistrusted and often hated," Richard wrote, "but not Greg Mortenson, a 41-year-old resident of Montana whose life's work is to build schools in remote villages of Pakistan's mountain valleys."

Richard related Mortenson's mission to his readers, arguing that aid work half a world away was having more of an effect on their lives than most Americans realized. "A politically volatile area, rural Pakistan is a breeding ground for terrorists who share anti-American sentiment," Richard explained. "Illiterate young boys often wind up in [terrorist] camps," he quoted Mortenson as saying. "When we increase literacy, we substantially reduce tensions."

"In one of the world's most volatile regions, "[Mortenson's] work already is making a difference," Richard concluded.

The following month, *San Francisco Examiner* travel editor John

Flinn wrote a piece promoting Mortenson's upcoming lecture in the Bay Area by summarizing his remarkable life story, concluding, "It's something to think about the next time you ask: What difference can one person make?" That winter, when Mortenson gave his slide show in Portland and San Francisco, event organizers had to turn hundreds of people away from packed venues.

By the millennium, Mortenson and the CAI had become a cause to which many of America's leading mountaineers were rallying. Before his October 1999 death in a freak avalanche on Nepal's Shishapangma, Mortenson's neighbor and friend Alex Lowe, at the time perhaps the world's most respected alpinist, introduced Mortenson at a Montana fundraiser. "While most of us are trying to scale new peaks," Lowe told an audience of climbers, "Greg has quietly been moving even greater mountains on his own. What he has accomplished, with pure tenacity and determination, is incredible. His kind of climb is one we should all attempt."

Lowe's message echoed throughout the mountaineering world. "A lot of us think about helping, but Mortenson just does it," says famed climber Jack Tackle, who donated twenty thousand dollars to help CAI establish the Jafarabad girls' elementary school in the Upper Shigar Valley.

But the more beloved Mortenson became in Pakistan, and the more admiration Mortenson inspired among the mountaineering community, the more he frustrated the people who worked with him in America.

When he wasn't bouncing down dirt roads in Pakistan or hauling his bags to slide shows in his own country, Mortenson jealously guarded his time with his family in Bozeman and cloaked himself in the silence of his basement.

"Even when he was home, we often wouldn't hear from Greg for weeks," says former CAI board chairman Tom Vaughan. "And he wouldn't return phone calls or e-mails. The board had a discussion about trying to make Greg account for how he spent his time, but we realized that would never work. Greg just does whatever he wants."

"What we really needed to do was train a few Greg Juniors," says Hoerni's widow, Jennifer Wilson, "some people Greg could delegate projects to. But he refused to do that. He said we didn't have enough money to rent an office or hire staff. And then he'd just bog down in the details of one project and neglect another. That's why I decided to distance myself from CAI. He accomplished a lot. But I felt we could do so much more if Greg agreed to run CAI more responsibly."

"Let's be honest," says Tom Vaughan. "The fact is the CAI is Greg. I didn't mind rubber-stamping whatever he wanted to work on. But without Greg, the CAI is finished. The risks he takes in that part of the world I understand—that's part of the job. But I began to get angry about the terrible way he took care of himself. He stopped climbing and exercising. He stopped sleeping. He began to gain so much weight that he didn't even look like a mountaineer anymore. I understand that he decided to pour everything into his work," Vaughan says, "But if he drops dead of a heart attack what's the point?"

Reluctantly, Mortenson agreed to hire an assistant, Christine Slaughter, to work with him a few hours each day organizing his basement, which even he could see was becoming an embarrassing mess. But throughout the winter of 2000, Mortenson was too alarmed by CAI's dwindling funds—their bank balance had dipped below one hundred thousand dollars—to expand CAI's American operations any further. "I mean, I'd gotten to the point where I could put up a school that would educate a village for generations for about twelve thousand dollars," Mortenson says. "Most of our staff in Pakistan were thrilled to make four hundred or five hundred dollars a year. It was hard to imagine paying someone an American salary when that money could do so much more over there."

Mortenson was then earning an annual salary of twenty-eight thousand dollars. Coupled with Tara's meager income as a part-time clinical psychologist at Montana State, they were just managing to tread water with their monthly expenses. But with CAI under serious financial strain, Mortenson says he couldn't, in good conscience, have accepted more, even if the board had offered him a raise.

The idea of a single rich donor solving all his problems with one flourish of a pen lodged in Mortenson's mind. Wealthy people aren't easily pried apart from their fortunes. He had learned that much since the comedy of the 580 letters. But Jean Hoerni had also taught him how much difference a single large donation could make. When a potential donor in Atlanta began calling CAI's office dangling monetary bait, Mortenson bit down on the hook and booked a flight.

"I've been saving money all my life," the elderly widow explained to Mortenson on the phone. "I've accumulated a fortune with at least six zeros behind it and after I read about the work you're doing I know what I was saving it for. Come down to Atlanta so we can discuss my donation."

At the Hartsfield International Airport arrivals hall, Mortenson switched on his cell phone and retrieved a message instructing him to take a shuttle to a hotel fifteen minutes away, then walk to a remote parking lot at the edge of the hotel's grounds.

In the lot, he found seventy-eight-year-old Vera Kurtz hunched over the wheel of her elderly Ford Fairlane. The trunk and rear seat were jammed with old newspapers and tin cans, so he climbed into the passenger seat and wedged his carry-on bag between the dashboard and his chest. "She'd sent me on this goose chase so she could avoid paying a few dollars to park at the airport. And when I saw that she couldn't even bear to part with the papers and cans in her car, I should have turned around and taken a plane home, but that line about the six zeros messed up my judgment. It made me get in and close the door."

While Mortenson squeezed the handles of his bag, Vera drove the wrong way down one-way streets, shaking her fist at the drivers who honked at her in warning. In her 1950s ranch home, Mortenson side-stepped through towering rows of decades-old magazines and newspapers until he reached Vera's kitchen table, beside a plugged sink full of filmy gray water. "She unscrewed a few of those minibottles of whiskey that she'd been collecting on airplanes for years, poured us a drink, and presented me with a bouquet of roses that looked recycled," Mortenson says. "The flowers were brown and almost completely dead."

After a decent interval, Mortenson tried to steer the conversation toward Vera's donation to the CAI, but his host had her own agenda. She laid out her plans for the next three days—a visit to the High Museum of Art, a stroll through the Atlanta Botanical Garden, and three talks she had arranged for Mortenson at a local library, a community college, and a travel club. Seventy-two hours had never offered such a bleak prospect to Mortenson before. He was weighing whether to stick them out when a knock on the door announced the arrival of a masseur Vera had hired.

"You work too hard, Greg," Vera told him, as the masseur set up his folding table in a clearing at the center of her living room. "You deserve to relax."

"They both expected me to strip naked right there," Mortenson says, "but I excused myself and went into the bathroom to think. I figured I'd been through enough getting CAI up and running that I could just roll with whatever Vera did for the next three days, especially if there was the chance of a big donation at the end of the tunnel."

Mortenson fished around in her cabinet for something large enough to wrap around his waist. Most of the towels Vera had stockpiled bore the fading logos of hotels, and were too small to cover him. He pulled a graying sheet from the linen closet, tucked it as securely as he could around his waist, and shuffled out to endure his massage.

At 2:00 A.M., Mortenson was out cold, snoring on Vera's sagging mattress, when the lights flicked on, waking him. Vera had insisted on sleeping on her couch and offering Mortenson the bed. He opened his eyes to the phantasmagorical vision of the seventy-eight-year-old Vera standing over him in a transparent negligee.

"She was right there in front of me," Mortenson says. "I was too shocked to say anything."

"I'm looking for my socks," Vera said, fishing interminably through the drawers of her dresser as Mortenson pulled a pillow over his head and cringed beneath it.

Back on the airplane to Bozeman, empty-handed, Mortenson realized that his hostess had never intended to donate any money. "She didn't even ask one question about my work, or the children of Pakistan," Mortenson says. "She was just a lonely woman who wanted a visitor, and I told myself I'd better be smarter in the future."

But Mortenson continued to snap at the bait wealthy admirers of his dangled. After a well-attended speech at the Mountain Film Festival in Banff, Mortenson accepted an invitation from Tom Lang, a wealthy local contractor, who hinted at a large donation he was prepared to make, and offered to hold a CAI fundraising party at his estate the following evening.

Lang had designed his ten-thousand-square-foot home himself, down to the faux marble paint on the walls of the great room where guests mingled with glasses of the cheap wine so often served by the very wealthy, and the twelve-foot-high white plaster statues of poodles that sat vigil at both ends of his twenty-foot fireplace.

Lang displayed Mortenson to his guests with the same pride of ownership with which he pointed out his custom bathroom fixtures and the fireplace poodles. And though Mortenson placed a large stack of CAI pamphlets prominently on the buffet table, at evening's end, he hadn't raised a cent from Lang for CAI. Having learned his lesson from Vera Kurtz, Mortenson pressed his host for details about his donation. "We'll work all that out tomorrow," Lang told him. "But first you're going dogsledding."

"Dogsledding?"

"Can't come to Canada without giving it a whirl," Lang said.

In a warming hut an hour west of Banff, where they sat after Mortenson had been dragged by a team of huskies on a cursory loop through the woods by himself, Mortenson spent the better part of the following afternoon listening to the man's self-aggrandizing epic about how a plucky contractor, armed only with grit and determination, had conquered the Banff housing market.

Mortenson, whose mother, Jerene, had flown from Wisconsin to hear his speech, hardly saw her son during her three-day visit. Mortenson, unsurprisingly, returned to Montana empty-handed.

"It just makes me sick to see Greg kowtowing to all those rich people," Jerene Mortenson says. "They should be bowing down to him."

By the spring of 2000, Tara Bishop had tired of her husband's flitting across the country on fool's errands when he wasn't away in Pakistan. Seven months pregnant with their second child, she called a summit meeting with her husband at their kitchen table.

"I told Greg I love how passionate he is about his work," Tara says. "But I told him he had a duty to his family, too. He needed to get more sleep, get some exercise, and get enough time at home to have a life with us." Until then, Mortenson had left home to be in Pakistan for three or four months at a time. "We agreed to set the limit at two months," Tara says. "After two months things just get too weird around here without him."

Mortenson also promised his wife he'd learn to manage his time better. The CAI board set aside a small budget each year for Mortenson to take college courses on subjects like management, development, and Asian politics. "I never had the time to take classes," Mortenson says. "So I spent the money on books. A lot of the time, when people thought I was just sitting in my basement doing nothing, I was reading those books. I would start my day at 3:30 A.M., trying to learn more about development theory finance, and how to be a better manager."

But the lessons he'd learned in the Karakoram had taught him there were some answers you couldn't find in print. So Mortenson designed a crash course on development for himself. From his reading, he decided that the two finest rural development programs then running in the world were in the Philippines and Bangladesh. For a rare untethered month he left Pakistan and Bozeman behind and flew to Southeast Asia.

In Cavite, an hour south of Manila, Mortenson visited the Institute of Rural Reconstruction, run by John Rigby, a friend of Lila Bishop's. Rigby taught Mortenson how to set up tiny businesses for the rural poor, like bicycle taxis and cigarette stands, that could quickly turn a profit on a small investment.

In the country that had once been called East Pakistan, Mortenson visited BARRA, the Bangladesh Rural Reconstruction Association. "A lot of people call Bangladesh the armpit of Asia," Mortenson says, "because of its extreme poverty. But the girls' education initiative is hugely successful there. I knocked on doors and visited NGOs that had been in the business of educating girls for a long time. I watched as amazing, strong women held village meetings and worked to empower their daughters.

"They were following the same philosophy as I was," Mortenson says. "Nobel Prize winner Amartya Sen's idea that you can change a culture by giving its girls the tools to grow up educated so they can help themselves. It was amazing to see the idea in action, working so well after only a generation, and it fired me up to fight for girls' education in Pakistan."

On the bumpy Biman Airways flight from Dacca to Calcutta, Mortenson had his notion of the desperate need to educate rural girls confirmed. The lone foreigner on the flight, he was shepherded by stewardesses to first class, where he sat among fifteen attractive Bangladeshi girls in bright new saris. "They were young and terrified," Mortenson says. "They didn't know how to use their seatbelts or silverware and when we got to the airport, I watched helplessly as corrupt officials whisked them off the plane and around the customs guards. I couldn't do anything for them. I could only imagine the kind of horrible life of prostitution they were heading to."

From the headlines of newspapers on stands at Calcutta International Airport, Mortenson learned that one of his heroes, Mother Teresa, had died after a long illness. He had a brief layover in Calcutta before heading home and decided to try to pay her his respects.

"Hashish? Heroin? Girl massage? Boy massage?" the taxi driver said, taking Mortenson's arm inside the arrivals hall, where he wasn't supposed to have access to passengers. "What you like? Anything, no problem."

Mortenson laughed, impressed by this shady wisp of a man's determination. "Mother Teresa just died. I'd like to visit her," Mortenson said. "Can you take me there?"

"No problem," he said, waggling his head as he took Mortenson's bag.

The driver smoked furiously as they rolled along in his black and yellow Ambassador cab, leaning so far out the window that Mortenson had an unobstructed view of Calcutta's doomsday traffic through the windshield. They stopped at a flower market where Mortenson gave the driver ten dollars' worth of rupees and asked him to select an appropriate funeral arrangement. "He left me sitting there, sweating, and came back at least thirty minutes later, carrying a huge gaudy mass of carnations and roses in his arms," Mortenson says. "We could hardly squeeze it into the backseat."

At dusk, outside the Missionaries of Charity Motherhouse, hundreds of hushed mourners crowded the gates, holding candles and arranging offerings of fruit and incense on the pavement.

The driver got out and rattled the metal gate loudly. *This Sahib has come all the way from America to pay his respects!* He shouted in Bengali. *Open up!* An elderly *chokidar* guarding the entrance stood up and returned with a young nun in a blue habit who looked the dusty traveler and his explosion of flowers up and down before waving him inside. Walking distastefully ahead, she led Mortenson down a dark hallway echoing with distant prayer, and pointed him toward a bathroom.

"Why don't you washing up first?" she said in Slavic-accented English.

She lay on a simple cot, at the center of a bright room full of flickering devotional candles. Mortenson gently nudged other bouquets aside, making room for his gaudy offering, and took a seat against a wall. The nun, backing out the door, left him alone with Mother Teresa.

"I sat in the corner with no idea what to do," Mortenson says. "Since I was a little boy she'd been one of my heroes."

An ethnic Albanian born to a successful contractor in Kosovo, Mother Teresa began her life as Agnes Gonxha Bojaxhiu. From the age of twelve, she said, she felt a calling to work with the poor, and began training for missionary work. As a teenager she joined the Sisters of Our Lady of Loreto, an Irish order of nuns, because of their commitment to provide education for girls. For two decades, she taught at St. Mary's High School in Calcutta, eventually becoming its principal. But in 1946, she said, she received a calling from God instructing her to serve the "poorest of the poor." In 1948, after receiving the special dispensation of Pope Pius XII to work independently, she founded an open-air school for Calcutta's homeless children.

In 1950, the woman by then known as Mother Teresa received permission from the Vatican to found her own order, the Missionaries of Charity, whose duty, she said, was to care for "the hungry, the naked, the homeless, the crippled, the blind, the lepers, all those people who feel unwanted, unloved, uncared for throughout society, people that have become a burden to the society and are shunned by everyone."

Mortenson, with his affection for society's underdogs, admired her determination to serve the world's most neglected populations. As a boy in Moshi, he'd learned about one of her first projects outside India, a hospice for the dying in Dar es Salaam, Tanzania. By the time she was awarded the Nobel Peace Prize in 1979, Mother Teresa's celebrity had become the engine that powered Missionaries of Charity orphanages, hospices, and schools around the world.

Mortenson had heard the criticism of the woman who lay on a cot before him ratchet up in the years before her death. He'd read her defense of her practice of taking donations from unsavory sources, like drug dealers, corporate criminals, and corrupt politicians hoping to purchase their own path to salvation. After his own struggle to raise funds for the children of Pakistan, he felt he understood what had driven her to famously dismiss her critics by saying, "I don't care where the money comes from. It's all washed clean in the service of God."

"I sat in the corner staring at this shrouded figure," Mortenson says. "She looked so small, draped in her cloth. And I remember thinking how amazing it was that such a tiny person had such a huge effect on humanity."

Nuns, visiting the room to pay their respects, had knelt to touch Mother Teresa's feet. He could see where the cream-colored muslin had been discolored from the laying on of hundreds of hands. But it didn't feel right to touch her feet. Mortenson knelt on the cool tiled floor next to Mother Teresa and placed his large palm over her small hand. It covered it completely.

The nun who'd showed him in returned, and found him kneeling. She nodded once, as if to say, "Ready?" And Mortenson followed her quiet footfalls down the dark hallway and out into the heat and clamor of Calcutta.

His taxi driver was squatting on his heels, smoking, and jumped up when he saw his payday approaching. "Success? Success?" he asked, leading the distracted American through a street thick with rickshaws and back to the waiting Ambassador. "Now," he said "you like some massage?"

Safely back in his basement, during the winter of 2000, Mortenson often reflected on those few rare moments with Mother Teresa. He marveled at how she lived her life without long trips home, away from misery and suffering, so she could rest up and prepare to resume the fight. That winter, Mortenson felt bone-tired. The shoulder he'd injured falling on Mount Sill, the day Christa had died, had never fully healed. Fruitlessly, he tried yoga and acupuncture. Sometimes it throbbed so unignorably that he popped fifteen or twenty Advil a day, trying to dull the pain enough to concentrate on his work.

Mortenson tried just as unsuccessfully to get comfortable with the process of becoming a public figure in America. But the endless ranks of people wanting to squeeze something from him sent him scurrying to his basement where he'd ignore the endlessly ringing phone and e-mails that piled up by the hundreds.

Climbers contacted him, wanting help arranging expeditions to Pakistan, miffed when a former climber wouldn't drop whatever he was doing to help them. Journalists and filmmakers called constantly, hoping to tag along with Mortenson on his next trip, wanting to exploit the contacts he'd made over the previous seven years to win access to restricted regions before their competitors could. Physicians, glaciologists, seismologists, ethnologists, and wildlife biologists wrote lengthy letters, unintelligible to laymen, wanting detailed answers to academic questions they had about Pakistan.

Tara recommended a fellow therapist in Bozeman whom Mortenson began talking to regularly when he was home, trying to mine the root causes of his desire to hide when he wasn't in Pakistan, and strategizing about ways to cope with the increasing anger of those who wanted more time than he was able to give.

His mother-in-law Lila Bishop's house became another of Mortenson's havens, especially its basement, where he would spend hours poring over Barry Bishop's mountaineering library, reading about the Balti migration out of Tibet, or studying a rare bound volume of the exquisite black-and-white plates of K2 and its accompanying peaks that Vittorio Sella shot on his large-format camera with the duke of Abruzzi's 1909 expedition.

Eventually, as his family gathered for dinner upstairs, Mortenson would permit himself to be coaxed away from his books. Lila Bishop, by then, shared her daughter's opinion of Mortenson. "I had to admit Tara was right, there was something to this 'Mr. Wonderful' stuff," Lila says. And like her daughter, she had come to the conclusion that the large, gentle man living two blocks away was cut from unusual cloth. "One snowy night we were barbecuing, and I asked Greg to go out and turn the salmon," Lila says. "I looked out the patio door a moment later and saw Greg, standing barefoot in the snow, scooping up the fish with a shovel, and flipping it, like that was the most normal thing in the world. And I guess, to him, it was. That's when I realized that he's just not one of us. He's his own species."

The rest of that winter, in his own basement, Mortenson obsessed about reports he was receiving detailing a calamity developing in northern Afghanistan. More than ten thousand Afghans, mostly women and children, had fled north ahead of advancing Taliban troops until they'd run out of real estate at the Tajik border. On islands in the middle of the Amu Darya River, these refugees scooped out mud huts and were slowly starving, eating grasses that grew by the riverbank out of desperation.

While they sickened and died, Taliban soldiers shot at them for sport, firing their rocket-propelled grenades up in great arcs until they'd come crashing down among the terrified refugees. When they tried to flee to Tajikistan, paddling logs across the river, they were shot by Russian troops guarding the border, determined not to let Afghanistan's growing chaos spill over into their backyard.

"Since I started working in Pakistan, I haven't slept much," Mortenson says. "But that winter I hardly slept at all. I was up all night, pacing my basement, trying to find some way to help them."

Mortenson fired off letters to newspaper editors and members of Congress, trying to stir up outrage. "But no one cared," Mortenson says. "The White House, Congress, the UN were all silent. I even started fantasizing about picking up an AK-47, getting Faisal Baig to round up some men, and crossing over to Afghanistan to fight for the refugees myself.

"Bottom line is I failed. I couldn't make anyone care. And Tara will tell you I was a nightmare. All I could think about was all those freezing children who'd never have the chance to grow up, helpless out there between groups of men with guns, dying from the dysentery they'd get from drinking river water or starving to death. I was actually going a bit crazy. It's amazing that Tara put up with me that winter.

"In times of war, you often hear leaders—Christian, Jewish, and Muslim—saying, 'God is on our side.' But that isn't true. In war, God is on the side of refugees, widows, and orphans."

It wasn't until July 24, 2000, that Mortenson felt his spirits lift. That day, he knelt in his kitchen and scooped up handfuls of warm water to dribble down his wife's bare back. He laid his hands on Tara's shoulders, kneading the taut muscles, but her mind was miles from his touch. She was concentrating on the hard labor ahead of her. Their new midwife, Vicky Cain, had suggested that Tara try an underwater birth for their second child. Their bathtub was too small so the midwife brought them a huge light-blue plastic horse trough she used, wedged it between their sink and kitchen table, and filled it with warm water.

They named their son Khyber Bishop Mortenson. Three years earlier, before the Korphe School inauguration, Mortenson had taken his wife and one-year-old daughter to see the Khyber Pass. Their Christmas card that year featured a photo of Greg and Tara at the Afghan border, in tribal dress, holding Amira and two AK-47s frontier guards had handed them as a joke. Beneath the photo, the card read "Peace on Earth."

Two hours after his son floated into the world out of his horse trough, Mortenson felt fully happy for the first time in months. Just the feeling of his hand on his son's head seemed to pour a current of contentment into him. Mortenson wrapped his brand-new boy in a fuzzy blanket and brought Khyber to his daughter's preschool class so Amira could dazzle her classmates at show-and-tell.

Amira, already a more comfortable public speaker than her father would ever be, revealed to her classmates the miracle of her brother's tiny fingers and toes while her father held him bundled in his big hands like a football.

"He's so small and wrinkly," a blonde four-year-old with pigtails said. "Do little babies like that grow up to be big like us?"

"*Inshallah,*" Mortenson said.

"Huh?"

"I hope so, sweetie," Mortenson said. "I sure hope so."

CHAPTER 19

A VILLAGE CALLED NEW YORK

The time of arithmetic and poetry is past. Nowadays, my brothers,
take your lessons from the Kalashnikov and rocket-propelled grenade.

—Graffiti spray-painted on the courtyard wall of the Korphe School

"WHAT IS THAT?" Mortenson said. "What are we looking at?"

"A *madrassa*, Greg Sahib," Apo said.

Mortenson asked Hussain to stop the Land Cruiser so he could
see the new building better. He climbed out of the jeep and stretched
his back against the hood while Hussain idled behind the wheel, flicking cigarette ash carelessly between his feet, onto the wooden box of
dynamite.

Mortenson appreciated his driver's steady, methodical style of
navigating Pakistan's worst roads and was loath to criticize him. In all
their thousands of miles of mountain driving the man had never had
an accident. But it wouldn't do to go out with a bang. Mortenson
promised himself to wrap the dynamite in a plastic tarp when they got
back to Skardu.

Mortenson straightened up with a grunt and studied the new
structure dominating the west side of the Shigar Valley, in the town of
Gulapor. It was a compound, two hundred yards long, hidden from
passersby behind twenty-foot walls. It looked like something he'd expect to find in Waziristan, but not a few hours from Skardu. "You're
sure it's not an army base?" Mortenson said.

"This is the new place," Apo said. "A *Wahhabi madrassa*."

"Why do they need so much space?"

"*Wahhabi madrassa* is like a . . ." Apo trailed, off, searching for
the English word. He settled for producing a buzzing sound.

"Bee?" Mortenson asked.

"Yes, like the bee house. *Wahhabi madrassa* have many students hidden inside."

Mortenson climbed back in, behind the box of dynamite.

Eighty kilometers east of Skardu, Mortenson noticed two neat white minarets piercing the greenery on the outskirts of a poor village called Yugo. "Where do these people have the money for a new mosque like this?" Mortenson asked.

"This also *Wahhabi*," Apo said. "The sheikhs come from Kuwait and Saudi with suitcases of rupees. They take the best student back to them. When the boy come back to Baltistan he have to take four wives."

Twenty minutes down the road, Mortenson saw the spitting image of Yugu's new mosque presiding over the impoverished village of Xurd.

"*Wahhabi?*" Mortenson asked, with a gathering sense of dread.

"Yes, Greg," Apo said, acknowledging the obvious thickly through his mouthful of Copenhagen, "they're everywhere."

"I'd known that the Saudi *Wahhabi* sect was building mosques along the Afghan border for years," Mortenson says. "But that spring, the spring of 2001, I was amazed by all their new construction right here in the heart of Shiite Baltistan. For the first time I understood the scale of what they were trying to do and it scared me."

Wahhabism is a conservative, fundamentalist offshoot of Sunni Islam and the official state religion of Saudi Arabia's rulers. Many Saudi followers of the sect consider the term offensive and prefer to call themselves *al-Muwahhiddun*, "the monotheists." In Pakistan, and other impoverished countries most affected by *Wahhabi* proselytizing, though, the name has stuck.

"*Wahhabi*" is derived from the term *Al-Wahhab*, which means, literally, "generous giver" in Arabic, one of Allah's many pseudonyms. And it is this generous giving—the seemingly unlimited supply of cash that *Wahhabi* operatives smuggle into Pakistan, both in suitcases and through the untraceable *hawala* money-transfer system—that has shaped their image among Pakistan's population. The bulk of that oil wealth pouring in from the Gulf is aimed at Pakistan's most virulent incubator of religious extremism—*Wahhabi madrassas*.

Exact numbers are impossible to pin down in such a secretive endeavor, but one of the rare reports to appear in the heavily censored Saudi press hints at the massive change shrewdly invested petroleum profits are having on Pakistan's most impoverished students.

In December 2000, the Saudi publication *Ain-Al-Yaqeen* reported that one of the four major *Wahhabi* proselytizing organizations, the Al Haramain Foundation, had built "1,100 mosques, schools, and Islamic centers," in Pakistan and other Muslim countries, and employed three thousand paid proselytizers in the previous year.

The most active of the four groups, *Ain-Al-Yaqeen* reported, the International Islamic Relief Organization, which the 9/11 Commission would later accuse of directly supporting the Taliban and Al Qaeda, completed the construction of thirty-eight hundred mosques, spent $45 million on "Islamic Education," and employed six thousand teachers, many of them in Pakistan, throughout the same period.

"In 2001, CAI operations were scattered all the way across northern Pakistan, from the schools we were building along the Line of Control to the east to several new initiatives we were working on all the way west along the Afghan border," Mortenson says. "But our resources were peanuts compared to the *Wahhabi*. Every time I visited to check on one of our projects, it seemed ten *Wahhabi madrassas* had popped up nearby overnight."

Pakistan's dysfunctional educational system made advancing *Wahhabi* doctrine a simple matter of economics. A tiny percentage of the country's wealthy children attended elite private schools, a legacy of the British colonial system. But as Mortenson had learned, vast swaths of the country were barely served by Pakistan's struggling, inadequately funded public schools. The *madrassa* system targeted the impoverished students the public system failed. By offering free room and board and building schools in areas where none existed, *madrassas* provided millions of Pakistan's parents with their only opportunity to educate their children. "I don't want to give the impression that all *Wahhabi* are bad," Mortenson says. "Many of their schools and mosques are doing good work to help Pakistan's poor. But some of them seem to exist only to teach militant *jihad.*"

By 2001, a World Bank study estimated that at least twenty thousand *madrassas* were teaching as many as 2 million of Pakistan's students an Islamic-based curriculum. Lahore-based journalist Ahmed Rashid, perhaps the world's leading authority on the link between *madrassa* education and the rise of extremist Islam, estimates that more than eighty thousand of these young *madrassa* students became Taliban recruits. Not every *madrassa* was a hotbed of extremism. But the World Bank concluded that 15 to 20 percent of *madrassa* students were receiving military training, along with a curriculum that emphasized *jihad* and hatred of the West at the expense of subjects of like math, science, and literature.

Rashid recounts his experience among the *Wahhabi madrassas* of Peshawar in his bestselling book *Taliban*. The students spent their days studying "the Koran, the sayings of the Prophet Mohammed and the basics of Islamic law as interpreted by their barely literate teachers," he writes. "Neither teachers nor students had any formal grounding in maths, science, history or geography."

These *madrassa* students were "the rootless and restless, the jobless and the economically deprived with little self knowledge," Rashid concludes. "They admired war because it was the only occupation they could possibly adapt to. Their simple belief in a messianic, puritan Islam which had been drummed into them by simple village mullahs was the only prop they could hold on to and which gave their lives some meaning.

"The work Mortenson is doing building schools is giving thousands of students what they need most—a balanced education and the tools to pull themselves out of poverty," Rashid says. "But we need many more like them. His schools are just a drop in the bucket when you look at the scale of the problem in Pakistan. Essentially, the state is failing its students on a massive scale and making them far too easy for the extremists who run many of the *madrassas* to recruit."

The most famous of these *madrassas,* the three-thousand-student *Darul Uloom Haqqania,* in Attock City, near Peshawar, came to be nicknamed the "University of *Jihad*" because its graduates included the Taliban's supreme ruler, the secretive one-eyed cleric Mullah Omar, and much of his top leadership.

"Thinking about the *Wahhabi* strategy made my head spin," Mortenson says. "This wasn't just a few Arab sheikhs getting off Gulf Air flights with bags of cash. They were bringing the brightest *madrassa* students back to Saudi Arabia and Kuwait for a decade of indoctrination, then encouraging them to take four wives when they came home and breed like rabbits.

"Apo calling *Wahhabi madrassas* beehives is exactly right. They're churning out generation after generation of brainwashed students and thinking twenty, forty, even sixty years ahead to a time when their armies of extremism will have the numbers to swarm over Pakistan and the rest of the Islamic world."

By early September 2001, the stark red minaret of a recently completed *Wahhabi* mosque and *madrassa* compound had risen behind high stone walls in the center of Skardu itself, like an exclamation point to the growing anxiety Mortenson had felt all summer.

On the ninth of September, Mortenson rode in the back of his green Land Cruiser, heading for the Charpurson Valley, at the very tip of northern Pakistan. From the front passenger seat, George McCown admired the majesty of the Hunza Valley. "We'd come over the Khunjerab pass from China," he says. "And it was about the most beautiful trip on Earth, with wild camel herds roaming around pristine wilderness before you head down between Pakistan's incredible peaks."

They were driving toward Zuudkhan, to inaugurate three CAI-funded projects that had just been completed—a water project, a small hydropower plant, and a health dispensary—in the ancestral home of Mortenson's bodyguard Faisal Baig. McCown, who had personally donated eight thousand dollars toward the projects, was accompanying Mortenson, to see what changes his money had wrought. Behind them, McCown's son Dan and daughter-in-law Susan rode in a second jeep.

They stopped for the night at Sost, a former Silk Road caravansary reincarnated as a truck stop for Bedfords plying the road to China. Mortenson cracked open the brand-new satellite phone he'd purchased for the trip and called his friend Brigadier General Bashir in Islamabad, to confirm that a helicopter would be available two days later to pick them up in Zuudkhan.

Much had changed over Mortenson's last year in Pakistan. He now wore a photographer's vest over his simple *shalwar kamiz*, with pockets enough to accommodate the detritus that swirled nowadays around the frenzied director of the Central Asia Institute. There were different pockets for the dollars waiting to be changed, for the stacks of small rupee notes that fueled daily transactions, pockets into which he could tuck the letters he was handed, pleading for new projects, and pockets for the receipts the projects already underway were generating, receipts that had to be conveyed to finicky American accountants. In the vest's voluminous pockets were both a film and a digital camera, means of documenting his work for the donors he had to court whenever he returned home.

Pakistan had changed, too. The blow to the nation's pride caused by the rout of Pakistan's forces during the Kargil Conflict had driven the democratically elected prime minister Nawaz Sharif from office. And in the bloodless military coup that ousted him, General Pervez Musharraf had been installed in his place. Pakistan now operated under martial law. And Musharraf had taken office pledging to beat back the forces of Islamic extremism he blamed for the country's recent decline.

Mortenson had yet to understand Musharraf's motives. But he was grateful for the support the new military government offered the CAI. "Musharraf gained respect right away by cracking down on corruption," he explains. "For the first time since I'd been in Pakistan, I began to meet military auditors in remote mountain villages who were there to ascertain if schools and clinics that the government had paid for actually existed. And for the first time ever, villagers in the Braldu told me a few funds had trickled to them all the way from Islamabad. That spoke more to me than the neglect and the empty rhetoric of the Sharif and Bhutto governments."

As the scope of his operations spread across all of northern Pakistan, military pilots offered their services to the dogged American whose work they admired, ferrying him in hours from Skardu to villages that would have taken days to reach in his Land Cruiser.

Brigadier General Bashir Baz, a close confidant of Musharraf's, had pioneered helicopter sling drops of men and material on the Siachen Glacier's ridgetop fighting posts, the world's highest battleground. After helping to turn back India's troops, he retired from active duty to run a private army-sponsored air charter service called Askari Aviation. When he had time and aircraft free, he and his men volunteered to fly Mortenson to the more remote corners of his country. "I've met a lot of people in my life, but no one like Greg Mortenson," Bashir says. "Taking into account how hard he works for the children of my country, offering him a flight now and then is the least I can do."

Mortenson dialed, and aimed the antenna of the sat phone south until he heard Bashir's cultivated voice arrive strained through static. The news from the country whose peaks he could see over the ridges to the west was shocking. "Say again!" Mortenson shouted. "Massoud is dead?"

Bashir had just received an unconfirmed report from Pakistani intelligence sources that Ahmed Shah Massoud had been murdered by Al Qaeda assassins posing as journalists. The helicopter pickup, Bashir added, was still on schedule.

"If the news is true," Mortenson thought, "Afghanistan will explode."

The information turned out to be accurate. Massoud, the charismatic leader of the Northern Alliance, the ragtag group of former *mujahadeen* whose military skill had kept the Taliban from taking northernmost Afghanistan, had been killed on September 9 by two Al Qaeda–trained Algerians claiming to be Belgian documentary filmmakers of Moroccan descent. After tracing serial numbers, French Intelligence would later reveal that they had stolen the video camera of photojournalist Jean-Pierre Vincendet the previous winter, while he was working on a puff piece about department store Christmas window displays in Grenoble.

The suicide assassins packed the camera with explosives and detonated it during an interview with Massoud at his base in Khvajeh Ba Odin, an hour by helicopter to the west of Sost, where Mortenson had just spent the night. Massoud died fifteen minutes later, in his Land Cruiser, as his men were rushing him toward a helicopter primed to fly him to a hospital in Dushanbe, Tajikistan. But they cloaked the news from the world for as long as possible, fearing his death would embolden the Taliban to launch a new offensive against the last free enclave in the country.

Ahmed Shah Massoud was known as the Lion of the Panjshir, for the ferocious way he had defended his country from Soviet invaders, repelling superior forces from his ancestral Panjshir Valley nine times with brilliant guerilla warfare tactics. Beloved by his supporters, and despised by those who lived through his brutal siege of Kabul, he was his country's Che Guevara. Though beneath his brown woolen cap, his scruffily bearded, haggardly handsome face more closely resembled Bob Marley.

And for Osama Bin Laden and his apocalyptic emissaries, the nineteen mostly Saudi men about to board American airliners carrying box-cutters, Massoud's death meant that the one leader most capable of uniting northern Afghanistan's warlords around the American military aid sure to pour in was toppled, like the towers about to fall half a world away.

The next morning, the tenth, Mortenson's convoy climbed the Charpurson Valley in high-altitude air that brought the rust-red ranges of Afghanistan's Hindu Kush into acute focus. Traveling only twenty kilometers an hour, they coaxed their jeeps up the rough dirt track, between shattered glaciers that hung like half-chewed meals from the flanks of shark-toothed twenty-thousand-foot peaks.

Zuudkhan, the last settlement in Pakistan, appeared at the end of the valley. Its dun-colored mud-block homes so closely matched the dusty valley floor that they barely noticed the village until they were within it. On Zuudkhan's polo field, Mortenson saw his bodyguard Faisal Baig standing proudly among a mass of his people, waiting to greet his guests. Here at home, he wore traditional Wakhi tribal dress, a rough-hewn brown woolen vest, a floppy white wool *skiihd* on his head, and knee-high riding boots. Towering over the crowd gathered to greet the Americans, he stood straight behind the dark aviator glasses McCown had sent him as a gift.

George McCown is a big man. But Baig lifted him effortlessly off the ground and crushed him in an embrace. "Faisal is a true gem," McCown says. "We'd stayed in touch ever since our trip to K2, when he got me and my bum knee down the Baltoro and practically saved the life of my daughter Amy, who he carried most of the way down after she got sick. There in his home village he was so proud to show us around. He organized a royal welcome."

A band of musicians blowing horns and banging drums accompanied the visitors' progress down a long, curling reception line of Zuudkhan's three hundred residents. Mortenson, who'd been to the village half a dozen times to prod along the projects, and had shared dozens of cups of tea in the process, was welcomed as family. Zuudkhan's men embraced him somewhat less bone-shatteringly than Faisal Baig. The women, in the flamboyantly colored *shalwar kamiz* and shawls common among the Wakhi, performed the *dast ba* greeting, laying their palms tenderly on Mortenson's cheek and kissing the back of their own hands as local custom dictated.

With Baig leading the way, Mortenson and McCown inspected the newly laid pipes carrying water down a steep culvert from a mountain stream to the north of the valley, and ceremonially switched on the small generator the water turned, enough to break the monotony of darkness a few hours each evening for the few dozen homes in Zuudkhan where newly wired light fixtures dangled from the ceiling.

Mortenson lingered at the new dispensary, where Zuudkhan village's first health care worker had just returned from the six months of training 150 kilometers downside at the Gulmit Medical Clinic CAI had arranged for her. Aziza Hussain, twenty-eight, beamed as she displayed the medical supplies in the room CAI funds had paid to have added on to her home. Balancing her infant son on her lap, while her five-year-old daughter clung to her neck, she proudly pointed out the cases containing antibiotics, cough syrup, and rehydration salts that CAI donations had bought.

With the nearest medical facility two days' drive down often impassible jeep tracks, illness in Zuudkhan could quickly turn to crisis. In the year before Aziza took charge of her village's health, three women had died during the delivery of their children. "Also, many people died from the diarrhea," Aziza says. "After I got training and Dr. Greg provided the medicines, we were able to control these things.

"After five years, with good water from the new pipes, and teaching the people how to clean their children, and use clean food, not a single person has died here from these problems. It's my great interest to continue to develop myself in this field," Aziza says. "And pass on my training to other women. Now that we have made such progress, not a single person in this area believes women should not be educated."

"Your money buys a lot in the hands of Greg Mortenson," McCown says. "I come from a world where corporations throw millions of dollars at problems and often nothing happens. For the price of a cheap car, he was able to turn all these people's lives around."

The next day, September 11, 2001, the entire village gathered at a stage set up at the edge of the polo ground. Under a banner that read "Welcome the Honourable Guest," Mortenson and McCown were seated while the mustachioed village elders, known as *puhps*, wearing long white wool robes embroidered with pink flowers, performed the whirling Wakhi dance of welcome. Mortenson, grinning, got up to join them, and, dancing with surprising grace despite his bulk, he had the entire village howling in appreciation.

Zuudkhan, under the progressive leadership of Faisal Baig, and the eight other elders who formed the *tanzeem*, or village council, had established their own school a decade earlier. And that afternoon, Zuudkhan's best students flaunted their facility with English as the endless speechmaking that attended the inauguration of all CAI projects wore on through the warm afternoon. "Thank you for spending your precious time in the far-flung region of northern Pakistan," one teenaged boy enunciated shyly into an amplified microphone attached to a tractor battery.

His handsome classmate tried to outdo him with his prepared remarks. "This was an isolate and cut-off area," he said, gripping the microphone with pop-star swagger. "We were lonely here in the Zuudkhan. But Dr. Greg and Mr. George wanted to improving our village. For the benefit of the poor and needy of this world like this Zuudkhan people, we tell our benefactors thank you. We are very, very graceful."

The festivities concluded with a polo match, staged, ostensibly, for the entertainment of the visiting dignitaries. The short, muscular mountain ponies had been gathered from eight villages down the isolated valley, and the Wakhi played a brand of polo as rugged as the lives they lead. As the bareback riders galloped up and down the clearing, pursuing the goat skull that served as a ball, they swiped at each other with their mallets and slammed their horses into each other like drivers at a demolition derby. Villagers howled and cheered lustily every time the players thundered past. Only when the last light had drained over the ridge into Afghanistan did the riders dismount and the crowd disperse.

Faisal Baig, tolerant of other cultures' traditions, had acquired a bottle of Chinese vodka, which he offered the guests he housed in his bunkerlike home, but he and Mortenson abstained from drinking. The talk with village elders visiting before bed was of Massoud's murder, and what it would mean for Baig's people. If the remainder of Afghanistan—just thirty kilometers distant over the Irshad Pass—fell to a Taliban assault, their lives would be transformed. The border would be sealed, their traditional trade routes would be blocked, and they would be cut off from the rest of their tribe, which roamed freely across the high passes and valleys of both nations.

The fall before, when Mortenson had visited Zuudkhan to deliver pipe for the water project, he'd had a taste of Afghanistan's proximity.

With Baig, Mortenson had stood on a meadow high above Zuudkhan, watching a dust cloud descend from the Irshad Pass. The horsemen had spotted Mortenson and rode straight for him like a pack of rampaging bandits. There were a dozen of them coming fast, with bandoliers bulging across their chests, matted beards, and homemade riding boots that rose above their knees.

"They jumped off their horses and came right at me," Mortenson says. "They were the wildest-looking men I'd ever seen. My detention in Waziristan flashed into my mind and I thought, 'Uh-oh! Here we go again.'"

The leader, a hard man with a hunting rifle slung over his shoulder, strode toward Mortenson, and Baig stepped into his path, willing to lay down his life. But a moment later the two men were embracing and speaking excitedly.

"My friend," Baig told Mortenson. "He looks for you many times."

Mortenson learned the men were Kirghiz nomads from the Wakhan, the thin projection at Afghanistan's remote northeast, which lays its brotherly arm over Pakistan's Charpurson Valley, where many of the Kirghiz families also roam. Adrift in this wild corridor, between Pakistan and Tajikistan, and hemmed into the corner of their country by the Taliban, they received neither foreign aid nor help from their own government. They had ridden for six days to reach him after hearing that Mortenson was due in the Charpurson.

The village chief stepped close to Mortenson. "For me hard life is no problem," he said through Baig. "But for children no good. We have not much food, not much house, and no school. We know about Dr. Greg build school in Pakistan so you can come build for us? We give land, stone, men, everything. Come now and stay with us for the winter so we can have good discuss and make a school?"

Mortenson thought of this man's neighbors to the west, the ten thousand refugees stranded on islands of the Amu Darya River that he'd failed. Even though Afghanistan at war was hardly the place to launch a new development initiative, he swore to himself he'd find some way to help these Afghans.

Tortuously, through Baig, Mortenson explained his wife was expecting him home in a few days, and that all CAI projects had to be approved by the board. But he laid his own hand on the man's shoulder, squeezing the grime-blackened sheep's-wool vest he wore. "Tell him I need go home now. Tell him working in Afghanistan is very difficult for me," he told Baig. "But I promise I come visit his family as soon as I can. Then we discuss if building some school is possible."

The Kirghiz listened carefully to Baig, frowning with concentration before his weathered face cracked open in a smile. He placed his muscular hand on Mortenson's shoulder, sealing the promise, before mounting his horse and leading his men on the long trip home over the Hindu Kush to report to his warlord, Abdul Rashid Khan.

Mortenson, in Baig's house a year later, lay back on the comfortable *charpoy* his host had built for his guests, even though Baig and his family slept on the floor. Dan and Susan slept soundly, while McCown snored from his bed by the window. Mortenson, half awake, had lost the thread of the village elders' conversation. Sleepily, he meditated on his promise to the Kirghiz horsemen and wondered whether Massoud's murder would make it impossible to keep.

Baig blew out the lanterns long after midnight, insisting that in the small hours, faced with the unknowable affairs of men, there was only one proper course of action: Ask for the protection of all-merciful Allah, then sleep.

In the dark, as Mortenson drifted toward the end of his long day, the last sound he heard was Baig, whispering quietly out of respect for his guests, praying urgently to Allah for peace.

At 4:30 that morning, Mortenson was shaken awake. Faisal Baig held a cheap plastic Russian shortwave radio pressed against his ear. And in the green underwater light cast by the dial, Mortenson saw an expression on his bodyguard's handsome face he had never witnessed there before—fear.

"Dr. Sahib! Dr. Sahib! Big problem," Baig said. "Up! Up!"

The army training that had never completely abandoned him made Mortenson swing his feet onto the floor even though he'd only snatched two hours of sleep. "*As-Salaam Alaaikum,* Faisal," Mortenson said, trying to rub the sleep out of his eyes. "*Baaf Ateya,* how are you?"

Baig, usually courteous, clenched his jaw without answering. "*Uzum Mofsar,*" he said after a long moment of locking eyes with Mortenson. "I'm sorry."

"Why?" Mortenson asked. He saw warily that his bodyguard,

whose bulk had always been enough to ward off any conceivable danger, had an AK-47 in his hands.

"A village called New York has been bombed."

Mortenson pulled a yak-hair blanket over his shoulders, slipped on his frozen sandals, and stepped outside. Around the house, in the bitter cold before first light, he saw that Baig had posted a guard around his American guests. Faisal's brother Alam Jan, a dashing blond-haired, blue-eyed high-altitude porter, held a Kalashnikov, covering the home's single window. Haidar, the village mullah, stood scanning the darkness toward Afghanistan. And Sarfraz, a lean, lanky former Pakistan army commando, watched the main road for any approaching vehicles while he fiddled with the dial of his own shortwave.

Mortenson learned that Sarfraz had heard a broadcast in Uighur, one of the half dozen languages he spoke, on a Chinese channel saying two great towers had fallen. He didn't understand what that meant, but knew that terrorists had killed many, many Americans. Now he was trying to find more news but, no matter how he spun the dial, the radio picked up only melancholy Uighur music from a station across the Chinese border in Kashgar.

Mortenson called for the satellite phone he'd bought specially for this trip, and Sarfraz, the most technically adept among them, rode off on his horse to retrieve it from his home, where he'd been learning to use it.

Faisal Baig needed no more information. With his AK-47 in one hand and the other balled into a fist by his side, he stared at the first blood-hued light brushing the tips of Afghanistan's peaks. For years he'd seen it coming, the storm building. It would take months and millions of dollars poured into the flailing serpentine arms of the U.S. Intelligence apparatus to untangle for certain what this illiterate man who lived in the last village at the end of a dirt road, without an Internet connection or even a phone, knew instinctively.

"Your problem in New York village comes from there," he said, snarling at the border. "From this Al Qaeda *shetan*," he said, spitting toward Afghanistan, "Osama."

The huge Russian-made MI-17 helicopter arrived at exactly 8:00 A.M., as Brigadier General Bashir had promised Mortenson it would. Bashir's top lieutenant, Colonel Ilyas Mirza, jumped down before the rotor stopped and snapped the Americans a salute. "Dr. Greg, Mr. George, sir, reporting for duty," he said, as army commandos leaped out of the MI-17 to form a perimeter around the Americans.

Ilyas was tall and dashing in the way Hollywood imagines its heroes. His black hair silvered precisely at the temples of his chiseled face. Otherwise he looked much like he had as a young man, when he served as one of his country's finest combat pilots. Ilyas was also a Wazir, from Bannu, the settlement Mortenson had passed through just before his kidnapping, and the colonel's knowledge of how Mortenson had been treated by his tribe at first made him determined to see that no further harm befell his American friend.

Faisal Baig raised his hands to Allah and performed a *dua,* thanking him for sending the army to protect the Americans. Packing no bag, with no idea where he was headed, he climbed into the helicopter with McCown's family and Mortenson, just to be sure their cordon of security was unbreachable.

From the air, they called America on Mortenson's phone, trying to keep calls short because of its forty-minute battery life. From Tara and McCown's wife, Karen, they learned the details of the terror attacks.

Jamming the receiver's headphone attachment deeper into his ear, Mortenson squinted at the cut-and-pasted vistas of peaks he could make out through the MI-17's small portholes, trying to keep the phone's antenna oriented toward the south, where satellites reflecting his wife's voice circled.

Tara was so relieved to hear from her husband she burst into tears, telling him how much she loved him through the maddening static and delay. "I know you're with your second family and they'll keep you safe," she shouted. "Finish you work and then come home to me, my love."

McCown, who'd served in the U.S. Air Force Strategic Command, refueling B52s carrying nuclear payloads in midair, had an unusually vivid sense of the fate awaiting Afghanistan. "I know Rumsfeld and Rice and Powell all personally, so I knew we were about to go to war," McCown says. "And I figured if that Al Qaeda bunch was behind it we were going to start bombing what was left of Afghanistan into oblivion any minute.

"If that happened, I didn't know which way Musharraf would go. Even if he jumped in the direction of the U.S., I didn't know if the

Pakistani military would jump with him, because they had supported the Taliban. I realized we could end up hostages and I was anxious to get the hell out of Dodge."

The flight engineer apologized that there weren't enough headsets to go around and offered Mortenson a pair of yellow plastic ear protectors. He put them on and pressed his face to a porthole, enjoying the way the silence seemed to amplify the view. Below them, the steeply terraced hillsides of the Hunza Valley rose like a crazy quilt patched together of all known shades of green, draped over the gray elephantine flanks of stony mountainsides.

From the air, the problems of Pakistan appeared simple. There were the hanging green glaciers of Rakaposhi, splintering under a tropical sun. There, the stream carrying the offspring of the snows. Below were the villages lacking water. Mortenson squinted, following the traceries of irrigation channels carrying water to each village's terraced fields. From this height, nurturing life and prosperity in each isolated settlement seemed simply a matter of drawing straight lines to divert water.

The intricate obstinacies of village mullahs opposed to educating girls were invisible from this altitude, Mortenson thought. As was the webwork of local politics that could ensnare the progress of a women's vocational center or slow the construction of a school. And how could you even hope to identify the hotbeds of extremism, growing like malignancies in these vulnerable valleys, when they took such care to hide behind high walls and cloak themselves in the excuse of education?

The MI-17 touched down at the Shangri-La, an expensive fishing resort patronized by Pakistan's generals on a lake an hour west of Skardu. In the owner's home, where a satellite dish dragged in a snowy version of CNN, McCown spent a numbing afternoon and evening watching footage of silvery fuselages turned missiles slamming into Lower Manhattan, and buildings sinking like torpedoed ships into a sea of ash.

In the *Jamia Darul Uloom Haqqania madrassa* in Peshawar, which translates as the "University of All Righteous Knowledge," students later boasted to the *New York Times* how they celebrated that day after hearing of the attack—running gleefully through the sprawling compound, stabbing their fingers into the palms of their hands, simulating what their teachers taught them was Allah's will in action—the impact of righteous airplanes on infidel office buildings.

Now, more than ever, Mortenson saw the need to dedicate himself to education. McCown was anxious to leave Pakistan by any possible route, and burned up the sat phone's batteries, trying to have business associates meet him at the Indian border, or arrange flights to China. But all the border posts were sealed tight and all international flights grounded. "I told George, 'You're in the safest place on Earth right now.'" Mortenson says. "'These people will protect you with their lives. Since we can't go anywhere, why don't we stick to the original program until we can put you on a plane?'"

The following day, General Bashir arranged for the MI-17 to take McCown's party on a flyby of K2, to entertain them while he searched for a way to send McCown and his family home. Face pressed to the porthole once again, Mortenson saw the Korphe School pass by far below, a yellow crescent glimmering faintly, like hope, among the village's emerald fields. It had become his custom to return to Korphe and share a cup of tea with Haji Ali each fall before returning to America. He promised himself he'd visit as soon as he'd escorted his guests safely out of the country.

On Friday, September 14, Mortenson and McCown drove an hour west to Kuardu in the Land Cruiser, at the head of a convoy that had grown much larger than usual as the grim news from the far side of the world washed over Baltistan. "It seemed like every politician, policeman, and military and religious leader in northern Pakistan came along to help us inaugurate the Kuardu School," Mortenson says.

Kuardu's primary school had been finished and educating students for years. But Changazi had delayed its official inauguration until an event promising sufficient pomp could be arranged, Mortenson says.

So many people crowded into the courtyard, munching apricot kernels as they milled around, that the school itself was hard to see. But the subject this day wasn't a building. Syed Abbas himself was the featured speaker. And with the Islamic world awash in crisis, the people of Baltistan hung on their supreme religious leader's every word.

"*Bismillah ir-Rahman ir-Rahim,*" he began, "In the name of Allah Almighty, the Beneficent, the Merciful." "*As-Salaam Alaaikum,*" "Peace be upon you."

"It is by fate that Allah the Almighty has brought us together in this hour," Syed Abbas said. The stage he stood on, invisible in the crush of bodies, made him seem to float above the crowd in his black cloak and turban. "Today is a day that you children will remember forever and tell your children and grandchildren. Today, from the darkness of illiteracy, the light of education shines bright.

"We share in the sorrow as people weep and suffer in America today," he said, pushing his thick glasses firmly into place, "as we inaugurate this school. Those who have committed this evil act against the innocent, the women and children, to create thousands of widows and orphans do not do so in the name of Islam. By the grace of Allah the Almighty, may justice be served upon them.

"For this tragedy, I humbly ask Mr. George and Dr. Greg Sahib for their forgiveness. All of you, my brethren: Protect and embrace these two American brothers in our midst. Let no harm come to them. Share all you have to make their mission successful.

"These two Christian men have come halfway around the world to show our Muslim children the light of education," Abbas said. "Why have we not been able to bring education to our children on our own? Fathers and parents, I implore you to dedicate your full effort and commitment to see that all your children are educated. Otherwise, they will merely graze like sheep in the field, at the mercy of nature and the world changing so terrifyingly around us."

Syed Abbas paused, considering what to say next, and somehow, even the youngest children among the hundreds of people packed into the courtyard were absolutely silent.

"I request America to look into our hearts," Abbas continued, his voice straining with emotion, "and see that the great majority of us are not terrorists, but good and simple people. Our land is stricken with poverty because we are without education. But today, another candle of knowledge has been lit. In the name of Allah the Almighty, may it light our way out of the darkness we find ourselves in."

"It was an incredible speech," Mortenson says. "And by the time Syed Abbas had finished he had the entire crowd in tears. I wish all the Americans who think 'Muslim' is just another way of saying 'terrorist' could have been there that day. The true core tenants of Islam are justice, tolerance, and charity, and Syed Abbas represented the moderate center of Muslim faith eloquently."

After the ceremony, Kuardu's many widows lined up to offer Mortenson and McCown their condolences. They pressed eggs into the Americans' hands, begging them to carry these tokens of grief to the faraway sisters they longed to comfort themselves, the widows of New York village.

Mortenson looked at the pile of freshly laid eggs trembling in his palms. He cupped his large hands around them protectively as he headed back toward the Land Cruiser, thinking about the children who must have been on the planes, and his own children at home. Now, he thought, walking through the crowd of well-wishers, over a carpet of cracked apricot husks that littered the ground, unable, even, to wave good-bye, everything in the world was fragile.

The next day, Colonel Ilyas escorted them to Islamabad in the MI-17, where they landed at President Musharraf's personal helipad, for the heightened security it offered. The Americans sat in the heavily guarded waiting room, next to an ornate marble fireplace that looked as if it had never been used, under an oil portrait of the general in full dress uniform.

General Bashir himself landed outside in a Vietnam-era Alouette helicopter nicknamed the "French Fluke" by Pakistan's military, because it was more reliable than the American Hueys of the same vintage they also flew. "The eagle has landed," Ilyas announced theatrically, as Bashir, balding and bull-like in his flight suit, jumped onto the tarmac to wave them in.

Bashir flew low and fast, hugging the scrubby hillsides, and by the time Islamabad's most noticeable landmark, the Saudi-financed Faisal Mosque, with its four minarets and massive, tentlike prayer hall capable of accommodating seventy-thousand worshipers, had faded behind them, they were practically in Lahore. The general set the Alouette down in the middle of a taxiway at Lahore International, fifty meters from the Singapore Airlines 747 that would carry McCown and his family away from the region that was clearly about to become a war zone.

After embracing Mortenson and Faisal Baig, McCown and his children were escorted to their first-class seats by Bashir, who, offering his apologies to the other passengers whose flight he'd helped to delay, remained with the Americans until the plane was ready to depart.

"Thinking back on all of it," McCown says, "no one in Pakistan was anything but wonderful to us. I was so worried about what might happen to me in this, quote, scary Islamic country. But nothing did. The bad part came only after I left."

For the next week, McCown was laid up at the posh Raffles Hotel in Singapore, recovering from the intestinal poisoning he got from Singapore Airlines' first-class food.

Mortenson returned north toward Haji Ali, catching a ride on a military transport flight to Skardu before sleeping most of the way up the Shigar and Braldu valleys in the back of his Land Cruiser while Hussain drove and Baig bored into the horizon with his watchful eyes.

The crowd standing on the far bluff of the Braldu to welcome him seemed somehow wrong. Then, walking over the swaying bridge, Mortenson felt his breath catch as he scanned the far right side of the ledge. The high point where Haji Ali had always stood, dependably as a boulder, was empty. Twaha met Mortenson at the riverbank and gave him the news.

In the month since his father's death, Twaha had shaved his head in mourning and grown a beard. With facial hair, the family resemblance was stronger than ever. The previous fall, when he'd come to take tea with Haji Ali, Mortenson had found Korphe's old *nurmadhar* distraught. His wife, Sakina had taken to her bed that summer, suffering agonizing stomach pain, weathering her illness with Balti patience. She died refusing to make the long trip downside to a hospital.

With Haji Ali, Mortenson had visited Korphe's cemetery, in a field not far from the school. Haji Ali, slowed by age, knelt laboriously to touch the simple stone placed above the spot where Sakina had been buried facing Mecca. When he rose, his eyes were wet. "I'm nothing without her," Haji Ali told his American son. "Nothing at all."

"From a conservative Shia Muslim, that was an incredible tribute," Mortenson says. "Many men might have felt that way about their wives. But very few would have the courage to say so."

Then Haji Ali put his arm on Mortenson's shoulder, and from the way his body trembled, Mortenson presumed he was still crying. But Haji Ali's hoarse laugh, honed by decades of chewing *naswar*, was unmistakable.

"One day soon, you're going to come here looking for me and find me planted in the ground, too," Haji Ali said, chuckling.

"I couldn't find anything funny about the idea of Haji Ali dying," Mortenson says, his voice breaking just trying to talk about the loss of the man years later. He wrapped the tutor who'd already taught him so much in an embrace and asked for one lesson more.

"What should I do, a long time from now, when that day comes?" he asked.

Haji Ali looked up toward the summit of Korphe K2, weighing his words. "Listen to the wind," he said.

With Twaha, Mortenson knelt by the fresh grave to pay his respects to Korphe's fallen chief, whose heart had given out sometime in what Twaha thought was his father's eighth decade. Nothing lasts, Mortenson thought. Despite all our work, nothing is permanent.

His own father's heart hadn't let him live beyond forty-eight, far too soon for Mortenson to ask enough of the questions that life kept piling up around him. And now, the irreplaceable Balti man who had helped to fill some of that hollowness, who had offered so many lessons he might never have learned, moldered in the ground at his wife's side.

Mortenson stood up, trying to imagine what Haji Ali would say at such a moment, at such a black time in history, when all that you cherished was as breakable as an egg. His words came drifting back with an hallucinogenic clarity.

"Listen to the wind."

So, straining for what he might otherwise miss, Mortenson did. He heard it whistling down the Braldu Gorge, carrying rumors of snow and the season's death. But in the breeze whipping across this fragile shelf where humans survived, somehow, in the high Himalaya, he also heard the musical trill of children's voices, at play in the courtyard of Korphe's school. Here was his last lesson, Mortenson realized, stabbing at the hot tears with his fingertips. "Think of them," he thought. "Think always of them."

CHAPTER 20

TEA WITH THE TALIBAN

Nuke 'Em All—Let Allah Sort Them Out.

—Bumper sticker seen on cab window of Ford-F150 pickup
truck in Bozeman, Montana

"LET'S GO SEE the circus," Suleman said.

Mortenson sat in the back of the white Toyota Corolla CAI rented for his Rawalpindi taxi driver turned fixer, leaning against one of the lace slipcovers Suleman had lovingly fitted to his car's headrests. Faisal Baig rode shotgun. Suleman had picked them up at the airport, where they'd flown down from Skardu on a PIA 737, commercial flights having resumed in Pakistan, as they had in America by late September 2001.

"The what?" Mortenson said.

"You'll see," Suleman said, grinning. Compared to the tiny Suzuki rustbucket he'd wielded as his taxi, the Toyota handled like a Ferrari. Suleman slalomed through slow-moving traffic on the highway connecting 'Pindi to its twin city, Islamabad, steering one-handed, while he speed-dialed his prize possession, a burgundy Sony cell phone the size of a book of matches, alerting the manager of the Home Sweet Home Guest House to hold their room because his sahib would be arriving late.

Suleman slowed, reluctantly, to present his documents at a police barricade protecting the Blue Area, the modern diplomatic enclave where Islamabad's government buildings, embassies, and business hotels were arranged between grids of boulevards built on a heroic scale. Mortenson leaned out the window to show a foreign face. The lawns of Islamabad were so supernaturally green, the shade trees so lush, in such an otherwise dry, dusty place, that they hinted at forces powerful enough to transform even nature's intentions. Seeing Mortenson, the policemen waved them on.

Islamabad was a planned city, built in the 1960s and 1970s as a world apart for Pakistan's rich and powerful. In the glossy shops that lined the edges of the avenues, like rows of pulsing LEDs, Japan's latest consumer electronics were available, as were the exotic delicacies of Kentucky Fried Chicken and Pizza Hut.

The city's throbbing cosmopolitan heart was the five-star Marriot Hotel, a fortress of luxury protected from the country's poverty by concrete crash gates and a force of 150 security guards in light-blue uniforms who loitered behind every bush and tree in the hotel's park-like setting, with weapons slung. At night, the burning ends of their cigarettes glowed from the greenery like deadly fireflies.

Suleman wheeled the Toyota up to the concrete crash barrier where two of the fireflies, M3 grease guns drawn, probed under the car with mirrored poles and inspected the contents of the trunk before unbolting a steel gate and sending them in.

"When I need to get things done I go to the Marriot," Mortenson says. "They always have a working fax and a fast Internet connection. And usually, when someone was visiting Pakistan for the first time, I'd take them straight to the Marriot from the airport, so they could get their bearings without too much culture shock."

But now, passing through a metal detector, and having his jam-packed photojournalist's vest patted down by two efficient security men wearing suits and earpieces, it was Mortenson's turn to be shocked. The ballroom-sized, marble-floored lobby, usually empty, except for a pianist and a few knots of foreign businessmen whispering into cell phones from islands of overstuffed furniture, was a solid mass of caffeine and deadline-fueled humanity; the world's press corps had arrived.

"The circus," Suleman said, smiling proudly up at Mortenson, like a student demonstrating an impressive project at a science fair. Everywhere he looked, Mortenson saw cameras and logos and the tense people beholden to them: CNN, BBC, NBC, ABC, Al-Jazeera. Pushing his way past a cameraman shouting into his satellite phone with Teutonic fury, Mortenson made it to the entrance of the Nadia Coffee Shop, separated from the lobby by a fragrant hedge of potted plants.

Around the buffet, where he ordinarily ate attended by five underworked waiters who raced each other to refill his glass of mineral water, Mortenson saw that every table was taken.

"Seems like our little corner of the world has become interesting all of a sudden." Mortenson turned to see the blonde Canadian journalist Kathy Gannon, Islamabad's longtime AP bureau chief, smiling next to him in a conservatively cut *shalwar kamiz*, waiting for a table, too. He hugged her hello.

"How long has it been like this?" Mortenson said, trying to make himself heard over the shouting German cameraman.

"A few days," Gannon said. "But wait until the bombs start falling. Then they'll be able to charge a thousand dollars a room."

"What are they now?"

"Up from $150 to $320 and still rising," Gannon said. "These guys have never had it so good. All the networks are doing stand-ups on the roof, and the hotel's charging each crew five hundred dollars a day just to film up there."

Mortenson shook his head. He'd never spent the night at the Marriot. Running the CAI on expenses as lean as the organization's everdipping bank balance meant staying at the hotel he'd become partial to since Suleman had first taken him there. The Home Sweet Home Guest House, a solidly built villa abandoned when its former owner ran out of funds before it could be completed, sat on a weedy lot near the Nepali Embassy. The tariff there, for a room with unpredictable plumbing and sticky pink carpets suffering from cigarette burns, ran twelve dollars a night.

"Dr. Greg, Sahib, Madame Kathy, come," a tuxedoed waiter who knew them whispered. "A table is nearly awailable, and I fear these . . ." he searched for the right word, "foreigners . . . will simply grasp it."

Gannon was widely known and admired for her fearlessness. Her blue eyes bored into everything like a challenge. Once, a Taliban border guard, unsuccessfully trying to point out imaginary flaws with her passport to keep her out of Afghanistan had been amazed by her persistence. "You're strong," he told her. "We have a word for someone like you: a man."

Gannon replied that she didn't consider that a compliment.

At a pink-clothed table by the Nadia's bursting buffet, Gannon filled Mortenson in on the clowns, jugglers, and high-wire acts who'd recently arrived in town. "It's pitiful," she said. "Green reporters who know nothing about the region stand up on the roof in flak jackets and act like their backdrop of the Margala Hills is some kind of war zone instead of a place to take the kids on weekends. Most of them don't want to get anywhere near the border and are running stories without checking them out. And those that do want to go are out of luck. The Taliban just closed Afghanistan to all foreign reporters."

"Are you going to try to get in?" Mortenson asked.

"I've just come from Kabul," she said. "I was on the phone with my editor in New York when the second plane hit the tower and filed a few stories before they 'escorted' me out."

"What's the Taliban going to do?"

"Hard to say. I heard they held a *shura* and decided to hand over Osama, but at the last minute, Mullah Omar overruled them and said he'd protect him with his life. So you know what that means. A lot of them seem scared. But the diehards are ready to fight it out," she said, grimacing. "Lucky for these guys, though," she said, nodding at the reporters massing by the maitre d's desk.

"Will you try to go back?" Mortenson asked.

"If I can go aboveboard," she said. "I'm not going to slip on a *burkha* like one of these cowboys, and get arrested or worse. I hear the Taliban are already holding two French reporters they caught sneaking in."

Suleman and Baig returned from the buffet with lavishly piled plates of mutton curry. Suleman brought a bonus—a bowl full of trembling pink trifle for dessert.

"Good?" Mortenson asked, and Suleman, his jaws working methodically, nodded. Before heading over to graze at the buffet, Mortenson scooped up a few spoonfuls of Suleman's dessert for himself. The pink custard reminded him of the British-style desserts he'd grown up with in East Africa.

Suleman ate with especial gusto any time mutton was on offer. When he was growing up in a family of seven children, in the modest village of Dhok Luna on the Punjab plain between Islamabad and Lahore, mutton was served only on very special occasions. And even then, not much fast-dwindling sheep ever survived to reach the mouth of the family's fourth child.

Suleman excused himself and returned to the buffet for seconds.

For the next week, Mortenson slept at the Home Sweet Home, but spent every waking hour at the Marriot, caught up, as he had been five years earlier in war-crazed Peshawar, in the sense of inhabiting the eye of history's storm. And with the world's media camped out on his doorstep, he decided to do what he could to promote the CAI.

Days after the terror attacks on New York and Washington, the two countries other than Pakistan that had maintained diplomatic relations with the Taliban, Saudi Arabia and the United Arab Emirates, cut them off. With Afghanistan now closed, Pakistan was the only place the Taliban could make their case to their world. They held lengthy daily press conferences on the lawn of their crumbling embassy, two kilometers from the Marriot. Taxis, which had once happily plied that route for about eighty cents, were now press-ganging reporters into paying ten dollars a trip.

Each afternoon, the United Nations held a briefing on conditions in Afghanistan at the Marriot, and the tide of sunstruck reporters washed happily back into the Marriot's air-conditioning.

Mortenson, by the fall of 2001, knew Pakistan more intimately than all but a few other foreigners, especially the far-flung border areas reporters were trying to reach. He was constantly cajoled and offered bribes by reporters hoping he could arrange their passage into Afghanistan.

"It seemed like the reporters were at war with each other almost as much as they wanted the fighting to start in Afghanistan," Mortenson says. "CNN teamed up with the BBC against ABC and CBS. Pakistani stringers would run into the lobby with stories like news about an American Predator drone the Taliban had shot down and the bidding wars would begin.

"An NBC producer and on-camera reporter took me to dinner at a Chinese restaurant in the Marriot to 'pick my brain' about Pakistan," Mortenson remembers. "But they were really after the same thing as everyone else. They wanted to go to Afghanistan and offered me more money than I make in a year if I could get them in. Then they looked around like the table might be miked and whispered, 'Don't tell CNN or CBS.' "

Instead, Mortenson gave interview after interview to reporters who rarely ranged beyond the Marriot and the Taliban Embassy for their material and needed some local color to fill out their stories about bland press conferences. "I tried to talk about root causes of the conflict—the lack of education in Pakistan, and the rise of the *Wahhabi madrassas,* and how that led to problems like terrorism," Mortenson says. "But that stuff hardly ever made it into print. They only wanted sound bites about the top Taliban leaders so they could turn them into villains in the run-up to war."

Each evening like clockwork, a group of the top Taliban leadership in Islamabad walked through the marble lobby of the Marriot in their turbans and flowing black robes and waited for a table at the Nadia Coffee Shop, coming to see the circus, too. "They'd sit there all night nursing cups of green tea," Mortenson says. "Because that was the cheapest thing on the menu. On their Taliban salaries they couldn't afford the twenty-dollar buffet. I always thought a reporter would be able to get quite a story if they just offered to buy them all dinner, but I never saw that happen."

Finally, Mortenson sat down with them himself. Asem Mustafa, who covered all the Karakoram expeditions for Pakistan's *Nation* newspaper, often contacted Mortenson in Skardu for the latest climbing news. Mustafa was acquainted with the Taliban ambassador, Mullah Abdul Salaam Zaeef, and introduced Mortenson one evening at the Nadia.

With Mustafa, Mortenson sat down at a table with four Taliban, in the seat next to Mullah Zaeef, under a hand-painted banner that read "Ole! Ole! Ole!" The Nadia, where foreign businessmen often ate seven evenings a week while they were in Islamabad, offered theme nights to break up the monotony. This was Mexican night at the Marriot.

A mustachioed Pakistani waiter, looking humiliated under his massive sombrero, stopped at the table to ask if they were ordering from the Continental buffet, or if the sahibs would perhaps like to take dinner from the taco bar.

"Only tea," Mullah Zaeef said in Urdu. With a flourish of his brightly striped Mexican serape, the waiter went to fetch it.

"Zaeef was one of the few Taliban leaders with a formal education and a little Western savvy," Mortenson says. "He had children about my kids' age so we talked about them for a while. I was curious what a Taliban leader would have to say about educating children, especially girls, so I asked him. He answered like a politician, and talked in a general way about the importance of education."

The waiter returned with a silver service and poured green *kawah* tea for the table while Mortenson made small talk with the other Taliban in Pashto, asking after the health of their families, who they said were well. In a few weeks, Mortenson thought grimly, their answers would probably be different.

The waiter, whose capelike serape kept falling over the teapot as he poured, tucked the edge out of the way into the imitation ammunition belts he wore across his chest.

Mortenson looked at the four serious bearded men in their black turbans, imagining the experience they had with actual weapons, and wondered what they made of the waiter's costume. "They probably didn't think he looked any weirder than all the foreign journalists standing near our table, trying to hear what we were talking about," Mortenson says.

Mullah Zaeef was in an impossible situation, Mortenson realized, as their talk turned to the coming war. Living in Islamabad's Blue Area, he had enough contact with the outside world that he could see what was coming. But the Taliban's top leadership in Kabul and Kandahar weren't as worldly. Mullah Omar, the supreme Taliban leader, like most of the high-ranking diehards who surrounded him, had only a *madrassa* education. Mohammed Sayed Ghiasuddin, the Taliban's minister of education, had no formal education at all, according to Ahmed Rashid.

"Perhaps we should turn in Bin Laden to save Afghanistan," Mullah Zaeef said to Mortenson, as he waved to the sombreroed waiter for the bill he insisted on paying. "Mullah Omar thinks there is still time to talk our way out of war," Zaeef said wearily. Then, as if aware of letting down his façade, he straightened up. "Make no mistake," he declared, his voice thick with bravado, "we will fight to the finish if we are attacked."

Mullah Omar would continue to think he could talk his way out of war until American cruise missiles began obliterating his personal residences. Not having established any formal channel to Washington, the Taliban leader would reportedly dial the White House's public information line from his satellite phone twice that October, offering to sit down for a *jirga*, at long last, with George Bush. The American president, predictably, never returned the calls.

Reluctantly, Mortenson tore himself away from the Marriot and went back to work. At the Home Sweet Home, phone messages had been piling up from the American Embassy, warning him that Pakistan was no longer considered safe for Americans. But Mortenson needed to visit the schools CAI funded in the refugee camps outside Peshawar and see if they had the capacity to deal with the influx of new refugees the fighting was sure to send their way. So he rounded up Baig and Suleman and packed for the short road trip past Peshawar, to the Afghan border.

Bruce Finley, a *Denver Post* reporter Mortenson knew, was sick of the steady diet of no news at the Marriot and asked to accompany him to Peshawar. Together, they visited the Shamshatoo Refugee Camp and the nearly one hundred CAI-supported teachers who were struggling to work there under almost impossible conditions.

Finley filed a story about the visit, describing the work Mortenson was doing and quoting him about the coming war. Mortenson urged Finley's readers not to lump all Muslims together. The Afghan children flocking to refugee camps with their families were victims, Mortenson argued, deserving our sympathy. "These aren't the terrorists. These aren't the bad people." Blaming all Muslims for the horror of 9/11, Mortenson argued, is "causing innocent people to panic.

"The only way we can defeat terrorism is if people in this country where terrorists exist learn to respect and love Americans," Mortenson concluded, "and if we can respect and love these people here. What's the difference between them becoming a productive local citizen or a terrorist? I think the key is education."

After Finley returned to Islamabad to file his story, Mortenson approached the Afghan border post, to see what would happen. A teenaged Taliban sentry swung open a green metal gate and flipped through Mortenson's passport suspiciously, while his colleagues waved the barrels of their Kalashnikovs from side to side, covering the entire party. Suleman rolled his eyes at the guns, waggling his head as he scolded the boys, suggesting they show their elders more respect. But weeks of waiting for war to begin had set the guards on a knife's edge and they ignored him.

The sentry in charge, his eyes so thickly chalked with black *surma* that he squinted out through dark slits, grunted when he came to a page in Mortenson's passport containing several handwritten visas from London's Afghan Embassy.

The London Embassy, run by Wali Massoud, the brother of slain

Northern Alliance leader Shah Ahmed Massoud, was dedicated to overthrowing the Taliban. Mortenson often had tea with Wali Massoud when he passed through London on his way to Islamabad, discussing the girls' schools he hoped to build in Afghanistan if the country ever became stable enough for him to work there.

"This is number-two visa," the sentry said, tearing a page out of Mortenson's passport, instantly rendering the entire document invalid. "You go to Islamabad and get number-one visa, Taliban visa," he said, unslinging his gun, and with it, waving Mortenson on his way.

The American Embassy in Islamabad declined to issue Mortenson another passport, since his was "suspiciously mutilated." The consular officer he made his case to told Mortenson he'd issue a ten-day temporary document that would allow him to return to America, where he could apply for another passport. But Mortenson, who had another month of CAI business planned before returning home, refused. Instead, he flew to Katmandu, Nepal, where the American Consulate was reputed to be more accommodating.

But after waiting his turn hopefully in line, and explaining his situation to an initially polite consular official, Mortenson saw a look flit over his face as he inspected his passport that told him coming to Katmandu wasn't going to make any difference. The official thumbed past dozens of the imposing black-and-white visas from the Islamic Republic of Pakistan that were glued onto every other page, and scrawled Afghan visas issued by the Northern Alliance, the questions in his mind mounting, and left Mortenson to speak to his superior.

By the time he returned, Mortenson already knew what he would say. "You need to come back tomorrow to talk to someone else about this," he said nervously, not meeting Mortenson's eyes. "Until then, I'm going to hold on to your passport."

The next morning, a detachment of Marine guards escorted Mortenson across the lawn of the American diplomatic compound in Katmandu, from the consular office to the main embassy building, deposited him in an empty room at a long conference table, and locked the door on their way out.

Mortenson sat at the table for forty-five minutes, alone with an American flag and a large portrait of the president who'd taken the oath of office ten months earlier, George W. Bush. "I knew what they were trying to do," Mortenson says. "I've never watched much television but even I could tell this was a scene straight out of a bad cop show. I figured someone was watching me to see if I acted guilty, so I just smiled, saluted Bush, and waited."

Finally three clean-cut men in suits and ties walked in and pulled up swivel chairs across the table from Mortenson. "They all had nice American names like Bob or Bill or Pete, and they smiled a lot as they introduced themselves, but this was clearly an interrogation and they were obviously Intelligence officers," Mortenson says.

The agent clearly in charge began the questioning. He slid Mortenson a business card across the polished tabletop. It read "Political-Military Attaché, Southeast Asia," under the name the agent used. "I'm sure we can clear all this up," he said, flashing a grin meant to be disarming as he took a pen out of his pocket and slid a notebook into place like a soldier ramming an ammunition cartridge into a military sidearm. "Now why do you want to go to Pakistan?" he asked, buckling down to business. "It's very dangerous there right now and we've advised all Americans to leave."

"I know," Mortenson said. "My work is there. I just left Islamabad two days ago."

All three men scribbled in their notebooks. "What sort of business did you have there?" BobBillPete asked.

"I've been working there for eight years," Mortenson said, "And I've got another month of work to do before I go home."

"What kind of work?"

"I build elementary schools, mostly for girls, in northern Pakistan."

"How many schools do you run right now?"

"I'm not exactly sure."

"Why?"

"Thing is, the number is always changing. If all the construction gets done this fall, which you never know, we'll have finished our twenty-second and twenty-third independent schools. But lots of times we add extensions to government schools, if they have too many kids crammed into their classrooms. And we find a lot of schools, run by the government or other foreign NGOs, where the teachers haven't been paid for months or years. So we sort of take them under our umbrella until they get straightened out. Also, we pay teachers in Afghan refugee camps to hold class where there aren't any schools. So the number changes from week to week. Did I answer your question?"

The three men looked at their notebooks, as if they were searching for something that should have been there in black and white, but wasn't.

"How many students do you have right now, total?"

"That's hard to say."

"Why is that hard to say?"

"Have you ever to been to a rural village in northern Pakistan?"

"What's your point?"

"Well, right now it's harvest time. Most families need their kids to help them in the fields so they pull them out of school for a while. And in winter, especially if it's really cold, they might close their schools for a few months because they can't afford to heat them. Then in the spring, some students—"

"A ballpark figure," the agent in charge interrupted.

"Somewhere between ten and fifteen thousand students."

Three pens scratched in unison, pinioning the rare hard fact to paper.

"Do you have maps of the places you work?"

"In Pakistan," Mortenson said.

One of the agents picked up a phone and a few minutes later an atlas was delivered to the conference room.

"So this area near Kashmir is called . . ."

"Baltistan," Mortenson said.

"And the people there are . . ."

"Shia, like in Iran," Mortenson said, watching the three idle pens come alive.

"And these areas near Afghanistan where you're starting to build schools are called the Northwest what?"

"Northwest Frontier Provinces," Mortenson said.

"And they're part of Pakistan?"

"That depends who you ask."

"But they're Sunni Muslims there, basically the same people as the Pashtuns in Afghanistan?"

"Well, in the lowlands, mostly they are Pashtun. But there are a lot of Ismaelis and some Shia, too. Then in the mountains you've got a lot of tribes with their own customs, the Khowar, the Kohistani, the Shina, Torwali, and Kalami. There's even one animist tribe, the Kalash, who live way up in an isolated valley beyond this dot I'm drawing here, which, if you had a better map, would be labeled Chitral."

The head interrogator blew out his breath. The more you probed into Pakistani politics, the more simple labels splintered into finer and finer strands, refusing to be reduced to a few black pen marks on white notebook paper. He slid his pen and notebook across the table-top to Mortenson. "I want you to write up a list of all the names and numbers of your contacts in Pakistan," he said.

"I'd like to call my attorney," Mortenson said.

"I wasn't trying to be difficult. These guys had a serious job to do, ecspecially after 9/11," Mortenson says, pronouncing the word the way he does. "But I also knew what could happen to innocent people who got put on that kind of list. And if these guys were who I think they were, I couldn't afford to have anyone in Pakistan think I was working with them, or the next time I went there I'd be a dead man."

"Go call your lawyer," BobBillPete said, unlocking the door, look-ing relieved to finally slip his notebook back in his suit pocket. "But come back at nine tomorrow morning. Sharp."

The following morning, an unusually punctual Mortenson sat down at the conference table. This time, he was alone with the head interrogator. "Let's clear up a few things right away," he said. "You know who I am?"

"I know who you are."

"You know what will happen to you if you don't tell me the truth?"

"I know what will happen."

"Okay. Are any of the parents of your students terrorists?"

"There's no way I could know that," Mortenson said. "I have thousands of students."

"Where's Osama?"

"What?"

"You heard me. Do you know where Osama is?"

Mortenson told himself not to laugh, not to let the agent even see him smile at the absurdity of the question. "I hope I never know a thing like that," he said seriously enough to bring the interrogation to an end.

Mortenson returned to Islamabad with the temporary one-year passport the Katmandu Consulate had grudgingly issued him. As he checked back into the Home Sweet Home, the manager handed Mortenson a stack of phone messages from the American Embassy.

Mortenson flipped through them as he walked down the hallway's worn pink carpet toward his room. The tone of the warnings ratcheted up day by day. And the most recent message hit a note of near hysteria. It ordered all American civilians to immediately evacuate the country the embassy called "the most dangerous place for American nationals on Earth." Mortenson threw his duffel bag on the bed and asked Suleman to find him a seat on the next flight to Skardu.

One of Mortenson's many admirers in the mountaineering community is Charlie Shimanski, the former executive director of the American Alpine Club, who championed a CAI fundraising drive among his organization's members that year. He likens the moment Mortenson returned to post-9/11 Pakistan, two months before Daniel Pearl's kidnapping and beheading, to New York City firefighters rushing into the wounded World Trade Center. "When Greg wins the Nobel Peace Prize, I hope the judges in Oslo point to that day," Shimanski says. "This guy Greg quietly, doggedly heading back into a war zone to do battle with the real causes of terror is every bit as heroic as those firemen running up the stairs of the burning towers while everyone else was frantically trying to get out."

For the next month, as American bombers and cruise missiles began to pummel the country to his west, Mortenson criss-crossed northern Pakistan in his Land Cruiser, making sure all the CAI projects underway were completed before cold weather set in. "Sometimes, at night, I'd be driving with Faisal and we'd hear military planes passing overhead, in Pakistan's airspace, where American aircraft weren't technically supposed to be. We'd see the whole western horizon flare up like we were looking at heat lightning. And Faisal, who would spit on a picture of Osama Bin Laden any time he saw one, would shudder at the thought of what people under those bombs must be going through and raise his hands in a *dua*, asking Allah to spare them any unnecessary suffering."

After dark on October 29, 2001, Baig escorted Mortenson to the Peshawar International Airport. At the security gate, only passengers were allowed past the military guards. When Mortenson took his bag from his bodyguard, he saw Baig's eyes were brimming with tears. Faisal Baig had sworn an oath to protect Mortenson anywhere his work took him in Pakistan, and was prepared, in an instant, to lay down his life.

"What is it, Faisal?" Mortenson said, squeezing his bodyguard's broad shoulder.

"Now your country is at war," Baig said. "What can I do? How can I protect you there?"

From his window seat in the mostly empty first-class cabin of the flight from Peshawar to Riyadh, where stewards had smilingly instructed Mortenson to sit, he saw the sky over Afghanistan pulsing with deadly light.

Steady turbulence announced they had left the land and were over the waters of the Arabian Sea. Across the aisle, Mortenson saw a bearded man in a black turban staring out the window through a high-powered pair of binoculars. When the lights of ships at sea appeared below them, he spoke animatedly to the turbaned man in the seat next to him. And pulling a satellite phone out of the pocket of his *shalwar kamiz,* this man rushed to the bathroom, presumably to place a call.

"Down there in the dark," Mortenson says, "was the most technologically sophisticated navy strike force in the world, launching fighters and cruise missiles into Afghanistan. I didn't have much sympathy for the Taliban, and I didn't have any for Al Qaeda, but I had to admit that what they were doing was brilliant. Without satellites, without an air force, with even their primitive radar knocked out, they were ingenious enough to use plain old commercial flights to keep track of the Fifth Fleet's positions. I realized that if we were counting on our military technology alone to win the war on terror, we had a lot of lessons to learn."

Mortenson emerged from an hour-long customs inspection courtesy of his temporary passport and Pakistani visa into the main terminal of the Denver International Airport. It was Halloween. Walking through a forest of American flags that had sprouted from every surface, adorning every doorway and hanging from every arch, he wondered if the explosion of red, white, and blue meant he hadn't arrived on a different holiday. Calling Tara from his cell phone as he walked toward his connecting flight to Bozeman, he asked her about the flags.

"What's up, Tara? It looks like the Fourth of July here."

"Welcome to the new America, sweetie," she said.

Late that night, discombobulated by too much travel, Mortenson crept out of bed without waking Tara and slipped down to the basement to confront the stacks of mail that had accumulated while he was away. The interviews he'd given at the Marriot, his trip to the refugee camps with Bruce Finley, and a letter he'd e-mailed to his friend, *Seattle Post Intelligencer* columnist Joel Connelly, urging sympathy for the innocent Muslims caught in the crossfire, had been picked up by dozens of American newspapers during his absence.

Mortenson's repeated pleas not to lump all Muslims together, and his arguments for a multipronged attack on terror—the need to educate Muslim children, rather than just dropping bombs—hit a nerve with a nation newly at war. For the first time in his life, Mortenson found himself opening envelope after envelope of hate mail.

A letter with a Denver postmark but no return address said, "I wish some of our bombs had hit you because you're counterproductive to our military efforts."

Another unsigned letter with a Minnesota postmark attacked Mortenson in a spidery hand. "Our Lord will see that you pay dearly for being a traitor," it began, before warning Mortenson that "soon you will suffer more excruciating pain than our brave soldiers."

Mortenson opened dozens of similar unsigned letters until he became too depressed to keep reading. "That night, for the first time since starting my work in Pakistan, I thought about quitting," he says. "I expected something like this from an ignorant village mullah, but to get those kinds of letters from my fellow Americans made me wonder whether I should just give up."

While his family slept upstairs, Mortenson began to obsess about their safety. "I could deal with taking some risks over there," Mortenson says. "Sometimes I had no choice. But to put Tara and Amira and Khyber in harm's way here at home was just unacceptable. I couldn't believe I'd let it happen."

Mortenson made a pot of coffee and kept reading. Many of the letters lauded his efforts, too. And he was encouraged to learn that in a time of national crisis, his message was at least being heard by a few Americans.

The next afternoon, November 1, 2001, Mortenson said good-bye to his family before he'd even had a chance to say a proper hello, stuffed a change of clothes into an overnight bag, and caught a commuter flight to Seattle, where he was due to deliver a speech that evening. Jon Krakauer, at the height of his celebrity after the success of *Into Thin Air,* his book about the deadly effect commercialization has had on the process of climbing Mount Everest, volunteered to introduce Mortenson at a twenty-five-dollar-a-ticket fundraiser for the Central Asia Institute. Quietly, Krakauer had become one of the CAI's biggest supporters.

In a piece promoting the event, titled "Jon Krakauer Reappears Out of Thin Air," the *Seattle Post Intelligencer's* John Marshall explained that the reclusive writer had agreed to a rare public appearance because he believed people needed to know about Mortenson's work. "What Greg's doing is just as important as any bombs that are being dropped," Marshall quoted Krakauer as saying. "If the Central Asia Institute were not doing what it's doing, people in that region would probably be chanting, 'We hate Americans!' Instead, they see us as agents of their salvation."

At Seattle's Town Hall, which sits atop the city's First Hill neighborhood like an Athenian temple, Mortenson arrived fifteen minutes late, wearing a *shalwar kamiz*. Inside the building's Great Hall, he was humbled to see every seat taken and crowds of people jostling for a glimpse of the stage from Town Hall's Romanesque archways. He hurried to take his place on a chair behind the podium.

"You paid twenty-five bucks to be here, which is a lot of money, but I'm not going to read from any of my own books tonight," Krakauer said, once the crowd had quieted. "Instead, I'm going to read from works that speak more directly to the current state of the world, and the growing importance of Greg's work."

He began with William Butler Yeats's "The Second Coming."

"Things fall apart; the centre cannot hold," Krakauer read in his thin, strangled-sounding voice, as uncomfortable in front of a big crowd as Mortenson. "Mere anarchy is loosed upon the world,/The blood-dimmed tide is loosed, and everywhere/The ceremony of innocence is drowned;/The best lack all conviction, while the worst/Are full of passionate intensity."

Yeats's lamentation had lost none of its power since its publication in 1920. The Great Hall might have been empty for all the sound in it after the last line hung in the domed space above the audience's heads. Then Krakauer read a long excerpt from a recent *New York Times Magazine* story about child laborers in Peshawar, and how easy their unendurable economic conditions made them for extremist clerics to recruit.

"By the time Jon introduced me, the whole audience was in tears, including me," Mortenson says.

When it was time to introduce Mortenson, Krakauer took issue with one of Yeats's observations. "Though the worst may indeed be full of passionate intensity," he said, "I'm certain that the best most definitely do not lack all conviction. For proof you don't have to look any farther than that big guy sitting behind me. What Greg has accomplished, with very little money, verges on the miraculous. If it were possible to clone fifty more Gregs, there is no doubt in my mind Islamic terrorism would quickly become a thing of the past. There's only one of him, alas. Please join me in welcoming Greg Mortenson."

Mortenson hugged Krakauer, thanking him, then asked the projectionist for the first slide. K2 flashed onto the screen behind him, its otherworldly pyramid painfully white against the blue bowl of the atmosphere. Here, in front of scores of the world's leading alpinists, was his failure, projected high as a three-story house for thousands of people to see. So why did he feel like his life had reached a new summit?

CHAPTER 21

RUMSFELD'S SHOES

Today in Kabul, clean-shaven men rubbed their faces. An old man with a newly-trimmed grey beard danced in the street holding a small tape recorder blaring music to his ear. The Taliban—who had banned music and ordered men to wear beards—were gone.

—Kathy Gannon, November 13, 2001, reporting for the Associated Press

THE PILOTS PLAYED musical chairs at thirty-five thousand feet. Every ten minutes one of them surrendered the cockpit of the well-used 727 and another took his place. Eight of Ariana's eager captains huddled at the front of the half-empty cabin, patiently sipping tea and smoking while they waited their turn at the stick. With seven of the Afghan national airlines' eight Boeings out of commission after being hit by bombs and mortars, this two-hour-and-forty-five-minute trip from Dubai to Kabul was an opportunity for each of the pilots to log a little precious flight time on their country's only airworthy commercial airplane.

Mortenson was seated midway between the pilots and fifteen Ariana stewardesses clustered around the rear galley. Every two minutes since leaving Dubai, a rotating task force of shy Afghan women had sprinted forward to top off Mortenson's plastic cup of Coke. Between their visits, an increasingly caffeinated Mortenson pressed his nose to the scuffed windowpane, studying the country that had seeped into his dreams ever since he started working in Pakistan.

They approached Kabul from the south, and when the captain-of-the-moment announced they were passing over Kandahar, Mortenson strained both to keep his broken seat upright, and to make out details of the former Taliban stronghold. But from thirty thousand feet all he could see was a highway cutting across a broad plain between brown hills and a few shadows that might have been buildings. Maybe, Mortenson thought, this is what Secretary of Defense Rumsfeld was talking about when he complained there were no good targets in Afghanistan and suggested striking Iraq instead.

But American bombs, both smart and not-so, had soon rained down on this parched landscape. On the computer monitor in his basement Mortenson had studied photos of U.S. soldiers, in the captured Kandahar home of supreme Taliban leader Mullah Omar, sitting on his giant, gaudily painted Bavarian-style bed, displaying the steel footlockers they had found underneath it, stacked full of crisp hundred-dollar bills.

And at first, Mortenson had supported the war in Afghanistan. But as he read accounts of increasing civilian casualties, and heard details during phone calls to his staff in the Afghan refugee camps about the numbers of children who were being killed when they mistakenly picked up the bright yellow pods of unexploded cluster bombs, which closely resembled the yellow military food packets American planes were also dropping as a humanitarian gesture, his attitude began to change.

"Why do Pentagon officials give us numbers on Al Qaeda and Taliban operatives killed in bombing raids but throw their hands in the air when asked about civilian casualties?" Mortenson wrote in a letter to the editor published in the *Washington Post* on December 8, 2001. "Even more frightening is the media's reluctance to question Secretary of Defense Rumsfeld about this during his press briefings."

Each night, about 2.00 A.M., Mortenson would wake up and lie quietly next to Tara, trying to put the images of civilian casualties out of his mind and fall back asleep. But he knew that many of the civilians under America's bomb sights were children who had attended CAI-sponsored classes in the Shamshatoo Camp near Peshawar, before their families had tired of the harsh refugee life and returned to Afghanistan. While Mortenson lay in bed, their faces would come into acute focus despite the darkness, and inevitably, he'd creep down to his basement and start making calls to Pakistan trying to learn the latest news. From his contacts in the military, he learned that Taliban ambassador Mullah Abdul Salaam Zaeef, with whom he'd sipped tea at the Marriot, had been captured and sent, hooded and shackled, to the extralegal detention facility in Guantanamo, Cuba.

"During that winter, opening my mail was like playing Russian roulette," Mortenson says. "Each time I'd get a few encouraging notes and donations. Then the next envelope I opened would say that God would surely grant me a painful death for helping Muslims." Mortenson took what steps he could to protect his family and applied for an unlisted number. After his mail carrier learned of the death threats, with the anthrax scare still on everyone's mind, she began quarantining envelopes he received that were sent without return addresses and passing them on to the FBI.

One of the most encouraging notes came from an elderly philanthropist in Seattle named Patsy Collins, who had become a regular donor to CAI. "I'm old enough to remember this nonsense from World War II, when we turned on all the Japanese and interned them without good cause," she wrote. "These horrible hate letters are a mandate for you to get out and tell Americans what you know about Muslims. You represent the goodness and courage that America is all about. Get out, don't be afraid, and spread your message for peace. Make this your finest hour."

Though his mind was half a world away, Mortenson took Collins's advice and began scheduling speaking engagements, waging the most effective campaign he could muster. Throughout December and January, he beat back the butterflies and appeared before large crowds at Seattle's flagship REI outdoor store, at an AARP–sponsored talk in Minneapolis, at the Montana Librarians' state convention (with Julia Bergman), and at the Explorers Club in Manhattan.

Some speeches weren't so well attended. At the exclusive Yellowstone Club, at the Big Sky Ski Area south of Bozeman, Mortenson was directed to a small basement room where six people sat on overstuffed chairs around a gas fireplace, waiting to hear him speak. Remembering how even his address to Minnesota's sea of two hundred empty chairs had turned out well in the end, he shut off the fireplace, hung a wrinkled white sheet over it, and showed his slides while he spoke passionately about the mistakes he believed America was making in its conduct of the war.

Mortenson noticed an attractive woman in her thirties curled up in an armchair, wearing a sweatshirt, jeans, and a baseball cap, and listening to him with special intensity. While he was taking down the sheet she introduced herself. "I'm Mary Bono," she said. "Actually Representative Mary Bono. I'm a Republican from Palm Springs and I have to tell you

I learned more from you in the last hour than I have in all the briefings I've been to on Capitol Hill since 9/11. We've got to get you up there." Representative Bono handed Mortenson her business card and asked him to call her when Congress was back in session to schedule a speech in Washington.

In the hands of yet another captain, the Ariana 727 began a steep descent toward Kabul, diving into a dusty bowl ringed by rugged mountains. Nervously, the stewardesses performed *duas,* asking that Allah grant them a safe landing. They banked close to the Logar Hills, where Mortenson could make out the charred husks of Soviet-era Taliban tanks that had been concealed in the mouths of caves and hidden behind berms, where they had nonetheless been easy targets for modern laser-guided munitions.

For months, Mortenson had drunk in e-mail correspondence about this place from Kathy Gannon, who had bulled her way back to the Afghan capital after he had last seen her at the Marriot. From Gannon, he learned how the skittish Taliban forces had fled the city as Northern Alliance tanks swept south, supported by the American fighter planes that concentrated their fire on the city's "Street of Guests," Kabul's poshest neighborhood, where Arab fighters allied with the Taliban lived. And from Gannon, Mortenson learned how people danced in the streets and long-hidden radios and cassette players blared across Kabul on November 13, 2001, the day the Taliban, who had banned all music, finally fled town.

Now, by mid-February 2002, there were still intense firefights in the distant White Mountains Mortenson could make out through the window, where U.S. ground forces were trying to clear out entrenched pockets of resistance. But Mortenson judged that Kabul, in the hands of the Northern Alliance and their American allies, was at long last secure enough for him to visit.

The walk from the plane to the terminal, past teams of demining crews in armored bulldozers clearing the edges of the taxiways, made him question the wisdom of his trip. Pieces of Ariana's other planes remained where they'd been bombed. Tailfins, their paint blackened and bubbled, loomed over the scene like warning flags. And burned fuselages lay like the decomposing carcasses of whales along the cratered runway.

By the door to the terminal, rocking slightly in the stinging wind, the unmistakable frame of a charred Volkswagen Beetle balanced upside down, its engine and passenger compartment picked clean.

Kabul's lone customs officer slumped at his desk in the unelectrified terminal and inspected Mortenson's passport under a shaft of light pouring through one of the holes shells had torn in the roof. Satisfied, he stamped it lazily and waved Mortenson out past a peeling likeness of slain Northern Alliance leader Shah Ahmed Massoud that his fighters had plastered on the wall when they'd taken the airport.

Mortenson had grown used to being greeted at airports in Pakistan. Arriving in Islamabad, Suleman's grinning face was the first thing he'd see after clearing customs. In Skardu, Faisal Baig would intimidate airport security into letting him meet the plane on the tarmac, so he could begin guard duty the minute Mortenson hit the ground.

But outside the terminal of Kabul's airport, Mortenson found himself alone with a pack of aggressive taxi drivers. He relied on his old trick of choosing the one who seemed least interested, throwing his bag in the back and climbing in beside him.

Abdullah Rahman, like most of Kabul, had been disfigured by war. He had no eyelids. And the right side of his face was shiny and tight, where he'd been scorched by a land mine that exploded on the shoulder of the road as he drove his cab past. His hands had been so badly burned that he couldn't close them around the steering wheel. Nonetheless, he proved a skillful navigator of Kabul's chaotic traffic.

Abdullah, like most of Kabul's residents, held a variety of jobs to feed his family. For $1.20 a month, he worked at the city's Military Hospital Library, guarding three locked cases of musty hardcovers that somehow had survived the time of the Taliban, who were in the habit of burning any book but the Koran. He drove Mortenson to his home for the next week, the bullet-riddled Kabul Peace Guest House, which looked as unlikely as the name sounded so soon on the heels of war.

In his small room without electricity or running water, Mortenson peered out between the bars on his windows at the injured buildings lining the noisy Bagh-e-Bala Road, and the injured citizens limping between them, trying to imagine his next move. But a plan of action was as hard to discern as the features of the women who floated past his windows in all-enveloping ink-blue *burkhas*.

Before arriving, he'd had a vague notion of hiring a car and heading north, trying to make contact with the Kirghiz horsemen who'd asked him for help in Zuudkhan. But Kabul was still so obviously insecure that heading blindly out into the countryside seemed suicidal. At night, shivering in the unheated room, Mortenson listened to automatic weapons fire echoing across Kabul and the concussions of rockets Taliban holdouts fired into the city from the surrounding hills.

Abdullah introduced Mortenson to his Pathan friend Hashmatullah, a handsome young fixer who'd been a Taliban soldier, until his wounds made him a liability in the field. "Like a lot of Taliban, Hash, as he told me to call him, was a *jihadi* in theory only," Mortenson explains. "He was a smart guy who would much rather have worked as a telecommunications technician than a Taliban fighter, if a job like that had been available. But the Taliban offered him three hundred dollars when he graduated from his *madrassa* to join them. So he gave the money to his mother in Khost and reported for weapons training."

Hash had been wounded when a Northern Alliance rocket-propelled grenade exploded against a wall where he'd taken cover. Four months later, puncture wounds on his back still oozed infected pus and his torn lungs whistled when he exerted himself. But Hash was ecstatic to be free of the Taliban's rigid restrictions and had shaved off the beard he'd been obliged to grow. And after Mortenson dressed his wounds and treated him with a course of antibiotics, he was ready to swear allegiance to the only American he'd ever met.

Like most everything else in Kabul, the city's schools had been badly damaged in the fighting. They were officially slated to reopen later that spring. Mortenson told Hash and Abdullah that he wanted to see how Kabul's schools were coming along, so they set out together in Abdullah's yellow Toyota, trying to find them. Only 20 percent of Kabul's 159 schools were functional enough to begin holding classes, Mortenson learned. They would have to struggle to accommodate the city's three hundred thousand students in shifts, holding classes outdoors, or in buildings so shattered they provided only rubble around which to gather, not actual shelter.

The Durkhani High School was a typical example of Afghan students' unmet needs. The principal, Uzra Faizad, told Mortenson through her powder-blue *burkha* that when her school reopened she would try to accommodate forty-five hundred students in and around the shattered Soviet-era building where her staff of ninety teachers planned to teach

each day in three shifts. The Durkhani School's projected enrollment grew every day, Uzra said, as girls came out of hiding, convinced the Taliban, who'd outlawed education for females, were finally gone.

"I was just overwhelmed listening to Uzra's story," Mortenson says. "Here was this strong, proud woman trying to do the impossible. Her school's boundary wall had been blown to rubble. The roof had fallen in. Still, she was coming to work every day and putting the place back together because she was passionate about education being the only way to solve Afghanistan's problems."

Mortenson had intended to register the CAI in Kabul so he could arrange whatever official permission was necessary to begin building schools. But along with the city's electricity and phone system, its bureaucracy was out of order. "Abdullah drove me from ministry to ministry but no one was there," Mortenson said. "So I decided to head back to Pakistan, round up some school supplies, and start helping out wherever I could."

After a week in Kabul, Mortenson was offered a seat on a Red Cross charter flight to Peshawar. After Afghanistan, Pakistan's problems seemed manageable, Mortenson thought, as he toured the Shamshatoo Camp, making sure the teachers were receiving their CAI salaries. Between Shamshatoo and the border, he stopped to photograph three young boys sitting on sacks of potatoes. Through his viewfinder, he noticed something he hadn't with his bare eyes. The boys all wore identical haunted looks, the kind he'd seen in Kabul. Mortenson put down the camera and asked them, in Pashto, if there was anything they needed.

The oldest, a boy of about thirteen named Ahmed, seemed relieved to talk to a sympathetic adult. He explained that only a week earlier, his father had been bringing a cartful of potatoes he'd bought in Peshawar back to their small village outside Jalalabad to sell, when he had been killed by a missile fired from an American plane, along with fifteen other people carting food and supplies.

With his younger brothers, Ahmed had returned to Peshawar, bought another load of potatoes at a discount from sympathetic vendors who had known their father, and was trying to arrange a ride back to his mother and sisters, who remained at home in mourning.

Ahmed spoke so blankly about his father's death, and the fact that he was telling his story to a citizen of the country whose forces had killed his father made such a slight impression on him, that Mortenson felt sure the boy was suffering from shock.

In his own way, so was he. Mortenson spent three sleepless nights at the Home Sweet Home, after Suleman fetched him from Peshawar, trying to process what he'd seen in Afghanistan. And after the misery of Kabul and the refugee camp, Mortenson looked forward to visiting familiar Skardu. At least he did until he called Parvi for an update on the status of CAI's schools.

Parvi told Mortenson that a few days earlier, in the middle of the night, a band of thugs organized by Agha Mubarek, one of northern Pakistan's most powerful village mullahs, had attacked their newest project, a coed school that they had nearly completed in the village of Hemasil, in the Shigar Valley. They had tried to set it on fire, Parvi reported. But with the wooden roof beams and window frames not yet installed, it had blackened, but refused to burn. So, swinging sledgehammers, Agha Mubarek's thugs had reduced the school's walls—its carefully carved and mortared stone bricks—to a pile of rubble.

By the time Mortenson arrived in Skardu to hold an emergency meeting about the Hemasil School, he was greeted by more bad news. Agha Mubarek had issued a *fatwa*, banning Mortenson from working in Pakistan. More upsetting to Mortenson was the fact that a powerful local politician he knew named Imran Nadim, pandering to his conservative Shia base, had publicly declared his support for Mubarek.

Upstairs, over tea and sugar cookies in the private dining room of the Indus Hotel, Mortenson held a *jirga* of his core supporters. "Mubarek wants a spoonful of custard," Parvi said, sighing. "This mullah approached Hemasil's village council and asked for a bribe to allow the school to be built. When they refused, he had it destroyed and issued his *fatwa*."

Parvi explained that he had talked to Nadim, the politician who supported Mubarek, and he had hinted the problem could be resolved with a payment. "I was furious," Mortenson says. "I wanted to round up a whattayacallit, a posse, of my allies in the military, tear into Mubarek's village, and scare him into backing down." Parvi counseled a more permanent solution. "If you approach this brigand's house surrounded by soldiers, Mubarek will promise you anything, then reverse course as quickly as the guns are gone," Parvi said. "We need to settle this once and for all in court. Shariat Court."

Mortenson had learned to rely on Parvi's advice. With Mortenson's old friend, Mehdi Ali, the village elder in Hemasil who had spearheaded the construction of the school, Parvi would press the case in Skardu's Islamic Court, Muslim against Muslim. Mortenson, Parvi advised, should keep his distance from the legal battle, and continue his critical work in Afghanistan.

Mortenson called his board from Skardu, reporting on what he'd seen in Afghanistan and requesting permission to purchase school supplies to carry back to Kabul. To his amazement, Julia Bergman offered to fly to Pakistan and accompany him on the trip he planned to take by road from Peshawar to Kabul. "It was a very courageous thing to do," Mortenson says. "There was still fighting along our route, but I couldn't talk Julia out of coming. She knew how the women of Afghanistan had suffered under the Taliban and she was desperate to help them."

In April 2002, blond Julia Bergman, wearing a flowing *shalwar kamiz* and a porcelain pendant around her neck that read "I want to be thoroughly used up when I die," stepped across the Landi Khotal border post with Mortenson and climbed into the minivan Suleman's Peshawar taxi-driver friend Monir had arranged for their trip to Kabul. The vehicle's rear seats and cargo area were packed to the ceiling with school supplies Bergman and Mortenson purchased in Peshawar. Suleman, lacking a passport, was frantic that he couldn't come along to look after them. At his urging, Monir, a Pashtun, leaned into the minivan and squeezed the back of the Pashtun driver's neck. "I swear a blood oath," he said. "If anything happens to this sahib and memsahib, I will kill you myself."

"I was surprised to see that the whole border area was wide open," Mortenson says. "I didn't see security anywhere. Osama and one hundred of his fighters could have walked right into Pakistan without anyone stopping them."

The two-hundred-mile trip to Kabul took eleven hours. "All along the road we saw burned-out, bombed tanks and other military vehicles," Bergman says. "They contrasted with the landscape, which was beautiful. Everywhere, fields were full of red and white opium poppies, and beyond them, snowcapped mountains made the countryside seem more serene than it really was."

"We stopped for bread and tea at the Spin Ghar Hotel in Jalalabad," Mortenson says, "which had been a Taliban headquarters. It looked like World War II photos I'd seen of Dresden after the fire-bombing. From my friends who had fled to Shamshatoo I knew the U.S. Air Force had carpet-bombed the region extensively with B52s. In Jalalabad, I was worried about Julia's safety. I saw absolute hate for us in people's eyes and I wondered how many of our bombs had hit innocent people like the potato salesman."

After they reached Kabul safely, Mortenson took Bergman to the Intercontinental Hotel, on a crest with a sweeping view over the wounded city. The Intercontinental was the closest thing Kabul had to fully functional lodgings. Only half of it had been reduced to rubble. For fifty dollars a night they were shown to a room in the "intact" wing, where blown-out windows had been patched with plastic sheeting and the staff brought warm buckets of water once a day for them to wash.

With Hash and Abdullah, the Americans toured Kabul's overburdened educational system. At the Kabul Medical Institute, the country's most prestigious training center for physicians, they stopped to donate medical books that an American CAI donor had asked Mortenson to carry to Kabul. Kim Trudell, from Marblehead, Massachusetts, had lost her husband, Frederick Rimmele, when, on his way to a medical conference in California on September 11, his flight, United Airlines 175, vaporized in a cloud of jet fuel against the south tower of the World Trade Center. Trudell asked Mortenson to carry her husband's medical books to Kabul, believing education was the key to resolving the crisis with militant Islam.

In the institute's cavernous, unheated lecture hall, beneath a sagging ceiling, Mortenson and Bergman found five hundred students listening attentively to a lecture. They were grateful for the donated books, because they only had ten of the textbooks required for the advanced anatomy course, Mortenson learned. And the 500 future doctors, 470 men and 30 intrepid women, took turns carrying them home and copying out chapters and sketching diagrams by hand.

But even that laborious process was an improvement from the school's status a few months earlier. Dr. Nazir Abdul, a pediatrician, explained that while the Taliban had ruled Kabul, they had banned all books with illustrations and publicly burned any they found. Armed Taliban enforcers from the despised Department of the Promotion of Virtue and the Prevention of Vice had stood at the rear of the lecture hall during class, making sure the school's professors didn't draw anatomical diagrams on the blackboard.

"We are textbook physicians only," Dr. Abdul said. "We don't have the most basic tools of our profession. We have no money for blood pressure cuffs or stethoscopes. And I, a physician, have never in my life looked through a microscope."

With Abdullah's scarred hands steering them around bomb craters, Mortenson and Bergman toured a cluster of eighty villages to the west of Kabul called Maidan Shah. Mortenson knew that most of the foreign aid now trickling into Afghanistan would never make it out of Kabul, and as was his strategy in Pakistan, he was anxious to serve Afghanistan's rural poor. The three hundred students at the Shahabudeen Middle School were in need of much more than the pencils and notebooks that Hash helped Mortenson unload from Abdullah's taxi.

Shahabudeen teachers held class for the younger boys in rusty shipping containers. The school's eldest students, nine ninth-grade boys, studied in the back of a scorched armored personnel carrier that had had its treads blown off by an antitank round. Wedged carefully into the gunner's hatch, which they used as a window, the class displayed their prize possession—a volleyball that a Swedish aid worker had given them as a gift. "Sweetish man have the long golden hairs, like a mountain goat," one bright-eyed boy with lice jumping from his close-cropped scalp told Mortenson, showing off his progress studying English.

But it was the lack of shelter for the school's female students that tore, particularly, at Mortenson's heart. "Eighty girls were forced to study outside," Mortenson says. "They were trying to hold class, but the wind kept whipping sand in their eyes and tipping over their blackboard." They were thrilled with their new notebooks and pencils, and clutched the notebooks tightly to keep them from blowing away.

As Mortenson walked back toward his taxi, four U.S. Army Cobra Attack Helicopters buzzed the school at high speed, streaking fifty feet above the terrified students with full payloads of Hellfire missiles bristling from their weapons pods. The girls' blackboard blew over in the blast of their rotor wash, shattering against the stony ground.

"Everywhere we went, we saw U.S. planes and helicopters. And I can only imagine the money we were spending on our military," Julia Bergman says. "But where was the aid? I'd heard so much about what

America promised Afghanistan's people while I was at home—how rebuilding the country was one of our top priorities. But being there, and seeing so little evidence of help for Afghanistan's children, particularly from the United States, was really embarrassing and frustrating for me."

The next day, Mortenson brought Bergman to meet the principal of the Durkhani School, and to drop off supplies for Uzra Faizad's forty-five hundred students. He saw that Faizad's students had to climb up crude log ladders into the second-story classrooms that had survived the shelling, because the stairs had been blown away and were not yet rebuilt, but the school was operating beyond capacity, teaching three shifts every day. Delighted to see Mortenson again, Uzra invited the Americans to tea in her home.

A widow, whose *mujahadeen* husband had been killed fighting the Soviets with Massoud's forces, Uzra lived with nunnish simplicity in a one-room shed on the school grounds. During the time of the Taliban, she had fled north to Taloqan, and tutored girls secretly after the city fell. But now, back home, she advocated female education openly. Uzra rolled up the flap of burlap shading the single window, removed her all-enveloping *burkha*, and hung it on a hook above one of her few worldly possessions, a neatly folded wool blanket. Then she crouched by a small propane stove to make tea.

"You know, in my country women would ask, " 'If the Taliban is gone, why do women in Afghanistan still wear the *burkha*?' " Bergman said.

"I'm a conservative lady," Uzra said, "and it suits me. Also, I feel safer in it. In fact, I insist that all my lady teachers wear the *burkha* in the bazaar. We don't want to give anyone an excuse to interfere with our girls' studies."

"Still, the emancipated women from the United States would want to know whether you feel oppressed having to look out through that little slit," Bergman continued her inquiry.

Uzra smiled broadly for the first time since Mortenson met her, and as she freed herself from her *burkha*, he was struck by how beautiful she still was at fifty despite the hardships she'd endured. "We women of Afghanistan see the light through education," Uzra replied. "Not through this or that hole in a piece of cloth."

When the green tea was ready, Uzra served her guests, apologizing that she had no sugar to offer them. "There is one favor I must ask you," Uzra said, after everyone had tasted their tea. "We're very grateful that the Americans chased out the Taliban. But for five months now, I haven't received my salary, even though I was told to expect it soon. Can you discuss my problem with someone in America to see if they know what happened?"

After distributing forty dollars of CAI's money to Uzra and twenty dollars to each of her ninety teachers, who hadn't been receiving their salaries either, Mortenson saw Bergman safely onto a United Nations charter flight to Islamabad and began trying to track down Uzra's money. On his third odyssey through the echoing halls of the crumbling Ministry of Finance, he met Afghanistan's deputy minister of finance, who threw up his hands when Mortenson asked him why Uzra and her teachers weren't receiving their pay.

"He told me that less than a quarter of the aid money President Bush had promised his country had actually arrived in Afghanistan. And of those insufficient funds, he said that $680 million had been 'redirected,' to build runways and bulk up supply depots in Bahrain, Kuwait, and Qatar for the invasion of Iraq everyone expected would soon begin."

On the Ariana 727 to Dubai, the British Air 777 to London, and the Delta 767 to D.C., Mortenson felt like a heat-seeking missile speeding toward his own government, fueled by outrage. "The time for us to turn all the suffering we'd helped to cause in Afghanistan into something positive was slipping away. I was so upset I paced the aisles of the planes all the way to Washington," Mortenson says. "If we couldn't do something as simple as seeing that a hero like Uzra gets her forty-dollar a-month salary, then how could we ever hope to do the hard work it takes to win the war on terror?"

It was impossible for Mortenson to aim his anger at Mary Bono. When the congresswoman's former pop-star husband Sonny Bono, a Republican representative from Palm Springs, California, had died skiing into a tree in 1998, she was urged to run for her husband's seat by Newt Gingrich. And like her late husband, she was initially dismissed as a joke by her opponents, before proving to be politically adept. A former gymnast, rock climber, and fitness instructor, Bono hardly resembled a run-of-the mill Republican when she arrived in Washington at the age of thirty-seven, especially when she displayed her honed physique in an evening gown at official functions.

And soon Mary Bono, with an intelligence as unsettling as her looks, was being talked of as a rising star in the Republican party. By the time Mortenson landed in her office on Capitol Hill, Bono had overwhelmingly won reelection and the respect of her peers on both sides of the aisle. And in testosterone-dominated D.C., her appearance wasn't exactly a handicap.

"When I arrived in Washington, I had no idea what to do. I felt like I had been dropped in a remote Afghan village where I didn't know the customs," Mortenson says. "Mary spent an entire day with me, showing me how everything worked. She walked me through a tunnel between her office and the Capitol, with dozens of other representatives on their way to vote, and along the way, introduced me to everyone. She had all these congressmen blushing like schoolboys. And me, too, especially once she started introducing me around, saying, "Here's someone you need to meet. This is Greg Mortenson. He's a real American hero.""

In a congressional hearing room in the Capitol, Bono had arranged a lecture for Mortenson, and sent a bulletin to every member of Congress inviting them to "come meet an American fighting terror in Pakistan and Afghanistan by building girls' schools."

"After I heard Greg speak, it was the least I could do," Bono says. "I meet so many people day in and day out who say they're trying to do good and help people. But Greg is the real thing. He's walking the walk. And I'm his biggest fan. The sacrifices that he and his family have made are staggering. He represents the best of America. I just wanted to do what I could to see that his humanity had a chance to rub off on as many people as possible."

After setting up his old slide projector, which was held together by a fresh application of duct tape, Mortenson turned to face a room full of members of Congress and their senior staff. He was wearing his only suit, a brown plaid, and a pair of worn brown suede after-ski moccasins. Mortenson would have rather faced a sea of two hundred empty seats, but he remembered how Uzra's innocent question about her missing salary had sent him on this mission, so he projected his first slide. Mortenson showed images of both the stark beauty and poverty of Pakistan, and spoke with growing heat about Uzra's missing salary and the importance of America keeping its promise to rebuild Afghanistan.

A Republican congressman from California interrupted Mortenson in midsentence, challenging him. "Building schools for kids is just fine and dandy," Mortenson remembers the congressman saying. "But our primary need as a nation now is security. Without security, what does all this matter?"

Mortenson took a breath. He felt an ember of the anger he'd carried all the way from Kabul flare. "I don't do what I'm doing to fight terror," Mortenson said, measuring his words, trying not to get himself kicked out of the Capitol. "I do it because I care about kids. Fighting terror is maybe seventh or eighth on my list of priorities. But working over there, I've learned a few things. I've learned that terror doesn't happen because some group of people somewhere like Pakistan or Afghanistan simply decide to hate us. It happens because children aren't being offered a bright enough future that they have a reason to choose life over death."

Then Mortenson continued with unusual eloquence, the rawness he felt after his passage through Afghanistan scouring away his self-consciousness. He spoke about Pakistan's impoverished public schools. He spoke about the *Wahhabi madrassas* sprouting like cancerous cells, and the billions of dollars Saudi sheikhs carried into the region in suitcases to fuel the factories of *jihad*. As he hit his stride, the conference room became quiet, except for the sound of pens and pencils furiously scratching.

After he'd finished, and answered several questions, a legislative aid to a congresswoman from New York City introduced herself while Mortenson was scrambling to pack his slides. "This is amazing," she said. "How come we never hear about this stuff in the news or our briefings? You need to write a book."

"I don't have time to write," Mortenson said, as General Anthony Zinni, the former head of CentCom, arrived surrounded by uniformed officers, to give another scheduled briefing.

"You should make time," she said.

"Ask my wife if you don't believe me. I don't even have time to sleep."

After his talk, Mortenson walked the Mall, wandering aimlessly toward the Potomac, wondering if his message had been heard. Knots of tourists strolled leisurely over the rolling lawns, between the frank black V of the Vietnam memorial and the white marble palace where a likeness of Lincoln brooded, waiting for time to bind up the nation's newest wounds.

A few months later, Mortenson found himself on the other side of the Potomac, invited to the Pentagon by a Marine general who had donated one thousand dollars to the CAI after reading about Mortenson's work.

The general escorted Mortenson down a polished marble hallway toward the office of the secretary of defense. "What I remember most is that the people we passed didn't make eye contact," Mortenson says. "They walked quickly, most of them clutching laptops under their arms, speeding toward their next task like missiles, like there wasn't time to look at me. And I remember thinking I was in the army once, but this didn't have anything to do with the military I knew. This was a laptop army."

In the secretary of defense's office, Mortenson remembers being surprised that he wasn't offered a seat. In Pakistan, meetings with high officials, even cursory meetings, meant, at minimum, being escorted to a chair and offered tea. Standing uncomfortably in his unfamiliar suit, Mortenson felt at a loss for what to do or say.

"We only stayed a minute, while I was introduced," Mortenson says. "And I wish I could tell you I said something amazing to Donald Rumsfeld, the kind of thing that made him question the whole conduct of the war on terror, but mostly what I did was stare at his shoes.

"I don't know much about that kind of thing, but even I could tell they were really nice shoes. They looked expensive and they were perfectly shined. I remember also that Rumsfeld had on a fancy-looking gray suit, and he smelled like cologne. And I remember thinking, even though I knew that the Pentagon had been hit by a hijacked plane, that we were very far away from the fighting, from the heat and dust I'd come from in Kabul."

Back in the inhospitable hallway again, walking toward a room where Mortenson was scheduled to brief top military planners, he wondered how the distance that he felt in the Pentagon affected the decisions made in the building. How would his feelings about the conduct of the war change if everything he'd just seen, the boys who had lost their potato salesman father, the girls with the blowing-over blackboard, and all the wounded attempting to walk the streets of Kabul with the pieces of limbs the land mines and cluster-bombs had left them, were just numbers on a laptop screen?

In a small lecture hall half full of uniformed officers and sprinkled with civilians in suits, Mortenson pulled no punches. "I felt like whatever I had to say was sort of futile. I wasn't going to change the way the Bush administration had decided to fight its wars," he says, "so I decided to just let it rip.

"I supported the war in Afghanistan," Mortenson said after he introduced himself. "I believed in it because I believed we were serious when we said we planned to rebuild Afghanistan. I'm here because I know that military victory is only the first phase of winning the war on terror and I'm afraid we're not willing to take the next steps."

Then Mortenson talked of the tribal traditions that attended conflict in the region—the way warring parties held a *jirga* before doing battle, to discuss how many losses they were willing to accept, since victors were expected to care for the widows and orphans of the rivals they have vanquished.

"People in that part of the world are used to death and violence," Mortenson said. "And if you tell them, 'We're sorry your father died, but he died a martyr so Afghanistan could be free,' and if you offer them compensation and honor their sacrifice, I think people will support us, even now. But the worst thing you can do is what we're doing—ignoring the victims. To call them 'collateral damage' and not even try to count the numbers of the dead. Because to ignore them is to deny they ever existed, and there is no greater insult in the Islamic world. For that, we will never be forgiven."

After an hour, reiterating his warning about the legions of *jihadis* being forged in extremist *madrassas*, Mortenson wound up his speech with an idea that had come to him while touring the twisted wreckage of a home he'd seen at the site of a cruise missile strike on Kabul's Street of Guests.

"I'm no military expert," Mortenson said. "And these figures might not be exactly right. But as best as I can tell, we've launched 114 Tomahawk cruise missiles into Afghanistan so far. Now take the cost of one of those missiles tipped with a Raytheon guidance system, which I think is about $840,000. For that much money, you could build dozens of schools that could provide tens of thousands of students with a balanced nonextremist education over the course of a generation. Which do you think will make us more secure?"

After his speech, Mortenson was approached by a noticeably fit man whose military bloodlines were obvious, even in the well-tailored civilian suit he wore.

"Could you draw us a map of all the *Wahhabi madrassas*?" he asked.

"Not if I wanted to live," Mortenson said.

"Could you put up a school next to each of the *madrassas*?"

"Sort of like a Starbucks? To drive the *jihadis* out of business?"

"I'm serious. We can get you the money. How about $2.2 million? How many schools could you build with that?" the man asked.

"About one hundred," Mortenson said.

"Isn't that what you want?"

"People there would find out the money came from the military and I'd be out of business."

"Not a problem. We could make it look like a private donation from a businessman in Hong Kong." The man flipped through a notebook that listed miscellaneous military appropriations. Mortenson saw foreign names he didn't recognize and numbers streaming down the margins of the pages: $15 million, $4.7 million, $27 million. "Think about it and call me," he said, jotting a few lines in the notebook and handing Mortenson his card.

Mortenson did think about it. The good that would radiate out from one hundred schools was constantly on his mind and he toyed with taking the military's money throughout much of 2002, though he knew he never could. "I realized my credibility in that part of the world depended on me not being associated with the American government," Mortenson says, "especially its military."

The well-attended slide shows he continued to give that year brought CAI's bank balance up appreciably, but the organization's finances were as shaky as ever. Just maintaining CAI's schools in Pakistan, while launching a new initiative for Afghanistan's children, could wipe out CAI's resources if Mortenson wasn't careful.

So Mortenson decided to defer the raise the board had approved for him, from twenty-eight thousand dollars to thirty-five thousand dollars a year, until CAI's finances were on firmer footing. And as 2002 turned into 2003, and the headlines about weapons of mass destruction and the approaching war with Iraq battered Mortenson early every morning as he sat down at his computer, he was increasingly glad he'd steered clear of the military's money.

In those charged days after 9/11, Mortenson's elderly donor, Patsy Collins, had urged him to speak out and fight for peace, just before she'd died, to make this time of national crisis his finest hour. And traveling across America, through the turbulence the attacks had left behind, Mortenson had certainly overcome his shyness and done his share of talking. But, he asked himself, packing his duffel bag for his twenty-seventh trip to Pakistan, preparing to take wrenching leave, once again, of his family, who knew if anyone was listening?

CHAPTER 22

"THE ENEMY IS IGNORANCE"

As the U.S. confronts Saddam Hussein's regime in Iraq,
Greg Mortenson, 45, is quietly waging his own campaign against Islamic
fundamentalists, who often recruit members
through religious schools called madrassas. Mortenson's approach
hinges on a simple idea: that by building secular
schools and helping to promote education—particularly for girls—in the
world's most volatile war zone, support for the
Taliban and other extremist sects eventually will dry up.

—Kevin Fedarko, *Parade* cover story, April 6, 2003

HUSSAIN HIT THE brakes where the road ended, and his passengers climbed out over the plastic-wrapped box of dynamite. It was dark where the dirt road they'd bounced up for ten hours petered out into a footpath between boulders—the trailhead to the High Karakoram. To Mortenson, Hussain, Apo, and Baig, arriving at the last settlement before the Baltoro was a comforting homecoming. But to Kevin Fedarko, it seemed he'd been dropped at the wild edge of the Earth.

Fedarko, a former editor for *Outside* magazine, had quit his office job in favor of reporting from the field. And that cold September evening, Fedarko and photographer Teru Kuwayama found themselves about as far outside as it was possible to get. "The stars over the Karakoram that night were incredible, like a solid mass of light," Fedarko remembers. Then three of the stars detached themselves from the heavens and drifted down to welcome the village of Korphe's visitors.

"The headman of Korphe and two of his friends came switchbacking down the cliff above us," Fedarko says. "They carried Chinese hurricane lanterns and escorted us across a suspension bridge and up into the darkness. It was the sort of thing you don't forget; it was like entering a medieval village, walking through stone and mud alleys by the faint light of the lamps."

Fedarko had come to Pakistan to report a story he would eventually publish in *Outside*, called "The Coldest War." After nineteen years of fighting, no journalist had ever reported from bases on both sides of the high-altitude conflict between India and Pakistan. But with Mortenson's help, he was about to be the first.

"Greg bent over backward to help me," Fedarko says. "He arranged my permits with the Pakistan army, introduced me to everyone, and organized helicopter pickups for me and Teru. I had no connections in Pakistan and never could have done it myself. Greg showed me an overwhelming generosity that went beyond anything I'd ever experienced as a journalist."

But as Fedarko crawled into bed that night and wrapped himself against the cold in "dirty wool blankets that smelled like dead goats," he had no way of knowing that soon, he would more than repay Mortenson's kindness.

"In the morning, when I opened my eyes," Fedarko says, "I felt like I was in the middle of a carnival."

"Before Haji Ali died, he had constructed a small building next to his house, and told me to consider it my home in Baltistan," Mortenson says. "Twaha had decorated it himself with different-colored scraps of fabric, covered the floor with blankets and pillows, and plastered pictures on the wall from all my different trips to Korphe. It had sort of become a combination of a men's club and Korphe's unofficial town hall."

When Fedarko sat up to accept a cup of tea, a town meeting was about to begin. "The people were so excited to see Greg that they had crept in all around us while we were sleeping," Fedarko says, "and once they had pressed a cup of tea into each of our hands the meeting got going full blast, with everyone laughing, shouting, and arguing like we'd been awake for hours."

"Whenever I came to Korphe or any village where we worked, I'd usually spend a few days meeting with the village council," Mortenson says. "There was always a lot to work out. I had to get reports about the school, find out if anything needed fixing, if the students needed supplies, if the teachers were getting their pay regularly. There were also always a few requests for other things—another sewing machine for the women's center, requests for some pipe to repair a water project. That sort of thing. Business as usual."

But this morning, something far from usual happened in the Braldu Valley's last village. A pretty, self-assured young woman burst into the room, stepped through the circle of thirty tea-sipping men sitting cross-legged on cushions, and approached the man who had built Korphe a school. Taking a seat boldly in front of Mortenson, Jahan interrupted the rollicking meeting of her village's elders.

"Dr. Greg," she said in Balti, her voice unwavering. "You made our village a promise once and you fulfilled it when you built our school. But you made me another promise the day the school was completed," she said. "Do you remember it?"

Mortenson smiled. Whenever he visited one of CAI's schools, he made time to ask all the students a little about themselves and their goals for the future, especially girls. Local village leaders accompanying him would shake their heads at first, amazed that a grown man would waste hours inquiring about the hopes and dreams of girls. But on return visits, they soon chalked the talk up to Mortenson's eccentricity and settled in to wait while he shook the hand of every student and asked them what they wanted to be one day, promising to help them reach those goals if they studied hard. Jahan had been one of the Korphe School's best students, and Mortenson had often listened to her talk about the hopes she had for her career.

"I told you my dream was to become a doctor one day and you said you would help," Jahan said, at the center of the circle of men. "Well, that day is here. You must keep your promise to me. I'm ready to begin my medical training and I need twenty thousand rupees."

Jahan unfolded a piece of paper on which she'd written a petition, carefully worded in English, detailing the course of study in maternal health care she proposed to attend in Skardu. Mortenson, impressed, noticed that she'd even bullet-pointed the tuition fee and cost of school supplies.

"This is great, Jahan," Mortenson said. "I'll read this when I have time and discuss it with your father."

"No!" Jahan said forcefully, in English, before switching back to Balti so she could explain herself clearly. "You don't understand. My class starts next week. I need money now!"

Mortenson grinned at the girl's pluck. The first graduate of his first school's first class had obviously learned the lesson he'd hoped all of his female students would absorb eventually—not to take a backseat to men. Mortenson asked Apo for the pouch of CAI's rupees the old cook carried, incongruously, in a pink child's daypack and counted out twenty thousand rupees, about four hundred dollars, before handing them to Jahan's father for his daughter's tuition.

"It was one of the most incredible things I've ever seen in my life," Fedarko says. "Here comes this teenage girl, in the center of a conservative Islamic village, waltzing into a circle of men, breaking through about sixteen layers of traditions at once: She had graduated from school and was the first educated woman in a valley of three thousand people. She didn't defer to anyone, sat down right in front of Greg, and handed him the product of the revolutionary skills she'd acquired— a proposal, in English, to better herself, and improve the life of her village.

"At that moment," Fedarko says, "for the first time in sixteen years of working as a journalist, I lost all objectivity. I told Greg, 'What you're doing here is a much more important story than the one I've come to report. I have to find some way to tell it.'"

Later that fall, stopping off in New York City on his way home to recuperate from spending two months, at altitude, among Pakistan and India's soldiers, Fedarko had lunch with his old friend Lamar Graham, then the managing editor of *Parade* magazine. "Lamar asked me about my war story, but I just found myself blurting out everything I'd seen and done during my time with Greg," Fedarko says.

"It was one of the most amazing stories I've ever heard," Graham says. "I told Kevin, if even half of it was true, we had to tell it in *Parade*."

The next day, the office phone rang in Mortenson's basement. "Man, are you for real," Graham asked in his Missouri drawl. "Have you really done all the things Kevin's told me about? In Pakistan? On your own? 'Cause if you have, you're my hero."

It had never taken much to embarrass Mortenson. This day was no different. "Well, I guess so," he said slowly, feeling the blood creep into his face, "but I had a lot of help."

On Sunday, April 6, with American ground forces massing on the outskirts of Baghdad, fighting their way into position for their final assault on Saddam Hussein's capital, 34 million copies of a magazine with

Mortenson's picture on the cover and a headline declaring "He Fights Terror With Books" saturated the nation's newspapers.

Never had Mortenson reached so many people, at such a critical time. The message he'd fought to publicize, ever since the morning he'd been shaken awake in Zuudkhan to hear the news from New York, had finally been delivered. Fedarko's story led with Jahan's breaking into a circle of men in Korphe, then connected Mortenson's work on the other side of the world with the well-being of Americans at home. "If we try to resolve terrorism with military might and nothing else," Mortenson argued to *Parade*'s readers, "then we will be no safer than we were before 9/11. If we truly want a legacy of peace for our children, we need to understand that this is a war that will ultimately be won with books, not with bombs."

Mortenson's message hit a national nerve, proposing, as it did, another way for a deeply divided nation to approach the war on terror. More than eighteen thousand letters and e-mails flooded in from all fifty states and twenty foreign countries.

"Greg's story created one of the most powerful reader responses in *Parade*'s sixty-four years of publishing," says *Parade* editor-in-chief Lee Kravitz. "I think it's because people understand that he's a real American hero. Greg Mortenson is fighting a personal war on terror that has an impact on all of us, and his weapon is not guns or bombs, but schools. What could be a better story than that?"

American readers agreed. Each day, for weeks after the article appeared, the wave of e-mails, letters, and telephone calls of support surged higher, threatening to swamp a small charitable organization run out of a basement in Montana.

Mortenson turned for help to his pragmatic family friend Anne Beyersdorfer, a liberal Democrat who would later serve as a media consultant for Arnold Schwarzenegger's successful campaign for governor of California. Beyersdorfer flew from Washington, D.C., to set up a "shock and awe" center in Mortenson's basement. She hired a phone bank in Omaha, Nebraska, to answer calls, and bumped up the bandwidth of the Central Asia Institute's website to handle the traffic that threatened to shut it down.

The Tuesday after the story appeared, Mortenson went to pick up mail addressed to Central Asia Institute's PO Box 7209. Eighty letters were stuffed inside. When Mortenson returned on Thursday, he found a note taped to his box telling him to pick up his mail at the counter. "So you're Greg Mortenson," the postmaster said. "I hope you brought a wheelbarrow." Mortenson loaded five canvas sacks of letters into his Toyota and returned the next day to haul home four more. For the next three months, the letters from *Parade* readers kept Bozeman's postal workers unusually busy.

By the time images of Saddam Hussein's statue falling had been beamed around the world, Mortenson realized that his life had been forever changed—the outpouring of support left him no choice but to embrace his new national prominence. "I felt like America had spoken. My tribe had spoken," Mortenson says. "And the most amazing thing was that after I finished reading every message, there was only one negative letter in the whole bunch."

The response was so overwhelmingly positive that it salved the wounds of the death threats he'd received soon after 9/11. "What really humbled me was how the response came from all sorts of people, from church groups, Muslims, Hindus, and Jews," Mortenson says. "I got letters of support from a lesbian political organization in Marin County, a Baptist youth group in Alabama, a general in the U.S. Air Force, and just about every other kind of group you can imagine."

Jake Greenberg, a thirteen-year-old from the suburbs of Philadelphia, was so fired up by reading about Mortenson's work that he donated more than one thousand dollars of his bar mitzvah money to the CAI and volunteered to come to Pakistan and help out himself. "When I heard about Greg's story," Greenberg says, "I realized that, unlike me, children in the Muslim world might not have educational opportunities. It makes no difference that I'm a Jew sending money to help Muslims. We all need to work together to plant the seeds of peace."

A woman who identified herself only as Sufiya e-mailed the following to CAI's website: "As a Muslim woman, born in America, I am showered with God's blessings, unlike my sisters around the world who endure oppression. Arab nations should look at your tremendous work and wallow in shame for never helping their own people. With sincere respect and admiration, I thank you."

Letters poured in from American servicemen and women, embracing Mortenson as a comrade on the front lines of the fight against terror. "As a captain in the U.S. Army and a veteran of the war in

Afghanistan with the Eighty-second Airborne Division I have had a very unique and up-close perspective on life in the rural portions of Central Asia," wrote Jason B. Nicholson from Fayetteville, North Carolina. "The war in Afghanistan was, and continues to be, bloody and destructive; most of all on those who deserve it least—the innocent civilians who only wish to make a wage and live a decent life with their families. CAI's projects provide a good alternative to the education offered in many of the radicalized *madrassas* from where the Taliban sprung forth with their so-called 'fundamental Islamacism.' What can be better than a future world made safe for us all by education? The Central Asia Institute is now my charity of choice."

Thousands of people felt the same way. By the time U.S. forces had settled in to endure their long occupation of Iraq, and Anne Beyersdorfer had dismantled the "shock and awe" operation and returned home, the CAI had gone from wallowing near financial insolvency to possessing a bank balance of more than one million dollars.

"It had been so long since the CAI had some real money that I wanted to get right back over there and put it to work," Mortenson says. "But the board pressed me to make some changes we'd been talking about for years, and I agreed it was time."

For six hundred dollars a month, Mortenson rented a small wood-paneled office space in a nondescript building a block from Bozeman's Main Street, and hired four employees to schedule his speaking engagements, produce a newsletter, maintain a website, and manage CAI's growing database of donors. And, at the board's insistence, after a decade of living paycheck to paycheck, Mortenson accepted a long-overdue raise that nearly doubled his salary.

Tara Bishop appreciated that her husband's salary finally began to reflect the hardships her family had endured for almost a decade. But she was far from happy about how frequently her husband would now be away, launching ambitious new projects the *Parade* money made possible.

"After Greg's kidnapping, and after 9/11, I didn't bother trying to talk Greg out of going back because I knew he'd go no matter what," Tara says. "So I've learned to live in what I call 'functional denial' while he's away. I just keep telling myself that he'll be fine. I trust the people he has around him, and I trust his cultural intelligence after working over there for so long. Still, I know it only takes one fundamentalist whack job to kill him. But I refuse to let myself think about that while he's away," she says with a strained laugh.

Christiane Letinger, whose mountaineer husband, Charlie Shimanski, predicts Mortenson will win the Nobel Peace Prize one day, argues that Tara Bishop's calm endurance is every bit as heroic as the risks her husband takes overseas. "How many women would have the strength and vision to let the father of their children work in such a dangerous place for months at a time?" Letinger asks. "Tara not only allows it, but supports it, because she believes so strongly in Greg's mission. If that's not heroism I don't know what is."

Suleman was the first person in Pakistan to get the good news. As they drove past the scale model of the mountain where Pakistan had detonated its "Muslim Bomb," Mortenson told his friend and fixer about the explosion of support Americans had provided to the CAI. Mortenson, whose staff in Pakistan had worked long hours alongside him for years, without benefiting personally the way locals allied with a foreigner might have expected to, was determined to share CAI's good fortune with his troops.

Mortenson told Suleman his salary would increase immediately, from eight hundred dollars to sixteen hundred dollars a year. That would be more than enough money for Suleman to achieve the dream he had been saving for, to move his family to Rawalpindi from his home village of Dhok Luna, and send his son Imran to private school. Suleman stole a glance from the road ahead to look at Mortenson, waggling his head with delight.

In the years since they'd been working together, both men had put on considerable weight, and Suleman's hair had gone mostly gray. But unlike Mortenson, once armed with his new salary, Suleman refused to let age have its way without a fight.

Suleman drove to the Jinnah Super Market, a fancy shopping center, walked into a hairdresser's, and ordered the most extravagant treatment on the menu. When he stepped outside two hours later, and found Mortenson browsing at his favorite bookstore, the thick thatch of graying hair over Suleman's grinning face had been dyed a shocking shade of orange.

In Skardu, Mortenson called a *jirga* in the upstairs dining room of the Indus to announce the good news. Gathering his staff around two tables, he announced that Apo, Hussain, and Faisal would now receive the raises they had deserved for years, and their salaries would double, from five hundred dollars to one thousand dollars a year. Parvi, who already made two thousand dollars annually as CAI's director in Pakistan, would now receive four thousand dollars a year, a formidable salary in Skardu for the man who made all of CAI's projects in Pakistan possible.

To Hussain, Mortenson disbursed an additional five hundred dollars, so he could have the engine of the aging Land Cruiser that had logged so many miles overhauled. Parvi suggested renting a warehouse in Skardu, now that they had sufficient funds, so they could buy cement and building supplies in bulk and store them until they were needed.

Mortenson hadn't felt so fired up and frantic to work since the day, six years earlier, that he had gathered his staff around one of the plank tables downstairs in the lobby and told them to start spending the *Parade* readers' money as quickly as they could construct schools. Before leaving town on a series of jeep rides and helicopter trips to jump-start two dozen new schools, women's centers, and water schemes, Mortenson proposed one project more: "For a long time, I've been worrying about what to do when our students graduate," he said. "Mr. Parvi, would you look into what it would cost to build a hostel in Skardu, so our best students would have someplace to stay if we give them scholarships to continue their education?"

"I'd be delighted, Dr. Sahib," Parvi said, smiling, freed finally to organize the project he'd been advocating for years.

"Oh, and one more thing," Mortenson said.

"Yes, Dr. Greg, sir."

"Yasmine would be a perfect candidate to receive one of CAI's first scholarships. Can you let me know what her tuition would be if she went to private high school in the fall?"

Yasmine, fifteen, was Parvi's daughter, a straight-A student who had obviously inherited her father's fierce intelligence, and just as obviously inspired his fierce devotion. "Well?"

For a rare, elongated moment, Ghulam Parvi, the most eloquent man in Skardu, was struck silent, his mouth hanging open. "I don't know what to say," he said.

"*Allah-u-Akbhar!*" Apo shouted, throwing up his hands in theatrical rapture, as the table exploded in laughter. "How long . . ." he croaked between giggles in his gravelly voice, "I've waited . . . for this day!"

Throughout the summer of 2003, Mortenson worked feverishly, testing the limits of the Land Cruiser's rebuilt engine as he and his reenergized crew visited each of the new construction sites that the *Parade* money had made possible, smoothing out obstacles, and delivering supplies. Nine new schools in northern Pakistan were progressing smoothly, but one of CAI's established projects, the Halde School, which the aging Mouzafer had helped bring to his village, had hit a roadblock, Mortenson learned. The five-room school had done so well that its operation was now entrusted to the increasingly effective local government.

Yakub, who had seen Mortenson's team member Scott Darsney safely off the Baltoro back in 1993, had created a crisis. An aging porter whose upside days were done, like his neighbor Mouzafer, Yakub wanted to be appointed the school's *chokidar*, or watchman. He had petitioned the government, requesting the job. But after receiving no reply, he chained the doors of the school, demanding payment.

A day after the news reached him in Skardu, Mortenson arrived in the Land Cruiser, dusty and exhausted from the eight-hour trip. Grinning with his sudden inspiration, Mortenson reached under his driver Hussain's seat.

He found Yakub standing uncertainly by the chained and padlocked door to the Halde School as a crowd of villagers gathered. Smilingly, Mortenson patted Yakub's shoulder with his right hand, before holding out the two sticks of dynamite he clenched in his left fist.

After exchanging pleasantries and inquiries about friends and family, Yakub's voice shook as he asked the question he knew he must: "What is that for, Dr. Greg, Sahib, sir?"

Mortenson handed the two sticks of dynamite to Yakub, still smiling. Perhaps, he thought, the explosives could clear up obstacles more intractable than a road covered with rocks. "I want you take these, Yakub," Mortenson said in Balti, pressing them into Yakub's shaking hand. "I'm leaving now for Khanday, to check on the progress of another school. When I come back tomorrow, I'll be bringing a match. If I don't see that the school is open and the students are going to class, we're going to make an announcement at the village mosque for everyone to gather here and watch you blow it up."

Mortenson left Yakub holding the dynamite in both trembling

hands and walked back toward the jeep. "The choice is yours," he said over his shoulder, climbing back in. "See you tomorrow. *Khuda hafiz!*"

Mortenson returned the next afternoon and delivered new pencils and notebooks to Halde's students, who were happily reinstalled at their desks. His old friend Mouzafer was not yet too feeble to assert his will on the school he helped to build. From Apo, Mortenson learned that Mouzafer, whose two grandchildren attended the Halde School, had also offered Yakub a choice after Mortenson left. "Get your keys and open the school," he'd told Yakub, "or I'll personally tie you to a tree and blow you up with Dr. Greg's dynamite." As punishment, Mortenson later learned, Halde's village council forced Yakub to sweep the school early each morning without pay.

Not every obstacle to education in northern Pakistan was so easily overcome. Mortenson would have liked to deliver dynamite to Agha Mubarek, but struggled to follow Parvi's advice, and observe, from afar, as the case against the mullah for destroying the Hemasil School progressed in Shariat Court.

After Korphe, no CAI project in Pakistan was closer to Mortenson's heart than the Hemasil School. In 1998, Ned Gillette, an American climber and former Olympic skier Mortenson admired, was killed while trekking in the Haramosh Valley, between Hemasil and Hunza, with his wife, Susan. The details of his death are still disputed by Pakistan's authorities, but the story Mortenson had pieced together from talking to Haramosh villagers was this: Gillette and his wife had been approached by porters who insisted that they hire them. Gillette, committed to traveling alpiniste-style, with only two light backpacks, refused, a bit too forcefully for the porters' taste. Late that night, the two men returned with a shotgun to the tent where the couple was sleeping.

"My guess is that perhaps they were just planning to rob them," Mortenson says. "To take something that, in their minds, would avenge their wounded honor. But, unfortunately, things got out of hand." Gillette was killed by a shotgun blast to the abdomen. Susan, badly wounded by buckshot in the thigh, survived.

"As far as I know," Mortenson says, "Ned Gillette was the first Westerner ever murdered in northern Pakistan. When his sister, Debbie Law, contacted me, and asked to donate money so a school could be built in her brother's honor, I jumped to make it happen. I couldn't imagine a more meaningful tribute."

But the site the elders of Shigar Valley chose for the Ned Gillette School was not only near the pass where he was murdered, it was adjacent to Chutran, mullah Agha Mubarek's village.

"After we had the walls built, and the men of our village were about to begin putting on the roof, Agha Mubarek and his men arrived to block the project," says Mehdi Ali, the village elder who oversaw the construction of the Hemasil School. Mehdi was an activist for education whose father, Sheikh Mohammed, had written asking for a ruling from Iran after the first *fatwa* had been declared against Mortenson. "Mubarek told us, 'This *kafir* school is no good. It is the non-Muslim school. It is to recruit Christians.' I told him, 'I know Mr. Greg Mortenson for a long time and he never does such like that,' but Mubarek wouldn't hear me. So after midnight, his men came with their hammers and tried to take away our children's future."

Mehdi, along with Parvi, had paraded character witnesses for Mortenson through the high Shariat Court all spring and summer, and testified themselves. "I told the mullah in charge that Agha Mubarek collects money from my people and never provides any *zakat* for our children," Mehdi Ali says. "I told them Agha Mubarek has no business making a *fatwa* on a saintly man like Dr. Greg. It is he who should be judged in the eyes of Allah Almighty."

In August 2003, when the Shariat Court issued its final ruling, it sided firmly with Mehdi Ali and Mortenson. The court declared Agha Mubarek's *fatwa* illegitimate and ordered him to pay for the eight hundred bricks his men destroyed.

"It was a very humbling victory," Mortenson says. "Here you have this Islamic court in conservative Shia Pakistan offering protection for an American, at a time when America is holding Muslims without charges in Guantanamo, Cuba, for years, under our so-called system of justice."

After a decade of struggle, Mortenson felt that finally, all the tea leaves in Pakistan were swirling his way. That summer, Mortenson gained a powerful new ally when Mohammed Fareed Khan was appointed the new chief secretary of the Northern Areas. Khan, a Wazir from Miram Shah, took office determined to declare war on northern Pakistan's poverty with his tribe's traditional aggressiveness.

At a meeting over tea, trout, and cucumber sandwiches in his headquarters, a nineteenth-century British colonial villa in Gilgit, he sought

Mortenson's advice about where to spend the money now finally flowing north from Musharraf's government in Islamabad. And to demonstrate his support for girls' education, he pledged to accompany Mortenson and personally inaugurate the Ned Gillette School after his police force had insured that it was rebuilt.

Another forceful personality, Brigadier General Bhangoo, had a more novel way of demonstrating his support for Mortenson. Brigadier Bhangoo had been President Musharraf's personal helicopter pilot before retiring from the military to join General Bashir's civil aviation company. By the summer of 2003, he regularly volunteered for the honor of transporting Mortenson to far-flung projects in his aging Alouette helicopter.

The general still wore his military flight suit, but substituted a pair of bright-blue jogging shoes for his combat boots, which he said gave him a better feel for the pedals.

Flying down the Shigar Valley toward Skardu, after retrieving Mortenson from a remote village, Bhangoo became enraged when Mortenson pointed out the ruins of Hemasil's school and related the story of his feud with Agha Mubarek.

"Point out this gentleman's house, will you?" Bhangoo said, increasing power to the Alouette's turbine. After Mortenson leveled a finger at the large walled compound where Mubarek lived, far beyond the means of a simple village mullah, Bhangoo set his lips firmly below his precisely clipped mustache and nudged his control stick forward, dive-bombing toward Mubarek's house.

People on the rooftops ran inside to take shelter as Bhangoo buzzed the compound half a dozen times, like an angry hornet preparing to sting, leaving welts of dust in his wake after each pass. His thumb drifted to the red button marked "missile" and he toyed with it idly. "Pity we're not armed," he said, banking toward Skardu, "Still, that should give him something to think about."

Six months later, the red buttons would be connected to actual armaments, when fifteen military helicopters flew in formation up the Daryle Valley, a haven of Taliban and Al Qaeda holdouts two hundred miles to the west, hunting extremists who had bombed eight government girls' schools. Mortenson, by then, had come to admire Musharraf, gratified to see that Pakistan's government was prepared to fight for the education of its girls.

In the fall of 2003, at the desk of his aviation company in Rawalpindi, as he tried to arrange a flight for Mortenson to Afghanistan, now that the CAI's work in Pakistan was on firm enough footing for him to leave, Bhangoo's boss, the bull-like Brigadier General Bashir Baz, ruminated on the importance of educating all of Pakistan's children, and the progress America was making in the war on terror.

"You know Greg, I have to thank your president," Bashir, said, paging through flight schedules on his high-tech flat-screen computer monitor. "A nightmare was growing on our western border, and he's paid to put it to an end. I can't imagine why. The only gainer in the whole equation is Pakistan."

Bashir paused to watch a live CNN feed from Baghdad. Staring at a small video window inset into the flight manifests scrolling down his monitor, Bashir was struck silent by the images of wailing Iraqi women carrying children's bodies out of the rubble of a bombed building.

As he studied the screen, Bashir's bullish shoulders slumped. "People like me are America's best friends in the region," Bashir said at last, shaking his head ruefully. "I'm a moderate Muslim, an educated man. But watching this, even I could become a *jihadi*. How can Americans say they are making themselves safer?" Bashir asked, struggling not to direct his anger toward the large American target on the other side of his desk. "Your President Bush has done a wonderful job of uniting one billion Muslims against America for the next two hundred years."

"Osama had something to do with it, too," Mortenson said.

"Osama, baah!" Bashir roared. "Osama is not a product of Pakistan or Afghanistan. He is a creation of America. Thanks to America, Osama is in every home. As a military man, I know you can never fight and win against someone who can shoot at you once and then run off and hide while you have to remain eternally on guard. You have to attack the source of your enemy's strength. In America's case, that's not Osama or Saddam or anyone else. The enemy is ignorance. The only way to defeat it is to build relationships with these people, to draw them into the modern world with education and business. Otherwise the fight will go on forever."

Bashir took a breath, and peered back through his tiny window to Baghdad, where a camera crew was filming radicalized young Iraqi men shaking their fists and firing their weapons into the air after setting off a roadside bomb. "Sorry, sir," he said, "I'm really inexcusably rude. Of course you know this as well as I do. Shall we have lunch?" Then Bashir pushed a button on his intercom and asked his lieutenant to send in the tubs of Kentucky Fried Chicken he'd ordered from the Blue Area especially for his American guest.

Skardu can be a depressing place when weather sets in. But in October 2003, making his last visit of the year to the Northern Areas before leaving to launch his new CAI initiative in Afghanistan, Mortenson felt perfectly content, despite the low cloud cover and encroaching chill.

Before Mortenson left Rawalpindi, Brigadier General Bashir had pledged four *lakh* rupees, or about six thousand dollars, a considerable sum in Pakistan, toward a new CAI school to be built in his home village southeast of Peshawar, where *Wahhabi madrassas* were plentiful. And he had promised to press his friends in the military for further donations, voicing his confidence that at least one American's war on terror was being fought in an effective fashion.

Mortenson had also won a landmark victory in Shariat Court, overcome his second *fatwa,* and humbled his most vocal opponent. Ten more schools would open their doors in the spring, once the nine new schools funded by *Parade* readers were completed, and the Ned Gillette School in Hemasil was rebuilt. Already, as Mortenson prepared to leave for Afghanistan, more than forty CAI schools were tucked into the high valleys of the Karakoram and Hindu Kush, where they were thriving. Thanks to Mortenson, the students who studied within their stone walls had become each village's most carefully tended crop.

And downside in bustling Skardu, in a small mud-block house Twaha had rented, with a view of a broad field where neighborhood children played soccer around clusters of grazing cattle, the new *nurmadhar* of Korphe's daughter was now living with her former classmate, chaperoned by two male cousins who'd come down from upside to see that the boldest young women in the entire Braldu were well looked after while they pursued their dreams.

Jahan and her classmate Tahira, the Korphe School's first two female graduates, had come to Skardu together, as two of the CAI's first harvest of scholarship students. And on his last day in Skardu, when

Mortenson stopped by with Jahan's father, Twaha, to inquire about the girls' progress, Jahan took pride in preparing tea for him herself, in her own home, as her grandmother Sakina had so often done.

While Mortenson sipped the Lipton Tea, brewed, not from handfuls of torn leaves and rancid yak milk, but from tap water and bags bought in Skardu's bazaar, he wondered what Sakina would have made of it. He imagined she would prefer her *paiyu cha*. Of her granddaughter, he was certain, she would be very proud. Jahan had completed her maternal health training course, but elected to stay in Skardu and continue her studies.

Courtesy of the CAI, both Jahan and Tahira were taking a full complement of classes at the private Girls' Model High School, including English grammar, formal Urdu, Arabic, physics, economics, and history.

Tahira, wearing a spotless white headscarf and sandals that wouldn't have been practical in the mountains, told Mortenson that once she graduated, she planned to return to Korphe and teach alongside her father, Master Hussein. "I've had this chance," she said. "Now when we go upside, all the people look at us, at our clothes, and think we are fashionable ladies. I think every girl of the Braldu deserves the chance to come downside at least once. Then their life will change. I think the greatest service I can perform is to go back and insure that this happens for all of them."

Jahan, who had come to Skardu planning to become a simple health worker and return to Korphe, was in the process of revising her goals upward. "Before I met you, Dr. Greg, I had no idea what education was," Jahan said, refilling his teacup. "But now I think it is like water. It is important for everything in life."

"What about marriage?" Mortenson asked, knowing that a *nurmadhar's* daughter would always be in demand, especially a pretty girl of seventeen, and a Balti husband might not support his brash young wife's ambitions.

"Don't worry, Dr. Greg," Twaha said, laughing in the rasping fashion that he'd inherited from Haji Ali. "The girl has learned your lesson too well. She has already made it clear she must finish her studies before we can even discuss marrying her to a suitable boy. And I agree. I will sell all my land if necessary so she can complete her education. I owe that to the memory of my father."

"So what will you do?" Mortenson asked Jahan.

"You won't laugh?" she said.

"I might," Mortenson teased.

Jahan took a breath and composed herself. "When I was a little sort of girl and I would see a gentleman or a lady with good, clean clothes I would run away and hide my face. But after I graduated from the Korphe School, I felt a big change in my life. I felt I was clear and clean and could go before anybody and discuss anything.

"And now that I am already in Skardu, I feel that anything is possible. I don't want to be just a health worker. I want to be such a woman that I can start a hospital and be an executive, and look over all the health problems of all the women in the Braldu. I want to become a very famous woman of this area," Jahan said, twirling the hem of her maroon silk headscarf around her finger as she peered out the window, past a soccer player sprinting through the drizzle toward a makeshift goal built of stacked stones, searching for the exact word with which to envision her future. "I want to be a . . . 'Superlady,' " she said, grinning defiantly, daring anyone, any man, to tell her she couldn't.

Mortenson didn't laugh after all. Instead, he beamed at the bold granddaughter of Haji Ali and imagined the contented look that would have been on the old *nurmadhar*'s face if he had lived long enough to see this day, to see the seed they planted together bear such splendid fruit.

Five hundred and eighty letters, twelve rams, and ten years of work was a small price to pay, Mortenson thought, for such a moment.

CHAPTER 23

STONES INTO SCHOOLS

Our earth is wounded. Her oceans and lakes are sick; her rivers
are like running sores; The air is filled with subtle poisons. And the oily
smoke of countless hellish fires blackens the sun. Men and women,
scattered from homeland, family, friends, wander desolate and uncertain,
scorched by a toxic sun. . . .

In this desert of frightened, blind uncertainty, some take refuge in
the pursuit of power. Some become manipulators of illusion and deceit.

If wisdom and harmony still dwell in this world, as other than a dream lost
in an unopened book, they are hidden in our heartbeat.

And it is from our hearts that we cry out. We cry out and our voices
are the single voice of this wounded earth. Our cries are a
great wind across the earth.

—From *The Warrior Song of King Gezar*

THE KING SAT in the window seat. Mortenson recognized him from
pictures on the old Afghan currency he'd seen for sale in the bazaars.
At eighty-nine, Zahir Shah looked far older than his official portrait
as he stared out the window of the PIA 737 at the country he'd been
exiled from for nearly thirty years.

Aside from the king's security detail and a small crew of stewardesses, Mortenson was alone on the short flight from Islamabad to
Kabul with Afghanistan's former monarch. When Shah turned away
from the window, he locked eyes with Mortenson across the aisle.

"*As-Salaam Alaaikum*, sir," Mortenson said.

"And to you, sir," Shah replied. During his exile in Rome, Shah
had become conversant with many cultures and had no trouble

pinpointing the place the large fair-haired man in the photographer's vest came from. "American?" he inquired.

"Yes, sir," Mortenson said.

Zahir Shah sighed, an old man's sound, born of decades of dashed hopes. "Are you a journalist?" he asked across the aisle.

"No," Mortenson said, "I build schools, for girls."

"And what is your business in my country, if I may ask?"

"I begin construction on five or six schools in the spring, *Inshallah*. I'm coming to deliver the money to get them going."

"In Kabul?"

"No," Mortenson said. "Up in Badakshan, and in the Wakhan Corridor."

Shah's eyebrows lifted toward the brown dome of his hairless head. He patted the seat next to him and Mortenson moved over. "Do you know someone in the area?" Shah said.

"It's a long story, but a few years ago, Kirghiz men rode over the Irshad Pass to the Charpurson Valley, where I work in Pakistan, and asked me to build schools for their villages. I promised them I'd come . . . discuss schools with them, but I couldn't get there until now."

"An American in the Wakhan," Shah said. "I'm told I have a hunting lodge the people built me there somewhere, but I've never been to it. Too hard to reach. We don't see many Americans in Afghanistan anymore. A year ago this plane would have been full of journalists and aid workers. But now they are all in Iraq. America has forgotten us," the King said. "Again."

A year earlier, Shah had flown into Kabul fresh from exile and was greeted by a cheering crowd who saw his return as a tiding that life would once again resume its normal course, free from the violence that had marked the decades of misrule by the Soviets, the feuding warlords, and the Taliban. Before being ousted by his cousin Mohammad Daud Khan, Shah had presided, from 1933 to 1973, over Afghanistan's most enduring modern period of peace. He had overseen the drafting of a constitution in 1964, which turned Afghanistan into a democracy, offering universal suffrage and emancipating women. He had founded Afghanistan's first modern university and recruited foreign academics and aid workers to assist with his campaign to develop the country. To many Afghans, Shah was a symbol of the life they hoped to lead again.

But by the fall of 2003, those hopes were fading. American troops still in Afghanistan were largely sequestered, hunting for Bin Laden and his supporters or providing security for the new government of Hamid Karzai. The level of violence across the country was, once again, escalating, and the Taliban was said to be regrouping.

"Just like we abandoned the *mujahadeen* after the Soviets pulled out, I was afraid we were in the process of abandoning Afghanistan again," Mortenson says. "As best I could tell, only a third of the aid money we'd promised had ever made it over there. With Mary Bono, I found one of the people in Congress who was responsible for Afghan appropriations. I told him about Uzra Faizad and all the teachers who weren't being paid, and asked him why the money wasn't getting there."

" 'It's difficult,' he told me. 'There is no central banking in Afghanistan. And no way to wire money.'

"But that didn't sound like much of an excuse to me," Mortenson says. "We had no problem flying in bags of cash to pay the warlords to fight against the Taliban. I wondered why we couldn't do the same thing to build roads, and sewers, and schools. If promises are not fulfilled, and cash not delivered, it sends a powerful message that the U.S. government simply does not care."

Zahir Shah placed his hand, with its enormous lapis ring, on Mortenson's. "I'm glad one American is here at least," he said. "The man you want to see up north is Sadhar Khan. He's a *mujahid.* But he cares about his people."

"So I've heard," Mortenson said.

Zahir Shah pulled a calling card out of the breast pocket of the business suit he wore under his striped robe and called for one of his security guards to bring his valise. Then the king held his thumb to an ink pad and pressed his print on the back of his card. "It may be helpful if you give this to *Commandhan* Khan," he said. "Allah be with you. And go with my blessing."

The 737 dove for the Kabul airport in a tight spiral. The capital wasn't as secure as it had been a year earlier, and pilots now took this precaution to make themselves difficult targets for the many Stinger missiles still unaccounted for in the country.

Mortenson found Kabul's traffic more frightening. With Abdullah calmly spinning the wheel of his Toyota between his clawed hands, they managed to survive four near-collisions on the short drive to the

Kabul Peace Guest House. "A government supported by America was supposedly in control of Kabul," Mortenson says. "But their power barely extended to the city limits, and they couldn't even control the traffic. Drivers just ignored road signs and a few shouting traffic cops and went where they wanted."

Where Mortenson wanted to go was Faizabad, the largest city in the Badakshan Province of northeastern Afghanistan, which would be his base for venturing out to the sites of possible rural school projects. And to get there, he'd have to go by road, braving not just chaotic traffic, but a two-day trip through the insecure countryside. But Mortenson had no other choice. On this, his third trip to Afghanistan, he was determined to keep his promise to the Kirghiz horsemen. In his absence, they had conducted a complete survey of the Wakhan Corridor, and again ridden six days each way to deliver it to Faisal Baig in Zuudkhan. The survey reported that fifty-two hundred elementary-age children had no school of any kind available, and were waiting, *Inshallah*, for Mortenson to start building them.

General Bashir had offered to have one of his pilots fly Mortenson directly to Faizabad, in a small twin-engine Cessna Golden Eagle that Askari Aviation contracted to fly ice cream, mineral water, protein bars, and other supplies to American operatives in Afghanistan. But the American CentCom headquarters, based in Doha, Qatar, which controlled Afghanistan's airspace, denied Bashir's request to send his plane into Afghanistan on a humanitarian mission.

Mortenson paced his powerless room in the Kabul Peace Guest House, annoyed that he hadn't remembered to charge his laptop and camera batteries in Islamabad. Power was predictably unpredictable in the Afghan capital and he might not find a working outlet between this room and Badakshan.

He planned to set off on the long drive north in the morning, traveling by day for safety, and had sent Abdullah out to look for a vehicle to rent that was capable of negotiating the gauntlet of bomb craters and mud bogs lining the only road north.

When Abdullah didn't return by dinnertime, Mortenson considered going out to look for food, but instead, lay down with his feet dangling over the edge of the narrow bed, pulled a hard pillow that smelled like hair pomade over his face, and fell asleep.

Just before midnight, Mortenson sat up abruptly, trying to make sense of the knocking on the door. In his dream it had been incoming RPG rounds exploding against the guest house walls.

Abdullah had both good and bad news. He'd managed to rent a Russian jeep and found a young Tajik named Kais to come along and translate, since his usual companion, Hash, wouldn't be welcome where they were going, because of his time with the Taliban. The only problem, Abdullah explained, was that the Salang Tunnel, the only passage north through the mountains, would be closing at 6:00 A.M.

"When will it open?" Mortenson asked, still clinging to his hope of a full night's sleep.

Abdullah shrugged. With his burned face and singed eyebrows, it was difficult to read his expression. But his hunched shoulders told Mortenson he should have known better than to ask. "Twe-lev hour? Two day?" he guessed. "Who can know?"

Mortenson began repacking his bags.

As they drove north through the unelectrified city, Kabul seemed deceptively peaceful. Groups of men in flowing white robes floated between the town's lantern-lit all-night tea stands like benevolent spirits, ready to leave on early morning flights for Saudi Arabia. Every Muslim of means is expected to perform the Haj, a pilgrimage to Mecca, at least once in his life. And the mood on the city's dim streets was festive, as so many men prepared to embark on the trip that was meant to be the high point of their earthly existence.

The last thing Mortenson remembers seeing, after circling the streets searching for an open gas station, was Afghanistan's former Ministry of Defense. He'd passed it by day, a looming shell so gutted by the bombs and missiles of three different wars that it seemed too unstable to stand. At night, the cooking fires of squatters living in it gave the structure a sinister jack-o-lantern glow. The building's jagged shell holes and rows of glassless windows gaped like eyeless sockets over a gap-toothed grin as firelight flickered behind them.

Drowsily, Mortenson watched the ministry's leer die in the darkness behind him, and drifted, picturing a laptop army racing through the halls of the Pentagon, and endless marble floors buffed to the same brilliant gloss as Donald Rumsfeld's shoes.

The Salang Tunnel was only one hundred kilometers north of Kabul, but the low-geared Soviet-era jeep ground up the distance so slowly as it climbed into the Hindu Kush Mountains that, despite the danger of ambush, Mortenson was lulled back to sleep hours before they entered it. This rocky spine of fifteen-thousand-foot peaks separating northern Afghanistan from the central Shomali Plain had been Massoud's most formidable line of defense from the Taliban.

On his orders, Massoud's men dynamited the two-kilometer tunnel Red Army engineers had built in the 1960s so they could open a trade route south through Uzbekistan. Leaving only the barely navigable twelve-thousand-foot-high dirt roads open to his stronghold, the Panjshir Valley, Massoud's outgunned and outnumbered *mujahadeen* prevented the Taliban from driving their tanks and fleets of Japanese pickup trucks north in force. Afghanistan's new government was employing Turkish construction crews to clear the tunnel of all the concrete rubble deposited by the explosions and to buttress the sagging structure against further collapse.

Motionlessness woke Mortenson. He rubbed his eyes, but the blackness surrounding him was seamless. Then he heard voices beyond what he guessed was the front of the jeep, and in the flare of a match, Abdullah's scorched, expressionless face appeared next to the worried pout of the Tajik teenager named Kais.

"We were right in the middle of the tunnel when the radiator blew," Mortenson says, "on an uphill curve, so traffic couldn't see us until the last second. It was the worst place we could possibly get stuck."

Mortenson grabbed his rucksack and fished through it for a flashlight. Then he remembered that in the rush to repack, he'd left it at the guest house in Kabul, with his laptop and cameras. Mortenson climbed out and bent over the open hood with Abdullah. And by the light of the matches that blew out in the frigid breeze swirling through the tunnel almost as soon as Abdullah lit them, Mortenson saw that the jeep's rubber radiator hose had disintegrated.

He was wondering whether he had any duct tape to attempt a repair when, with a panicked shrill from its airhorns, a Russian Kamaz III cargo truck roared downhill, down the center of the tunnel, right toward them. There was no time to move. Mortenson braced for the collision and the truck swerved back into its lane, missing the jeep's hood by inches and tearing off its sideview mirror.

"Let's go!" Mortenson ordered, pushing Abdullah and Kais toward the tunnel wall. Mortenson felt the wintry air blowing harder and held his hands out toward it like a dowser, jogging flush with the tunnel wall, searching for its source. As the headlights of another truck careening toward them scraped along the tunnel's uneven rock face, Mortenson saw a slash of blackness that he took for a door and pushed his companions through it.

"We stepped outside, into snow at the top of a mountain pass," Mortenson says. "There was a moon, so we could see clearly enough. And I tried to get a bearing on which side of the pass we were on, so we could start hiking down."

Then Mortenson saw the first red stone. It was almost obscured by snow, but once Mortenson spotted it, he could clearly make out the dozens of other reddish depressions stippling the white snowfield.

Afghanistan is the most heavily mined country on earth. With millions of tiny explosives buried by half a dozen different armies over decades, no one knows exactly where the patient devices lie in wait. And after a goat or a cow or a child loses its life locating them, demining teams paint rocks in the area red before they can spare the months it can take to laboriously clear them.

Kais saw the red rocks surrounding them, too, and began to panic. Mortenson held the boy's arm, in case he was tempted to run. Abdullah, who'd had more than enough experience with mines already, pronounced the inevitable.

"Slowly, slowly," he said, turning and retracing his steps through the snow. "We must go back inside."

"I figured it was fifty-fifty we'd get killed in the tunnel," Mortenson says. "But we would definitely die out there." Kais was frozen in place, but gently, Mortenson led the boy back into the blackness.

"I don't know what would have happened if the next vehicle wasn't a truck, climbing slowly uphill," Mortenson says. "But thank God it was. I jumped out in front of it to flag it down."

Mortenson and Kais rode, wedged between the five men in the cab of the Bedford. Abdullah steered the powerless jeep as the truck pushed it uphill. "They were rough guys, smugglers," Mortenson says, "but they seemed all right. They were taking dozens of new refrigerators up to Mazir-i-Sharif, so the truck was overloaded and we were barely moving, but that was fine with me."

Kais stared at the men anxiously and whispered in English to Mortenson. "These the bad men," he said. "Teef."

"I told Kais to be quiet," Mortenson says. "I was trying to concentrate, to use all the skills I'd acquired over a decade of working in Pakistan to get us out of there. The smugglers were Pashtun and Kais was a Tajik, so he was going to be suspicious of them no matter what. I just decided to trust them and make small talk. After a few minutes, everyone relaxed and even Kais could see they were okay, especially after they offered us a bunch of grapes."

As they climbed to the crest of the tunnel, Mortenson crunched the juicy fruit between his teeth greedily, realizing he hadn't eaten since breakfast the previous day and watched the back of the rented white jeep turning black as the Bedford's grill scraped the paint from the Russian vehicle's tailgate.

After the road pitched down toward the other side of the pass, Mortenson thanked the crew of refrigerator smugglers for the rescue and the delicious grapes, and, along with Kais, climbed back in behind Abdullah. The driver had managed to get the headlights on faintly, even with the engine off, by turning the ignition switch, and Mortenson slumped back on the cargo bench, exhausted. In Abdullah's capable hands, they coasted silently downhill all the way to daylight.

To Taliban and Soviet troops, the Panjshir Valley, to their east, beneath mountains brushed by the gathering light, was a shadowland of suffering and death. The soldiers' predictable progress between the gorge's rock escarpments made them easy targets for bands of Massoud's *mujahadeen* aiming rocket launchers from vantage points high above the valley floor. But to Mortenson, with dawn limning the sharp tips of the snowy peaks mauve, the distant valley looked like Shangri-La.

"I was so happy to get out of that tunnel and into the light that I hugged Abdullah so hard I almost made him crash the jeep," Mortenson says. After his driver managed to stop just short of a roadside boulder, they climbed out to attempt a repair. As the sun rose, it became easy to see the problem—a section of radiator hose six inches long would have to be patched. Abdullah, a veteran not only of war, but of countless roadside repairs, cut away a section of the spare tire's inner tube, wrapped it around the damaged section of hose, and secured it with a roll of duct tape that Mortenson found stuck to a package of cough drops in his rucksack.

After refilling the radiator from his precious bottles of mineral water, Mortenson was once again on his way north. It was the holy month of Ramadan, and Abdullah drove fast, hoping to reach a tea stand where they could be served breakfast before the day's fast officially began. But by the time they reached the first settlement, a former Soviet garrison named Pol-e-Kamri, both roadside restaurants were shuttered for the day. So Mortenson shared out a bag of peanuts he had squirreled away for such an occasion, and Kais and Abdullah munched them hungrily until the sun breached the valley's eastern wall.

After their breakfast, Abdullah left to search on foot for someone willing to sell them gas. He returned and drove the jeep up into the courtyard of a crude mud home, where he parked next to a rusting barrel. An old man shuffled out toward them, bent almost double and walking with a cane. It took him two minutes to remove the cap from the gas tank with his enfeebled hands. He began cranking the barrel's pump himself, but as Abdullah saw how much effort the task cost him, he leaped out to take over.

While Abdullah pumped, Mortenson spoke to the old man as Kais translated from Dari, the close relative of Farsi that was the most common language in northern Afghanistan. "I used to live in the Shomali," the man, who introduced himself as Mohammed, said, referring to the vast plain north of Kabul that had once been Afghanistan's breadbasket. "Our land used to be a paradise. Kabulis would come to their country homes near my village on weekends, and even King Zahir Shah, blessed be his name, had a palace built nearby. In my garden, I had every kind of tree and grew even grapes and melons," Mohammed said, his mouth, toothless except for two tusklike canines, working at the memory of his vanished delicacies.

"Once the Taliban came, it was too dangerous to stay," he continued, "so I moved my family north of the Salang for their safety. Last spring, I returned to see if my home had survived, but at first, I couldn't find it. I was born there as a boy and had lived in that place for seventy years, but I couldn't recognize my own village. All the houses were destroyed. And all the crops were dead. The Taliban had burned not only our homes, but every bush and tree as well. I recognized my own garden only by the shape of a burned apricot tree's trunk, which forked in a very peculiar way, like a human hand." Mohammed said, wheezing with indignation at the memory.

"I can understand shooting men and bombing buildings. In a time of war these things happen, as they always have. But why?" Mohammed said, putting his question not to Mortenson, but letting the unanswerable lament hang in the air between them. "Why did the Taliban have to kill our land?"

On their passage north, it became increasingly clear to Mortenson just how much killing had been done in Afghanistan, and how thoroughly not just the civilians, but the combatants, must have suffered. They passed a Soviet T-51 tank, its turret blown askew by fearsome forces, which served as a magnet for village children who climbed on top of it to play at war.

They rolled along a graveyard whose headstones were the charred carcasses of heavily armed Soviet Hind helicopters. Their crews, Mortenson thought, had been unlucky enough to fly near Massoud's stronghold after the CIA made Stinger missiles and the training to fire them effectively available to *mujahadeen* leaders battling America's Cold War enemy here, leaders like Osama Bin Laden.

Pasted to the flanks of every piece of rusting war materiel, the face of Shah Ahmed Massoud regarded their progress from posters, a secular saint of northern Afghanistan, insinuating from somewhere beyond life that these sacrifices had been necessary.

By dusk, they had passed through the towns of Khanabad and Konduz, and were approaching Taloqan, where they planned to stop for their first real meal in days, after evening prayer released them from the fast of Ramadan. Mortenson, who was due to address an important group of donors in Denver a week later, was weighing whether to press Abdullah to drive on toward Faizabad after dinner or wait for the security of daylight to proceed, when a fusillade of machine-gun fire fifty yards ahead of them forced Abdullah to slam on the brakes.

Abdullah jammed the gearshift into reverse and stomped on the gas, sending them careening backward, away from the red stream of tracer bullets pulsing through the gathering dark. But gunfire erupted behind them and Abdullah hit the brakes once again. "Come!" he commanded, pulling Kais and Mortenson out of the jeep and into a muddy ditch at the side of the road, where he pressed his companions into the oozing earth with his clawed hands. Then Abdullah raised them in a *dua*, beseeching Allah for protection.

"We had driven straight into a turf battle between opium smugglers," Mortenson says. "It was trafficking time and there were always skirmishes that time of year to control the mule trains that transported the crop. They fired back and forth at each other over our heads with their Kalashnikovs, which make a real distinctive stuttering sound. I could see by the red glow of their tracer bullets that Kais was totally panicking. But Abdullah was angry. He was a real Pashtun. He lay there muttering, blaming himself for putting me, his guest, in danger."

Mortenson lay prone in the cool mud, trying to think his way out of the firefight, but there was nothing to be done. Several new gunners joined the battle, and the intensity of fire above their heads surged, tearing the air into shreds. "I stopped thinking about escape and started thinking about my kids," Mortenson says, "trying to imagine how Tara would explain the way I'd died to them, and wondering if they would understand what I was trying to do—how I didn't mean to leave them, that I was trying to help kids like them over here. I decided Tara would make them understand. And that was a pretty good feeling."

The headlights of an approaching vehicle illuminated the berms on both sides of the road where the warring squads of opium smugglers crouched, and their fire tapered off as they took cover. The truck appeared, traveling toward Taloqan, and Abdullah jumped up out of the ditch to flag it down. It was a poor vehicle, an aged pickup that listed to the side on its damaged suspension, carrying a load of freshly harvested goat hides on their way to a tannery, and Mortenson could smell the stench of putrefying flesh before it stopped.

Abdullah ran forward to the cab, as sporadic bursts of gunfire crackled from both sides of the road, then shouted toward the ditch for Kais to translate. The boy's thin, trembling voice, speaking Dari, requested a ride for the foreigner. Abdullah called for Mortenson to come and waved frantically toward the bed of the truck. Mortenson, crouching as he'd been trained two decades earlier, ran toward him, weaving to make himself a tougher target. He jumped in the back and Abdullah threw a blanket of goat hides over Mortenson, pressing him down beneath the moist skins.

"What about you and the boy?"

"Allah will watch over us," Abdullah said. "These *Shetans* shoot at each other, not us. We wait, then take the jeep back to Kabul." Mortenson hoped his friend was right. Abdullah slapped the tailgate with his claw and the truck jolted into gear.

From his berth beneath a pile of rotting goatskins, Mortenson held his hand over his nose and watched the road behind him unwind as the rattletrap truck picked up speed. After they'd traveled half a kilometer, he saw the firefight resume. The widely spaced streams of tracers leaped across the road like ellipses. But to Mortenson, who wouldn't learn his friends had survived until the following week, when he returned to Kabul, they looked more like question marks.

The truck rolled on through Taloqan toward Faizabad, so Mortenson did without dinner once again. The stench in the back of the truck wasn't conducive to hunger, but eventually, rolling slowly through the night, his animal instincts won out. He thought of his peanuts, and only at that moment realized he'd left his bag in the jeep. Anxiously, Mortenson sat up and patted the pockets of his vest until he felt the outline of his passport and a brick of American dollars. Then, with a jolt, he remembered that the king's calling card was in his abandoned bag. There was nothing to be done, he realized, sighing. He'd just have to approach *Commandhan* Khan without an introduction. So Mortenson wrapped his checkered headscarf over his nose and mouth and watched the truck's passage under the starry sky.

"I was alone. I was covered in mud and goat blood. I'd lost my luggage. I didn't speak the local language. I hadn't had a meal for days, but I felt surprisingly good," Mortenson says. "I felt like I had all those years earlier, riding on top of the Bedford up the Indus Gorge with my supplies for the Korphe School, having no clue what was ahead of me. My plan for the next few days was vague. And I had no idea if I'd succeed. But you know what? It wasn't a bad feeling at all."

The goatskin sellers dropped Mortenson at Faizabad's Uliah Hotel. At the peak of the opium-trafficking season, all the rooms were full, so the sleepy *chokidar* offered Mortenson a blanket and a berth in the hall, next to thirty other sleeping men. The hotel had no running water, and Mortenson was desperate to wash the goat stink off his clothes, so he walked outside, opened the spigot on a tanker truck of water parked beside the hotel, and slopped the icy stream of water over his clothes.

"I didn't bother trying to dry off," Mortenson says. "I just wrapped myself in my blanket and lay down in the hotel hallway. It was about the most disgusting place to sleep you could imagine, with all these seedy opium smugglers and unemployed *mujahadeen* burping up a storm. But after all I'd been through I slept as well as if I'd been in a five-star hotel."

Before four in the morning, the *chokidar* woke the hallway full of sleeping men with a meal. Ramadan dictated no food could be consumed after morning prayer, and Mortenson, so far beyond hunger that he had no taste for food, nonetheless joined the men, shoveling a full day's supply of lentil curry and four flat loaves of chewy *chapatti* down his throat.

In the frosty predawn, the country surrounding Faizabad reminded Mortenson of Baltistan. The day to come insinuated itself along the peaks of the Great Pamir range to the north. He was in his familiar mountains again, and if he didn't take in the details, he could almost imagine he'd returned to his second home. But the differences were unavoidable. Women were much more visibly a part of public life, moving freely along the streets, though most of them cloaked themselves within white *burkhas*. And the proximity to the former Soviet Republics was obvious, as gangs of heavily armed Chechens, speaking in Slavic cadences that sounded especially foreign to Mortenson's ear, marched in businesslike fashion toward mosques for morning prayer.

With few resources available, Faizabad's economy revolved around the opium trade. Raw paste was collected in bulk from the poppy fields of Badakshan, refined into heroin in the factories around Faizabad, then shipped through Central Asia to Chechnya and on to Moscow. For all their flaws, the Taliban had harshly suppressed the production of opium. And with them gone, especially in northern Afghanistan, poppy planting had resumed with a vengeance.

According to a study by Human Rights Watch, Afghanistan's opium harvest had spiked from nearly nonexistent under the Taliban to almost four thousand tons by the end of 2003. Afghanistan by then produced two-thirds of the world's raw material for heroin. And those opium profits, funneled back to the warlords, as they were called in the West, or *commandhans,* as they were known in Afghanistan, enabled them to recruit and equip formidable private militias, making the feeble central government of Hamid Karzai increasingly irrelevant the farther you traveled from Kabul.

In Badakshan, as far from Kabul as one could get in Afghanistan, absolute power resided with *Commandhan* Sadhar Khan. Mortenson had heard stories about Khan for years. His people spoke of him glowingly, as they still talked about his martyred comrade in the struggle against the Soviets and the Taliban, Shah Ahmed Massoud. Khan, like all *commandhans,* took a tariff from opium traffickers whose mule trains passed through his lands. But unlike many, he plowed the profits back into his people's welfare. For his former fighters, he'd built a thriving bazaar and disbursed small loans so they could start businesses, helping to ease the transition from *mujahid* to merchant. Khan was as beloved by his people as he was feared by his rivals for the harsh judgments he was in the habit of meting out.

Sarfraz, the former Pakistani commando from Zuudkhan who had helped to protect Mortenson when the news from 9/11 arrived over his shortwave radio, had met Khan on his own less-than-legal travels in the Wakhan Corridor as a smuggler. "Is he a good man? Yes, good. But dangerous," Sarfraz said. "If his enemy doesn't agree to surrender and join him, he ties him between two jeeps and pulls him apart. In such a way he has become like the president of Badakshan."

In the afternoon, Mortenson changed some money and hired another jeep from a devout father and son who agreed to make the two-hour trip to Khan's headquarters in Baharak, as long as Mortenson was prepared to leave immediately, so they could arrive in time for evening prayer.

"I can go now," Mortenson said.

"What about your luggages?" said the boy, who spoke a few words of English.

Mortenson shrugged and climbed into the jeep.

"The trip to Baharak couldn't have been more than sixty miles," Mortenson said. "But it took three hours. We were back in country that reminded me of the Indus Gorge, creeping along ledges over a river that wound through a rocky canyon. I was glad we had a good vehicle. All those SUVs Americans drive are made to get groceries and take kids to soccer practice. You need something like a real Russian jeep to get over that kind of terrain."

Twenty minutes before Baharak, the river gorge opened into lush benchland between rolling hills. Bands of farmers blanketed the slopes, planting poppies on every arable surface. "Except for the poppies, we could have been driving up the mouth of the Shigar Valley," Mortenson says, "heading for Korphe. I realized how close to Pakistan we were and even though I'd never been in that spot before, it felt like a homecoming, like I was among my people again."

The town of Baharak reinforced that feeling. Ringed by the snowy peaks of the Hindu Kush, Baharak was the gateway to the Wakhan. The mouth of its narrow valley was only a few kilometers to the east, and Mortenson was warmed with the knowledge that so many people he cared about in Zuudkhan were so close by.

The driver and his son drove to Baharak's bazaar, to ask the way to Sadhar Khan's home. In the bazaar, Mortenson could see that the people of Baharak, who grew, rather than trafficked, opium, lived in a subsistence economy like the Balti. Food in the stalls was simple and scarce and the overburdened miniature donkeys that carried wares to and from the market looked unhealthy and underfed. From his reading, Mortenson knew how cut off all of Badakshan had been from the world during the reign of the Taliban. But he hadn't realized just how poor a place it was.

Through the middle of the market, where the only other traffic traveled on four hooves, a well-worn white Russian jeep rolled toward them. Mortenson flagged it down, figuring anyone who could afford such a vehicle in Baharak would know the way to Sadhar Khan.

The jeep was packed with menacing-looking *mujahadeen,* but the driver, a man of middle age with piercing eyes and a precisely trimmed black beard, got out to address Mortenson.

"I'm looking for Sadhar Khan," Mortenson said, in the rudimentary Dari he'd coaxed Kais to teach him on the drive out of Kabul.

"He is here," the man said, in English.

"Where?"

"I am he. I am *Commandhan* Khan."

On the roof of Sadhar Khan's compound, under the browned hills of Baharak, Mortenson paced nervously around the chair he'd been led to, waiting for the *commandhan* to return from *Juma* prayers. Khan lived simply, but the apparatus of his power was everywhere apparent. The antenna of a powerful radio transmitter jutted up beyond the edge of the roof like a flagless pole, announcing Khan's affiliation with modernity. Several small satellite dishes were trained toward the southern sky. And on the rooftops of surrounding buildings, Mortenson watched Khan's gunmen watching him through the scopes of their sniper rifles.

To the southeast, he could see the snow peaks of his Pakistan, and made himself imagine Faisal Baig standing guard beneath them, so that the snipers wouldn't unnerve him. From Faisal, Mortenson drew a mental line from school to school, community to community, down the Hunza Valley, to Gilgit, across the Indus Gorge all the way to Skardu, connecting people and places he knew and loved to this lonely rooftop, telling himself he was far from alone.

Just before sunset, Mortenson saw hundreds of men streaming out of Baharak's plain bunkerlike mosque, which looked more like a military barracks than a house of worship. Khan was the last to leave, deep in conversation with the village mullah. He bent to embrace the elderly man and turned to walk toward the foreigner waiting on his roof.

"Sadhar Khan came up without any guards. He only brought one of his young lieutenants to translate. I know the gunmen watching me would have dropped me in a second if I even looked at him the wrong way, but I appreciated the gesture," Mortenson says. "Just as he had when he met me in the bazaar, he was willing to tackle things head on, by himself."

"I'm sorry I can't offer you any tea," Khan said through his translator, who spoke excellent English. "But in a few moments," he said, indicating the sun sinking behind a boulderfield to the west, "you may have whatever you wish."

"That's fine," Mortenson said. "I've come a long way to speak with you. I'm just honored to be here."

"And what has an American come so far from Kabul to talk about?" Khan said, straightening the brown woolen robe, embroidered with scarlet seams, that served as his badge of office.

So Mortenson told the *commandhan* his story, beginning with the arrival of the Kirghiz horsemen, in a dust cloud descending the Irshad Pass, and finishing with an account of the firefight he had passed through the evening before, and his escape under goatskins. Then, to Mortenson's astonishment, the fearsome leader of Badakshan's *mujahadeen* shouted with joy and wrapped the startled American in an embrace.

"Yes! Yes! You're Dr. Greg! My *commandhan* Abdul Rashid has told me about you. This is incredible," Khan said, pacing with excitement, "and to think, I didn't even arrange a meal or a welcome from the village elders. Forgive me."

Mortenson grinned. And the tension of the terrible trip north, if not the dust and goat smell, melted away. Khan pulled a late-model satellite phone out of the pocket of the photographer's vest he wore under his robe and ordered his staff to start preparing a feast. Then he and Mortenson paced circles in the roof, discussing potential sites for schools.

Khan's knowledge of the Wakhan Corridor, where Mortenson was most anxious to begin working, was encyclopedic. And he ticked off the five communities that would benefit immediately from primary education. Then Khan catalogued a sea of schoolless girls, far more vast than anything Mortenson had imagined. In Faizabad alone, Khan said, five thousand teenaged girls were attempting to hold classes in a field beside the boys' high school. The story was the same, he said, across Badakshan, and he detailed a vast litany of need that could keep Mortenson busy for decades.

As the sun slipped behind the western ridges, Khan placed one hand on Mortenson's back as he pointed with the other. "We fought with Americans, here in these mountains, against the Russians. And though we heard many promises, they never returned to help us when the dying was done."

"Look here, look at these hills." Khan indicated the boulderfields that marched up from the dirt streets of Baharak like irregularly spaced headstones, arrayed like a vast army of the dead as they climbed toward the deepening sunset. "There has been far too much dying in these hills," Sadhar Khan said, somberly. "Every rock, every boulder that you see before you is one of my *mujahadeen, shahids,* martyrs, who sacrificed their lives fighting the Russians and the Taliban. Now we must make their sacrifice worthwhile," Khan said, turning to face Mortenson. "We must turn these stones into schools."

Mortenson had always doubted that the entire life a person led could flash before him in the moment before death. There didn't seem to be enough time. But in the second it took to look into Sadhar Khan's dark eyes, and then through them, as he contemplated the vow he was being asked to take, Mortenson saw the rest of the life he had yet to live unreel before him.

This rooftop, surrounded by these harsh, stony hills, was a fork where he had to choose his way. And if he turned in the direction of this man, and these stones, he could see the path ahead painted more vividly than the decade-long detour he'd begun one distant day in Korphe.

There would be new languages to learn, new customs to blunder through before they could be mastered. There were months of absences from his family, scattered like blank spots on the bright canvas that stretched before him, this sunlit prospect that rose like an untrodden snowfield, and dangers he couldn't yet imagine, which loomed over his route like thunderheads. He saw this life rising before him as clearly as he'd seen the summit of Kilimanjaro as a boy, as brilliantly as the peerless pyramid of K2 still haunted his dreams.

Mortenson put his hands on the shoulders of Sadhar Khan's brown robe, as he'd done a decade earlier, among other mountains, with another leader, named Haji Ali, conscious, not of the gunmen still observing him through their sniperscopes, nor of the *shahid* stones, warmed to amber by the sun's late rays, but of the inner mountain he'd committed, in that instant, to climb.

Acknowledgments

When your heart speaks, take good notes.

—Judith Campbell

It is my vision that we all will dedicate the next decade to achieve universal literacy and education for all children, especially for girls. More than 145 million of the world's children are deprived of education due to poverty, exploitation, slavery, gender discrimination, religious extremism, and corrupt governments. May *Three Cups of Tea* be a catalyst to bring the gift of literacy to each of those children who deserves a chance to go to school.

All the pages of this book could be filled with acknowledgments to the thousands of incredible souls who were a vital part of the creation of this story and book. I regret—and will lose many nights of sleep—that I cannot acknowledge each one of you in this limited space. Thank you for blessing my life and know that a tribute to each of you lives on in the education of a child.

The coauthor of this book, David Oliver Relin, persevered for two years to bring *Three Cups of Tea* to fruition. Without you, this story in its entirety never would have been told. *Shukuria* Relin sahib.

A special thanks to Viking Penguin editor, Paul Slovak, who worked diligently to guide this paperback edition to completion, and for patiently heeding our multiple requests to change the hardcover subtitle version of "One Man's Mission to Fight Terrorism and Build Nations . . . One School at a Time," to the present Penguin paperback subtitle, "One Man's Mission to Promote Peace . . . One School at a Time."

Viking Penguin publicist Louise Braverman provided extraordinary assistance that helped *Three Cups of Tea* become a bestseller.

Thank you for your eternal optimism. Thanks also to Susan Kennedy (President, Penguin Group (USA)), Carolyn Coleburn (Viking publicity director), Nancy Sheppard (Viking marketing director), and Ray Roberts (the original Viking editor of this book).

Our literary agent, Elizabeth Kaplan, was a stalwart force that guided *Three Cups of Tea* for two years from a mere proposal to full publication. We are forever grateful for your support.

Thanks to the devoted "Montana women" at the Central Asia Institute (CAI) office, Jennifer Sipes and Laura Anderson, who work diligently for our grassroots mission to bring education to more than 24,000 children. A special thanks also to Christiane Leitinger, the director of the "Pennies for Peace" program that builds bridges between children halfway around the world.

CAI Board Directors Dr. Abdul Jabbar, Julia Bergman, and Karen McCown, are a vital part of our endeavors. Thanks to you and your families for your steadfast support, encouragement, and commitment through the years.

To Jean Hoerni, Haji Ali, and Christa—this is to humbly honor your legacies!

Our unlikely, indefatigable CAI staff in Pakistan moves mountains tirelessly to keep the ball rolling. *Bohot Shukuria* to Apo Cha Cha Abdul Razak, Ghulam Parvi sahib, Suleman Minhas, Saidullah Baig, Faisal Baig, Mohammed Nazir, and in Afghanistan, Sarfraz Khan, Abdul Waqil, Parvin Bibi, and Mullah Mohammed. May Allah bless you and your families for the noble work you do for humanity!

To my beloved friends, mentors, elders, teachers, guides, and brothers and sisters in Pakistan and Afghanistan: there are no words adequate to express my gratitude, except to say that each of you are a star that lights up the night sky, and that your loyalty, ardor, and perseverance bring education to your children. *Shukuria, Rahmat, Manana, Shakkeram, Baf, Bakshish, Thanks!*

Thanks to my grandparents, Regina Mortenson and Al and Lyria Doerring, for their wisdom. Thanks to my sisters, Sonja and Kari, their husbands, Dan and Dean, and their families for their love and tribal loyalty, which bring true meaning to "family values."

As a child in Tanzania, my parents, Dempsey and Jerene Mortenson, read fastidiously to us at bedtime by candlelight and, later, electricity. Those stories filled us with curiosity about the world and other cultures. They inspired the humanitarian adventure that shaped my life. My mother's lifelong dedication to education is an immense inspiration. Although cancer took my forty-eight-year-old father in 1980, his legacy of compassion lives on forever in our spirits.

What motivates me to do this? The answer is simple: when I look into the eyes of the children in Pakistan and Afghanistan, I see the eyes of my own children full of wonder—and hope that we each do our part to leave them a legacy of peace instead of the perpetual cycle of violence, war, terrorism, racism, exploitation, and bigotry that we have yet to conquer.

To my amazing children, Amira Eliana and Khyber, who give me courage, unconditional love, and the hope that inspires me to try to make a difference, one child at a time.

Most of all, I owe immeasurable gratitude to my incredible wife, Tara. I'm glad we took a leap of faith together. You are an amazing companion, confidante, mother, and friend. In my frequent absences over the eleven years of our marriage—to the rugged Pakistan and Afghan hinterland—your love has made it possible for me to follow my heart. I love you.

—*Greg Mortenson*
Neelam Valley, Azad Kashmir, Pakistan
November 2006

I'd like to thank Greg Mortenson, both for telling me one of the most remarkable stories I've ever heard, and then for inviting me to tell it to others. I'd also like to thank Tara, Amira, Khyber, and the entire extended Mortenson/Bishop clan, for making my frequent visits to Bozeman such a family affair.

Brigadier General Bashir Baz and Colonel Ilyas Mirza at Askari Aviation not only arranged for me to reach some of the most remote valleys of the Northern Areas, they also helped me reach at least a rudimentary understanding of the challenges currently facing Pakistan's military. Brigadier General Bhangoo flew me to the high-altitude treasures of the Karakoram and Hindu Kush in his trusty Alouette and entertained me late into the night with high-minded conversation about his country's future.

Suleman Minhas sped me past police barricades and into the most interesting areas of Islamabad and Rawalpindi, where, with great good humor, he helped an outsider to see more clearly. Ghulam Parvi worked tirelessly as both tutor and translator, making the rich culture of the Balti people bristle with life. Apo, Faisal, Nazir, and Sarfraz anticipated and catered to my every need as I traveled throughout the Northern Areas. Twaha, Jahan, and Tahira, along with the other rightly proud people of Korphe, helped me understand that isolation and poverty can't prevent a determined community from achieving the goals it sets for its children. And, repeatedly, relentlessly, the people of Pakistan proved to me that there is no more hospitable country anywhere on earth.

In Madrid, Ahmed Rashid was good enough to sneak away from the podium at the world summit on terrorism and treat me to a crash course in both the intricacies of Pakistan's political system and the relation between the rise of the *madrassas* and extremism. Conrad Anker, Doug Chabot, Scott Darsney, Jon Krakauer, Jenny Lowe, Dan Mazur, and Charlie Shimanski each gave me meaningful glimpses into the high-wire world of mountaineering. Jim "Mapman" McMahon deserves kudos for both the professional job he did drawing the book's maps and for his offer to mud wrestle anyone at Fox News who doesn't like *Three Cups of Tea*'s message.

I owe my old friend Lee Kravitz at *Parade* a debt for the day he said, "There's someone I think you should meet," and for his wise counsel as the book came together. I'd like to thank him also for having the good sense to marry Elizabeth Kaplan, who gracefully shepherded this book through the publishing process and educated a rube about the book business, all while simultaneously eating, walking, talking on her cell phone, and caring for her children. I'm grateful to Ray Roberts at Viking both for his erudition and his courtly attitude toward all the minor catastrophes involved in preparing this book for publication.

I need to thank the Murphy-Goode Winery, for lubricating so much of the interview process. Thanks also to Victor Ichioka at Mountain Hardwear for outfitting our trips to the Northern Areas. And I'm grateful to the coffee shops of Portland, Oregon, some of the finest on earth, for allowing an overcaffeinated writer to mutter to himself throughout so many long afternoons.

Finally, I want to thank Dawn, for far too many things to list here, but especially for the look on her lovely firelit face that evening in the Salmon-Huckleberry Wilderness when I read her the first few completed chapters.

—*David Oliver Relin*

If *Three Cups of Tea* inspires you to do more, here are suggestions for how to help:

1. Visit the www.threecupsoftea.com Web site for more info, book reviews, events, and ideas. If you purchase books online, go through this Web site and 7 percent of all your book purchases will go toward a girls' education scholarship fund in Pakistan and Afghanistan.
2. Suggest *Three Cups of Tea* to a friend, colleague, book club, women's group, church, civic group, synagogue, mosque, university or high school class, or a group interested in education, literacy, adventure, cross-cultural issues, Islam, or Pakistan and Afghanistan.
3. Check if *Three Cups of Tea* is in your local library. If not, either donate a book or suggest to the library to add *Three Cups of Tea* to their collection. Ask your friends or family in other states to do this also. As of late 2006, *Three Cups of Tea* was only in 1,100 out of 8,400 U.S. public libraries. In several libraries, there is a backlog of more than ten to twenty people to read this book.
4. Encourage your local independent or chain bookstore to carry this book.
5. Write a *Three Cups of Tea* book review for Amazon.com, Barnes & Noble, Borders, or a blog. Your candid comments will help the buzz with this (or any) book.
6. Ask the book editor of your local newspaper or radio to consider reviewing the book.

7. Pennies for Peace, www.penniesforpeace.org, is designed for schoolchildren. Get your local school involved to make a difference, one penny, one pencil at a time. Since 1994, more than eight million pennies have been raised through Pennies for Peace!

8. If you want to support our efforts to promote education and literacy, especially for girls, you can make a tax-deductible contribution to our nonprofit organization, Central Asia Institute, P.O. Box 7209, Bozeman, MT 59771, phone 406-585-7841, www.ikat.org. It costs us $1.00 per month for one child's education in Pakistan or Afghanistan, a penny to buy a pencil, and a teacher's salary averages $1.00 per day.

9. Please direct media or *Three Cups of Tea* inquiries to info@threecupsoftea.com or call 406-585-7841.

For more information contact: Central Asia Institute
P.O. Box 7209
Bozeman, MT 59771
406-585-7841
www.ikat.org

INDEX